Computer Communications and Networks

For further volumes:
http://www.springer.com/series/4198

The Computer Communications and Networks series is a range of textbooks, monographs and handbooks. It sets out to provide students, researchers and non-specialists alike with a sure grounding in current knowledge, together with comprehensible access to the latest developments in computer communications and networking.

Emphasis is placed on clear and explanatory styles that support a tutorial approach, so that even the most complex of topics is presented in a lucid and intelligible manner.

Zaigham Mahmood • Richard Hill

Editors

Cloud Computing
for Enterprise Architectures

Editors
Zaigham Mahmood
School of Computing and Mathematics
University of Derby
Kedleston Road
DE22 1GB Derby
UK
z.mahmood@derby.ac.uk

Richard Hill
School of Computing and Mathematics
University of Derby
Kedleston Road
DE22 1GB Derby
UK
r.hill@derby.ac.uk

Series Editor
A.J. Sammes
Centre for Forensic Computing
Cranfield University, DCMT, Shrivenham
Swindon SN6 8LA
UK

ISSN 1617-7975
ISBN 978-1-4471-2235-7   e-ISBN 978-1-4471-2236-4
DOI 10.1007/978-1-4471-2236-4
Springer London Dordrecht Heidelberg New York

British Library Cataloguing in Publication Data
A catalogue record for this book is available from the British Library

Library of Congress Control Number: 2011943560

Printed on acid-free paper

Springer is part of Springer Science+Business Media (www.springer.com)

*In memory of my parents
whose guidance and words of wisdom
I miss more each year.*

–Zaigham Mahmood

For Daniel and Megan. Keep asking 'why?'

–Richard Hill

Foreword

Understanding cloud technology innovation is becoming essential for most IT practitioners. Mechanisms, platforms and models have established themselves as concrete architectural building blocks that enable us to position and leverage cloud computing advances, when and where we can justify their benefits over their risks. However, many in the IT community continue to focus on immediate solutions when considering cloud environments. SaaS offerings, for example, have become common, yet limited demonstrations of what harnessing cloud technologies can truly accomplish. As a result, there is the on-going danger that, with a consistent focus on individual, single-purpose applications, we will end up repeating mistakes from the past by creating "silos in the sky."

It is critical for us to gain an enterprise perspective of cloud computing. Viewing cloud platforms as extensions of IT enterprises empowers us to creatively evolve our ecosystems to encompass cloud-based resources, as they prove themselves to better increase our business requirements fulfilment potential. There are countless ways we can safely augment traditional, controlled on-premise environments into effective hybrid technology architectures that can scale out into or simply incorporate remote cloud platforms. In some cases, this may be a gradual evolution that takes years to occur, while in other situations the adoption may be rapid, driven aggressively by uncompromising business demands and the need to overcome hard on-premise resource limitations. Either way, the opportunity is there for us today to explore these options, and make educated and (hopefully) intelligent decisions as to how to best leverage what cloud computing can truly offer.

This book addresses areas of technology architecture that go beyond individual solution design and implementation in order to broaden the understanding of how and where the building blocks of cloud computing technology can be added to support immediate, tactical goals, while planning for long-term, strategic incorporation at the same time. This evolutionary approach to adopting cloud technology innovation is necessary for us to maintain the vitality of an enterprise architecture. It gives us control over the usage and governance of cloud mechanisms, as they may enhance or even replace existing, corresponding parts of on-premise environments. The topic areas covered in the upcoming chapters will equip you with essential knowledge to help tackle these types of decision points, while maintaining that ever-important enterprise-level perspective.

Thomas Erl
Arcitura Education Inc. and CloudSchool.com

About Thomas Erl:

Thomas Erl is a renown IT author, a speaker of international fame and founder of SOASchool.com® and CloudSchool.com™. Thomas is also the editor of the Service Technology Magazine. With over 140,000 copies in print world-wide, his seven published books in SOA related area have become international bestsellers. As CEO of Arcitura Education Inc. and SOA Systems Inc. Thomas has led the development of curricula for the internationally recognized SOA Certified Professional (SOACP) and Cloud Certified Professional (CCP) accreditation programs.

Preface

Overview and Goals

Cloud Computing is emerging as a pervasive and consumer-driven utility that is attracting great interest from entrepreneurs, innovators and technology evangelists, as well as the 'connected' public at large. The shift from a focus upon IT, to a more assertive focus upon business, further strengthens the case for cloud adoption, and enterprises need to understand how they can best prepare themselves to fully exploit this exciting technological advance.

Cloud Computing for Enterprise Architectures addresses the need for a single point of reference for state-of-the-art cloud computing design and implementation techniques. It considers Cloud Computing from the perspective of Enterprise Architecture: how do we realize new business potential, with our existing enterprises?

Key objectives for this book include:

- Capturing the state of the art in Enterprise Architecture approaches with respect to Cloud Computing models, frameworks, technologies and applications
- Identifying potential research directions and technologies to facilitate the realization of emerging business models through Enterprise Architecture approaches
- Providing relevant theoretical frameworks and the latest empirical research findings
- Advancing the understanding of the field of Enterprise Cloud Computing

Organization and Features

This book is organized in four parts:

- Part I refers to Cloud Computing and Enterprise Architecture concepts and principles.
- Part II discusses architectural approaches and frameworks for the adoption of Cloud Computing.

- Part III is devoted to issues and challenges with Cloud Computing for Enterprise Architecture.
- Part IV presents future directions and ideas for further research.

Target Audiences

We have written this book to support a number of potential audiences. *Enterprise Architects* and *Business Analysts* will both have a need to understand how Cloud Computing can impact upon their work, both in terms of potential benefits and constraints.

Similarly, *Business Leaders* and *IT Infrastructure Managers* will have a desire to appreciate where Cloud Computing fits in to their current thinking, and to appreciate how Enterprise Architecture can assist the making of critical decisions for an enterprise.

Those involved in system design and implementation as *Application Developers* will observe how the adoption of architectures that support Cloud Computing can positively affect the means by which customers are satisfied.

Finally, as a collection of the latest theoretical, practical and evaluative work in the field of Enterprise Cloud Computing, we anticipate that this book will be of direct interest to *Researchers* and also *University Instructors* for adoption as a course textbook.

Suggested Uses

Cloud Computing for Enterprise Architectures can be used as an introduction to the topics of Cloud Computing and Enterprise Architecture, and as such the reader is advised to consult Part I for a thorough overview of the fundamental concepts.

Part II considers frameworks and approaches for the adoption of Cloud Computing, building upon the concepts presented in Part I.

Issues and challenges in this emerging area are considered in Part III, and then research and future directions are presented in Part IV.

Readers can use the book as a 'primer' if they have no prior knowledge, and then consult individual chapters at will as a reference text. Alternatively, for *University Instructors*, we suggest the following programme of study for a 12-week semester format:

- Weeks 1–3: Part I
- Weeks 4–7: Part II
- Weeks 7–9: Part III
- Weeks 9–11: Part IV
- Week 12: Assessment

Instructors are encouraged to make use of the various case studies within the book to provide the starting point for seminar or tutorial discussions, and as a means of summatively assessing learners at the end of the course.

Acknowledgements

The editors acknowledge the help and support of the following colleagues during the review and editing phases of this book:

- Raymond Slot, Utrecht Univ of Applied Sciences, Netherlands
- S Parthasarathy, Thiagarajar College of Eng, India
- Constandinos X. Mavromoustakis, University of Nicosia, Cyprus
- Khandakar Entenam Unayes Ahmed School of Electrical & Computer Engineering, RMIT University, Melbourne, Australia
- Nahed A Azab, The American University in Cairo, Egypt
- D Jeya Mala, Thiagarajar College of Eng, India
- Claudio Sartori, University of Bologna, Italy
- Stephen Woodruff, University of Glasgow, UK
- Alfredo Cuzzocrea, ICAR-CNR & Univ of Calabria, Italy
- Hamed Haddadi, University of London, UK
- Harjinder Singh Lallie, University of Warwick, UK

The editors also acknowledge the efforts of the authors of the individual chapters, without whose work this book would not have been possible.

School of Computing and Mathematics   Zaigham Mahmood
University of Derby, UK   Richard Hill

Contents

Contributors

Khandakar Entenam Unayes Ahmed School of Electrical & Computer Engineering, RMIT University, Melbourne, Australia, khandakar.ahmed@rmit.edu.au

Vassil Alexandrov ICREA Research Professor in Computational Science at Barcelona Supercomputing Centre, Barcelona, Spain, vassil.alexandrov@bsc.es

Shaun Bridges Open-SEA.org, Shaun.Bridges@Open-Sea.org

Eleri Cardozo School of Electrical and Computer Engineering, State University of Campinas – UNICAMP, Campinas, Brazil

Yu Chen Department of Electrical and Computer Engineering, Binghamton University, SUNY, Binghamton, NY 1390

Neil Cooke Department of Computing, University of Surrey, Guildford, Surrey, UK, N.Cooke@surrey.ac.uk

Guilherme Feliciano School of Electrical and Computer Engineering, State University of Campinas – UNICAMP, Campinas, Brazil

Jun Feng Department of Electrical and Computer Engineering, Binghamton University, SUNY Binghamton, NY 13902

G.R. Gangadharan Institute for Development & Research in Banking Technology [IDRBT], Castle Hills, Road No.1, Masab Tank, Hyderabad 500057, India, gangadharan@in.ibm.com

Lee Gillam Department of Computing, University of Surrey, Guildford, Surrey, UK, L.Gillam@surrey.ac.uk

Eliane G. Guimarães Information Technology Center Renato Archer, 13083-970, Campinas, SP, Brazil

Richard Hill School of Computing and Mathematics, University of Derby, Room E516, Kedleston Road, Derby, Derbyshire DE22 1GB, UK, r.hill@derby.ac.uk

Kai Hwang Department of Electrical Engineering – Systems,University of Southern California, Los Angeles, CA 90089, USA

Helen D. Karatza Department of Informatics, Aristotle University of Thessaloniki, 54124 Thessaloniki, Greece, karatza@csd.auth.gr

Zaigham Mahmood Distributed and Intelligent Systems Research Group, School of Computing and Mathematics, University of Derby, Kedleston Road, DE22 1GB, Derby, UK, z.mahmood@derby.ac.uk

Ioannis A. Moschakis Department of Informatics, Aristotle University of Thessaloniki, 54124 Thessaloniki, Greece, imoschak@csd.auth.gr

Siavash Moshiri Sheffield Business School, Sheffield Hallam University, Howard St, Sheffield, S1 1WB, UK, a.moshiri@shu.ac.uk

Leonardo R. Olivi School of Electrical and Computer Engineering, State University of Campinas – UNICAMP, Campinas, Brazil

Fernando Paolieri School of Electrical and Computer Engineering, State University of Campinas – UNICAMP, Campinas, Brazil

Davide Maria Parrilli time.lex Information & Technology law firm, Congresstraat 35 1000 Brussels, Belgium, davide.parrilli@timelex.eu

Mohanavadivu Periasamy Scientific Research Invision (SRI) Inc., Canada, 4872 Bourret Ave. Apt. # 407 Montreal, QC H3W1L1, Canada , sriinccanada@gmail.com

Fernando Pinho School of Electrical and Computer Engineering, State University of Campinas – UNICAMP, Campinas, Brazil

Pethuru Raj Enterprise Architect, Sify Software Ltd., 2nd Floor, TIDEL Park, Taramani, Chennai, Tamil Nadu 600113, India, peterindia@gmail.com

Muthu Ramachandran School of Computing and Creative Technologies, The Faculty of Arts, Environment and Technology, Leeds Metropolitan University, Leeds LS6 3QS, UK, m.ramachandran@leedsmet.ac.uk

N. Raghavendra Rao Advisor, FINAIT, Consultancy Services, Chennai, India

Amir R. Razavi Department of Computing, School of Electronics and Physical Sciences, University of Surrey, Guildford, Surrey GU2 7XH, UK

Lucio A. Rocha School of Electrical and Computer Engineering, State University of Campinas – UNICAMP, Campinas, Brazil

Diego Rodrigues School of Electrical and Computer Engineering, State University of Campinas – UNICAMP, Campinas, Brazil

Jeffrey A. Schiffel The Boeing Company – Wichita Division, jeffrey.a.schiffel@boeing.com

Ricardo S. Souza School of Electrical and Computer Engineering, State University of Campinas – UNICAMP, Campinas, Brazil

Abbas Strømmen-Bakhtiar Centre for Enterprise Architecture and Information Systems, Bodø Graduate School of Business, University of Nordland, 80049, Bodø, Norway, abbas.strommen.bakhtiar@gmail.com

Douglas H. Summerville Department of Electrical and Computer Engineering, Binghamton University, SUNY, Binghamton, NY 13902

Fábio Teixeira School of Electrical and Computer Engineering, State University of Campinas – UNICAMP, Campinas, Brazil

J. Doug Thomson Graduate School of Business and Law, RMIT University, Melbourne, Australia

Part I
Concepts and Principles

Chapter 1
Cloud Computing for Enterprise Architectures: Concepts, Principles and Approaches

Zaigham Mahmood

Abstract Cloud Computing is the latest paradigm that involves delivering hosted services over the Internet, based on a pay-as-you-go approach. It allows for provision of a variety of business and customer services. Consumers, especially the business organizations, can extend their existing computing provision and easily scale up Information Technology (IT) facilities by consuming services available in the Cloud. There are generally three varieties of services, namely, Software as a Service (SaaS), Platform as a Service (PaaS) and Infrastructure as a Service (IaaS), and four types of deployment approaches, viz., Private Clouds, Public Clouds, Community Clouds and Hybrid Clouds. Enterprises, who have implemented appropriate Enterprise Architectures (EA), can scale up their 'technical architectures' by integrating the existing infrastructure with the PaaS and IaaS provisions. Similarly, they can extend 'information and application architectures' by utilizing the PaaS and SaaS offerings. Thus, Cloud Computing can provide a useful extension to existing EAs, on demand and without the additional capital investment. This chapter discusses the Cloud and EA concepts, principles, technologies, deployment approaches and associated frameworks. It provides a basic overview and sets the background for the rest of the chapters in this book.

1.1 Introduction

Cloud Computing is a generic term that involves delivering hosted services over the Internet. The name *Cloud Computing* was inspired by the cloud symbol that is often used to represent the Internet. Gartner [1] defines Cloud Computing as *a style*

Z. Mahmood (✉)

Distributed and Intelligent Systems Research Group, School of Computing and Mathematics, University of Derby, Kedleston Road, DE22 1GB Derby, UK
e-mail: z.mahmood@derby.ac.uk

Z. Mahmood and R. Hill (eds.), *Cloud Computing for Enterprise Architectures*,
Computer Communications and Networks, DOI 10.1007/978-1-4471-2236-4_1,
© Springer-Verlag London Limited 2011

of computing where massively scalable IT-enabled capabilities are delivered 'as a service' to external customers using Internet technologies. According to NIST (National Institute of Standards and Technology), Cloud Computing is *on-demand access to a shared pool of computing resources* [2]. It is an *all-inclusive solution in which all computing resources (hardware, software, networking, storage, and so on) are provided rapidly to users as demand dictates* [3]. It promises to revolution-ize information technology (IT) and commerce by making computing available, in a fashion very similar to other utilities such as gas and electricity, over the Internet. Forrester (in Rhoton [4]) suggests that Cloud Computing refers to a *pool of abstracted, highly scalable and managed infrastructure capable of hosting end-customer applications and billed by consumption.* This follows a pay-as-you-use approach; the broader aim of Cloud Computing is to make *supercomputing* avail-able to the masses.

Whereas large organizations are being drawn to the Cloud technologies and infrastructures, SMEs (small- and medium-sized enterprises) have been using Cloud Computing for some time. Consumers such as general public have also readily embraced Cloud Computing in the form of services like *Facebook* (since about 2006), *YouTube* (since about 2005) and *Gmail* (since about 2007). In fact, consum-ers have been using Cloud Computing in the form of services like *Hotmail* since about 1996. Some of the reasons why more and more companies are shifting towards Cloud Computing IT solutions include:

- Reduction in costs associated with delivering IT services and, thus, diverting such resources to other activities such as integration of services
- Reduction in management responsibilities and, thereby, allowing key personnel in the enterprise to focus more on production and innovation
- Increased business agility and scalability and, thus, allowing enterprises to satisfactorily meet the needs of rapidly changing environments

Business organizations, who have already implemented appropriate Enterprise Architectures (EA), e.g. an approach based on Zachman's framework [5, 6] or other market favourite approaches such as TOGAF [7], are well placed to take advantages offered by Cloud provisions, the advantages being those of scalability, flexibility, availability and utilization of services on demand.

In the rest of this chapter, we first outline the characteristics, promise and bene-fits associated with Cloud Computing and discuss the deployment and delivery approaches, as well as the inherent issues and challenges in Sects. 1.1 and 1.2. Then, in Sects. 1.3 and 1.4, we provide a discussion on Enterprise Architectures (EA), develop a link between the Cloud environment and EA and suggest a way forward to extend the on-premises IT provision to combine with Cloud solutions. Section 1.5 presents a brief summary.

1.2 Cloud Computing

1.2.1 Characteristics, Promise and Benefits

Large organizations such as IBM, Dell, Microsoft, Google, Amazon and Sun have already started to take strong positions with respect to Cloud Computing provision [8]. They are so much behind this latest paradigm that the success is virtually guaranteed. The essential characteristics of Cloud environment include [2, 9]:

- On-demand self-service that enables users to consume computing capabilities (e.g. applications, server time, network storage) as and when required
- Multi-tenancy and resource pooling that allows combining heterogeneous computing resources (e.g. hardware, software, processing, servers, network bandwidth) to serve multiple consumers – such resources being dynamically assigned
- Rapid elasticity and scalability that allows functionalities and resources to be rapidly, elastically and automatically scaled out or in, as demand rises or drops
- Measured provision to automatically control and optimize resource allocation and to provide a metering capability to determine the usage for billing purpose, allowing easy monitoring, controlling and reporting

Cloud Computing is an attractive paradigm that promises numerous benefits, inherent in the characteristics, as mentioned above. These include:

- Optimization of a company's capital investment by reducing costs of purchasing hardware and software, resulting in a much lower total cost of ownership and, ultimately, a whole new way of looking at the economics of scale and operational IT
- Simplicity and agility of operations and use, requiring minimal time and effort to provision additional resources
- Enabling an enterprise to tap into a talent pool, as and when needed, for a fraction of the cost of hiring staff or retaining the existing staff and, thus, enabling the key personnel in the organizations to focus more on producing value and innovation for the business
- Enabling small organizations to access the IT services and resources that would otherwise be out of their reach, thus placing large organizations and small businesses on a level playing field
- Providing novel and complex computing architectures and innovation potential
- Providing mechanism for disaster recovery and business continuity through a variety of fully outsourced ICT services and resources

Cloud Computing can be massively scalable, and there are built-in benefits of efficiency, availability and high utilization that, in turn, result in reduced capital expenditure and reduced operational costs. It permits seamless sharing and collaboration through virtualization. In general, Cloud Computing promises cost savings, agility, innovation, flexibility and simplicity. The offerings from vendors, in terms of services of the application, platform and infrastructure nature, are continuing to mature, and the cost savings are becoming particularly attractive in the current competitive economic climate. Another broader aim of Cloud technology is to make *supercomputing* available to the enterprises, in particular, and the public, in general.

1.2.2 Deployment Approaches

Cloud deployment approaches represent specific types of Cloud environments – the way the Cloud delivery models (i.e. software, platforms and infrastructures as *services*) are deployed by the Cloud providers to make the Cloud provisions available to Cloud consumers. Organizations choose deployment models for IT solutions based on their specific business, operational and technical requirements. Cloud Computing can be classified and deployed in a number of ways, typically, as *Public, Private* or *Hybrid* Clouds.

Public Clouds are Cloud services provided by third parties but hosted and managed by the service providers. The Cloud providers take on the responsibility of installation, management, provisioning and maintenance. The customers access and use the services and physical resources. Consumers are charged only for the resources and services they use. It follows a pay-as-you-go approach to determine the usage – and this is the main attraction of Cloud environment. Lack of appropriate security and regulatory compliance is often a major issue here. Amazon Web Services, Microsoft Azure, Google Apps, SalesForce.com are some of the well-known Public Cloud providers and products.

Private Clouds are proprietary networks, often data centres, residing within the enterprise for the exclusive use of the organization. These are shared and multi-tenant environments built on highly efficient, automated and virtualized infrastructures. In case of a Private Cloud environment, the enterprise is in charge of setting up and maintaining the Cloud resources and, thus, the enterprise can take better control of security and regulatory compliance issues. The added advantage is in terms of better control of security (including security of sensitive data), more effective regulatory compliance and improved quality of services.

When a service provider uses Public Cloud resources to develop a Private Cloud environment, the result is called a *Virtual Private Cloud.* A *Community Cloud* is a semiprivate Cloud that is used by a defined group of tenants with similar backgrounds and requirements [9].

Hybrid Clouds are a combination of Private and Public Clouds. They combine on-demand external capacity with on-premises resources and in-house compliance. In this case, the management responsibilities are often split between the enterprise and the Public Cloud providers, which can often become an issue of concern. For mission-critical processes, this type of Cloud infrastructure is much more effective because of enhanced control and management by the enterprise itself. Organizations can keep their sensitive data and mission-critical applications in the Private Cloud and migrate other applications and data to a Public Cloud. The integration of external provision with the on-premise environment is often far from easy.

The Cloud environment consists of, generally, three core components which refer to three types of services, namely, *Software Services, Platform Services* and *Infrastructure Services*. Presenting the model as a pyramid, the *Software Services* will be at the top and the *Infrastructure Services* will be at the bottom of the pyramid [3, 10]. The abstraction increases as we move upwards towards the software services, and the element of control increases as we move downwards. Based on this anatomy, the Cloud services may be defined as follows:

- Software as a Service (SaaS)
- Platform as a Service (PaaS)
- Infrastructure as a Service (IaaS)

These are generally accepted groups of generic services. However, a number of other specialized services have also been suggested, e.g. Storage as a Service, Database as a Service, Security as a Service, Communication as a Service, Management as a Service, Integration as a Service, Testing as a Service, Business Process as a Service, etc.

1.2.2.1   Software as a Service (SaaS)

SaaS, often pronounced as 'saas', refers to prebuilt, functionally independent, vertically integrated and universally available applications (e.g. an e-mail system, human resource management, payroll processing, database processing and other application processes) delivered to and used by customers as *services*. Microsoft [11] defines SaaS as *software deployed as a hosted service and accessed over the Internet*. These services normally run behind a firewall on a network and provide *on-demand* usage, employing *pay-as-you-go* delivery approach which is based on a paradigm, generally known as *Utility Computing*. Here, customers are looking to purchase functionality and pay for its use. Sometimes, such service is available to general public totally free of charge, e.g. *Gmail* and *Facebook* services where e-mails, e-mail attachments, photographs, music and video files are stored on a remotely accessible server. Applications, especially the *line of business services* (large, customizable business solutions aimed at facilitating business processes, such as finances, supply-chain management and customer relations), are normally designed for ease of use and based upon proven business architectures. The advantages of this approach include readily available well-tested functionality, ease of use, faster implementation, multi-tenant efficiency, scalability, reliability and ease of management. The prerequisite is that services and other provision are appropriately organized and provided. In practice, though, there are issues in all these respects, especially in terms of reliability as well as security and confidentiality of data and information. It is for this reason that another variation of SaaS, known as 'Software as a Secure Service' (SaaSS), is also becoming a popular approach where provision of security becomes an added element of the service. Chong and Carraro [11] suggest that there are four maturity levels for SaaS applications, viz.:

- Ad hoc
- Configurable
- Configurable and multi-tenant-efficient
- Scalable, configurable and multi-tenant-efficient

Here, *multi-tenant efficiency* refers to a Cloud vendor providing virtual instances of services to many Cloud customers.

SaaS is a broad market where services can be anything from web-based e-mail to inventory control, even in some cases online banking services, as well as database processing. Gmail, Hotmail, Quicken Online, IBM® WebSphere, Boomi, SalesForce.com and Microsoft Office Online are some of the well-known SaaS products and providers.

1.2.2.2 Platform as a Service (PaaS)

This refers to software and product development tools (e.g. application servers, database servers, portal servers, middleware, etc.) which clients lease so they can build and deploy their own applications for their specific use. This provides an increased flexibility and control for the Cloud consumer. PaaS offerings may include the following:

- Deployment of complete applications, including tailor-made platforms
- Management of underlying hardware and software and hosting capabilities
- Facilities for application design, development, testing, deployment and hosting

In general, PaaS is the deliverance of a computer platform and resolution stack as a service. Cost is the major driver for customers signing up to a PaaS offering. Although too much reliance on the platform and infrastructure providers may result in a certain amount of dependence upon the Cloud vendors, the benefits of PaaS include support for development, reduction in development costs, multi-tenant architectures and scalability. Since platform is also software, there is often an overlap with SaaS and PaaS. It is possible that a SaaS provider subcontracts to a PaaS provider or incorporates the PaaS provision within the SaaS and provides it as part of the SaaS stack. Also, it is not uncommon to build PaaS solutions on top of an IaaS-based environment. This allows the platform to respond to demands, dynamically, by taking advantage of IaaS capabilities. The services in this environment are intended to support the 'software services' top layer of the pyramid. The customers are looking to buy time and cost savings in developing and deploying their own applications.

Google App Engine, Heroku, Mosso, Force.com, Engine Yard, Amazon Simple Storage Service (S3), Eccentex's AppBase and Windows Azure are examples of PaaS products and providers.

1.2.2.3   Infrastructure as a Service (IaaS)

IaaS is essentially hardware devices, e.g. visualized servers, storage, network devices, etc. It generally refers to a virtualization environment where services enable the Cloud platforms and applications to connect and operate. IaaS delivers compute services, typically in the form of a set of virtual machines with associated storage, processing capability, other relevant services and network connectivity. This enables multiple applications, owned by different Cloud consumers, to transparently share common underlying physical resources, such as servers and storage. Ideally, this layer should provide a pool of highly available processing units, utilization data and chargeback data. Rather than purchasing servers, software, data-centre space or network equipment, consumers lease such resources as part of a fully outsourced service. These services generally support the 'software services' top layer of the pyramid.

IaaS layer is at the bottom of the pyramid, just below the PaaS. As mentioned before, it is common to build PaaS solutions on top of the IaaS environment to allow the platform to dynamically respond to demand by taking advantage of the IaaS functionality. Customers get full control over server infrastructure; however, this often comes with a price premium as well as a certain amount of dependency on the infrastructure provider. In case of IaaS, customers are looking to buy 'computing'. Since the infrastructure is offered on pay-as-you-go basis, it is sometimes referred to as *Utility Computing*.

Amazon Elastic Cloud Compute (EC2), IBM BlueHouse, VMWare, GoGrid, RightScale and Linode are some of the IaaS products and providers.

1.2.2.4   Extended Frameworks

Several researchers have attempted to define Cloud frameworks by adding other essential components, such as management, quality, security and communication. Following the Cloud framework as suggested by David Linthicum [12], we can also include storage, database, information and process as additional services extending the basic structure (consisting of SaaS, PaaS and IaaS, as already explained in the previous sections).

Whereas the basic structure (consisting of SaaS, PaaS and IaaS) is reasonably distinct, there is a considerable overlap of Cloud provision between the three layers of the pyramid. For example, a software system (as SaaS) may be considered as part of a software platform (as PaaS); similarly, a component of information system platform (as PaaS) may be regarded as part of information system infrastructure (as IaaS). Thus, the following combinations of Cloud delivery models have also been suggested:

- SaaS + PaaS
- SaaS + IaaS
- IaaS + PaaS
- SaaS + PaaS + IaaS

1.2.3 Issues and Challenges

Notwithstanding the benefits that Cloud Computing offers, there are numerous issues and challenges for organizations embracing this new paradigm. Zhen [13] lists a number of major challenges with respect to the following:

- Data management and governance
- Service management and governance
- Product and process control and monitoring
- Infrastructure and system reliability and availability
- Information and visualization security

The Expert Group Report [14] mentions a number of issues including the following:

- Concerns over security with respect to knowledge, information and data residing on an external service device
- Concerns over services' and resources' availability and business continuity
- Concerns over data transmission across anticipated broadband speeds

Other shortcomings include no native security attributes, inadequate or no security provisioning by providers, lack of understanding of Cloud legal issues, and the failure to recognize potential liability from either legal issues or because of lack of security.

Issues with respect to "control" are also real concerns. Numerous questions that arise in this regard include (1) what happens to data and information held on a Cloud resource when the company that owns it goes out of business; how these data will be retrieved and returned to the owner organization; (2) what is the guarantee that the vendor has appropriate resilience arrangements in place with respect to the Cloud consumer organization's business continuity viewpoint, etc.

In spite of the limitation and inherent issues, Cloud Computing is becoming an attractive paradigm for large and small enterprises alike:

- In 2008, it was predicted [8] that *Cloud Computing initiatives could affect the enterprise within 2–3 years as it has the potential to significantly change IT.*
- In 2009, Gartner listed Cloud Computing as number 1 in its top 10 strategic technology areas for 2010 (in Amrhein [15] and Shankland [16]).
- In another report, Gartner suggested that *by 2012, 80% of Fortune companies will pay for some Cloud Computing service and 30% of them will pay for Cloud Computing infrastructure* (in Rhoton [4]).

1.2.4 Cloud Technologies

Numerous vendors have come up with tools and frameworks for deployment by organizations, to make effective use of the resources available, through different varieties of Cloud provision. These tools can be grouped into three general classes: (1) those that enable IT specialists and enterprise architects to create new applications, models and infrastructures, (2) tools that enable the movement and inking of existing and establishment applications, models and infrastructures to a Cloud environment and (3) tools that provide facilities to monitor and manage such applications and infrastructures. Some of these are briefly explained below:

- Cloud Foundation: This is the first major set of tools released by Red Hat, a lead Linux vendor [17], to provide a comprehensive set of products including virtualization, Cloud management, operating system, middleware and applications management software. Cloud consumers can use it for the following purposes: (1) build a private Cloud using Red Hat Enterprise Virtualization or VMware ESX Server, (2) manage the internal Cloud software infrastructure and (3) leverage the existing infrastructure using Red Hat's unique open-source products.
- JBoss Enterprise Middleware: This is another offering from Red Hat, which provides a comprehensive set of middleware software for building and deploying composite applications into Private and Public Clouds. It provides lightweight Java-based application platform that enables architects to deploy, manage and orchestrate cloud-based services into composite applications. JBoss presentation services enable users to create user interaction capabilities composed of disparate Cloud services [18].
- Eucalyptus Enterprise Edition (Eucalyptus EE): This is offered by Eucalyptus Systems. It is built on their open-source software infrastructure for implementing a Private Cloud using Cloud consumers' existing IT infrastructure, without modification that requires special-purpose hardware or reconfiguration [19]. Eucalyptus EE is compatible with the Amazon Web Services (AWS) Cloud infrastructure. According to [19], Eucalyptus EE enables the following: (1) cross-platform operating systems including Microsoft Windows and Linux, (2) connection and management of organization's existing storage systems from within the Eucalyptus Cloud and (3) appropriate control of resources within a Private Cloud.
- OpenNebula: This is a fully open-source toolkit to build an IaaS, whether Private, Public or Hybrid. The toolkit 'orchestrates storage, network, virtualization, monitoring and security technologies to enable the dynamic placement of multi-tier services on distributed infrastructures' [20]. The benefits include centralized management, higher utilization of existing resources, scalability of services to meet dynamic demands and seamless integration of IT resources.
- CA 3Tera AppLogic: This is an application-centric Cloud Computing platform and a key component of Cloud solutions provided by CA Technologies [21]. It allows for composing, running and scaling distributed applications and uses virtualization technologies to be completely compatible with existing operating systems, middleware and web applications. The platform eliminates the binding of software and hardware through virtualization. The applications are assembled using completely self-contained independent software components. Monitoring and metering tools are also available as part of the package. The framework 'enables Cloud Computing by making applications completely self-contained, scalable and portable' [21].

1.3   Enterprise Architectures

A well-established enterprise has a *Strategic Vision* that sets a future direction. This helps the enterprise to move from *where it is* (current position) to *where it wants to be* (future state) and provides a guidance to develop the enterprise's *Business Strategy*. It is the business strategy that drives the *Information System (or IT) Strategy*. The IT Strategy, considered in terms of enterprise's vision, guides the development of what is called *Enterprise Architecture (EA)*, which attempts to address enterprise-wide concerns such as:

- Enterprise strategic goals, objectives and strategies
- Meeting stakeholders' requirements
- Aligning IT with the business vision
- Extracting timely information from enterprise data
- Improving operating efficiency and decision making
- Adoption strategy for future development
- Integration of business systems, processes and data sharing
- Organizing technology infrastructure and information systems
- Ensuring data integrity, quality, consistency and security
- Reducing duplication and complexity of business functions

EA is a method and organizing principle that aligns functional business mission with the IT strategy and execution plans. Zachman [5] defines architecture as 'the set of principles, guidelines, policies, models, standards and processes that, aligned to business strategy and information requirements, guides the selection, creation and implementation of solutions that are aligned with future business directions'. Harrison [22] defines EA more fully as 'the capture of all behavior that goes on in an organization i.e. the who, what, why, when, where and how of the business at every level from high-level corporate goals to the code of low-level programs that implement business processes used to achieve those goals'. According to the Reference Model for Open Distributed Processing (ODP) [23–25], architecture of a system is 'a set of rules to define the structure of the system and the interrelationships between its parts' [23]. Thus, EA is a high-level view of an organization's information-related components that conveys an overall understanding of each component and an understanding of the relationship and the interaction between these components.

1.3.1   Enterprise Architecture Frameworks

A framework provides a generic problem space and a common vocabulary within which individuals can operate to solve specific problems. These are not always comprehensive, but they can be leveraged to provide at least a starter set of issues and concerns to be addressed in architecture development. The various frameworks generally share the same objectives but vary in focus, scope and intent. Each business sector (e.g. manufacturing, service, financial) operates differently and has its own objectives and goals. Thus, there are many frameworks or *architecture models*, e.g.:

- Zachman's Framework [5, 6]:This is a widely used approach for developing enterprise-wise IS architectures and is considered as a reference model against which other frameworks can map themselves.
- RM-ODP [23–26]: This uses a well-understood object-modelling technique (OMT) and is developed by highly reputable agencies such as ISO and International Telecommunications Unit.
- TOGAF [7]:This is an industry standard generic framework and is freely available.
- C4ISR/DoDAF [7, 27, 28]:These are frameworks developed mainly for the use of US Department of Defense.

For a comparison and review, refer to [29–32].

1.4   Cloud Computing and Enterprise Architectures

As mentioned before, an EA provides a high-level corporate view of an enterprise. It is the capture of all behaviour that goes in an organization: the data that are processed, the information that is kept, who does what and why, etc. In essence, it is the *what, how, who* and *why* of the business at every level of the organization, where:

- What – determines business objects, data and materials
- How – establishes control flows, business functions and procedures
- Who – refers to staff, stakeholders and their responsibilities
- Why – provides mission aims and objectives of the enterprise

These elements can be referred to as the way the various specific architectural representations can be described. Some of these *descriptions* refer to the business mission and the goals of the organization; some refer to the business and governance processes and the rest to the information and application systems.

This suggests that the EA should be based on the strategic vision of the enterprise. It also suggests that an EA is a multi-tier model employing several tightly coupled architectures, which provide or represent different *perspectives* of an organization. In this context, Malhotra [33] identifies the following core components of an EA:

- Strategic Capabilities Architecture – a guiding architecture based on the strategic vision
- Business Architecture – based on the long-term strategy, goals and objectives
- Information Architecture – based on the Business Architecture to define the IS strategy that implements the business strategy

- Data, Systems and Computer Architectures – to determine the Information
  Architecture, consisting of:

  - Data Architecture – relates to and aligns the firm's data-related aspects with
    the business applications
  - Systems Architecture – refers to the specific information and data systems
  - Computer Architecture – refers to the specific hardware and software

Zachman [4] suggests three fundamental architectures to be the *Business model*,
the *IS model* and the *Technology model* from the perspectives of the *owner*, the
designer and the *builder* of the system, respectively.

Based on the above and following, the ideas presented by other researchers [e.g.
34–36], Mahmood [37] suggests the following components, in terms of *what, how,
who* and *why,* as the minimum set of core *architectural representations*:

- Business Architecture – to address the business mission, strategy, governance,
  business process models and business functions
- Application (or Solution or Software or Functional) Architecture – to focus on
  the information systems to support the business mission and information
  requirements
- Data (or Information) Architecture – to define the data and information that
  needs to be made available to accomplish the mission and to provide to other
  agencies
- Technical (or IT or Infrastructure) Architecture – to define the technology infrastructure needed to support the Data and Application architectures and to document the required technical standards

A closer examination of the above reveals that a clear connection exists between
the different architectural representations of an EA (e.g. business, applications, data
and technical architectures) and the Cloud environment (as consisting of software,
platforms and infrastructure services). Whilst most organizations understand what
the Cloud environment offers and what an EA is, few have managed to make a successful connection. If an organization's EA is mature, i.e. its different architectural
representations are loosely coupled, then the specific architectures can be built using
the Cloud offerings as follows:

- To build the *technical* layer of an EA, use the Cloud IaaS and PaaS offerings. In
  this case, although organizations need to understand their EA, they do not need
  to concern themselves with the detail and governance of technology and platform infrastructures, thus reducing the size, dependence and maintenance of on-
  premises IT resources.
- To help with the *applications* layer, use the Cloud SaaS offerings. In this case,
  the software services in the form of software components and complete applications are available to consumers, as they require.
- To organize the *data* layer, use the Cloud PaaS and IaaS offerings or access other
  specialized services, such as Database as a Service, and make use of cloud-based
  virtual storage and servers.

- For the *business* layer of an EA, other specialized Cloud provision such as Management as a Service can prove highly useful. However, it is important that the business strategy and vision as well as the governance control remain with the organization.

Because of certain synergies, Cloud technologies and EA can be suitably linked to provide organization better flexibility, availability and scalability. In this scenario, the Cloud directly and beneficially impacts on the organization, and the organization becomes a Cloud Enterprise with business functions and IT resources provided through the Cloud.

1.4.1   The Way Forward

Because of the savings and business agility that Cloud environment offers, large enterprises are already integrating Cloud Computing into their existing IT systems and resources. For the newcomers aiming to migrate to the Cloud, the recommendation is that they plan well as there are also integration challenges besides the security and other issues. Sasson [38] suggests the following best practices as a way forward:

- Develop a strategy – keeping in view the broader aim and the mission of the business
- Learn from others' mistakes – adopting the practices that have been successful elsewhere
- Avoid upfront costs – using the pay-as-you-go approach as much as possible
- Ensure autonomy – minimizing the development and maintenance activities
- Ensure security of data and information – noting that this a major concern on Public Clouds

When deciding whether to deploy existing resources on a Public Cloud or develop a Private Cloud, Spinola [39] provides the following practical suggestions:

- Consider the enterprise applications, other systems and IT resources and divide them into core and non-core business practices, systems and resources. As an example, HR services will be considered as non-core, and services that would provide competitive differentiation will be considered as core and business critical.
- If non-core, then they can be deployed on a Public Cloud. Otherwise, they can be deployed in a Private Cloud or perhaps left within the organization, as they are.
- Also, in applications that require the use of a network outside of the organization (e.g. Internet), then Public Cloud is the place for deployment. Similarly, Applications that involve extremely sensitive data, particularly where there is a regulatory or legal risk involved, should be kept well behind the firewall, i.e. on a Private Cloud or perhaps left within the organization, as they are.

In case of aligning the organization's business vision with its IT strategy, the following suggestion may be considered:

- Develop enterprise architecture in terms of business, data, applications and technology architectures.
- Understand the structure well and ensure reasonably loose coupling between the specific architectures.
- Align the individual components of EA architecture with cloud-based provision for migrating to the Cloud in terms of accessing its infrastructures, platform and software services.
- Integrate appropriately to gain the benefits that Cloud environment offers.

When deploying data and services or consuming services from a Public Cloud, enterprises need to ensure that they know (1) where their data will be kept and who else would have permission to use it, (2) how the data will be protected and how its integrity will be ensured, (3) what mechanisms will be used to ensure that unauthorized personnel will not be able to access it, (4) who has the responsibility for management and maintenance of services and platforms contracted, (5) what are the support facilities, (6) will the services and data remain available 24 h a day, 7 days a week, (7) what is the exit strategy, (8) how can the contract be terminated, (9) what are any relevant penalties, etc.

There are a number of related infrastructures that also need to be in place to take the full advantage. Linthicum [40] points out that *Cloud Computing won't necessarily work without SOA* (service-oriented architecture) as this provides an appropriate infrastructure within the organization for integrating services and components from outside (say, form a public cloud). Grid Computing (GC), which involves networking of hardware devices, is another architecture that can be usefully deployed for the most effective integration of in-house and Public or Hybrid Cloud platforms or infrastructure services. The IaaS component of a Cloud may be designed around the concept of Grid Computing [10]. Similarly, PaaS and SaaS components, developed as web services and layered on top of the IaaS component, become an SOA approach [10]. Appropriate implementation and connection of SOA and GC will then provide the infrastructure for developing and deploying an effective Cloud Computing environment.

Cloud Computing is, in fact, the realization of combining many existing technologies (SOA, GC, utility computing, virtualization, autonomic computing) with new ideas to create efficient and more effective IT solutions [15]. A report on Cloud Computing published in Jan 2010 [41] suggested that (1) enterprises are moving beyond experimentation, (2) they are beginning to develop management software to deal with scaled Cloud environments and (3) they are beginning to develop enterprise-level policies for dealing with Public and Hybrid Clouds.

Enterprises are excited about the opportunities that Cloud Computing presents and, as the evidence suggests [4, 8, 15, 16, 41], Enterprise Cloud Computing is firmly poised to be the *next big thing*.

1.5   Conclusion

Cloud Computing is *on-demand access to a shared pool of computing resources.* It helps consumers to reduce costs, reduce management responsibilities and increase business agility. For this reason, it is becoming a popular paradigm, and increasingly more companies are shifting towards IT Cloud Computing solutions. Advantages are many but, being a new paradigm, there are also challenges and inherent issues. These relate to data governance, service management, process monitoring, infrastructure reliability, information security, data integrity and business continuity. The way forward for an enterprise is to plan a strategy for integrating existing resources to Cloud offerings, to have appropriate enterprise architectures in place to correctly align the IT resources with business applications, to follow best practices suggested by other organizations and think in terms of moving towards SOA and Grid Computing. Once this is done, the enterprise is well on its way to migrate to the Cloud environment and gain the benefits that Cloud technologies offer.

This chapter discusses the deployment approaches, benefits, issues, challenges, relevant tools and technologies, as well as the importance of enterprise architectures (EA). The chapter also provides a link between the Cloud environment and an organization's EA and suggests a practical way forward. The aim is to provide some general information for enterprises who wish to integrate existing IT provision with Cloud infrastructures available outside the organizational boundaries. There is no doubt that Cloud Computing is firmly poised to be the *next big thing* for enterprises, large and small.

References

1. Cearley, D.W.: Cloud computing: key initiative overview. Gartner Report (2010)
2. Mell, P., Grance, T.: The NIST definition of cloud computing, version 15. National Institute of Standards and Technology (NIST), Information Technology Laboratory. www.csrc.nist.gov (2009). Accessed 7 Oct 2009
3. Amrhein, D., Quint, S.: Cloud computing for the enterprise: part 1: capturing the cloud, DeveloperWorks, IBM. www.ibm.com/developerworks/websphere/techjournal/0904_amrhein/0904_amrhein.html (2009). Accessed 8 Apr 2009
4. Rhoton, J.: Cloud Computing Explained: Implementation Handbook for Enterprises. Recursive Press, London (2010). 3 May 2010
5. Zachman, J.: The framework for information systems architecture. IBM Syst. J. **26**(3), 276–292 (1987)
6. Zachman, J.: A framework for information systems architecture. IBM Syst. J. **38**(2/3), 454–470 (1999)
7. The Open Group: TOGAF Version 9 Enterprise Edition, https://www2.opengroup.org/ogsys/jsp/publications/PublicationDetails.jsp?catalogno=g091 (2009). Accessed 25 Oct 2011
8. Willis, J.M.: Cloud computing and the enterprise. IT Management and Cloud. www.johnmwillis.com/ibm/cloud-computing-and-the-enterprise/ (2008). Accessed 13 Feb 2008
9. Kvitka, C.: Clouds bring agility to the enterprise. http://www.oracle.com/technology/oramag/oracle/10-mar/o20interview.html (2010). Accessed 28 Sept 2010

10. Sheehan, M.: Cloud computing expo: introducing the cloud pyramid. Cloud Comput. J. (2008)
11. Chong, F., Carraro, G.: Architecture strategies for catching the Long Tail, Microsoft Corporation. (2006). Accessed Apr 2006
12. Linthicum, D.: Defining the cloud computing framework. Cloud J. (2009)
13. Zhen, J.: Five key challenges of enterprise cloud computing. Cloud Comput. J. (2008)
14. Schubert. L.: The future of cloud computing. Expert Group Report. www.cordis.europa.eu/fp7/ict/ssai/docs/executivesummary-forweb_en.pdf (2010). Accessed 28 Sept 2010
15. Amrhein, D., Quint, S.: Cloud computing for the enterprise: part 1: capturing the cloud, understanding cloud computing and related technologies, IBM. www.ibm.com/developerworks/websphere/techjournal/0904_amrhein/0904_amrhein.html (2010). Accessed 28 Sept 2010
16. Shankland, S.: Brace yourself for cloud computing. CNET News. http://news.cnet.com/8301-30685_3-10378782-264.html (2009). Accessed Oct 2009
17. Red Hat: Cloud foundations: edition one. www.redhat.com/solutions/cloud/foundations/ (2010). Accessed 20 Sept 2010
18. Red Hat: Cloud solutions. http://www.redhat.com/solutions/cloud/products/ (2010). Accessed 20 Sept 2010
19. Eucalyptus Systems: Eucalyptus enterprise edition. www.eucalyptus.com/products/eee (2010). Accessed 20 Sept 2010
20. OpenNebula: About the OpenNebula technology. www.opennebula.org/about:technology (2010). Accessed 20 Sept 2010
21. CA Technologies: Turnkey cloud computing. www.3tera.com/AppLogic/ (2010). Accessed 20 Sept 2010
22. Harrison, D. Varveris, L.: TOGAF: establishing itself as the definitive method for building enterprise architectures in the commercial world, Popkin Software (1995)
23. ODP: ISO/IEC JTC1/SC21 Open distributed processing – reference model – part 1: foundations, IS 10746–1/ITU-T Recommendations X.901 (1995a)
24. ODP: ISO/IEC JTC1/SC21 Open distributed processing – reference model – part 2: foundations, IS 10746–2/ITU-T Recommendations X.902 (1995b)
25. ODP: ISO/IEC JTC1/SC21 Open distributed processing – reference model – part 3: architecture IS 10746–3/ITU-T Recommendations X.903 (1995c)
26. Putman, J.: Architecting with RM-ODP. Prentice Hall, Upper Saddle River (2001)
27. C4ISR Architecture Working Group: C4ISR Architecture Framework Version 2, http://www.afcea.org/education/courses/archfwk2.pdf (1997). Accessed 25 Oct 2011
28. DODAF: DOD Architecture Framework Version 2.02, http://cio-nii.defense.gov/sites/dodaf20/ (2010). Accessed 25 Oct 2011
29. Allen, B., Boynton, A.: Information architecture: in search of efficient flexibility. MIS Q. **15**(4), 435–442 (1991)
30. Ross, J.W., Rockart, J.F.: Reconceptualising IT. MIT CSR working paper 302, MIT, USA (1999)
31. Rowley, J.: Towards a framework for information management. Int. J. Info. Manag. **18**(5), 359–369 (1998)
32. Shah, M., Mahmood, Z.: Frameworks for building enterprise information architectures. In: Proceedings 17th IRMA international conference, Washington, DC, 22–24 May 2006
33. Malhotra, Y.: Enterprise architecture: an overview [www document], BRINT Institute. http://www.kmbrook.com/enterarch.htm (1996)
34. Adaptive Inc.: The road to enterprise architecture. http://www.adaptive-solutions.com/links/papers.html (2002). Accessed 24 Apr 2011
35. Office of the Secretary of Defence Working Group: C4ISR Architecture Framework, Version 2.0. Office of the Secretary of Defence Working Group, Washington, DC (1997)
36. C4ISR Architecture Working Group: C4ISR architecture framework version 2. www.afcea.org/education/courses/archfwk2.pdf (2010). Accessed 24 Apr 2011
37. Mahmood, Z.: Architectural representations for describing enterprise information and data. In: Proceedings 10th WSEAS conference on computers, pp. 728–733. Athens, Greece, July 2006

38. Sasson, S.: Seven best practices for cloud computing. Enterprise Systems, Aug 2008. http://esj. com/articles/2009/08/18/cloud-best-practices.aspx (2008). Accessed 24 Sept 2010
39. Spinola, M.: Cloud computing implementation roadmap. Cloud Comput. J. (2009)
40. Linthicum, D.: Cloud computing? Thank SOA. www.thecloudtutorial.com/cloud-computing-soa.html (2010). Accessed 28 Sept 2010
41. Mhatre, R.: Top 5 trends for enterprise cloud computing in 2010. Lightspeed Venuter Partners. http://lsvp.wordpress.com/2010/01/05/top-5-trends-for-enterprise-cloud-computing-in-2010/ (2010). Accessed Jan 2010

Chapter 2
Enterprise Architecture Fundamentals

Siavash Moshiri and Richard Hill

Abstract The concept of Enterprise Architecture and the associated architecture design principles and practice of service orientation has gained popularity of late. However, many implementation attempts do not realize the intended SOA promise, and whilst software application vendors' implementations of SOA are maturing, there is a need to understand issues relating to scoping and delivery. First and foremost, the broader context of Enterprise Architecture must be understood in the context of emerging models such as Cloud Computing, to ensure sustained alignment of business and IT assets.

2.1 Introduction

The justification of technology as a key business driver is drawing renewed attention as enterprises look to build Service-Oriented Architectures (SOA [5, 21]) to meet the needs of their dynamic enterprises in an ever complex and competitive business environment. The challenge of Service-Oriented Architecture (SOA) (as a significant step towards achieving business value) has been raising the context and application of service enablement beyond technology functions. Nearly all technology vendors propose and deliver their SOA solutions reliant on the work of Enterprise Architecture (EA [24]), Business Process Analysis (BPA) and Business Process Management (BPM). These frameworks help to define, analyze and execute

S. Moshiri (✉)
Sheffield Business School, Sheffield Hallam University, Howard St, Sheffield, S1 1WB, UK
e-mail: a.moshiri@shu.ac.uk

R. Hill
School of Computing and Mathematics, University of Derby,
Room E516, Kedleston Road, Derby, Derbyshire DE22 1GB, UK
e-mail: r.hill@derby.ac.uk

Z. Mahmood and R. Hill (eds.), *Cloud Computing for Enterprise Architectures*,
Computer Communications and Networks, DOI 10.1007/978-1-4471-2236-4_2,
© Springer-Verlag London Limited 2011

resources where SOA has the best effect. When EA and SOA disciplines combine, SOA can encompass disparate applications and platforms, orchestrating and controlling them in the context of business processes. The result should be an agile enterprise in which business models drive executable business processes, powered by a portfolio of services.

While SOA can go so far in addressing the important security, reliability and reusability of services, it is nonetheless more of a technical approach. SOA offers limited business value unless it encompasses disparate applications and platforms, moving beyond technology to be orchestrated and controlled in the context of business processes. SOA technology and methods provide a foundation for service enablement in an orderly fashion and allow an organization to avoid the pitfalls of deploying an uncontrolled maze of services. Forrester [6] reinforces the importance of binding SOA to a bigger architecture vision:

> No prior industry initiative for IT architecture has had an impact as positive and broad-reaching as service-oriented architecture (SOA). But SOA's impact is only part of the story: You have many more technology initiatives besides SOA. You need a bigger architectural vision that encompasses SOA, business process management, event processing, Web 2.0, and much more besides. Although SOA is far from dead, it should be buried inside a larger vision.

This chapter takes a preliminary look at SOA and EA, identifying and examining crucial characteristics that can inform effective implementation in the light of emerging models and technologies such as Cloud Computing (CC), and describes an assessment tool to assist EA planning and implementation.

2.2 Aligning Business and Technological Needs

Ross et al.'s [12] work illustrates that there is a:

> significant correlation between strategic agility and IT-infrastructure capability of an organization. If managers can describe their desired strategic agility, they can identify the IT infrastructure service clusters that need to be above the industry average – and thus can create a distinctive competence.

As such, the development of Information Technology (IT) capabilities requires an architecture that is flexible, *elastic* (or scalable up or down as in CC), modular and easily integrated. In today's rapidly changing, competitive business environment, organizations need an IT landscape that enables managers and their employees to effectively manage the processes they work with from design and configuration to executing, monitoring and analysis. The dynamism of the business environment means that the typical value chains are no longer constrained by the traditional boundaries of an enterprise. To support this, the corporate IT landscape is constantly changing as the systems and applications are added and upgraded and functions outsourced. This has the effect of merging the information architecture of both supplier and customer systems, in order that new business demands can be accommodated in markets whose behaviours are difficult to predict.

Thus, the underlying business logic and IT infrastructure that supports the organization's business processes must be highly adaptive and dynamic to fulfil this challenge. To support a specific business process, there is a mandate for the flexible selection and utilization of the most efficient and effective system and application configuration, coupled with a consistent implementation approach that does not disrupt business logic and technical implementation [13, 14].

Homogenous Information Systems architectures are no longer practical options, and organizations are moving away from the traditional point-to-point integration approach to building and evolving standardized enterprise architecture capabilities to address efficient and effective strategic enterprise management beyond the traditional approach to business-IT alignment. EA has come to exist since the early 1980s as a concept of enabling improved business-IT alignment, and has become more important as technologies such as CC have emerged and developed, and as such has been an attempt to address the underlying issues which have surfaced as systems capabilities have increased. Opinion surveys of Chief Executive Officers for the last 15 years consistently had 'alignment' as one of the top ten objectives they identified for the IT community. In fact, since 2006, alignment has been *the top issue* in these surveys [9].

2.3   Towards a Framework for EA

The Zachman Framework [22–24] has guided many enterprise architects in their endeavours to better align IT infrastructure with business objectives. It is a two-dimensional matrix that that identifies critical architectural artefacts. In his first article, and subsequent elaboration in 1992, Zachman proposed that there are six descriptive foci (data, function, network, people, time and motivation) and six player perspectives (planner, owner, designer, builder, subcontractor and enterprise).

The term taxonomy might better describe Zachman's framework as it proposes a system to organize architectural artefacts (i.e. design documents, specifications and models) that takes into account both who the artefact targets (e.g. the business owner) and what particular issue (e.g. data and functionality) is being addressed. As John Zachman retrospectively describes his work:

The (Enterprise Architecture) Framework as it applies to Enterprises is simply a logical structure for classifying and organizing the descriptive representations of an Enterprise that are significant to the management of the Enterprise, as well as to the development of the Enterprise's systems [22].

Many proponents of the Zachman Framework see it as cross-disciplinary, with influence extending far beyond IT. One popular book [11] on Zachman, for example, says:

…in due course, you will discover that the Framework exists in everything you do, not only IT projects. When you thoroughly understand the Framework, you can become more effective in everything you do. This means everything. This statement is not made lightly.

According to O'Rourke et al. [11], since its development in 1983 and extension in the 1990s, the Zachman Framework has been referred to as a base framework, and many of its concepts have been borrowed in other approaches to enterprise architecture methodologies.

With the development of this framework, John Zachman revolutionized the study of enterprise architecture. However, his framework did not offer a methodology for implementation. With its unique aspects, this framework is faced with two issues. First, a lack of a common modelling notation such as UML, and second, there is no methodology or toolkit for implementation of EA associated with the framework. There is a notable lack of academic literature on the subject, especially in the context of methodology.

Industry solution providers and IT vendors have been developing their own tools and methodological approaches based on their preferred or extended frameworks. Examples include SAP [14] in the commercial sector and government bodies such as the US DoD in the public sector [4].

Clearly, a framework, however complete or well designed, if not implemented effectively, cannot deliver the proposed benefits. Although Zachman does not mention methodology in his framework, there have been attempts, in academia and industry, to develop a practical approach towards EA implementation. One such work is Enterprise Architecture Planning (EAP) by [16], again based on the Zachman framework. The application of Spewak's EAP methodology has been widely used in the IT domain which demonstrates its strength in EA design, development and implementation. EAP is used in some of the widely used and commonly referenced EA methodologies such as the Federal Enterprise Architecture Framework (FEAF [2]). EAP defines the blueprint for subsequent design and implementation, and it places the planning/defining stages into a framework.

While the Zachman Framework provides the broad context and taxonomy of the architecture layers,

> EAP focuses on planning and managing the process of establishing the business alignment of the architectures. EAP is planning that focuses on the development of matrixes for comparing and analyzing data, applications, and technology. Most important, EAP produces an implementation plan [2].

The fast pace of development in IT, emergence of new technologies, new and extended EA frameworks such as DoDAF (US Department of Defense Architecture Framework [4]), FEAF (Federal Enterprise Architecture Framework [3]), TEAF (Treasury Enterprise Architecture Framework [1]), TOGAF (The Open Group Architecture Framework), modern modelling techniques, propagation of object-oriented application development methodologies and especially the growing interest and maturity of Service-Oriented Architecture (SOA) thus necessitate a new mandate for EA.

2.4 Service-Oriented Architecture

Service-Oriented Architecture (SOA) uses the concept of loosely coupled integration between software components using web services. Services are callable entities or application functionalities accessed via the exchange of messages. In a broad sense, a service exposes certain functionalities that can be consumed by another software application or service. This facilitates service reuse and a gradual and organic adoption of new services as and when required, to respond quickly to changing business requirements. Essentially, SOA is a system architecture based upon services and standards. In the context of EA, SOA plays an important role in directly supporting the operational domain of the architecture. In this way, an EA defines the interactions and articulations between business and information technology and their alignment or congruence [12, 17, 19, 20, 24].

A Service-Oriented Enterprise Architecture (SOEA) uses services to describe the articulations of business and information technology. It has to identify the business services needed to support the business processes of the enterprise, and to map the business services to technology and software services. Such new developments and innovation in the context of IT systems and enterprise integration (especially SOA in the context of CC initiatives) calls for a methodology corresponding to a base EA framework such as Zachman's to respond to the evolving enterprise requirement for an implementation methodology.

This chapter considers pertinent literature of the theory and application of EA, and how this presents opportunities for emerging models such as CC. The next section describes some of the fundamental concepts of EA.

2.5   Some Definitions

Large software application vendors such as SAP and Oracle have proposed approaches and toolsets that utilize SOA to realize EA principles. This tends to support the perspective that EA should be technology-driven, and can be seen as opposing the EA perspective that business-IT alignment results in improvements *to the business*, SOA merely being an enabler, rather than a driver. Before we can consider this in the context of emerging technologies and models such as CC, we need to establish some definitions for the fundamental concepts of EA.

2.5.1   What Is an Architecture?

When people talk about architecture, they typically refer to it in the context of buildings. In its purest sense, it has far broader connotations. Specifying and sharing a set of design principles of an artefact is at the core of the concept of architecture. Zachman [22] maintains:

> Architecture is the set of descriptive representations that are required in order to create an object.

In a typical specification, decisions span parameters such as specific requirements that need to be met, resource requirements, scope, dimensions, extensibility and complexities in relation to the fit within the micro and macro environment. According to American National Standards Institute/Institute of Electrical and Electronics Engineers (ANSI/IEEE) standard 1471–2000, an architecture is:

> the fundamental organization of a system embodied in its components, their relationships to each other and the environment, and the principles governing its design and evolution.

According to The Open Group [10], *architecture* has two meanings depending upon its contextual usage:

> 1. A formal description of a system, or a detailed plan of the system at component level to guide its implementation. 2. The structure of components, their inter-relationships, and the principles and guidelines governing their design and evolution over time.

A metaphor can be drawn by thinking of a blueprint for the planning of a large-scale residential or commercial property development. In this light, the blueprint provides the macro view of how various elements (roads, structures, utilities, etc.) fit coherently together.

2.5.2 What Is an Enterprise?

In the context of EA, an enterprise is more than just a business organization. An enterprise is any collection of systematic and purposeful functional corporate entities. In this context, an enterprise is, but not necessarily limited to, an entire organization, functional areas, divisions and business units, linked together by common governance and administrative ownership.

2.5.3 Enterprise Architecture

From the analysis so far, we can conclude that an EA provides the symbiotic blueprint of the business and IT environment, together with governance principles, with the goal of alignment, standardization, reuse of existing IT and organizational assets and processes and the sharing of common methods and practices, within an enterprise.

Zachman regards EA to be the total set of logically linked and structured descriptive representations (i.e. models or design artefacts) for an enterprise based on its strategic and operational requirements maintainable during its useful life cycle.

> Enterprise Architectures are an emerging approach for capturing complex knowledge about organizations and technology. Enterprise Architectural approaches range from broad, enterprise focused approaches, through to approaches aimed at specific domains. The focus of enterprise architecture efforts is now shifting to become more holistic, thereby necessitating the use of comprehensive modeling tools to analyze and optimize the portfolio of business strategies, organizational structures, business processes/tasks and activities, information flows, applications, and technology infrastructure [8].

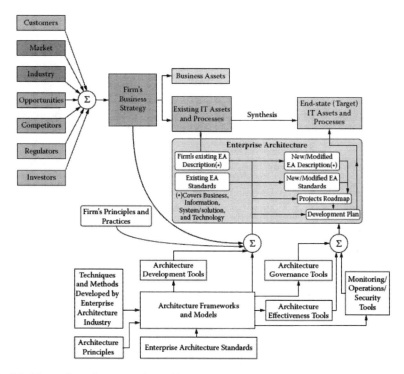

Fig. 2.1 Macro view of an enterprise architecture in the environment

Figure 2.1 depicts the macro view of the business environment. The external entities that may drive a firm are shown on the left. They include the customers, the market, the industry the enterprise is in, the opportunities that may exist or may develop, competitors, regulators and investors, amongst others. An enterprise has an existing or newly developed business strategy. The enterprise also has an existing set of business assets. The goal is to develop the IT infrastructure to support an end-state IT environment that enables, supports and facilitates the business strategy. To this end, the enterprise may have developed an architecture, which is a blueprint of its information, systems and technology environment. The blueprint also specifies the standards as related to these three categories (e.g. equipment standards, protocols standards, interface standards, etc.)

The enterprise may have developed the architecture using the industry mechanisms shown towards the bottom of Fig. 2.1. These include IT industry techniques and methods to develop an EA, architecture principles, enterprise architecture IT industry standards, IT industry enterprise architecture frameworks and models and architecture development tools.

As a new business strategy is developed by the enterprise, a new or modified EA may be needed (this could be determined by a gap analysis). This preliminary EA needs to take into account the existing embedded base of IT assets, the existing EA, the existing EA standards, the principles and practices of the enterprise, the desired business strategy and the available frameworks/tools to develop a new EA or modify the existing one.

The output of this synthesis will be a set of derived IT strategies, a new/modified EA, a new/modified set of EA standards, a roadmap describing the IT projects needed to implement the new architecture and achieve the target state and a development or deployment plan. As Fig. 2.1 also illustrates, there are governance and effectiveness-assessment capabilities as well as an environment-monitoring function.

EA therefore is about making sense of the architectural building blocks of the enterprise and their existing dynamics in relation to one another. A suitable definition might be:

> a set of organizational units with the common principles and objectives. The definition of the architectural elements consists of all people, processes, business and (information-) technology infrastructures [8].

Thus, EA is an operational plan for organizing business processes and required systems and technological infrastructure to achieve efficient process implementation. It is important to consider the EA as an active operational plan rather than only a set of descriptions or organizational artefacts and associated models.

2.6 Towards an EA Typology

Since EA has emerged from a set of principles, and these principles are usually described within a framework, there are many ways in which an EA can be developed, implemented and maintained. There are, however, two principal perspectives. One view is to consider the IT first – what systems are already in place and what opportunities they can afford the business. The opposing view is that of 'business first' – what business goals should the IT infrastructure realize.

Within the business-first perspective, there are two further sub-categories: business process-centric and governance-centric. Table 2.1 summarizes the key differences between the perspectives.

2.6.1 IT-Centric EA

The core objective of an IT-centric EA approach is to improve business-IT alignment. EA is mainly used to achieve effectiveness and efficiency by a systematic and structured approach to the coordination of IT in such a way that it realizes its efficiency goals. Harmon [7] introduces an 'Enterprise Architecture Pyramid' which shows how all of the different elements in an architecture are related within an organization.

Table 2.1 Comparison between "IT-centric" and "business-centric" perspectives of EA

	IT-centric	Business process-centric	Governance-centric
Objective	Business–IT alignment	To manage and improve business processes	To understand the business better, to be able to govern it better
Provide	An overview, from an IT perspective, of all the different IT and business models and resources and how they relate	An overview of all the different business processes and the relations between processes and the environment	An overview of all the domains within the enterprise described from different viewpoints
Focus is on	IT systems and their architecture	Business processes	Communication between business and IT; collaboration between all the divisions and managers
Initiators	IT managers	Business managers	All the managers of the enterprise
Users	IT department	Business departments	All departments

The focus of IT-centric EA lies in the corner of the pyramid which is the implementation level of the IT systems. Enterprises, which are using an IT-centric EA, will only consider other areas of the enterprise if that is necessary to define the IT. Business architecture in this context refers to models of the business, which are usually its processes and data models that support the design of IT solutions [7].

The IT-centric EA is an approach that is mostly used in the IT world, and it is used for generating an architecture that provides an overview of all the different IT models and resources and how they relate to one another. In this architecture, there is a focus on the IT systems and the architecture. The business is only described to lay down the demand for IT, and this demand is considered as given, and this is not discussed. IT only influences the business when new technology enables new business processes.

The IT architecture has to link up to the business processes, and the EA is a tool to do that as good as possible. Thus, there is a potential lack of integrated communication between the business and the IT. The initiators of an IT-centric EA are the IT managers, and this architecture is mainly used by the IT department.

Harmon also describes a model of EA that consists of the four layers from the IAF framework which can be adopted in an EA with an IT-centric perspective. The four layers each have their own dynamics, and they each need their own architectural description. The purpose of this model is to align IT with business. The division in these four layers, their level of detail and traceability through the layers (bottom up and top down) is sufficient to develop a holistic EA that leads to the proper alignment, validation and implementation of changing business strategies, tasks and activities, information and technology. If necessary, the EA elements can easily be extended on in more detailed domain-specific solution architectures; however, there is little or no consideration in terms of business process management [15].

As discussed, the most important goal of an IT-centric approach is business-IT alignment, and by definition, an enterprise has to be described with all its different architectures and the relationships between them. In this way, the Business Architecture (including the business processes) can be aligned with the System Architecture, Application Architecture, Software Architecture or Information Architecture. This way it will become clear which part of the business (processes) will be influenced by IT and vice versa.

2.6.2   Business Process-Centric Enterprise Architecture

In a business process-centric Enterprise Architecture, the prime objective is to adopt a business-oriented approach to integrally enhance and manage business processes top down by translating business objectives in actual operations including the IT support. This approach will result in the whole organizational processes to become optimally organized by designing business processes in a more abstract manner without implementation considerations followed by design of the relevant information systems and the organization in parallel [18].

In this manner the processes are first optimized and then each task in the process will be allocated to an IT system. Although the pyramid is in consideration as a whole, the core focus of business process-centric Enterprise Architecture lies in the middle layer of the Business Process Level [7]. Since the most important objective of a business process-centric approach is business processes improvement and management, it helps the enterprise to be market-led and customer-focused; hence, business processes are managed and improved to add value to the customers through continuous enhancement of value-adding business processes. It also creates opportunities for double-loop learning on every level in the enterprise. In this way, EA is used to fulfil the needs and demands of the customer.

2.6.3   Governance-Centric Enterprise Architecture

The most important objective of a governance-centric EA is a better understanding of the whole business and what makes better governance of it possible. By deconstructing the enterprise business model, it is possible to assess business results per business domain (instead of functional contributions to the whole) and compare them with relevant benchmarks.

The implementation of EA as a management tool has the benefit that sensitivity for the context is structured at every level of the enterprise. This increases the adaptability and agility of the enterprise to respond more adequately to the dynamics of the business environment. With the help of EA, entrepreneurial autonomy and initiative can be managed at all levels resulting in better exploitation of the creativity potential of an enterprise. In the same way, business principles and conformance will become clear for all the stakeholders.

2.7   Assessing the Benefits of Enterprise Architecture

Advocates of EA often see it as a 'smart' approach towards delivering increased value to an enterprise. Though, like any large-scale enterprise-wide initiatives, embracing EA consumes much needed enterprise resources. It is therefore essential to consider the realizable benefits of EA as well as measurable indicators to avoid generalities. It is important to consider EA benefits from different viewpoints of multiple stakeholders if an EA initiative is to succeed.

The stakeholders can be divided into business users and IT practitioners with varying requirements. From a business perspective, IT must be aligned with the business strategy to improve business process performance, whereas IT users want to deliver results that work and are reliable, reducing complexity and minimizing cost.

Recognizing that the auditing and monitoring aspects of managing EA implementation is challenging, the authors have adopted key characteristics identified by SAP in their own EA Framework [14] to produce an assessment tool that is illustrated below in the following sections.

For each contribution identified, there is a benefit, rationale and, importantly for the purposes of monitoring, one or more Key Performance Indicators (KPI).

2.7.1 EA Contributions for the Business

EA Contrib.	Benefit	Rationale	KPI
Helps achieve business strategy	Without an understanding of business, application and technical architecture, a business does not know what it is going to take to align and to implement IT to execute its business strategy. In essence, it does not know what it has or does not have. This ensures when planning programmes and projects that effort is targeted onto those aspects that really matter, and this adds to the strengths of the enterprise. It means that IT investment is targeted on the key business goals and performance. It ensures the business can be early adopters of new innovations and is not held back by IT	This is the ability of IT to leverage an organization's capability by a direct focus through understanding the strategy and intent. If everyone sees the same future, more can be done to achieve it It is difficult to estimate this value in monetary terms, but it can be appreciated regardless Spin-off benefits also include eliminating changes required by heading in the wrong initial direction Without Enterprise Architecture, organizations frequently approve projects that, from all outwards appearance, are not associated with any business strategy Organizational clout, supposedly self-funding business cases, and compartmentalized decision processes drive these behaviours If you cannot easily identify the strategy supporting the funding decision, then there probably isn't one	Alignment of investment with business strategy. (This can be monitored qualitatively via opinion survey targeted at the CxO-level executives) Number of projects approved that are in compliance/not in compliance with business strategy

| Faster time-to-market of new innovations and capabilities | If IT can introduce new technologies faster and functionalities faster to key business areas, this ensures the organization can respond faster to competitive pressures and deploy differentiating capabilities faster

These areas are most likely to be spotted when business and IT staff collaborate closely in the EA process

The outcome is that technology is ready when it is needed, transitions are smoother and unnecessary change is minimized | EA gives users faster delivery of new functionality and modifications and easier access to higher-quality, more consistent and more reliable information. Well-architected systems can more quickly link with external business partners

A common symptom in organizations without a robust Enterprise Architecture is project overruns. When new, important strategic projects are created, without a comprehensive understanding of the current state, the desired state, or the interrelationships of processes, people and technology affected by that project, unforeseen problems will occur resulting in project overruns

If the architecture of the organization is known and familiar, the relative time to implement new systems or capabilities is reduced

Dependent opportunities to upgrade items or refresh the estate can be identified early, and their impact on projects reduced

There are many examples of organizations that are prepared to employ new technologies such as VoIP, single user sign-on, or web-based services, because their upfront work on the target architecture has been done and the means to get there has been defined. | New business capabilities or features or service implemented faster

Number of project overspends/overruns >x months or x% of budget |

(continued)

(continued)

EA Contrib.	Benefit	Rationale	KPI
More consistent business processes and information across business units	EA can unlock the power of information, unifying information silos that inhibit business processes It identifies the processes, applications and data that need to be consistent if consistent business decisions are to be made	If an organization does not have visibility of its business process information, and how this relates to IT infrastructure, information silos and inconsistent systems will result This symptom has been exacerbated in recent years by mergers and acquisitions. These have added to the complexity of an organization's IT estate resulting in duplicate processes	Relative ease of access to information. (This can be monitored qualitatively via opinion survey targeted at the specific user groups) Response time to business demands. (This can be monitored qualitatively via opinion survey targeted at the specific user groups)
	EA identifies opportunities for integration and reuse that prevents the development of inconsistent processes and information	Especially important to users is the capability of integrating the information among applications and across data warehouses and data marts. By understanding an organization's data architecture, it can develop a standard data dictionary and develop metadata standards to minimize data inconsistency	

| More reliability and security and less risk | EA provides clear traceability between business processes, data, user roles, applications and infrastructure

A reliable architecture model aids consistency and manageability, and an organization has a much better chance of implementing corporate standards and planning and managing to those standards on an ongoing basis | When changes occur that cause unplanned downtime or other problems, and no one understands who did it, how it happened or why it happened, then the odds are high that it will happen again

The IT environment itself is in a constant state of change. A change two or three cycles in the past may not have an impact until the worse possible moment sometime in the future, cascading across the enterprise

If an organization does not have a clear model of its business, application and technical architecture and the dependencies and interrelatedness and installed processes and standards to manage that environment, then there will be no traceability or accountability | Rate of disruptions, availability of systems, number of untraced security incidents |

2.7.2 EA Contributions for IT Infrastructure

EA Contrib.	Benefit	Rationale	KPI
Better traceability of IT costs	EA provides greater understanding of the interrelated nature of business, application and infrastructure assets This enables greater understanding of how the architecture is structured and enables more accurate cross-charging or service billing It enables high-cost areas of the IT estate to be identified more accurately and a fairer cost model to be developed	Most organizations can identify the individual cost of an asset. However, many cannot understand the cost of an asset as it relates within the organization with all its interrelatedness and interdependencies IT departments can typically identify that a server costs so much, but they cannot identify what organizations that server supports, what the maintenance costs are, or what critical business applications are using that server In many cases, organizations do not have a mechanism to understand holistically all the costs associated with those related assets	Percent of IT operational expenditure that can be allocated to specific applications or business units
Lower IT costs – design, buy, operate, support, change	A clear understanding of AS-IS and TO-BE architecture, and the migration plan of how to progress from one to the other, will enable the implementation of duplicate systems to be avoided and acquisition integration to be accomplished effectively By understanding what it has, what it needs, what is redundant, an organization can tailor its investment to the areas of most need and identify reuse more frequently	If development standards and guidelines are in place that define the boundaries of what is possible for the application developer or infrastructure builder to do, and in effect describe how to behave when creating new capabilities, this can increase the efficiency of development projects whilst also enable the solution designer to have considerable freedom of choice in creating a solution where appropriate	Costs for upgrades/conversions Support cost (reduced due to less asset diversity) Monitoring/tracking level (costs reduced)

Faster design and development	The development of enterprise architecture enables earlier preparation for new technologies, smarter timing of projects and the reuse of development best practices, standard designs and components	Level of reuse (leveraging costs, implement faster, better)
Less complexity	Enterprise Architecture is an ideal tool to identify duplicate and overlapping processes, services, data hardware and software Standardization drives IT procurement efficiencies due to economies of scale Reduced skills maintenance, training, fewer support staff and simpler upgrades also result	CIOs should regularly monitor the size and complexity of their IT infrastructure and application portfolios It is common to see organizations that have no defined management mechanism to identify an 'end of life' technology or optimize application portfolios. The increasing complexity adds overhead costs while also increasing risk to project delivery schedules Savings estimates range from 10% to 30% of infrastructure costs, which are typically 50% of IT operating budgets. A 2001 Meta Group survey reported a 30% average reduction in IT total cost of ownership for companies with mature IT architectures and standards	Product diversity (more of fewer products) (no. of products per class in place, guidelines, new systems) Number of consolidated multiple redundant systems
	To solve duplication and overlap, an organization needs a comprehensive view of its applications, software and infrastructure and their interrelatedness	Fewer products, as opposed to many, means higher unit volumes and better ability to support the products and plan timely transitions that respond both to the business need and the technology progress rate. Familiarity also provides experience on performance, risk and maintenance. Sound choices often enable an ability to monitor and track the system in consistent ways that help deliver better client service. Even IT personnel demands are made simpler	Number of avoided purchases (e.g. another enterprise RDBMS) Technical infrastructure skills diversity

(continued)

(continued)

EA Contrib.	Benefit	Rationale	KPI
Less IT risk	Developing a TO-BE architecture and a managed migration plan will mean that the IT function will be prepared to deliver the new capabilities in a timely manner – generally, faster than the competition The IT effort will be aligned with the strategy, and unexpected surprises and demands will be avoided. This will enable efficient transitions to new capabilities Capacity planning and monitoring improves as system retirements and upgrades can be planned in advance	A clear 2–3-year plan for the enterprise is a typical product on Enterprise Architecture. Using this, the organization can forecast the required budget, make realistic commitments and plan in good time for IT changes An organization without a strategic plan is often consumed day-to-day with the next 'emergency'. While some may say, 'What's wrong with that? Everyone is focused on what matters', the situation is not healthy for IT or for the business With focus on the short term, and without adequate time to plan, each new solution is at risk for becoming another silo. Increasingly, more time is spent trying to make each new solution 'fit in' than on the solution itself Capacity planning becomes very difficult in such environments, which in turn causes further unplanned capacity and system upgrades. This causes further project overruns	Rate of urgent infrastructure projects (reactive) Downtime/availability Occurrence of short-lived products (more stable) Number of projects in compliance, not in compliance, returned for modifications, proceeded without change, requested waiver(s), waivers granted/rejected Percent of projects accepted into Service Delivery without issue Cost/time vs. original budget adjusted by percent of original requirements/percent of high severity defects

2.8 Discussion

At definition level, as an architecture, SOA's association to EA can be regarded in each component architecture view from a Business Architecture right to technical and operational architecture. The concepts and artefacts described by an Enterprise Architecture are also central to SOAs in that they link the organizational relationships and roles in business processes to service points. On the other hand, representing services in an EA requires extensions to the existing architectural frameworks as for instance to support SOA interoperability. EA products need to be extended as specified in an SOA framework. In the same way, the core concept of SOA, namely services, need to be understood and be viewable across the multiple perspectives contained within an EA framework. EA frameworks comprise multiple views or perspectives such as business or technical, whereas SOA provides a single services view whether technical and business.

As SOA supports business processes through its focus on the business services, Enterprise Architectures can offer an integrated and abstract context to describe the enterprise's business services.

Just like its predecessor, SOA often requires upfront business process reengineering and change management to align services and subsequent Business Process Management to drive effective service management. SOA's properties such as loose coupling, reuse and modularity should be understood and accounted for in EA. The EA discipline offers depth and breadth of analysis; a top-down design Enterprise Architecture allows a more effective SOA design. This will imply governance and alignment of methodologies.

2.8.1 EA Contributions to SOA

The development of Enterprise Architecture provides the definition of initiatives and prioritization of those initiatives with each of these initiatives realized via enterprise SOA solutions. EA guides the development of the Solution Architecture of those individual enterprise SOA initiatives. In other words, EA defines the architectural requirements that can be fulfilled by individual enterprise SOA initiatives. EA provides a complete business-IT traceability and supports the alignment of enterprise web services with other enterprise-wide services within each architecture domain (business, data and platform services). EA enables the trace of enterprise services to business goals/objectives and strategy. One of the key benefits of EA is that it optimizes application and data portfolios at the enterprise level by defining the strategic architecture, helping enterprises avoid applications that have duplicated functionality and data structures. EA provides the necessary context, structure and governance for the individual initiatives and their solution development that would transform the enterprise from its *as-is* to *to-be* state. From the 'context' perspective, EA helps to define the business vision, goals and objectives, and prescribes the development of principles that will guide the subsequent architectural development.

2.8.2   SOA Contributions to EA

A Service-Oriented Enterprise Architecture can be a starting point for application architecture principles and guidelines, and is often deemed as a requirement for the adoption of CC. Enterprise SOA and, in general, SOA has expanded the concept of service orientation to other architectural domains within the enterprise. In other words, what is good for applications is good for business as well. The notion of encapsulating functionality and exposing it as a service can be expanded to other domains such as business or technology domains. EA discipline offers enterprises a structured approach to identifying the changes that are needed to realize their strategy, define what those changes are and finally guide or govern the implementation of those changes. Service-Oriented EA also offers a structured approach to develop flexible and open service based solutions for the change initiatives identified and prioritized during the development of enterprise architecture.

2.9   Conclusion

An EA based on SOA provides the necessary foundation for the exploitation of business-IT alignment. It represents a *to-be* blueprint of the enterprise. A well-designed EA can serve as an organizing mechanism providing a strategic architecture that will help steer the enterprise transformation to the desired target state. This can inform the development of CC and, subsequently, enterprise SOA initiatives to enable or operationalize corporate strategy.

As the disciplines of EA and SOA are still evolving and emerging and approaches such as CC appearing (such as Software as a Service, Business Process as a Service and the 'Enterprise 2.0' paradigm), there is scope for much research into the maturity of architectural models and approaches. In particular, research into critical success factors and best practice implementation of SOA and EA would serve to inform how enterprises can adopt CC to serve the business needs of an organization. As infrastructure interoperability becomes less of an issue in the technical sense, there is a greater need to understand the information and goal-direct aspirations of enterprises, in order that these may be exchanged, delegated and shared for tangible business advantage.

References

1. Chief Information Officers Council: TEAF, Treasury Enterprise Architecture Framework version 1.0. Architecture Working Group, US Department of Treasury, Washington, DC (2000)
2. Chief Information Officers Council: Federal Enterprise Architecture Framework (FEAF) version 1.1 (Sept 1999)
3. Chief Information Officers Council: A practical guide to Federal Enterprise Architecture, version 1.0 (2001)

4. DoD Architecture Framework Working Group, US Department of Defense: DoD Architecture Framework version 1.0 (2003)
5. Forrester Research: Service-oriented architecture: concepts, technology and design. Prentice Hall, Upper Saddle River (2006)
6. Forrester Research: SOA is not dead – but it should be buried: doing SOA right opens the door to a much bigger architecture vision. Forrester Research, Inc., Cambridge, MA, USA, May 11 (2009)
7. Harmon, P.: The human side of an Enterprise Architecture. Business Process Trends Newsletter, 2(10). www.bptrends.com (2004)
8. Institute for Enterprise Architecture Development (IEAD): Available at: www.enterprise-architecture.info. Last accessed May 2009
9. Mahon Smith, L.: Data analysis for business analysts: the Zachman Framework™ and data architecture. ModernAnalyst.com. The Premier online Community for Business Analysts (2009). Last accessed May 2011
10. The Open Group: The Open Group Architecture Framework (TOGAF) version 8, Enterprise Edition (2002)
11. O'Rourke, C., Fishman, N., Selkow, W.: Enterprise Architecture using the Zachman Framework. Course Technology, Boston (2003)
12. Ross, J.W., Weill, P., Robertson, D.C.: Enterprise Architecture as strategy, vol. 1. Harvard Business School Press, Cambridge (2006)
13. SAP Community Network: Methodology for accelerated transformation to SOA. https://www.sdn.sap.com/irj/sdn/soa-methodology (2009). Last accessed May 2011
14. SAP: SAP EAF overview guide, version 1.1 (2007). Access confidential Dec 2008
15. Schekkerman, J.: How to survive in the jungle of enterprise architecture frameworks: creating or choosing an enterprise architecture framework, 3rd edn. Trafford Publishing, Victoria (2006)
16. Spewak, S., Hill, S.C.: Enterprise Architecture planning: developing a blueprint for data, applications, and technology. Wiley, New York (1995)
17. US Department of Defense – C4ISR Architectures Working Group: C4ISR Architecture Framework version 2.0. Available at: http://www.c3i.osd.mil/org/cio/i3/AWG_Digital_Library/ (1997). Last accessed Dec 2011
18. Van Hee, K.M.: Information systems engineering: a formal approach. Cambridge University Press, Cambridge (1994)
19. Wegmann, A.: The systemic enterprise architecture methodology. In: The International Conference on Enterprise Information Systems (ICEIS 2003), Angers (2003)
20. Wegmann, A., et al.: Augmenting the Zachman Enterprise Architecture Framework with a systemic conceptualization. Presented at the 12th IEEE International EDOC Conference (EDOC 2008), München, Germany (2008)
21. Wilkes, L.: The essential guide to service orientation. CBDI Journal, CBDI Forum (2004)
22. Zachman, J.A.: Zachman on the Framework. Zachman Institute for Framework Advancement (ZIFA) at www.zifa.com (2008). Last accessed Dec 2010
23. Zachman, J.A.: The Framework for Enterprise Architecture: background, description and utility. Zachman Institute for Framework Advancement (ZIFA) at www.zifa.com (2000). Last accessed Dec 2010
24. Zachman, J.A., Sowa, J.F.: Extending and formalizing the framework for Information Systems Architecture. IBM Syst. J. **31**(3):590–616 (1992)

Chapter 3
Cloud Computing Business Models

Abbas Strømmen-Bakhtiar and Amir R. Razavi

Abstract This chapter is focused on business models for Cloud computing. The authors try to provide a clear picture of various available business models for both Cloud providers and consumers in terms of cost, necessary infrastructures, and expectations. The standard cost model for both service consumers and service providers (IaaS, PaaS, and SaaS) has been investigated while keeping in mind the existing interdependence of various levels. Meanwhile the various business models for different layers of the Cloud computing are listed, and their suitability is studied. In this regard, IaaS has been of particular interest since this layer clearly has the least barrier to entry (financing) and therefore presents the greatest opportunity to the SMBs who may be interested in competing in this layer. The chapter can be used as an adequate guideline for businesses who intend to enter the market as Cloud providers (investors, consultants, etc.), are already providers, or are either already Cloud consumers or intend to outsource their IT infrastructure and services using the Cloud.

3.1 Introduction

Cloud computing is often referred to as the fifth utility, bringing to mind the images of water, electricity, telephone, or radio and TV broadcasting companies with the associated products and services that are available almost anywhere, on demand. These references are based on the nature and promise of Cloud computing which is defined as "common, location-independent, online, utility that is available on – Demand" [1].

A. Strømmen-Bakhtiar (✉)
Centre for Enterprise Architecture and Information Systems, Bodø Graduate School of Business, University of Nordland, 80049 Bodø, Norway
e-mail: abbas.strommen.bakhtiar@gmail.com

A.R. Razavi
Department of Computing, School of Electronics and Physical Sciences, University of Surrey, Guildford, Surrey GU2 7XH, UK

Z. Mahmood and R. Hill (eds.), *Cloud Computing for Enterprise Architectures*,
Computer Communications and Networks, DOI 10.1007/978-1-4471-2236-4_3,
© Springer-Verlag London Limited 2011

Currently Cloud computing is being promoted as the latest outsourcing solution of the new century. But before businesses, be they service providers or service consumers, venture into the Cloud, they have to determine if it makes business sense; i.e., it is profitable. They have to know about pricing and cost structures of the Cloud.

They are also concerned with the nature of partnerships that will enter into. The advantages of the traditional outsourcing such as favourable cash flow profile, cost reduction in IT service chain, shifting to 24×7 operations, etc., are still there; but so are the original questions and problems, such as reliability, security, technological renewal, and legal responsibility, just to name a few.

The traditional outsourcing "contract" is evolving into something different, resulting in the need for redefining the emerging relationship. Bohm et al. [2] point out that the best way to address this critical question is to look at the current challenges of outsourcing. The customers expect a cost-effective and flexible delivery of IT services from their service providers at a lowest cost possible, while at the same time demanding customer-specific innovations. Out of these expectations and challenges, they argue, has the Cloud computing emerged, necessitating a new approach to the "relationship management," i.e., the maintenance of a good outsourcing relationship.

This chapter will look into these issues and try to present a balanced view of the existing pricing models and the evolving relationships in the Cloud. It will begin with a general review of the Cloud computing, its layers, and business models. The second section analyzes the business models with respect to IaaS (Infrastructure as a Service). The business model for Platform as a Service (PaaS) is discussed in the third section. The SaaS (Software as a Service) business models are explored in the fourth section. The fifth section discusses the evolving relationships (customer-provider) in the Cloud. And finally we will consider the remaining issues that are to be addressed before Cloud computing can be truly be called a utility.

3.2   Business Models and the Cloud Layers

The impetuses behind outsourcing have always been dependent on the evolving business models which emphasize creating sustainable advantage in the marketplace. Businesses look for ways to increase revenue growth, decrease costs, increase asset efficiency, build entry barriers, innovate, etc., all of which have become increasingly dependent on the IT technologies. These technologies are playing an increasing role in determining the success or failure of these businesses.

As the complexity and importance of having a functioning IT system has increased, so has the pressure on the managers to address various technical issues that in many instances are tangential to the core activities of the companies. In these cases, outsourcing has been an attractive solution.

But as internetworking has reshaped the marketplace, where geography and time zones have lost their meanings, and online access to markets, customers, and suppliers have become a must, the role of IT systems has changed from one of supporting role to becoming one of the key success factors.

With this change has come the problem of constructing, maintaining, and managing IT systems that are constantly evolving. For companies where focus should be on the core activities of the company, this can become a quite a distraction. For these companies, outsourcing has been, is, and will be a good solution.

But how about companies whose core activities are dependent on their IT systems or where IT is embedded in their products and services? How about those companies that use IT in innovative ways to differentiate themselves from others? Can outsourcing be a solution for them?

As can be seen, the questions of pricing and relationship management are only a part of a larger set of problems that have to be addressed before one can get a clearer picture of true advantages and disadvantages of Cloud computing for the businesses, governments, and individual user. This applies both to the providers and the consumers of the services at all levels.

3.3   Cloud Computing Layers

Cloud computing is composed of three layers. These layers are Software as a Service (SaaS), Platform as a Service (PaaS), and Infrastructure as a Service (IaaS). Each layer offers particular types of services to a particular segment of the market while at the same time paying for the services provided by the preceding layer (except IaaS) (Fig. 3.1).

The first layer or foundation of the Cloud computing is the IT level or IaaS. At this level, the product is the hardware and related services. Here we have general processing, servers, storage devices, database management, and all other hardware-related services offered as a service to the end user. As can be guessed, the necessary investment at this level is huge and requires a considerable financial planning and provisioning. Datacenters are expensive to build and maintain (Fig. 3.2).

The next layer is the Platform layer (PaaS). At this level, developers can design, build, and test applications that run on the IaaS. Those applications can be either for

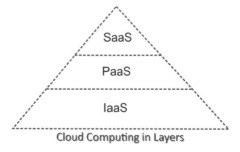

Fig. 3.1 SaaS, PaaS, and IaaS

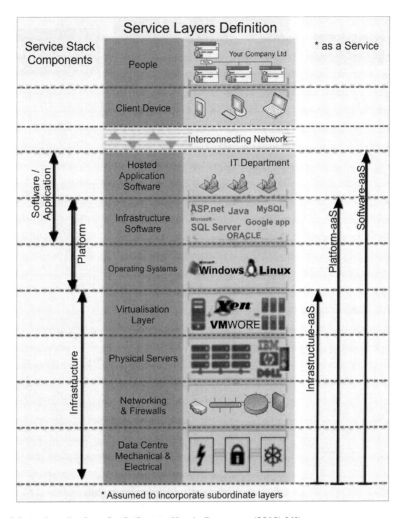

Fig. 3.2 IaaS vs. PaaS vs. SaaS (Source: Kate's Comments (2010) [4])

the IaaS itself or for the layer above (SaaS). This layer offers the same environment as the traditional software development environment except that the hardware is outsourced. So as far as the investment is concerned, the advantages are not as large as it is for other companies at other layers. But, the opportunity of providing new applications for the Cloud and distributed through SaaS can make this layer a very attractive layer for developers (Table 3.1).

The final layer (SaaS) deals exclusively with applications for the end users. This layer is the hosting layer, where companies host applications for the users. SaaS layer is where providers will face the largest challenge with regard to providing the range and quality of services that customers demand at competitive prices. Here one must plan for all exigencies.

Table 3.1 Variants of cloud computing

Level	Description
User level (Software-as-a-Service)	Companies host applications in the cloud that many users access through Internet connections. The service being sold or offered is a complete end-user application
Developer Level (Platform-as-a-Service)	Developer can design, build, and test applications that run on the cloud provider's infrastructure and then deliver those applications to end-users from the provider's servers
IT Level (Infrastructure-as-a-Service)	System administrators obtain general processing, storage, database management, and other resources and applications through the network and pay only for what gets used

Source: Adapted from: Rayport and Heyward [3]

3.4 Business Models of the Cloud

A business model is defined as "The plan implemented by a company to generate revenue and make a profit from operations. The model includes the components and functions of the business, as well as the revenues it generates and the expenses it incurs" [5].

Cloud computing is often referred to as the fifth utility, and as such we should start by looking at the models used by utility companies. In this respect, Rappa's [6] categories of business models of utility services can be a good starting point (Table 3.2).

As can be seen, water, electricity, and common carrier transportation utility companies all use the "metered usage of service" business model. While the rest (radio, TV, telephone, and Internet access) use mainly the "subscription" model with some metered usage for special services.

The metered usage model is used mainly for products that are standardized and quality of which is (to some extent) known or regulated. This applies perfectly to processing power, use of storage devices, servers, and other hardware that composes the IaaS layer. So it is assumed that for IaaS, the metering model is the best solution. The PaaS layer which can be compared to the water pipelines or electrical grids has their own model. It is difficult to apply the pay as you go to this layer since the final consumer hardly sees or thinks about this layer. Therefore, the costs associated with this layer have to be somehow baked in the infrastructure costs.

The SaaS layer with its myriad of products, and especially the quality of services, requires a different solution. Subscription and pay as you go (licensing fees) are the best available models for this layer. We shall now have a closer look at each layer and consider the available business models.

Table 3.2 Business models of utility services

Type of service	Business models
Water	Metered usage of service
Electricity	Metered usage of service
Common carrier transportation	Basic pay-as-you-go fare for one-way or roundtrip service; subscription for commuter service
Telephone:	
POTS	Subscription for local service; metered usage of long distance service; equipment is leased or purchased
Cellular	Subscription with usage limits; metered usage in excess of the subscription limit; equipment purchased or bundled with subscription
Radio and Television Broadcasting:	
Terrestrial	Advertiser-sponsored, community-sponsored
Satellite	Subscription with basic package and premium services
	Lease or purchase equipment
Cable	Subscription with basic package and premium services
	Pay-per-view for special event programming and movie selections
	Leased equipment is bundled with service
Internet Access:	
DSL	Subscription for unlimited ("always on") service
	Leased equipment is bundled with service
Cable	Subscription for unlimited ("always on") service
	Leased equipment is bundled with service
Dial-up	Subscription for limited service or metered usage based upon connection time
	Equipment is purchased

Source: M. A. Rappa [6]

3.5   Infrastructure as a Service (IaaS)

As was mentioned previously, the general consensus [7–9] is that infrastructure outsourcing business model should follow the utility model. But what makes a particular service a utility is shaped by a combination of requirements, which Rappa [6] lists as: necessity, reliability, usability, utilization rates, scalability, and service exclusivity.

We should also add commoditization to our list. All utility companies offer (more or less) products that are standardized/commoditized. According to Jaekel and Luhn [10] of Siemens IT Solutions and Services, "all IaaS models result in industrialization and commoditization of infrastructure services. A vital prerequisite is a high degree of automation in providing virtualized infrastructure services (dynamic services)."

IaaS providers need to consider these factors when deciding on investments and pricing models: (1) The infrastructure is necessary for the operation of the customer's company; any disruptions may have both financial and legal consequences. As the customer uses the infrastructure, soon it becomes a transparent part of their organization, which makes the second point vital. (2) The service (uptime) has to be readily available when and where the user needs it. (3) The interface should be easy, regardless of how complex the technology. This means that the user should not go through loops to get access. It should be flawless. (4) The user demand may fluctuate, but the service level should not. This means that if many customers suddenly require processing power, this should not create a bottleneck or increase response time. Capacity planning is extremely important, which brings us to the subject of scalability. (5) IaaS providers have to determine a realistic threshold. All utility companies face the same problem: as the demand for a service increases beyond some threshold, the quality of service may decline. It is paramount that the service provider makes provisions for such scenarios. (6) In addition, we have to consider the legal issues that arise from customers using physical infrastructures that are outside the customer's national boundaries.

Laurin H. Mills [11] of Nixon Peabody LLP (Attorneys at Law) lists six legal issues that may affect a Cloud provider, especially the IaaS provider. These issues are:

- Location (where is the data and what laws govern them)
- Operations (service level and security)
- Legislation or regulatory (including privacy)
- Third-party contractual limitations on use of Cloud
- Security
- Investigative/litigation (e-discovery)
- Risk allocation or risk mitigation/insurance

Mills points out that the provider may not be able to control the location of the infrastructure through the contract with the customer since in some countries the law may trump contractual provisions. Storing data in certain regions may also not be acceptable to the customer, especially the government. Other important issues, she argues, are the backup/data restoration and disaster recovery. Who is responsible for such costs and what are the limits and liabilities. There are also other regulatory/governance issues such as: Patriot Act/UK regulation of Investigatory Powers Act, Stored Communication Act (USA), HIPPA (health-related information – USA), FTC and state privacy laws (USA) and a host of other regulations (depending on national, regional, or international laws and agreements).

The IaaS providers should consider all these issues and include the costs in their pricing models. As far as the customers are concerned, it is the provider that has to meet the regulatory requirements. They are mainly concerned with their cash flow (Fig. 3.3), quality of services, and reliability, after all, that is why they are outsourcing their infrastructure (Fig. 3.4).

The pay as you go model or metering is perhaps the best model for the IaaS providers which can be packaged in several ways to allow for customization of the product. It can also be combined with subscription to allow for more flexibility (and revenue). For example, the provider can offer a certain level of basic

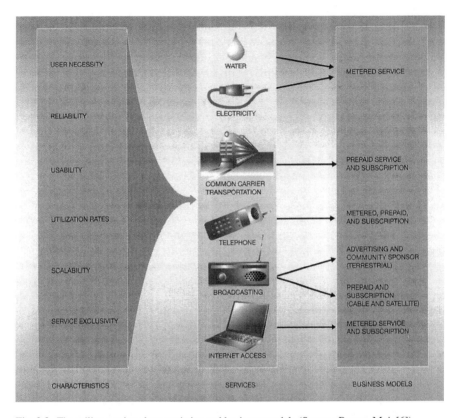

Fig. 3.3 The utility-service characteristics and business models (Source: Rappa, M.A.[6])

services at a fixed rate and then anything above can be metered. In another version, one can separate and meter individual services such as processing, storage, access, etc.

3.6 IaaS Variants

There is also the question of sharing resources. IaaS business model can take three forms: public, private, or hybrid. In public Cloud, the applications of different customers are hosted in a shared environment, which is suitable for nonbusiness-critical applications, individual users, and micro to small businesses. Private Cloud on the other hand is suitable for those businesses that have special requirements such as special security, maintenance of resource control, compliance with corporate or regulatory requirements, etc. And finally, it is possible to have a hybrid model where part of the infrastructure can be dedicated and the rest be on the shared Cloud (Fig. 3.5).

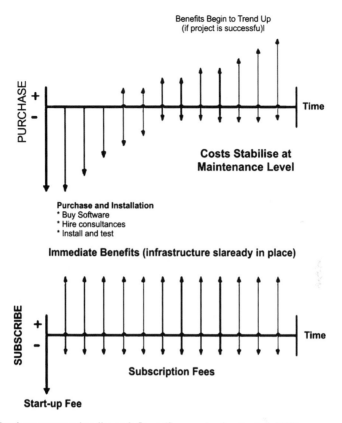

Fig. 3.4 Purchase versus subscribe cash flows (Source: Applegate et al. [12])

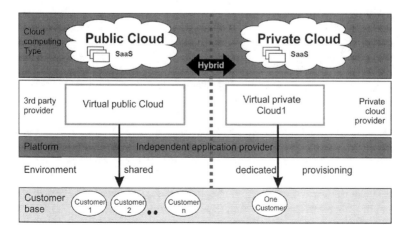

Fig. 3.5 IaaS Variants

3.7   Platform as a Service (PaaS)

PaaS is the sweet spot of the Cloud computing. It is where the infrastructure software and the operating systems are located. This layer provides the software environment where developers create Cloud applications. This layer also offers a host of benefits to the developers, from features like "automatic scaling and load balancing, authentication services and communication services, to graphical user interface (GUI) components. However, as long as there is no common standard for Cloud application development, lock-in effects arise, making the developer dependent on the proprietary software environment of the Cloud platform provider" [2].

A few examples of this are the Google App Engine, Microsoft Azure, Tibco Silver, IBM sMash, Mosso, and Retail One. Most providers lock in developers by offering flexible platform for almost no cost at all (at least to begin with). For example, Google App Engine offers 500 MB [13] of storage and enough CPU and bandwidth to support an efficient application serving around five million page views a month, absolutely free. When the application developer enables billing, then the free limits are raised and then the developer pays only for resources used above the free limit.

> All PaaS solutions are based on integration of SaaS applications in the underlying infrastructure via a Cloud-capable PaaS development environment. The largest variant involves extensive middleware components. A further aspect of PaaS will give rise to further business model variants: billing, metering and monitoring functionalities. These decide what the features of the pay-as-you-use component are. Creation of full-service platform solutions means that independent software vendors (ISVs) and IT departments of system integrators can develop and deliver applications online using third-party infrastructure services. [10]

PaaS layer can be an important source of future revenue by locking in the ISVs into the IaaS layer and in addition get part of the revenues accrued from the sale of the developed software. In other words, the PaaS provider allows the ISVs to develop their software and sell it for a percentage of the sales plus something extra for use of the environment.

Outsourcing key parts of business elsewhere carries risks. To reduce this risk, companies such as IBM, HP, and others sell virtualization and specialized management software to keep customers' new systems running as unified whole, in effect allowing customers to create their own private Clouds.

As can be seen, PaaS providers play an important role in determining the success or failure of a particular Cloud venture. The operating system/middleware that PaaS provides is the key to seamless integration of various systems. How to price a particular application will of course vary; but large corporations such as IBM or other hardware manufacturers will have to subsidize the costs, if it is bundled with their own hardware. But as in commercial Cloud, the cost is born by the infrastructure provider; i.e., there IaaS provider will pay licence fees to the PaaS provider.

3.8   Software as a Service (SaaS)

Software as a Service is basically a delivery model of software services on demand across the web. For years, software expenses (purchase price, licensing, etc.) have been a major part of IT expenses of companies. For many industries, 10% of their investments go into software. The fraction is higher in businesses such as banking, less in healthcare and education [14]. The SaaS promises to drastically reduce that. The result has been a steady increase in the number of companies that are outsourcing their software needs. This has been reflected in the revenue of companies that offer SaaS. According to *McKinsey Quarterly* "the companies whose main business is delivering software as a service saw their revenue rise from $295 million in 2002 to $485 million in 2005, an 18% increase. On the buyer's side, our fall 2006 survey of senior IT executives indicated a dramatic jump in the number of companies considering software-as-a-service applications during 2007" [15].

As of 2009, there were around 75,000 independent software vendors (ISVs) worldwide, with total sales of approximately $250 billion. Around 80% of the total revenue was generated by about 2% of these companies [16]. The rest comprise of small companies with limited resources for R&D, and specially, marketing.

Cloud computing offers these small companies a unique opportunity to lower their application development costs, reduce their development and time to market, extend the service offerings of other vendors, and create new and novel solutions to customers. These ISVs can also take advantage of virtualization of their own infrastructure, focusing their resources and attention on R&D, distribution, and marketing.

Most major software developers are already investing heavily in Cloud infrastructure, or cooperating with major IaaS providers, so a direct competition with these companies will be difficult. The best model for small ISVs would be to follow the models of mobile phone application developers, that is to say, build solutions around the offerings of the big players like Microsoft, Google, and others. The small ISVs can complement the existing solutions by offering specialized services, such as software + services (a strategy used by Microsoft) or offer on-demand versions of their existing software.

As far as the SaaS providers go, they have to be careful of how they design, build, and market their products. One of the global hands-on venture investment groups, Bessemer (Bessemer Venture Partners or BVP), has been investing in leading technology companies such as Ciena, Ingersoll, Skype, Verisign, Veritas, and others. In the recent years, Bessemer has invested in a number of Cloud computing companies, which has given BVP a good knowledge of what actually works out there. Based on this, BVP has come up with what they call the ten laws of Cloud computing and SaaS [17]. Bessemer suggests that the customer should put as much into the Cloud as possible and pay attention to the following:

1. Less is more
2. Trust the 6 C's of Cloud finance

   - Committed Monthly Recurring Revenue (CMRR)
   - Cash flow

- CPipe – CMRR pipeline
- Churn
- Customer Acquisition Cost (CAC) ratio and customer lifetime
- CLTV – Customer LifeTime Value

3. Study the sales learning curve (SLC) and only invest behind success
4. Forget everything you learned about software channels
5. Build employee software
6. Concentrate more on online marketing and sale
7. Concentrate on service: support, support, support
8. Leverage and monetize the data assets
9. Mind the GAAP (General Accepted Accounting Principles)
10. Need for several refueling (investments) along the way

These ten laws basically cover the full spectrum of investing in and using SaaS layer. *The first law* tells us to put as much as possible in the Cloud and reduce on-premises deployments as much as possible. *The second law* deals with the financial aspects, such as CMRR, cash flow, CPipe, Churn, CAC, and CLTV.

CMRR is analogous to the saying: a bird in the hand is worth two in the bush. One of the most important metrics for software executives is the "booking" value. Executives look at this booking to see the future health of their companies. Bessemer says that this is for suckers. In Cloud computing, one should concentrate on the Annual Contract Value (ACV) or Monthly Recurring Revenue (MRR), or the combined value of all of the current recurring subscription revenue, instead of bookings. It is the tracking of the forward view of CMRR that gives the executives a better picture of their future financial health and not the bookings.

The cash flow can be improved by offering customers discounts in exchange for quarterly or annual pre-payment; which in turn affects the CMRR pipeline. That is to say, define which pipeline (monthly, quarterly etc.) is best suited for the business.

Keeping track of customer churn is also a vital task for the executives. Customers are expensive to get and easy to lose simply because the switching costs in SaaS layer are relatively small. The churn ratio is of course dependent on the number of existing customers, which in turn is influenced by your marketing expenditure.

One major question which always arises, when discussing marketing, is one of return on investments; that is to say, how much bang do we get for each dollar spent on marketing. The CAC ratio can answer this question by identifying the amount of time it takes to get back the marketing investment. For example, a ratio of 0.5 will tell you that it will take half a year to recover the marketing costs.

$$\text{Customer Acquisition Cost Ratio (CAC)} = \frac{\text{New Committed Monthly Recurring Revenue (CRMM)} \times 12 \times \text{Gross Margin\%}}{\text{Sales and Marketing costs}}$$

(excluding account management costs)

But looking only at churn rate and CMRR do not answer the important question of what a customer is actually worth over the entire life of that relationship with the customer. We have to consider the lifetime value of the customer.

In finance, the Net Present Value (NPV) is the sum present value of all future cash in-flows minus all future outflows, that is to say all cash flows are discounted back to their present value. The Customer LifeTime Value (CLTV) is the net present value of all the recurring profit of a given customer minus the cost of acquisition.

The third law concerns the investment in sales and software channels. In sales, a salesperson is thought to have a certain personality; he is either a hunter or a farmer. A hunter is a salesperson (using aggressive sales techniques) who focuses mostly on bringing in new customers, while a farmer is someone who creates sales demand by activities that directly influence and alter the buying process [18, 19]. Of course sales people have a little of both, but in general, some may have more attributes of one than the other.

According to Bessemer, the software organizations that staff up their sales efforts too quickly before their sales model has been refined often fail. They suggest that software organizations should hire sales representatives slowly upfront and focus on their immediate geographical area until the business starts to scale considerably, while at the same time separating the hunters and farmers as the business starts to ramp, and pay them all on CMRR growth.

Once the company has got a sizable customer base, it should supplement its sales force with renewal-oriented account managers (farmers). One should be aware that both teams are important for the health and growth of the company, since CMRR is a function of new sales net of churn from the existing accounts.

The fourth law tells us to forget everything we have learned about software channels. This is simply because Cloud products do not "pull through" sizable amount of professional services, hardware, or infrastructure software. So there is no need for close relationships with traditional software and integration companies (e.g., IBM Oracle, etc.).

The fifth law tells us to redirect our focus from the managers of companies as decision makers to the employees. According to Bessemer, employees are now powerful customers, not just their managers. They argue that employees are now familiar with rich internet applications such as Facebook, Wikipedia, etc. They are tired of using the standard products that are offered by SAP or Oracle. If enough employees of a company go for the software, then the company will follow.

The sixth law concerns the online marketing. The future is online. People are now used to do most things, including window shopping, online. It is time for businesses to use the business-to-customer (B2C) marketing techniques for business-to-business (B2B) marketing as well.

The seventh law deals with services. Bessemer argues that the most important part of Software-as-a-Service isn't "Software" but "service". They argue that every Cloud computing company is in the service business and therefore should provide as good a service as possible. They suggest that a good place to start is the detailed usage statistics. Using this, the company can evolve the product each and every day.

The eighth law deals with monetizing the data assets. One of the consequences of providing software subscription to the customers is that you end up hosting their data. Bessemer argues that as a Cloud computing service, the company captures some peripheral information that can be interesting for the executives of those companies. These information can be packaged (e.g., through a dashboard) and sold for an incremental subscription fee. Another related benefit would be to identify key performance indicators across the board for your entire customer base.

The ninth law concerns GAAP. GAAP stands for Generally Accepted Accounting Principles which is "the common set of accounting principles, standards and procedures that companies use to compile their financial statements. GAAP is a combination of authoritative standards (set by policy boards) and simply the commonly accepted ways of recording and reporting accounting information" [20]. GAAP may differ from country to country, but generally, and at least in EU and USA, Canada, and other advanced economies, the rules are similar.

From the Cloud computing provider side, the revenue stream is composed of one or both of the following: subscription services and professional services, including implementation and training. Subscription services replace the old licensing fee for the software providers. For example, when an ERP software was sold, as soon as the software was shipped the fee could be recognized, just as if a product was shipped to the customer. This made accounting easy, for the costs and revenues could easily be aligned. One could also separate the professional services from the product.

For subscription fee, the rules are different. As was mentioned earlier, the officially recognized (GAAP) revenue lags the CMRR because one usually cannot (as far as accounting goes) recognize the revenue before the services go live, even if one has been paid in advance. Also "according to GAAP, professional services for recurring revenue businesses are tied to the subscription service, and therefore cannot be accounted for separately. In this respect, even if the professional services are delivered only over the first few months of the contract, the revenue recognition needs to match at least the length of the contract."

And finally, *the tenth law* states that Cloudonomics requires that one be very careful about how much investment is required and when. It is stated that since providers have to pay for everything up front and customers pay over time, in the short time, there will arise a cash flow problem that providers have to plan for. The providers have to determine their capital requirements carefully and plan for "refueling" stops along the way.

3.9 The Cloud and the Evolving Relationships

The traditional outsourcing "*contract*" is evolving into something different, resulting in the need for redefining of the emerging relationship. Bohm et al. [2] point out that the best way to address this critical question is to look at the current challenges of outsourcing. The customers expect a cost-effective and flexible delivery of IT services from their service providers at a lowest cost possible, while at the same time demanding customer-specific innovations. Out of these expectations and challenges, they argue, has the Cloud computing emerged, necessitating a new approach to the "relationship management," i.e., the maintenance of a good outsourcing relationship.

But what is a good outsourcing relationship? The answer lies perhaps in what each part in the relationship is after. The provider is interested to have a good return on its investment through long-term contracts that binds the customer to itself; while the customer is interested in receiving high-quality services at reasonable prices on demand.

Cloud pricing models that are based on pay as you go (utility model) can be confusing – and even off-putting – to IT managers and organizational executives. They have to think differently. They used to buy a blade server and could use it whenever and however they liked; now they have to think about CPU hours, etc.

Customers, as was mentioned earlier, expect tremendous cost savings, something that may not be the case. This does not necessarily mean that there are hidden costs (although they may be) in the contract, but that the anticipated usage may be grossly underestimated by the customer. How many people are shocked by the mobile phone bills? Underestimating utilization can quickly sour the relationship between the provider and the customer.

There is also the problem of perceptions. For example, as the cost of storage, CPUs, and other hardware declines, the customer will be left with a feeling that they are paying more for less.

All in all, the old IT outsourcing models still apply, only more complicated. Considering the pricing models and different layers of Cloud computing, one can state that a successful relationship will depend on realistic expectations of the customer including assessing the risks involved, and realistic presentation of the cost and quality of services by the provider.

A good example of what can go wrong is presented by the Australian Federal Government's attempt to outsource its IT infrastructure. In 2001, after a damning public report by the Auditor General, the Federal Government abandoned the outsourcing project. Rouse and Corbitt [21] conducted a 4-year study of this failure and identified several key underlying factors that led to the failure of this outsourcing project; factors that are still relevant today.

They put the blame partially on the providers, stating that the providers were overstating the advantages and understating the risks of outsourcing. But most of the blames fall on the customer (Australian Federal Government). The government is accused of underestimating the costs and the managerial effort required while overestimating the savings and effects on operational performance. They argue that "framing IT outsourcing as a quite risky venture (in contrast to the comfortable and reassuring message provided by many vendors and consultants) demands similar strategies to those undertaken when examining any potentially risky venture. Such framing suggests careful examination of assumptions, recognition of the high levels of uncertainty involved in estimates, sensitivity analysis, "risk-boxing" initial forays and, as was done by the Auditor-General, early, and ideally, independent, evaluation of the achievement of goals set for the venture."

3.10   Conclusion

The growth of Internet and personal computers, especially the mobile devices, has made computing ubiquitous today. Our dependence on computing services is such that our societies can no longer function without them. Our dependence on computing technologies and its ubiquity has made it one of the most important factors in our societies. Cloud computing is promising to do what the utility companies did for electricity, water, and telecommunication.

Cloud computing promises to be the ultimate outsourcing solution to all: from the individual users to small businesses, as well as to large enterprises and even governments. Many large corporations are already investing heavily in Cloud computing hoping to take advantage of being the first mover (technological leadership, preemption of assets, and buyer switching costs).

The Cloud computing's main attraction, similar to other utilities, stems from its cost and pricing structure, which relies on the economies of scale and its utility-like pricing model (for the most part, pay as you go and subscription fees).

We have listed various business models for different layers of the Cloud; what is suitable, where and when. However, many businesses and normal consumers are still hesitant. The Cloud industry is still in its infancy, and although major actors are investing heavily in infrastructure, others issues are yet to be answered.

One of the first and most important issues is the access to the Cloud. The current Internet infrastructure, especially the transmission medium (physical layer) is not capable of handling the vast bandwidth that a true Cloud computing environment would require.

No business will take the risk of putting its business-critical applications in the Cloud without the assurance of 100% (or 99.999%) access to those applications and associated data. Who will bear the burden of investing in the physical layer? ISPs, governments, or Cloud providers?

To ensure access, there is a strong possibility that Cloud providers opt for vertical integration throughout the layers all the way to the ISP level. We have seen this done in other utilities such as electricity and gas, where the power-generating company has moved both upstream and downstream, from oil and gas exploration to refining to owning and running the gas stations (e.g., Shell, or BP).

We can already see the early signs of this vertical move, by companies such as Amazon, Google, IBM, and Microsoft (just to name a few). Building mega datacenters is expensive and requires huge long-term investments. The pay-as-you-go and subscription fee models do not allow for a speedy return on those investments, making it attractive only to those with very strong financial positions.

These companies are investing heavily in several Cloud layers simultaneously, and they expect to sell their services to businesses and individuals, nearly all of which rely on Internet for access. Considering the current available bandwidth, we see that the present subscription fee–based business model of ISPs will create the bottleneck for the Cloud service providers.

The Cloud providers will have several options; they can acquire these ISPs, create their own, or come to some kind of agreement with the ISPs to prioritize Cloud customers. In all these cases, this will result in the death of "net neutrality."

Cloud computing is still in its infancy, and as such we are still faced with many challenges that are not clear today. As with other utilities, we will have to see if the major actors will push to create monopolies or oligopolies, or if the government will allow the "net neutrality" to die a quite death. Whatever the case may be, the current hype surrounding the Cloud computing will continue for some time to come, masking the potential problems facing us just under the surface.

The infrastructure (IaaS) business part of the Cloud, because of the heavy investment requirements) is already turning into a battle of Titans, which most likely will result in a few major actors dominating the heart of our IT future. They will also most likely control the PaaS layer as well. Here major software/hardware vendors will dominate, leaving the SaaS layer open to smaller businesses. This layer promises the greatest opportunity to SMBs. The great competition in this layer will most likely result in many innovations which will benefit both the consumers and providers alike. But all of these will depend on resolving the issues of security, regulations, and cheap access.

References

1. Weinhardt, C., Anandasivam, A., Blau, B., Borissov, N., Meinl, T., Michalk, W., Stößer, J.: Cloud computing–a classification, business models, and research directions. Bus. Info. Syst. Eng. **1**, 391–399 (2009)
2. Böhm, M., Leimeister, S., Riedl, C., Krcmar, H.: Cloud Computing-Outsourcing 2.0 or a new Business Model for IT Provisioning?, *Application Management*, pp. 31–56 (2011)
3. Rayport, J., Heyward, A.: Envisioning the cloud: the next computing paradigm. Int. J. Database Manage. Syst. (IJDMS) **1**(1) (2009)
4. Katy, "IaaS vs. PaaS vs. SaaS definition," *KATE'S COMMENT*, 18-May-2010. [Online]. Available: http://www.katescomment.com/iaas-paas-saas-definition/. Accessed: Nov 10 (2010)
5. Dictionary.com, "business model," in Investopedia.com. Source location: Investopedia Inc. http://dictionary.reference.com/browse/business model. Available: http://dictionary.reference. com. Accessed: Sept 20 (2011)
6. Rappa, M.A.: The utility business model and the future of computing services. IBM Syst. J. **43**(1), 32–42 (2004)
7. Andrzejak, A., Arlitt, M., Rolia, J.: Bounding the resource savings of utility computing models, *HP Laboratories Technical Report HPL-2002-339* (2002). Citeseer
8. Vazquez, T., Huedo, E., Montero, R., Llorente, I.: Evaluation of a utility computing model based on the federation of grid infrastructures. In: Euro-Par 2007 Parallel Processing, pp. 372–381. Springer, Berlin (2007)
9. Nurmi, D., Wolski, R., Grzegorczyk, C., Obertelli, G., Soman, S., Youseff, L., Zagorodnov, D.: Eucalyptus: a technical report on an elastic utility computing architecture linking your programs to useful systems, UCSB Technical Report (2008)
10. Jaekel, M., Luhn, A.: Cloud computing – business models value creation dynamics and advantages for customers, (2010)
11. Mills, L.H.: Legal issues associated with cloud computing (2009)
12. Applegate, L.M., Austin, R.D., McFarlan, F.W.: Corporate Information Strategy and Management: Text and Cases. McGraw-Hill/Irwin, Boston (2007)

13. "What is Google App Engine." Google Code. [Online]. Available: http://code.google.com/appengine/docs/whatisgoogleappengine.html/. Accessed: Dec 10 (2010)
14. Wiederhold, G.: What is your software worth? Commun. ACM **49**, 65–75 (2006)
15. Dubey, A., Wagle, D.: Delivering software as a service, *The McKinsey Quarterly*, vol. 6, pp. 1–12 (2007). [Online]. Available: http://saascatalog.com/sites/default/files/McKinsey_Study_on_SaaS.pdf. Accessed: Dec 10 (2010)
16. "How does Microsoft work with ISVs?," 22-Aug-2007. [Online]. Available: http://blogs.msdn.com/msftisvs/archive/2007/08/22/how-does-microsoft-work-with-isvs.aspx. Accessed: Mar 10 (2010)
17. Botteri, P.: Bessemer's top 10 laws of cloud computing and SaaS, Winter (2010)
18. Greening, J.: Selling Without Confrontation. The Haworth Press, Inc, New York (1993)
19. "Sales Training Home - Sales Training - ASTD," *American Society for Training and Development (ASTD)*. [Online]. Available: http://www.astd.org/communities/salestraining/. Accessed: Dec 5 (2010)
20. Dictionary.com, "Generally Accepted Accounting Principles," in WordNet® 3.0. Source location: Princeton University. http://dictionary.reference.com/browse/Generally Accepted Accounting Principles. Available: http://dictionary.reference.com. Accessed: Dec 5 (2010)
21. Rouse, A., Corbitt, B.: The Australian Government's Abandoned Infrastructure Outsourcing Program: "fiasco" or relatively typical?, Proceedings of the 13th Australiasian Conference on Information Systems, pp 699–710, Victoria University, Melbourne, Australia (2002)

Chapter 4
The Convergence of Enterprise Architecture (EA) and Cloud Computing

Pethuru Raj and Mohanavadivu Periasamy

Abstract Information Technology (IT) has become the critical and crucial component for providing the long-standing aspirations of the business community, namely, agility, adaptability, and affordability. That is, the coupling between IT and business is getting stronger and more solid. The well-articulated vision of business and IT alignment is definitely bound to raise a storm of innovations and improvizations for establishing and sustaining people-centric, process-based, service-oriented, model-driven, and Cloud-enabled enterprises that are destined to be dynamic, on-demand, autonomic, and real-time in their outlooks, operations, and offerings. As IT and business are getting interlinked very tightly, all kinds of advancements and accomplishments in IT are being expediently and easily replicated in business operations for the much-needed business disruption, augmentation, and transformation. There are several enabling and empowering technologies, and techniques emerging and elegantly evolving in order to close the inhibiting gap between IT and business. Practitioners and academics proudly project that Cloud Computing is the interruptive, inspiring, and inventive paradigm to fulfill this long-standing mission. In this chapter, we have written about the Enterprise Architecture (EA) frameworks facilitating the development and sustenance of flexible and futuristic EA. Furthermore, the chapter also discusses how the Cloud provision meets and molds EA and how the convergence of Cloud Computing with EA is to bring big success stories for small-, medium-, and large-scale enterprises.

P. Raj (✉)
Enterprise Architect, Sify Software Ltd., 2nd Floor, TIDEL Park, Taramani,
Chennai, Tamil Nadu 600113, India
e-mail: peterindia@gmail.com

M. Periasamy
Scientific Research Invision (SRI) Inc., Canada,
4872 Bourret Ave. Apt. # 407 Montreal, QC H3W1L1, Canada
e-mail: sriinccanada@gmail.com

Z. Mahmood and R. Hill (eds.), *Cloud Computing for Enterprise Architectures*,
Computer Communications and Networks, DOI 10.1007/978-1-4471-2236-4_4,
© Springer-Verlag London Limited 2011

4.1   Introduction

Cloud Computing has emerged with much promise and potential and is being positioned as the most strategic and sustainable IT paradigm facilitating the much-desired harmonization between the fast-changing business realities [9] and appreciable IT inventions. Business executives, entrepreneurs, and employees are highly optimistic about the unfolding concepts behind the Cloud methods, which are all set to deliver, definitely and decisively, and guarantee the spectacular success and sustenance of IT agility and autonomy in the extremely competitive and knowledge-driven society.

In this chapter, we would like to dig and dive deeper in extracting and elucidating the right and relevant details toward the venerable mission of precisely and concisely presenting the impacts and implications of the evolving Cloud concepts on the Enterprise Architecture (EA) of any growing and glowing organization. Enterprises are increasingly positive about the transformative nature of Cloud Computing. It is presumed and proclaimed that there will be noteworthy changes getting effected on any enterprise that smartly embraces the tectonic and telling shifts being advertised and offered by the pervasive and persuasive Cloud idea. The path-breaking and pioneering principles and philosophies of the Cloud technology are to result in connected, optimized, autonomic, and lean enterprises.

4.2   Next Generation Enterprises: The IT Requirements

On the ICT side, there are several important requirements [11] such as dynamic, virtualized, converged, automation-enabled, and shared infrastructures for structuring and sustaining next-generation enterprises [13]. Businesses are enthusiastic in capitalizing modern methodologies and technologies for smoothly transforming their passive, stagnant, closed, inflexible, and silo infrastructures to open, modular, dynamic, adaptive, and lean ones. In this section, we are to see how systems and their networks are being empowered to incorporate the needed capabilities to support future business needs.

Fueled by technological advancements and faced with an increasingly unpredictable and volatile economic climate, enterprises are forced to rethink, rearrange their priorities, and determine where to innovate. Without an iota of doubt, the enterprise endeavor has to be directed in a focused manner for unwrapping scores of business technologies. Business innovation has to be prioritized in such a way that the possible research outputs have to help halving IT development time and resources through automation of the phases of the engineering lifecycle. Another noteworthy area is simplified service delivery. There are four critical requirements to connect with customers, partners, and employees to gain business advantages:

- *Innovation* – To accelerate growth and produce higher-quality products and services, an organization must innovate. Tomorrow's leaders will do this through the smart applications of promising and potential technologies.

- *Agility* – To meet changing customer/citizen demands, enterprises have to accelerate time to market and time to service. In an age of "instant" expectations, we have to be able to sense and respond quickly and effectively to changing businesses' sentiments and citizens' needs.
- *Optimization* – Enterprises must optimize to reduce operating costs while improving operational processes. There is an urgent need to modernize and make strategic investments to improve the productivity of organizations and to drive higher return on investment (ROI).
- *Risk* – Risks are always there in several forms, but we have to have the armor to manage them very effectively and that mischief and mishap can be transformed to our advantages. Risks can originate from a variety of places and have to be identified proactively, and countermeasures need to be put in fast track to stop the cascading effectives of viruses, worms, malware, and malevolent attacks.

Organizations are expected to capitalize proven and potential technologies extensively for their betterment. Organization uses technologies to integrate and automate the value chain. It adapts easily and innovates rapidly. It complies with policies and rules quickly, interacts with stakeholder intelligently, and transacts without losing the integrity. It manages risk and environmental responsibilities effectively. The IT imperatives are therefore flexibility, automation, insight, speed, and security. There are five key steps in the path to next-generation enterprises:

- *Modernization* – To create a next-generation instant-on enterprise, we need to analyze and modernize the existing applications and re-architect them for enabling to accommodate changes. This will ensure that we can quickly and easily add new functionality. It also ensures that today's innovation does not become tomorrow's legacy problem. This approach also reduces the operational cost of the new solutions.
- *Transformation* – There is a need for breaking down the rigid IT silos. It is all about the realization of converged infrastructure that drives down cost and provides the foundation for agile service delivery. The transformed infrastructure is the core entity on which next-generation enterprises will run efficiently and exotically.
- *Security* – The environment has to be highly secure so that all kinds of IT systems, solutions, and services can be compactly insulated from hackers and other evil elements that are bent on creating and directing worms, bugs, and viruses to crash down compute servers. Thus, robust and resolute security solutions are the need of the hour to have unbreakable and impenetrable IT resources in order to ensure high availability, performance, tolerance, and assurance. The goal here is to ensure that the right people have the right access at the right time at the right quantity. The solutions need to provide customers, employees, partners, and consumers with instant access to the right enterprise assets securely.
- *Optimization* – Today we have massive data centers and server farms with a dynamic pool of heterogeneous storage appliances and systems. Everyday exabytes of digital information are getting created, captured, and recorded. The next-generation business therefore has to optimally capture, process,

analyze, and mine data from scores of distributed, disparate, and decentralized sources. The objective therefore is to come out with actionable and accountable insights. Further on, there are scores of tools being unfolded and utilized for transitioning data to information and to knowledge. In short, for enabling insights-driven decision making and actuation, infrastructure need is quite huge and growing steadily. There is a forward movement in unearthing optimization techniques and to apply them easily in order to enhance the infrastructure utilization rate.

- *Delivery* – With the adoption of service orientation and Cloud concepts, newer and nimbler delivery and consumption models have arrived on the horizon.

On summary, leading software and hardware providers are visualizing futuristic enterprises in their own perspectives and proficiencies such as technical competencies, focus areas, product offerings, and services. They are constantly articulating and advertising their offerings in artistic phrases for public consumption. IBM trumpets around the vision of "On-demand E-business," HP is banking on "Instant-On Enterprise," Dell is on "Efficient Enterprise," etc. Lately terms such as service-oriented and Cloud-enabled enterprises are going steady and getting popular. We have seen the major activities that have to be activated and accomplished to face instantly and instinctively those unpredictable business challenges and concerns.

4.2.1 Next-Generation Service Delivery Networks

Smart delivery of IT services requires a highly scalable and smart network that provides end-to-end automation of service delivery. Both users and service providers agree in unison that the network is the most critical asset in deploying and delivering services to user clients. Network efficiency, tolerance, availability, and optimization are being approached very vigorously in order to guarantee reliable and resilient service delivery.

- *Automated* – Automation is the key. A variety of multifaceted business and IT services can be combined. Business-aligned and sophisticated services can be constituted and constructed and conveyed out of a well-designed network. The network helps orchestrate and federate IT and business services. Its key role is to automate service delivery as well as integrate with other infrastructures to ensure that provisioning and other operational tasks too can be automated and transparent to the user. Network management tools are made available in order to provide high-quality network services.
- *Accessible* – Network accessibility has to be greatly simplified. Anytime anywhere, any network, any device connectivity and access to IT infrastructures are vehemently insisted. Highly competent and compact network solutions are the need of the hour considering the importance of providing Ubiquitous Information Access (UIA).

- *Dependence* – Availability and security are the crucial components for dependability. The underlying network has to be always available, secure, and trustworthy. If there is any kind of outage, deviation, and disruption in the network, then the total environment would come to an unpalatable and unproductive halt.
- *High performance* – Any futuristic network has to give higher throughput. As the phrase "more with less" is picking up fast everywhere, network product vendors, service providers, etc., are forced to come out with a series of network optimization techniques and tips. More and more intelligence is being embedded in network connectivity solutions such as routers, switches, gateways, proxies, load balancers, etc.

Cisco [2] is in the forefront in realizing next-generation network and connectivity solutions in order to ensure utmost quality such as fault tolerance, availability, security, accessibility, etc., in order to facilitate anytime anywhere, any device, and any medium delivery of services. Network adaptivity, dependability, and throughput are the prominent needs for future networks so that ubiquitous access is guaranteed.

4.3 Elucidating the Evolving Cloud Idea

Business is booming and IT infrastructure is subsequently added to readily grasp all the incoming and impending business opportunities. But the economy is tottering, and hence IT expenditure is being pruned. The moot question is how to enable a lean yet anticipative, accommodative, articulative, and adaptive IT in place so that business can grow without any breakdown, slowdown, and even letdown. The most recent and resilient Cloud concepts are being portrayed and prescribed as the savior and silver bullet for all the present and future needs of IT. Cloud in a way presents an illusion of infinite compute and storage capacity. The hotly pursued and greatly pampered Cloud paradigm is capable of decimating the age-old phrase "IT is a cost center" forever. That is the power and poise of the Cloud idea, which is penetrating and permeating into every tangible domain these days.

Cloud Computing is all about accomplishing myriad and changing computing needs by leveraging a dynamic pool of consolidated and virtualized compute and storage servers in association with scores of automated tools that are mainly for effective virtual machine monitoring and management, dynamic load balancing, adaptive resource provisioning, and advanced job scheduling. A bevy of versatile technologies smartly get combined and converged to realize the unique idea of computing and its pioneering ideals.

- *SOA as the business enabler* – In the recent past [12], Service Oriented Architecture (SOA) came along and has laid the sound and stable foundation for achieving a host of complete automation in tasks such as service composition, enterprise modernization, and business integration. That is, services, the most flexible and futuristic building block for adaptive, on-demand, and dynamic IT systems, can

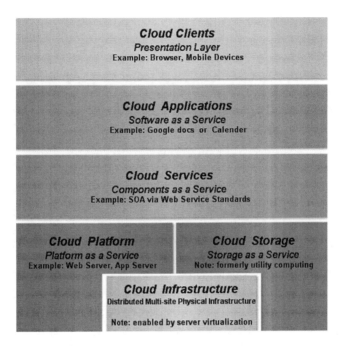

Figs. 4.1 The Cloud stack

dynamically find one another, bind, and compose to generate smart and sophisticated services that in turn lead to intelligent processes, mashups, and applications. Aspects and agents too contribute immeasurably for the much-anticipated self-adaptation in both personal as well as professional applications. Model-Driven Architecture (MDA) provides developmental automation. Autonomic computing is a strategic initiative for bringing tangible and perceptible autonomy in enterprise IT, which is heading toward elastic IT. Thus, every noteworthy aspect in IT and business is getting automated with competent and catalytic technologies.

- *Cloud as the IT enabler* – The most resilient and remarkable paradigm and platform for today and tomorrow's IT is nonetheless the Cloud, which is being proclaimed as the prominent and dominant contributor and contender in the long-drawn battle toward the IT autonomy and agility. The Cloud paradigm brings in several value-added qualities to IT: elasticity/scalability, performance/throughput, flexibility, affordability, agility, availability, autonomy, adaptability, etc. The Cloud model has certainly brought in scores of innovations and improvements to IT, which has been in the forefront in successfully fulfilling the fast-changing needs of the global business. The full Cloud stack [10] is pictorially represented in Figs. 4.1.

Several enterprise-scale and empowered technologies gelled well toward the creation and sustenance of the Cloud concept, which has been turning out to be strategically and significantly transformative and disruptive for individuals, innovators, and institutions.

4.3.1   The Cloud Realization Technologies

The much hyped and hoped Cloud Computing has attained greater heights and insights due to the maturity of the virtualization technology, which is mainly for decoupling hardware and software components. This loose coupling has done a lot of good for IT in bringing the much-needed elasticity, exuberance, and elegance. That is, the inhibiting dependencies among various IT modules get eliminated completely to bring in fresh possibilities and opportunities in tackling existing and emerging IT challenges. Another noteworthy factor is transparency. That is, location, technology, platform, and language transparency are being easily achieved with Cloud Computing. There are other contributive technologies and tools such as:

- Cluster, grid, utility, on-demand, and autonomic computing
- Consolidation, virtualization, and federation technologies
- Lean and green technologies
- Techniques and tools for automated resource provisioning, load balancing, and job scheduling
- Self-service technologies (virtual machine creation, expansion, contraction, retirement, monitoring, and management)
- Automation, monitoring, and billing

Cloud, being an enterprise-scale and energy-efficient technology, has to guarantee several quality attributes in its application. As Cloud is being touted as a kind of sophisticated server in the client/server realm, service and operation-level agreements come into the picture. Incidentally, several enterprise-level qualities are being realized with the adept leverage of Cloud technologies. Newer deployment and delivery models have been unearthed and are being rendered satisfactorily with the adoption of Clouds. Further on, the potential to cut down capital expenditure and rein in operating costs is so compelling that CIOs already started to push for Cloud adoption aggressively. However, good managers understand that cost savings is not the only variable to consider when evaluating for Cloud enablement. The significance of Cloud Computing is that enterprises are eligible for availing a tremendous amount of flexibility and scalability by deploying and managing their IT services and applications on Cloud servers.

As far as the service providers are concerned, they always want to have highly optimized, dynamic, converged, and on-demand Cloud infrastructures. To achieve the goal of an optimized Cloud, they seek to optimize the use of resources and assets in their environment – from servers to storage to software licenses. Service providers are also held responsible for compliance to rules, regulations, and other conditions being imposed by customers and government officials. For this reason, the final component in a mature and mellowed Cloud infrastructure is Cloud governance. With Cloud governance in place, they not only will deliver superior value through Cloud adoption but they will also prove that the use of resources is reasonable, responsible, and aligned with the requirements of the business.

4.3.2   The Cloud-Induced Innovations on Enterprise Architecture

Cloud Computing lays the foundation for originating a number of significant and strategic business and technical innovations as described below:

- *Technology cluster* – Clouds represent the seamless convergence of proven and potential technologies and techniques (miniaturization, automation, consolidation, virtualization, integration, federation, composition, provisioning, etc.).
- *Heterogeneity to homogeneity* – Clouds hide the multiplicity and heterogeneity-induced complexity of IT environments by leveraging a variety of optimized management platforms and tools such as Virtual Machine Monitor (VMM), power, resource, and workload management modules.
- *Service-oriented infrastructure (SOI)* – With the faster adoption of service orientation principles, newer delivery models have erupted and are evolving to meet up diverse needs of users. Software as a Service (SaaS) is the base, which is laying the foundation for encouraging enormous growth of every IT resource getting expressed and exposed as a service to general public via the web. The tendency ticking is nonetheless but IT as a Service (ITaaS). As the much-anticipated service era gradually and gracefully unfolds, Clouds' contribution as an elastic service platform is really tremendous and trendsetting for the forthcoming knowledge era. Clouds will become insightful infrastructure for service engineering, deployment, and delivery.
- *Business innovations* – Clouds lay a strong and stimulating foundation for emitting newer business, service, and pricing models that are more tuned to changing business sentiments and customers' liking. There will be a paramount shift from the current capital expenditure to operational expenditure. Consumption-based metering and billing will become common and casual. Ultimately, Service-Oriented Enterprises (SOEs) will see the light with the beneficial synchronization between SOA and Cloud infrastructure.
- *Green IT* – Due to the persistent voice for energy efficiency and clarion calls from different quarters for energy efficiency and reduction of greenhouse gas emission for minimizing climatic changes, Clouds are being established as the viable and valuable IT instrument for greener environments.
- *IT optimization* – Optimization of IT development and operations is gaining traction. Clouds contribute exceedingly well for this optimization goals. In short, Clouds fulfill lean, elastic, catalytic, agile, and adaptive IT. Further on, Cloud enables computing to be the fifth utility. Finally IT as a Service is a foregone conclusion with the maturity of Cloud standards, products, and technologies.

- *Extreme elasticity* – Capacity planning is a difficult exercise for IT as predicting exact usage, and acquiring just enough IT resources to avoid excessive under- or over-provisioning is really a tough call in this volatile world. Other internal as well as external factors contributing for this predicament and pain are season-specific usage spikes that demand additional compute resources that otherwise remain idle. Elasticity of IT resources leads to application scalability. Clouds offer resources on demand that can settle up or down with changing demands of businesses.
- *Tending toward the on-demand era* – The vision of everything on demand (computing, communication, intelligence, scalability, information, service, etc.) is set to see the light when Cloud reaches a level of maturity and stability.

The specialty of Cloud Computing clearly lies in the realm of dynamically and smartly provisioning expensive computational assets (processors/cores, memory, and storage) to meet the fluctuating needs of users. This allows global users to acquire and release the resources on demand and get accurately billed for the exact time or amount of usage. Cloud Computing could mean different things to different set of users. For businesses, it is scalability on demand. Other attributes include efficiency, sensitivity, and flexibility to meet unplanned business changes and emerging challenges. And for ordinary users, simplicity, consumability, and cost effectiveness are the key criteria.

4.3.3 Why Cloud Enablement?

The ground-breaking idea of Cloud has silently yet solidly percolated into diverse domains. Cloud enablement has become the most articulated modernization mechanism these days. Every tangible space is undergoing through the well-defined Cloud-enablement procedure. Not only the enterprise space but also the vast and untapped embedded space is, too, toeing the same line. Besides the key motivators and drivers, the unprecedented growth being attained in the web domain is being quoted widely for the great and grand adoption of the metamorphic Cloud concepts. There are four prominent trends happening in the Internet space:

- The Internet has emerged as the cheapest and global-scale communication infrastructure.
- The web is being stuffed with a wider variety of resources such as man- and machine-generated data, web pages, components, agents and services, and knowledge bases. The web is the largest digital information superhighway/digital library.
- The web is being positioned as the open, flexible, and affordable deployment, execution, provisioning, and delivery platform for personal as well as professional applications.
- The web is the next-generation connectivity, integration, composition, and collaboration environment.

These clearly vouch for employing the web beneficially for anything and everything. As Clouds are the most agile, autonomous, web-based, affordable, and adaptive infrastructure, nourishing and cherishing of Cloud gain immense momentum these days.

4.3.4 Implementing Smarter Environments via Clouds

We need smart devices and networks for smart spaces. Devices are accordingly enhanced to participate and contribute for the success and sustenance of smart spaces. Extreme and deeper connectivity, service enablement, Cloud infrastructure and platforms, and integration at service level of all kinds of devices are the differentiators for creating intelligent environments.

- Integration of new features within devices (internal integration)
- Attaching extra and external nanoscale modules (such as RFID tags, disappearing and diminutive sensors, actuators, etc.) onto devices (external integration)
- Device-to-device integration (local)
- Device-to-Cloud-device integration (global)

4.3.5 Application Domains

Clouds will be an inseparable part of the automation initiatives that are being implemented across the spectrum of industries:

- Manufacturing/process/factory/industrial automation
- Home and building automation
- Entertainment, education, and financial services
- Supply chain, energy, health care, retail, government, utilities, logistics and transports, physical security, homeland security, etc.

In a nutshell, the world of computing is undergoing a tectonic shift in order to guarantee extreme productivity and power to users. Not only large IT users, but also small and medium companies and even individuals are hooked to massive and scalable server clusters being offered in Cloud centers. Every IT infrastructural node individually and collectively is transitioned to be exposed as a usable, reusable, and composable service that is readily available for public discovery and consumption over any network. The dependency factor that kept IT resources as silos thus far is gone forever, and henceforth any software can run on any platform. Meshing and mashing up of heterogeneous IT resources will be very common, casual, and cheap. By seamlessly linking tens of thousands of servers and storage systems to power applications like search engines, social media, and online services, Clouds represent the next evolution and revolution of computing. There is a new awakening in order to develop services to support and streamline Cloud Computing for the increasingly connected age. Cloud intrinsically represents efficiency in order to achieve more with less and for clean and green next-generation IT centers.

4.4 Enterprise Architecture and Cloud Computing

Businesses are seriously and sincerely contemplating to have a small IT center locally (on-site or on-premise) by smartly modernizing and migrating the large chunk of business and IT services and applications to be deployed and delivered via a rented infrastructure from the third-party, massive, and well-managed public Clouds (online, on-demand, hosted, remote, and off-premise). This kind of segregation does a lot for companies on different accounts. One is to facilitate companies to realign their priorities in order to focus on their core competencies. Also there are other noteworthy benefits such as the transition from capital to operational expenditure. The richness and reach of Cloud-based applications are definitely greater. The objective of "more with less" is seeing the light. Cloud is elegantly enabling and empowering scores of innovations and improvizations in the pervasive and persuasive IT. IT simplicity and sensitivity are being given more thrust with the emergence of the Cloud technology.

Though the Cloud is tremendously popular, organizations still keep their customer, confidential, and corporate data locally in their own consolidated and virtualized data centers (private Clouds). Cloud represents another front being opened up for IT, and the boundary gets expanded with the involvement of enterprise as well as public Clouds. Further on, in order to overcome some specific concerns, community Cloud, hybrid Cloud, etc. too are being recommended and recognized. Thus, it is very clear that the adoption of Cloud Computing is to impact tactically as well as strategically on the Enterprise Architecture (EA) front.

4.4.1 Briefing Enterprise Architecture (EA)

An EA provides a clear and comprehensive picture of the structure and substance of any purposeful activity, whether it is an organization or a functional area that cuts across organizational boundaries (e.g., terrorism information sharing or homeland security). Accordingly, an EA is an essential tool for effectively and efficiently engineering business or functional processes and for implementing and evolving supporting systems. EA is the enterprise-wide architecture giving an integrated and harmonized view of any enterprise, which could be even distributed across the world. EA is all about the most efficient framework, knowledge base, and strategy for effective enterprise-scale initiation, implementation, and governance. In short, complexity and changes are being taken care of proactively, preemptively, and promptly. Several enabling EA frameworks [5] are being built and continuously enhanced.

TOGAF is one such prominent framework in the EA domain and is a detailed method and a set of supporting tools for developing EA. It describes a well-defined method for designing an information system in terms of a set of building blocks and for showing how the building blocks fit and interact together. It should contain a set of tools and provide a common vocabulary. It should also include a list of recommended standards and compliant products that can be used to implement the building blocks. There are several sub-architectures that need to be derived quickly and validated:

- Business architecture
- Data architecture
- Technology architecture
- Application architecture

Based on the business vision, mission, and objectives, business architecture defines the business strategy, roadmap, processes, and rules/policies, best practices, key guidelines and metrics, and governance mechanism. Business architecture directly or indirectly is able to meet up any kind of business contingency, complexity, and change. Data architecture describes the structure of an organization's logical and physical data assets. Data collection, storage, mining, and extraction of right and relevant information out of the data heap greatly decide the success of any corporate. Data management methods, tools, and systems are also decided via this architectural style. Thus, data architecture is an essential component in any EA. Application architecture provides a blueprint for applications and services, their interactions within one another as well as with the back-end databases, and their coupling with the business processes. This association between services and business processes ensures a process-centric organization. This effectively ensures that all sorts of changes can be initiated and implemented at process level. Technology architecture describes the underlying platforms (development, testing, deployment, delivery, and management), integration backbones, execution containers and engines, adaptors library, and infrastructures needed to install, administer, govern, profile, monitor, broker, mediate, secure, and enhance business data, applications, and services.

As the complexity of enterprise IT is constantly on the climb, it is imperative to devise means and ways of moderating and minimizing the bewildering and burgeoning IT complexity. Also system silos need to be seamlessly integrated in order to enable spontaneous interactions among distributed systems for producing business-aware and aligned composite applications. There are other mechanisms galore such as Enterprise Application Integration (EAI) hub, Enterprise Content Management (ECM), Enterprise Service Bus (ESB), Message-Oriented Middleware (MoM), application server, data warehouses, etc. However, enterprise architecture is given the highest priority in driving enterprises in an orderly fashion.

4.4.2 The Cloud Implications

As we all know, EA deals with the whole enterprise. EA not only insists on the IT part, but also it involves the business side. Subsequently EA is for business and IT alignment. Now as Cloud is being presented as the most versatile technology in the IT field, there are tremors among enterprise architects to quickly understand the implicit as well as the explicit transformations being brought in by the Cloud principles and to do the required twist and tweak on the EA. Increasingly enterprise architects are tasked to tune their EA to be Cloud-ready. Cloud enterprise is the new term in the industry circle. That is, apart from the matured and modernized enterprise and web spaces, a new, potential, and promising Cloud space is also emerging on the IT horizon. An enterprise architect has to take the Cloud front too very seriously before deciding, devising, depicting, and dictating a comprehensive, futuristic, flexible, and enterprise-wide architecture. Thus, in a way, the irresistible Cloud phenomenon is extending the horizon of any enterprise, which is to involve and invoke the Cloud principle. Some visionaries and experts argue that as many companies move to Cloud Computing, the workload of enterprise architects goes down significantly. But that is not the case as the boundary of IT is getting expansive with the Cloud incorporation, there are more things to be taken into account and analyzed, and hence the workload is bound to go up. Thus, in this section, we are to discuss how the much-hoped Cloud determines and deals with the complexities associated with framing and formulating EA. Besides the computing field, the Cloud concepts induce a significant improvization in the communication domain. As we are grappling with several technologies and terminologies such as ambient communication, autonomic communication, and unified communication, the Cloud breeze has set in more efficient and economical communication regime.

Shifting application and service portfolios to the Cloud should make a lot of behind-the-scenes process headaches easier, particularly when it comes to some of the complex technical implementation issues. But it does not eliminate the need for an effective strategy for putting together all the people, processes, and pieces that the Cloud supports in order to maintain business continuity. The business never really cared what it was running on, and it just cares about the business efficiency, resiliency, versatility, and throughput. That means, even in Cloud IT, the need for EA does not get diminished a bit. If anything, this further complicates things more. Not long ago IT departments had the luxury of having full control of their entire landscape – often times, built on top of mature and stable software packages. But the emerging enterprise scene is to depict an altogether different picture. Enterprise architecture is still a leading challenge. Now, EA is increasingly splintered into a bunch of smaller projects that are distributed all over the place. Cloud services, whether by way of Software as a Service (SaaS) or Infrastructure as a Service (IaaS), are simply another set of deployment and delivery options. If there is not a well-intended and defined EA in place to spell out which technology is required, how it has to be approached and accomplished, and how all fit into the big picture, eventually the enterprise suffers.

The good news is that the shift to Cloud services will actually free up IT to operate more systematically and strategically. Whether there is a separate group of professionals responsible for managing and overseeing it, or it is built into the group's DNA, EA will be one of the prime enablers of IT in this modern world. From the Cloud's ongoing journey, it can be inferred that the path-breaking Cloud idea is to take the enterprise architecture to the next level. That is, Cloud architecture is set to become an inseparable and indistinguishable part of EA. As Cloud Computing grows and matures, it materially and mesmerizingly influences any organization that leverages its unique concepts and capabilities. Cloud adoption is bound to bring in a number of significant modifications in enterprise analysis, planning, strategy, execution, and enhancement. Cloud Computing fully enables the integration of enterprise procedures, processes, patterns, platforms, and practices. Prominently there will be a few domains that get attracted and altered by the EA convergence with the exploding and expanding Cloud domain. Ultimately, the IT trend is toward the realization of Cloud enterprises such as:

- Cloud-inspired processes
- Cloud-empowered infrastructures
- Cloud-derived practices

4.4.3   Cloud Processes

Processes are the central nervous system for all kinds of IT systems. Processes facilitate modular application development and sustenance. With the widespread adoption of SOA, services are directly related to process and their subprocesses. Each process dictates the services to be used for the process implementation. In other words, a process is composed by aggregating multiple services via orchestration and/or choreography methods. That is, composite services are for completing a whole or partial business process or task. There are a plenty of process engineering, execution, and examination tools, engines, and containers embedded in any standard SOA suite. However, the traditional SOA processes face many challenges and issues such as high performance, on-demand scalability, large payloads, memory constraints, real-time interactions, high availability, and reliability. In a distributed SOA environment, the bottlenecks tend to occur in all, two, or one of the following three places:

- Shared intermediary services
- The services themselves
- SOA infrastructure operations

The scalability bottlenecks across all these SOA parts in a process are caused when disk I/O, memory, or CPU saturation levels are reached in most cases. Moreover the cluster technology, adopted by traditional SOA, can provide higher availability. However, it depends on static partitioning, where a single backup server is preassigned to service requests from a failing server. The grid-enabled SOA provides a way to improve the performance, scalability, and availability of SOA processes. Cloud Computing shares the same goal as grid computing. That is to allow service consumers to obtain computing resources on demand. However, Cloud Computing is a new style of distributed computing, which introduces many new architectural styles and technologies to SOA. There are four aspects that Cloud Computing differs from grid computing:

- It is massively scalable.
- It can be encapsulated as an abstract entity that delivers different levels of services to the customers outside of the Cloud.
- It is driven by econometrics.
- The services can be dynamically configured through virtualization or other methods and delivered on demand.

Cloud-enabled SOA process spectacularly improves SOA process' capabilities such as scalability, performance, and availability. In summary, processes are the core component in any functional system. Process engineering is too going through a number of upgrades, and today there are several subtopics that cater to process improvement, innovation, modeling, performance simulation, control, management, etc. Besides, distributed and decentralized processes are getting integrated seamlessly for multi-enterprise application engineering. Lean processes are the much sought-after ones these days.

4.4.4   Event-Driven Business Processes

Events are the latest entrant into enterprise systems. Enterprises are readying their infrastructures as well as processes in order to quickly capture incoming events, extract the actionable insights embedded in those events, and act on them in real time. Events lay the foundation for real-time enterprises. Business Event Processing (BEP) is a new kind of container capable of receiving millions of events from distributed sources and directing them to the appropriate recipients. Event-Driven Architecture (EDA) is the architectural style getting very popular and is being attached with SOA in order to guarantee event-driven, service-oriented enterprises. Processes too are accordingly strengthened to incorporate events and their passage.

4.4.5   Communication-Enabled Business Processes (CEBP)

As there are many kinds [8] of input/output devices for receiving and sending information, enterprise processes are attached with communication capability. That means, users as well as systems can be notified in real time about the sequence of events and any important messages.

4.4.6 Cloud-Impacted Business Processes

As indicated, the Cloud principle has impacted the process too. Processes are solidified so that achieving nonfunctional (quality of service) attributes of any system gets simpler and smarter.

That is, processes too are undergoing a number of positive transformations. Ultimately the target is to derive intelligent processes. Insights extracted by analytics are being fed to processes. Further on, the optimization, productivity efficiency, consolidation, and virtualization techniques being luxuriously leveraged by the Cloud paradigm are being used for sharply enhancing and sustaining process innovations. Besides the process-induced changes, there are several other noteworthy trends ticking for the much-deliberated Cloud enterprises. Some of them are given in detail in the latter part of this chapter.

4.5 A Strategy for Establishing Enterprise Private Clouds

Every enterprise architect has to set his agenda and make his vision clear for establishing technology-sponsored and splurged private (internal) Cloud within his/her organization. Given the performance and economic attractiveness of public Clouds, it is logical to ask if there is a way to take advantage of the benefits of public Clouds and somehow get around their concerns and challenges. One approach and certainly a recommended first step toward the Cloud era would be to construct a Cloud-like architecture within the organization's own data center. Clearly, if a commercial hosting entity is able to develop such an elastic and energy-efficient infrastructure, then the same ought to be possible to create an "internal Cloud" with equivalent performance and economics within the enterprise boundary.

Fortunately, in Figs. 4.2, solutions and technologies besides knowledge materials and know how guides are available in plenty today that can help revisit and remodel any existing and heterogeneous data centers to function as an enterprise-wide private Cloud [1]. The high-level expectation is that any internal Cloud architecture should not adversely impact any existing assets and processes. On the other hand, the private Cloud has to leverage the existing capabilities and capacities smartly. The major requirements and constraints for a typical internal architecture include:

- Managing diverse and disparate compute, storage, and networking infrastructures
- Managing multiple and heterogeneous virtualized infrastructures
- Providing service-centric features for designing, measuring, and maintaining a growing catalog of services and chargeback if necessary
- Not disrupting security processes and procedures, application architectures, and application code bases or configurations
- Being compatible with tracking, logging, and compliance systems
- Providing per-use resource cost metrics and usage metrics

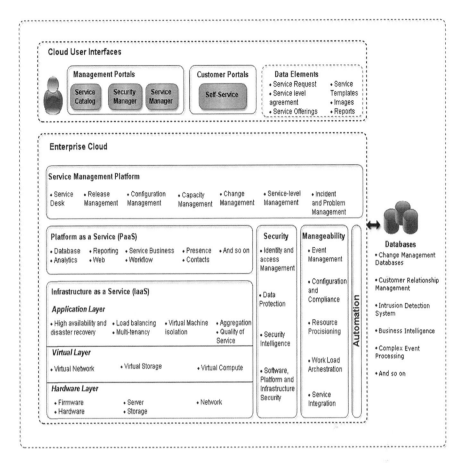

Figs. 4.2 The architectural stack of private Cloud

With these operational requirements, an enterprise private Cloud will generate the same capabilities of a public Cloud. Essentially, the only difference is that the internal Cloud is behind the firewall within our facility, and under our complete control.

The private Cloud is a shared and multi-tenant environment built on a highly efficient, automated, and virtualized infrastructure. Other key elements [6] of the Cloud include standardized application platforms provided as a service and a self-service portal that enables business analysts and managers to request and manage additional capacity for their applications. The short-term as well as long-term implications of Cloud enablement, embracement, and embarkation are definitely manifold. All the deployment and delivery models are bound to instigate and inspire numerous improvizations and improvements in the current IT establishments and their operations. Above all, the delivery system will undergo sharp turnaround toward the synchronized and simplified service delivery. In this section, we are to dig deeper in order to extract all kinds of technical, business, and user-centric benefits. Private Clouds are internal and enterprise-scale Cloud can be accessed by those in the corporate network only. Private Clouds [3] support:

- Elasticity and scalability
- Better capacity planning and management
- Fault tolerance, availability, and affordability
- High performance/throughput and workload predictability
- Improved infrastructure efficiency including energy efficiency
- Reduced provisioning times and higher utilization
- Agility, adaptability, and autonomy
- Easy manageability and malleability
- Report summary can be easily reviewed
- Maintain and improve industry/company industry standards

4.5.1   Why Private Clouds?

Besides fulfilling the above quality attributes of a generic Cloud system, private Clouds [4] are:

- Highly secure, auditable, accountable, and drillable
- Flexible and controllable
- Visible, traceable, and manageable
- Compliant to SLAs, OLAs, and government rules and regulations

There are ways and means for huge cost reduction in setting up and sustaining private Clouds.

Through the pioneering virtualization technology, IT resources can be managed as configurable pools of resources instead of islands/silos of independent elements. These pools can then be exposed in a granular manner for use by business applications and services. Fluctuations in the resource requirements of each application can be met by using fewer technology resources. The economic benefits here are profound. The risks of over-provisioning and under-provisioning are considerably reduced. The capital and operational expenses will come down as utilization rate goes up, and the number of data center devices and even data centers too come down. Plus the facility costs such as power, cooling, and space expenses get decreased. Smaller data center decrements energy consumption, heat dissipation, and lower CO_2 emissions.

Virtualized resources can run on any platform. There is a clear separation between applications and their run-time infrastructures. This light and loose coupling goes a long way toward increased utilization and decreased expense. By virtualizing storage, private Cloud Computing allows the physical location of data to be abstracted from the underlying platform, making data vastly easier to migrate. Data can be housed on the platform that best meets particular cost or the security criteria at a given point in time according to a given policy.

Implementing a common set of standardized, integrated system packages within a data center and across geographically distributed data centers makes workload migration and disaster recovery affordable options for more applications and data.

Use of a single-pane management view gives IT administrators a consistent and common interface for each step in a technology lifecycle: configuration, provisioning, compliance, management, and monitoring across platforms. These management tools let administrators set up and run automated utilization monitoring and workload-balancing policies. They also enable a smaller number of administrators to manage a larger pool of resources, lowering staff costs while enhancing resource utilization.

4.6 Cloud-Enabled Enterprise Communications

Enterprise architects not only focus on the computing front but also on the communication space in order to frame a comprehensive enterprise strategy. There are both evolutionary and revolutionary movements in the hot communication field. Cutting-edge technologies and state-of-the-art infrastructures contribute immensely for making communication pervasive and persuasive. Enterprise communication too has been through several remarkable and radical changes in the last decade, and the same is expected in the years to unfold. In the communication space, the often presented and pronounced buzzwords are ambient communication, autonomic communication, and unified communication (UC). As the respective implementation technologies mature and fresh requirements emerge, communication service providers, connectivity solution vendors, standards consortiums, service integrators, and other important stakeholders are cognitively and collaboratively working out the new-generation and people-centric communication services to keep up the revenue targets. Now with the game-changing Cloud technology sweeping the entire ICT industry, there are more expectations from providers as well as end users. The latest Forrester report on enterprise communications insists on Cloud-based multimodal services that directly provide the much-needed multimodal communication and collaboration facilities.

Businesses have been asking for a bevy of deft and disruptive technologies for accomplishing the real-time connectivity and collaboration capabilities for their workers to sharply enhance the productivity while fulfilling low-cost and real-time delivery. The other critical segment is end users, who aspire for context-aware services.

Technology advancements include innovative applications based on Session Initiation Protocol (SIP), multimodal devices that displace landline phones, increased adoption of open-source software, widespread video adoption, and mobile UC for contextual collaboration. Social networking sites supply more relevant content and information for workers. There is a rapid expansion of SIP for services and applications. Devices will provide greater functionality to replace or coexist with desktop phones. Remote working and telecommuting growth, which will create demand for secure mobile applications, will be facilitated by SIP. Video will become widespread, promoting conversations and collaboration across the enterprise. Video-based surveillance, security, and safety will get a strong boost. These changes will create an integrated workplace environment that facilitates real-time collaboration to fulfill business goals and to aid aware and aligned processes. Videoconferencing solutions will expand steadily as costs go down and options increase. More meetings will be scheduled via video as companies embrace cost-effective video solutions for internal meetings and engage more customers over videoconferencing devices. Video solutions will expand upward into large telepresence conference rooms and downward to individual desktops. The cost savings based on the reduction of travel costs often support the business case for video expansion.

Other noteworthy trends include the much-maligned convergence in the mobile space. Computer is becoming a communicator whereas communicator tends to be a computer. Cell phones are being empowered to be smart phones with the smooth synchronization of mobile phones and personal digital assistant (PDA) functionalities. The miniaturization technologies superbly contribute for very-large-scale integration of multiple digital modules to work together within a phone. This transformation helps mobile phones to be actively involved in business transactions. Professionals on the move are exceedingly benefited out of this great evolution. Wireless and mobile devices seamlessly bring together voice, Internet, and video to support business communications. Integration with UC software allows workers to use their mobile devices for contextual collaboration and enables access to features that indicate a coworker's availability and location.

4.6.1   Virtualization for the Communication Industry

Virtualization has become a highly impactful and insightful technology. Virtualization enables partitioning any IT resource into a collection of independently manageable modules. This means, handling and usage of modules is simpler, wastage of resources is substantially reduced, energy cost crashes down, complexity gets minimized, utilization goes up, etc. All communications activity needs to be capable of being virtualized, just like any other application. Communications servers and applications need to be virtualized and capable of being deployed over thin client virtual desktops. The ultimate business benefit is not only to reduce costs but also to facilitate novel and flexible working models. With virtualization zooms, the enterprise and the workers become less interested in where their platforms and applications are being hosted and run. Centralized systems connected to remote locations using high-speed networks allow services to be provided quickly. Centralization brings cost savings and effective management leading to new utility pricing and deployment models.

4.6.2   Cloud Inspires the UC Paradigm

The emerging UC concept is definitely compelling. UC is all about the seamless and spontaneous convergence of all methods of communicating between two or more people, from any application, using any device, at any location, via the most appropriate route, enabling effective and real-time collaboration with business-grade security. With UC, IT departments can offer streamlined communication solutions and advanced productivity-enhancing applications throughout the network. Because of the facets it incorporates and combines implicitly, UC is a definite value-add for organizations focusing on communication services. UC is such a powerful entity capable of creating ample business opportunities and fresh possibilities. Advanced UC applications, for example, provide the real-time status and availability of other staff, including preferred methods of contact. With this level of presence, employees can quickly determine who is accessible and in what capacity. Mobility solutions further extend the unprecedented capabilities of the communications network beyond the confines of the organization environment. Regardless of location, mobility can provide presence and voice communications via smart phones as if the employee were physically in the office. Video communications and desktop collaboration have also emerged as promising UC solutions. Both provide tremendous benefits. Around 90% of human communication is based on visual queuing. So video serves as a logical extension of the UC network. Add the functionality of desktop collaboration (the ability to share documents, presentations, and any stored media), UC becomes not only thoroughly versatile but increasingly indispensable in today's communication environment.

4.6.3   Communication as a Service (CaaS)

The transformational Cloud technology permeates into the money-spinning communication domain. Providing communication services from the Cloud will change the current communication landscape upside down. Communication as a Service (CaaS), an offshoot of Cloud enablement of communication services, is being projected as the next-generation communication method. Cloud empowerment brings the celebrated centralized service delivery. Although currently an emerging market, CaaS offers greater accessibility for UC applications and services. Network service providers will offer communication and collaboration solutions to companies as a fee-based service offering that incorporates Web 2.0 technology with solutions from traditional premises-based providers.

CaaS eliminates the need for acquiring and operating on-premises telephone equipments and does away the need for voice applications. Rather than overinvest, companies can focus on their competencies such as adding novel communication applications as needed from the Cloud providers, and pay for only what is actually used. The adoption of integrated applications allows workers to use advanced applications and will support a connected workforce and reduce business delays due to existing limitations of current applications. Information workers can quickly launch conferencing and collaboration sessions with their peers, partners, and people and accelerate decision making.

4.7 Cloud-Enablement Strategy

In today's knowledge-driven and globalized economy, the ability to be sensitive and responsive (S&R) to changes is more important than ever before. Information capturing, transmission, persistence, modeling, processing, mining, and analyzing toward knowledge extraction have become the key operational areas for most enterprises. Information is a vital asset to be taken care of in order to generate actionable insights for achieving several worthwhile and wonderful things such as shrinking cycle times, to be competitive in their offerings, outlooks, and operations and to be prompt, proactive, preemptive, and people-centric. The market imperative to be nimble, responsive, and collaborative has led to an increased interest in a next generation of enterprise services that can be provisioned from the Internet using Cloud services.

4.7.1 Cloud-Enabled Enterprise: The Transition Methodology

This segment describes the key areas an enterprise needs to address during the transformation into a Cloud-enabled enterprise. EA professionals have a bigger role in determining the specification of Cloud contracts in two distinct areas. They will lead enterprise solution contract specifications and also assist in the development of commercial contracts led by procurement organizations. This will require EA functions to engage more fully with business and procurement organizations. Cloud is simply business as usual to EA, but EA can assist in corporate integration by the use of contract models.

4.7.1.1 Service Categorization

As we discussed above, as per an EA perspective, the focus areas include business, information, technical, and application architectures and infrastructures. As services are the primary building block in service-driven and Cloud-enabled enterprises, services for each of these distinct architectures need to be identified systematically, modernized accordingly, and moved to Cloud. For example, technical architecture services such as storage, processing, and network can be availed on demand from one or more infrastructure Clouds as a service (IaaS).

4.7.1.2   Service Selection

Cloud services can provide services for the above four aspects of any company. However, which services need to be outsourced from external Cloud service providers (CSPs) have to be decided very carefully based on some of the criteria:

- Flexibility, visibility, dependability, and controllability
- Elasticity and availability
- Security, privacy, and time to market
- Business continuity via effective disaster recovery (DR)
- Standardized for avoiding vendor lock-in
- Service level agreement (SLA)
- Financial implications and brand value
- Auditability and accountability
- User-friendly interfaces and automation tools for self-service and auto-scaling

After the selection of the service and the CSP, an important issue is to define the contract with the CSP to ensure business versatility, robustness, and resiliency.

4.7.1.3   Service Selection Attributes for Cloud-Based Delivery

There has been a deeper deliberation on buying or building service components. There is a well-designed selection procedure to decide which services need to be outsourced from third-party providers. The criteria being imposed are:

- *Flexibility* – Services should be capable of adapting to business changes.
- *Costs* – It is much more expensive to industrialize corporate capabilities than to personalize targeted and tailored business offers.
- *Time to market* – It will take longer to organize and run the complete business on the Cloud than just tailored business offers.
- *Service level agreement (SLA)* – What SLAs are required between the services, can they be provided, and what are the location implications?
- *Security and compliance* – Challenges in dealing with security and compliance about provisioning service from a public and private Clouds.
- *Core business* – What is the core business and what services are willing to contract from other Clouds?
- *Integration in EA* – This is about the interaction between business services.

4.7.1.4   Right Services for Clouds: The Selection Approach

A viable strategy is to find, select, and start with those services that:

- Do not have big interaction with other services and information bases
- Bring high value to the business
- Are with lower security risks

The services that are fulfilling these attributes are the first candidate for transformation.

4.7.2   Cloud Participation

Typically there are Cloud service providers (CSPs) and Cloud service consumers (CSCs). However, with the considerable adoption of the pioneering and path-breaking Cloud paradigm across the world, Cloud Service Brokers (CSBs) are the new important entities in the burgeoning and bewildering Cloud space. Cloud brokers are for facilitating Cloud integration, intermediation, and arbitration purposes. Cloud brokers are the abstraction of common middleware services from both Cloud owners and users.

A *Cloud broker* is an organization or entity that creates and maintains relationships with multiple Cloud service providers. This makes it possible to access services provided by multiple providers with a consistent user experience and minimal configuration. Cloud brokers provide additional services. A Cloud broker might provide consolidated billing, seamless switching between Cloud Computing services, or simultaneous connection to different Cloud Computing services, as well as federated identity management or other added services.

A Cloud broker may also survey Cloud service providers to understand their capabilities, liabilities, business models, and costs. This allows avoiding multiple relationships in favor of forging just one relationship with a Cloud broker who would understand our particular IT service requirements. The Cloud broker could, in turn, select the best Cloud services for the IT organization and monitor those services on its behalf. A Cloud broker will provide with significant cost savings and enable us to better use Cloud Computing to provide business value.

4.7.3   Contract in the Cloud

Cloud services include products, applications, and solutions that are delivered via the Internet and consumed in real time by a growing array of client devices. Cloud services can interact with other local services within the Cloud, with remote services that are in the enterprise space, or with remote services in other Clouds. The evolving trend is that Cloud interaction is getting really global. Aspects such as Cloud service integration, composition, and collaboration are increasingly relevant and nearer to reality. The boundaryless flow of information is the centrality of Cloud Computing. All these movements clearly indicate and insist that contract issues need to be handled very carefully as the complexity is on the increase. Experts need to be involved for signing contractual obligations as contracts are getting murkier in the recent Cloud space. Further on, there are myriads of regulatory environments in order to deliver service globally. It is all about collaboration and how services can be delivered using Cloud in a reliable, efficient, and secured way.

4.7.3.1   Cloud Contract Characteristics

Liability and intellectual property are just a few of the issues that must be considered. Other contractual issues include:

- *End-of-service support (including reversibility clause)* – When the provider–customer relationship ends, customer assets, such as services, applications, and data, should be repackaged and delivered to the customer without any condition and any remaining copies of customer data should be erased from the provider's infrastructure.
- *Provisioning and scalability* – Resource provisioning has to be made simpler and smarter. Additional resources can be quickly supplied by the provider on just a click. That is, auto-scaling has to the inseparable part of infrastructure Clouds. Also unwanted resources can be immediately deleted. Supply and demand variance has to be very minimal.
- *Service level agreement (SLA)* – This includes defining the process of managing and monitoring the capacity, data protection, data privacy, operational integrity, vulnerability management, business continuity, disaster recovery, identity management, and ownership of intellectual properties. Similarly, Operation Level Agreement (OLA) requirements too have to be discussed threadbare and signed.
- *Payments and penalties models* – Define the payment contract between the providers of the service to the users. Some of the models can be pay-per-use and pay-for-capacity. What are the penalties for stopping the contract? Another challenge is the tracking and the billing processes.
- *Availability* – The availability of Cloud services has to be guaranteed by Cloud provider in sync with network provider.
- *Issue resolution/escalation* – How and by whom resolutions are handled? When and to whom issues are being escalated? How change requests are being handled? Who has the rights?
- *Liability* – The Cloud service provider is responsible for ensuring that the provided services are compliant to relevant regulations and that subcontractors are also compliant. These result in a situation whereby the organization only needs to negotiate a contract with the main Cloud provider.

4.7.3.2   Leveraging EA Frameworks for Cloud Strategy

We have several competent and compact EA frameworks such as TOGAF. These help immeasurably in arriving at a viable Cloud strategy that leads to closer business – IT alignment. There are fine-tuned knowledge base, best practices, and guidelines to be taken into account while framing valuable and usable Cloud strategy for grand glowing enterprises. In addition to that, the Integrated Architecture Framework (IAF) helps to calculate the business value of services. Also this EA framework [7] contains the relevant details of contract definition and management.

These contribute immensely toward better strategy. Another thing is to simplify and streamline the derivation of services across different areas ranging from business to technology.

4.7.3.3   Role of EA in Defining the Contracts with CSPs and CSBs

The EA has different roles to play in defining and maintaining contract definition. Obviously there is an activity related to "classical contract of collaboration" based on the behavior between services, like it is done in the EA of a company. There are new types of contracts (or new characteristics of existing services) which will involve new actors.

On summarizing, it is clear that top-down incremental rollout strategy supported by executive and business-led strategies will be more ideal and successful than IT-led initiatives for Cloud enablement. Business goals, constraints, and cases are the main pillars and factors while chalking out a competent enterprise-wide strategy. At the same time, IT investments and services need to be considered along with the direct and indirect risks involved in Cloud migration. At the end, it is all about business performance, competitiveness, and results that dictate technology adoption. In order to embark and embrace the sizzling Cloud technology, there are two main things to do:

- Set in place a team in order to define and govern the EA across the company and the Cloud.
- Define a strategy in order to accelerate the transformation, taking into account both the trends of the market and the values for the company.

There is a clarion call to evolve a company-specific accelerator framework that vividly helps in analyzing and articulating the capabilities and competencies of new technologies, the challenges and concerns related to their usage and utilization, the internal as well as the external effects of going for new technologies, the ultimate business outputs expected and elucidated, etc.

4.8   Conclusion

In this chapter, we have discussed about the distinct features of Cloud Computing and supplied a brief about the relevance of enterprise architecture for any fast-growing business organization. Also, we have explained how next-generation enterprises can leverage the stabilizing concepts of the ground-breaking Cloud idea toward better-prepared enterprises to take on business and technology-induced changes and challenges easily and quickly. Going forward, the soaring customer and consumers' expectations can be also cleanly and compactly incorporated into ICT systems speedily. In the minds of many, there were some lingering doubts about the need of Cloud Computing for enhancing the EA's value and power for simplifying and streamlining enterprise offerings and operations.

As we all know, the paradigm of Enterprise Architecture (EA) is being prescribed for ages as the best mechanism for building and enabling enterprises to be proactive, preemptive, and prompt in meeting newer requirements. However, it is recently found that the key principles of Cloud Computing contribute immensely in arriving and articulating at an extensible and elegant EA, and hence professionals are competing with one another in steadily bringing out brewing, beneficial, and dynamic relationship between Cloud and EA. This chapter has brought in the hidden connectivity between these hot topics and how this interdependence goes a long way in achieving and accomplishing next-generation enterprises.

References

1. Chahal, S. et al. An Enterprise Private Cloud Architecture and Implementation Roadmap, IT@Intel White Paper, USA (2010)
2. Cisco EMC VMware, Cloud Computing and the Economics of Enterprise IT REV 1.0, VCE Coalition © USA (2010)
3. Citrix, Is Your Load Balancer Cloud Ready? How NetScaler Helps EnterprisesAchieve Cloud Computing Benefits? White Paper: Citrix, Florida, USA (2010)
4. Doddavula, S.K., Gawande, A.W.: Adopting Cloud Computing: enterprise private clouds. SETLabs Briefings **7**(7), 18p (2009)
5. Ebneter, D., Gatziu Grivas, S., Kumar, T.U., Wache, H.: Enterprise architecture frameworks for enabling Cloud computing. IEEE 3rd International Conference on Cloud Computing (CLOUD), vol. 5, pp. 542–543. doi: 10.1109/CLOUD.2010.47 ISBN: 978–1–4244–8207–8
6. Grigoriu, A. The Cloud Enterprise, BPTrends publications, Wokingham, United Kingdom (2009)
7. McKendrick, J.: Deloitte de-bates: does Cloud Computing make enterprise architecture irrelevant? (2010)
8. NEC Publication, Converging Enterprise – Communications, IT and the Cloud. White Paper: NEC Publication, Tokyo, Japan (2010)
9. NEC Publication, Enterprise Communications and Collaboration in a Fast Changing World, White Paper: Tokyo, Japan (2009)
10. Raines, Geoffrey. Cloud computing and SOA, MITRE technical papers, MITRE Corp., Massachusetts, USA (2009)
11. Somashekar, Sam. Opportunities for the Cloud in the Enterprise, White Paper: CA, Inc., New York, USA (2010)
12. Tsai, W.-T., Sun, X., Balasooriya, J.: Service-oriented Cloud Computing architecture. Seventh International Conference on Information Technology, pp. 684–689. IEEE doi: 10.1109/ITNG.2010.214 isbn:978–1–4244–6270–4 (2010)
13. Verizon, Next-Generation Identity Management for Cloud-Enabled Ecosystems, SOLUTIONS BRIEF; White Paper: New York, USA (2010)

Part II
Approaches and Frameworks

Chapter 5
Component-Based Development
for Cloud Computing Architectures

Muthu Ramachandran

Abstract Cloud computing has been increasing its data centres due to demand. This newly emerging paradigm is heavily based on Software as a Service concept, which provides services on demand utilising resources more effectively within the Cloud environment. The Cloud architecture, its layers and its composition of components and services need to be designed for scalability and re-configurability, as they support services and their agreements (e.g. service level agreements). The resource management of Cloud computing is the key to achieving potential benefits. Therefore, it is essential to design Cloud applications as web service components based on well-proven CBSE (component-based software engineering) methods and techniques with appropriate security controls. This chapter proposes a number of component models which have been designed for supporting Cloud design characteristics and their associated architectural layers. We have also developed a number of best practice design guidelines for components-based design that supports componentising Cloud applications explicitly. This chapter also proposes a process model based on CBSE, which is specifically customised for developing Cloud applications. A case study on Amazon Cloud EC2 has been designed based on software component model for Cloud computing. The results show a number of good practice guidelines satisfaction index which is promising.

5.1 Introduction

Cloud computing has evolved to address the availability of computing resources which can be accessed from anywhere and anytime. In particular, computing hardware and software often gets outdated, and hence, it is wise to outsource computing

M. Ramachandran (✉)
School of Computing and Creative Technologies, The Faculty of Arts,
Environment and Technology, Leeds Metropolitan University, Leeds LS6 3QS, UK
e-mail: m.ramachandran@leedsmet.ac.uk

Z. Mahmood and R. Hill (eds.), *Cloud Computing for Enterprise Architectures*,
Computer Communications and Networks, DOI 10.1007/978-1-4471-2236-4_5,
© Springer-Verlag London Limited 2011

resources and to manage their IT infrastructures outside of their company premises, which is more cost effective than is the case at present. Applications can be leased (like pay-as-you-go service) rather than being purchased, and companies have increased their data centres due to demand (Amazon, Microsoft and IBM). Cloud computing is heavily based on 'software as a service' concept and needs high-speed web access. It provides services on demand utilising resources more effectively within the Cloud environment. The Cloud architecture, its layers and its composition of components and services need to be designed for scalability, security and re-configurability as they support services and its agreements (e.g. service level agreements). In this scenario, the resource management of Cloud computing is the key to achieving potential benefits.

Cloud computing is based on web access; therefore, we need to design web applications which are designed for security. Hence, it is essential to design Cloud applications as web service components based on well-proven software process, design methods and techniques such as component-based software engineering (CBSE). Wand and Laszewski [1] define Cloud computing as a set of network-enabled services which provides scalable, guaranteed QoS (Quality of Service), inexpensive computing platforms on demand, customisable (personalised) and all of which can be accessed in a simple and pervasive way. An overview of the different Cloud computing paradigms is discussed and presented with definitions, business models and technologies by Wand and Laszewski [1] and by many others [1–34].

Software components provide a good design rationale supporting various requirements of application developments, design flexibility, system composition, testability, reusability and other design characteristics. Component-based designs are customisable, and interfaces can be designed supporting SLA (service level agreement). SLAs vary between service providers which need to be customised without much effort. This can only be achieved using a component which has been designed for flexible interface that links to a number of SLAs. Each SLA and business rule can be represented as a set of interfaces that can be mapped onto knowledge-based database or a data server. This also allows reuse of SLAs for any individual service providers. Some of the important characteristics of the Cloud computing mentioned are:

- On-demand services
- Handling wide area network addresses
- Resource grouping
- Efficient elasticity
- Measurable service delivery

Our earlier work described by Ramachandran [22] on component model for web services and service-oriented architecture (SOA), grid computing and various other systems can become an integrated aspect of any Cloud computing architectures and application design. We also need to understand the basic differences amongst SOA (service-oriented architecture), grid and Cloud computing. *SOA* is to offer services which are based on open standard Internet services and virtualisation technology and have been running in a different environment; *grid* offers services from multiple environments and virtualisation, and *Cloud* combines both. We also need to identify a specific development process for capturing requirements, design and implementation strategies, security and testing Cloud applications. Cloud computing paradigm has lots to offer, but at the same time we need to consider building a secured and resilient architecture and services that are reliable and trustworthy. In this chapter, a generic component model and a web service component model have been developed, meeting the design demands for building Cloud application architectures. In this research, we have also proposed architectural composition strategies which can be customised for various Cloud services.

This chapter has developed a number of component models which have been designed for supporting Cloud characteristics that are discussed earlier and its architectural layers for customisation and flexibility of services. We have also developed a number of best practice design guidelines for components-based design that support componentising Cloud applications explicitly. This chapter will provide a process model based on agile methodology and a process model based on CBSE. A case study on Amazon Cloud EC2 has been designed based on software component model for Cloud computing. The results show a number of good practice guidelines satisfaction index which is promising.

5.2   Background and Characteristics of Cloud Computing

Cloud computing – a moderately new term – collaborates a decade of research which has been done on virtualisation, distributed computing, utility computing and very recently the sectors such as networking and software as a service. Vouk [30] mentioned that Cloud computing is a next answer in the development of on-demand characteristics of the information technology services and products. It basically implies service-oriented architecture, less information technology overhead for the end users, far more flexibility than that is present today, low cost of ownership and on-demand services to name a few. Naone [18] further discusses that Cloud computing depends to a large extent on the virtualisation of the resources. The predecessors of Cloud computing have been around for a time now, but the technology came into limelight in 2007 when the giants such as IBM, Google announced their entrance into the arena.

Cloud security standards have been established by organisations such as European Network and Information Security Agency (ENISA), National Institute of Standards and Technology (NIST) and Cloud Security Alliance (CSA). ENISA mentions Cloud computing as highly abstract, scalable and elastic where sources which are shared and thus the money are charged on the usage. CSA describes it as a growing technology where the different sectors such as applications, information resource and infrastructure are separated. CSA further mentions that these separations come with virtualisation and brigs flexibility to the business.

In other words, Cloud computing = autonomic computing (self management) + client-server model of distributed computing + grid computing (virtualisation +

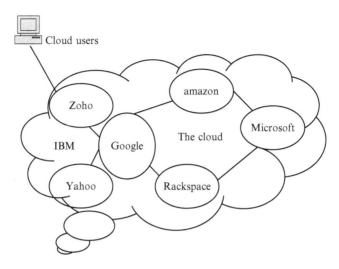

Fig. 5.1 Cloud computing service providers

distributed + parallel computing) + the power of a mainframe computing (enterprise resource planning (ERP) and management + transaction processing) + utility computing (packaging of computing resources (resources + metre/rates)) + peer-to-peer networking architecture (a distributed architecture without need for a central co-ordination). Figure 5.1 shows an illustration of a Cloud computing service providers where there are a number of Clouds provided by different vendors such as Zoho, Amazon, Google, Microsoft, Yahoo, Rackspac and IBM can all work together. Services from different vendors can be combined, requested, forwarded and delegated all on the go.

Cloud computing has emerged to offer services and resources cost-effectively. The main characteristics of a Cloud are to offer services that are dynamically scalable and to provide virtualised resources. Figure 5.2 shows a number of characteristics such as virtualisation, pay-per-service, based on grid infrastructure, failover, recoverability, re-configurability, resource management, scalability, data integrity, service customisation, elasticity, services and service level agreements, performance, availability and open standard that are required for any Cloud infrastructure to offer. The main reason for studying these characteristics is to develop Cloud services and applications from the user perspective throughout the development life cycle. These also help Cloud software engineers to capture non-functional requirements to map onto the functional requirements.

These characteristics are essential for us to understand before we start to build a Cloud service and application. These characteristics can also be used to capture non-functional and performance requirements as part of a Cloud application. A number of enabling technologies contribute to Cloud computing. In this section, we can look at few key principles and technology behind the emergence of Cloud computing. This set of characteristics allows us to derive requirements, design and testing as well as to build SaaS applications that are secured. Resilient Cloud service

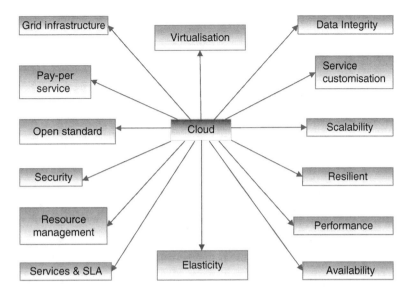

Fig. 5.2 Cloud characteristics

design helps to drive service request completion criteria which also provide support to software engineers to design scalable service and to test for resiliency.

Virtualisation technology is based on the concepts of having multiple servers, and elasticity is one of the key characteristics of a Cloud to provide resilient services on demand whereas the term Cloud itself means to provide a metaphor of on-demand services over the Internet (web services). Virtualisation technologies mainly perform the partition of hardware and thus provide flexible and scalable computing platforms. Virtual machine techniques, such as VMware and Hyper-V, offer virtualised IT infrastructures on demand. Virtual network advances, such as VPN, support users with a customised network environment to access Cloud resources. Virtualisation techniques are the bases of the Cloud computing since they render flexible and scalable hardware services.

Computing Cloud services are normally exposed as Web services, which follow the industry standards such as Web Service Definition Language (WSDL), Simple Object Access Protocol (SOAP) and Universal Description, Discovery and Integration (UDDI). The services organisation and orchestration inside Clouds could be managed in a service-oriented architecture (SOA). A set of Cloud services furthermore could be used in a SOA application environment, thus making them available on various distributed platforms and could be further accessed across the Internet. One of the key aspects of Cloud computing is to offer resources to buy-in rather than to purchase them. The key part of resources is the storage mechanism which is reliable, distributed, accessible and secured. Cloud computing services in nature are Web applications which render desirable computing services on demand. It is thus a natural technical evolution that the Cloud computing adopts the Web 2.0 technique.

We need to have a simplified programming model for Cloud users who can use and customise services on the fly. The MapReduce is a programming model and an associated implementation for processing and generating large data sets across the Google worldwide infrastructures. The MapReduce model first involves applying a 'map' operation to some data records a set of key/value pairs and then processes a 'reduce' operation to all the values that shared the same key. The Map-Reduce-Merge method evolves the MapReduce paradigm by adding a 'merge' operation. Hadoop is a framework for running applications on large clusters built of commodity hardware. It implements the MapReduce paradigm and provides a distributed file system the Hadoop Distributed File System. The MapReduce and the Hadoop are adopted by recently created international Cloud computing project of Yahoo!, Intel and HP.

Benefits of Cloud computing are discussed extensively in the current literatures [1–34]. The main benefits are secured data storage and cost-effective service and infrastructure management. The aim of this chapter is to apply Cloud characteristics to the development of Cloud services.

5.3   Cloud Services

Services are the basic principle behind the emergence of Cloud computing. Cloud computing has now been considered as a good business and enterprise model for the future of computing sectors. There are three main services that can be offered by any Cloud architecture and technology that can support, such as *Software as a Service (SaaS)*, a concept of providing software applications as a service on demand over the Internet which means it can be run anywhere and anytime and to pay per use rather than to buy; *Platform as a Service (PaaS)*, a concept of providing a complete service level application development environment as a service over the Internet right from requirements to the complete life cycle; and *Infrastructure as a Service (IaaS)*, a concept of providing the whole IT infrastructures such as storage, virtual environment, servers, platforms, and applications. This has been illustrated in Fig. 5.3 on Cloud services.

This is to understand the basic Cloud architecture so that we can map out application design artefacts across the core Cloud architecture. The following sections will discuss more on how to design them as software components by providing a model for each of these services. Before embarking on Cloud service models, we will also look at service-oriented architecture and components which have been established and hence can be used those services as it is and can also be embedded as part of any Cloud services. This provides us a basic structural mechanism by which we can build service level applications, security considerations and architectures. These three main services are to be protected, secured, available and also customisable to user need on the fly. This can only be achieved if those services are designed for supporting those characteristics explicitly across the service development life cycle, a notion that will be discussed, in detail, in the following sections.

Fig. 5.3 Cloud services

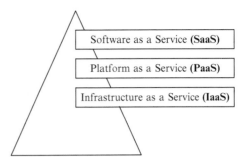

Fig. 5.4 Web services
component with architectural
composition

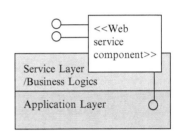

5.4   Service-Oriented Component Architectures

Component models and their architecture provide a framework for system composition and integration. A generic component model that is presented in this chapter provides a unique concept of two distinct sets of services: *providers and requires*. Software components are the basic unit of artefact that supports service composition with the Cloud computing architecture and its environment. However, each development paradigm and applications demands customisable and extendable component architectures that suit the needs of their applications. Figure 5.4 shows an example of composing web service component to service and/or system architecture. Each web service component interface is mapped onto different ports within architectural layers to request for services and offer services as and when required at run time.

As shown in this diagram, a web service component plugs into different layers of the application system using *require* (can be defined as a set of services that are required from other components in order to complete a service request) and *provider* (can be defined as a set of services that can be used by other components to complete a service request) *interfaces*. There are two models of service composition in SOAs, one is a *process-oriented composition model* which combines services using a workflow model to define new service component for which Business Process Execution Language (BPEL) (http://docs.oasis-open.org/wsbpel/2.0/OS/wsbpel-v2.0-OS.html) is used as a prototype model for specification, and second one is a *structural composition model* (also known as Service Component Architecture (SCA) model) which focuses on identifying the participating components and the

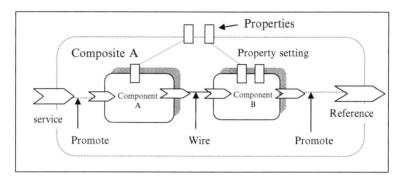

Fig. 5.5 Service component architecture (SCA) model

component connections that represent component interaction channels. To date, the SCA specification is under review for standardisation since it is the most comprehensive model for structural composition and addresses service composition explicitly. Curbera [8] has proposed a graphical representation for the SCA model which provides specification and implementation representing reusable services component that is capable of encapsulating business logic supporting one or more *services*. The SCA model is represented in Fig. 5.5 as a composition and assembly of components to form SaaS component architecture.

As shown in this model, implementations can be in many languages including Java, BPEL4WS (www.bpmi.org), and it represents the *references* as well as the call for configuration *properties* during normal operations. The properties are represented as interface ports that are described in WSDL port types (as shown as a small rectangle boxes in the diagram), services and references. Services and references use SCA bindings to configure the interaction protocol used for providing or using a service (e.g. web services binding). A composite SCA shown in the above diagram is a way of packaging a set of SCA component composition which in turn forms a system of services.

5.5   Characteristics of Service-Oriented Systems for the Cloud

Identifying a set of good design characteristics of a services-oriented system is vital for designers such that they can select, design and evaluate those characteristics that are applicable to their applications. Service-oriented computing (SoC) involves integration of several disciplines and subject areas. Therefore, some of the characteristics will overlap with each other. For example, granularity is important for reuse to maximise benefits, but at the same time it may conflict with flexibility and extensibility of services. Some of the identified services and components characteristics for Cloud services are as follows:

- Reusable web services and some other core services
- Enterprise integration services

- Dynamic binding and reconfigurable at run time
- Granularity
- Publish, subscribe and discover
- Open world where components must be able to connect and pluggable to third party software systems or components
- Heterogeneity supporting cross-platform applications
- Re-configurable
- Self-composable and recoverable
- Cloud computing infrastructure and resources management
- Autonomic framework
- Middleware
- QoS
- WS-security
- Availability
- Failover

These set of characteristics provide a clear guidelines for designers to use when developing Cloud components and architectures explicitly right from requirements to testing. The emergence of web services and SaaS has put tremendous demands on an array of security issues such as web security, network security, application security and software security. Web service security is paramount since web services allow interoperability and exchange of messages between different applications on the fly. Lakshminarayanan [16] discusses various WS-security standards when specifying web services. Developing SaaS is quite similar to web services, hence the main reason for this section to recap some of the SOA characteristics as they can be used as design heuristics. A web service application can be a part of a SaaS Cloud service. This chapter distinguishes these two aspects (between the concept of a web service and the concept of a Cloud service (SaaS)) clearly. SaaS Cloud service can be composed of a complex and over-linked set of web services. This is another good reason why we should use a component model discussed earlier to illustrate how a set of web services can be composed and contained as a SaaS component. Web services and SOA have been discussed more extensively by Erl [10] and Ramachandran [22].

5.6 Development Process Model for Cloud Applications

Cloud applications have emerged to provide cost-effective and efficient services. Currently, there is a lack of software development process model that has been applied and fine-tuned for Cloud applications, in particular, SaaS paradigm. The well-known classical process models such as waterfall and any other models cannot specify those characteristics explicitly. Therefore, it is essential to identify issues that address those needs early in the design process right from the requirements. This section aims to present a process framework that addresses these characteristics more explicitly so that practitioners can start identifying them early on.

Classical requirement techniques such as the use of case modelling and all other techniques can be used effectively, combined with some form of ethnography to understand the needs of Cloud applications and services to help design Cloud services. This will allow Cloud applications development engineers to specify SaaS business functions as well as the needs of the novice users who should be able to customise services. However, any such requirements engineering method for Cloud applications should include the following processes as part of the overall system requirements:

1. Identifying business process management (BPM). The main aim is to identify all possible scenarios on business processes so that the design of application can reflect sustainability and resilience of the system for years to come, thus achieving higher level of service level reusability. BPM can be modelled using BPMN (Business Process Modelling Notations) and can also be specified using a specification execution language known as BPEL (Business Process Execution Language).
2. Identifying service level agreements (SLA) – contract between a service provider and consumer (client). The SLAs are used to structure tasks such as process and service deployment, monitor services and event paradigm which has been used to develop distributed processes.
3. Specifying service-oriented requirements which are classified into a number of categories:

   • Technical infrastructure support
   • Load and response time
   • Service level infrastructure support

4. Specifying Cloud security. As discussed earlier, Cloud security is paramount in making Cloud computing as a successful paradigm. Therefore, this phase should consider building in security rather than adding security batches after the fact. Security should not only address the Cloud infrastructure but should also address any interfaces that are relevant to other systems, services or clients.

Figure 5.6 shows a development process model for identifying and developing Cloud services right from requirements, design, test and deploy. The main focus is on identifying security and service level agreements for Cloud services, as early, during requirements as they are part of a software engineering approach to Cloud applications development. It is also a well-known best practice that eliciting and validating service level requirements early can save cost as much as 70% of the overall test and development costs. As shown in the diagram, the Cloud development process model consists of a number of phases such as RE for Cloud, conducting BPM modelling and specification (using BPMN 2 standard and BPEL), identifying and specifying SLAs, building software security in, designing services and test and deploy.

We can always use classical software development life cyle (SDLC) models such as waterfall, spiral and others to capture functional and non-functional features for each SaaS services and web services. During the design stage, we could employ a set of good design rationales to compose SaaS as components. Alternatively, we can also directly design SaaS as components from service requirements. During business

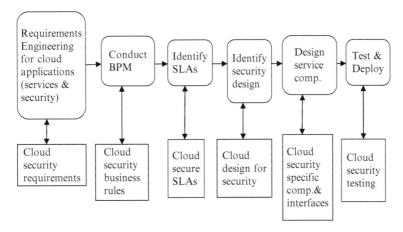

Fig. 5.6 Development process model for Cloud application

process modelling and service level specification, we can use BPMN for modelling and BPEL to specify service level workflows. These artefacts can then easily be transformed into a set of SaaS services. The model shown in this section is a security-driven Cloud development process. Hence, the main reason for identifying, specifying and designing service level software security specific issues has been addressed across all phases of the development process.

5.7 Best Practice Software Design Guidelines

Software guidelines have been with us in many forms within software engineering community such as knowledge, experiences, domain expertise, laws, software design principles, rules, design heuristics, hypothesis, experimental results, programming rules, best practices, observations, skills and algorithms. They have played a major role in software development for the past three decades of software engineering. However, our lack of experience in recording and reusing those best practices has led to re-inventing the wheel for every new applications and paradigms that emerge time to time. This section presents a new discipline known as guidelines-based software engineering where the main aim is to learn from well-known best practices when developing software systems across the life cycle. Thereby, it allows reuse of knowledge and experiences. Guidelines-based software engineering for developing highly reusable and customisable software components has been discussed by Ramachandran [22].

Software guidelines provide a precise set of steps based on underlying software design principles which help us to follow any course of disciplined set of activities. The term guidelines are defined in the dictionary as follows:

- A recommended approach, parameter, etc., for conducting an activity or task, utilising a product, etc.
- A statement of desired, good and best practice.

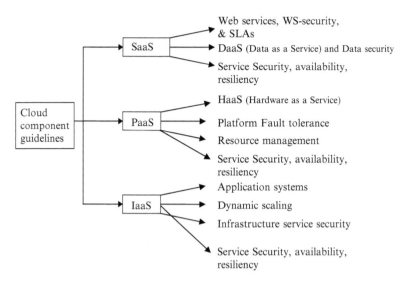

Fig. 5.7 Classifying Cloud component design guidelines

- Advice about how to design an interface.
- A document used to communicate the recommended procedures, processes or usage of a particular business practice.
- A recommendation that leads or directs a course of action to achieve a certain goal
- A written statement or outline of a policy, practice or conduct. Guidelines may propose options to enable a user to satisfy provisions of a code, standard, regulation or recommendation.

Software engineering is a set of disciplined activities that are based on well-defined standards and procedures. In software design, we use guidelines that help us to identify a suitable design criterion when faced with design decisions. Therefore, software guidelines summarise expert knowledge as a collection of design judgements, rationales and principles. This can be used by students/engineers as well as experts when learning about new design principles with examples. We have identified a classification model for categorising best practice Cloud service guidelines as shown in Fig. 5.7. Cloud service software components are classified into SaaS, PaaS and IaaS. SaaS component guidelines are further sub-categorised into web services and service level agreements.

Furthermore, one of the main aims of this research is to develop a knowledge-based system whereby best practices and Cloud component design guidelines can be applied, assessed and improved for SaaS, PaaS and IaaS components. The best practice guidelines can be encoded as knowledge into a knowledge base which can be used to automatically assess, advice and to improve component specifications perhaps written in BPEL or in any other implementation languages. Figure 5.8 shows an illustration of a knowledge-based system support for developing resilient (software resiliency means of supporting its existence) service level components for

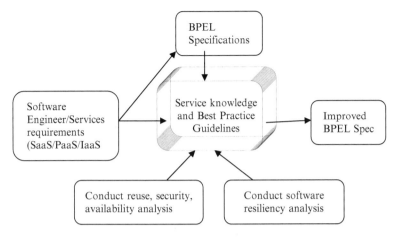

Fig. 5.8 Knowledge-based support for Cloud service components-based development

Cloud applications. The system can take any form of specification, and apply and analyse best practices on security, reusability, extensibility, re-configurability, availability and resiliency.

The idea is to develop and reuse a set of best practice Cloud guidelines from user requirements, design and testing. Currently, we have applied these guidelines manually to assess service level components against those best practices. This project has also developed a number of service level component models for SaaS, PaaS and IaaS and has been applied to the Amazon EC2 architecture which has been discussed in the later section. More on best practice guidelines are presented in the following section when selecting appropriate architectural design for Cloud services.

5.8   Component Model for Cloud Applications and Services

Some of the main reason for the emergence of software component is for customisation through interfaces, supporting reuse through extensibility by applying building block concepts and interoperability for distributed Cloud components. Service level components should support communication and exchange of messages to different systems and services on the fly, and therefore, componentising services will satisfy those criteria. Web services and SOA have been well established in the past few years with new technologies and architectures supporting service-oriented paradigm explicitly in the process, and they have also been proven to be a good design model. This section provides component models for Cloud services. Cloud applications development should primarily focus based on user perspective, their risks, and the design and architectural models should reflect user needs and their risks. Clarke [9] has proposed an architectural model based on user risks and their expectations such

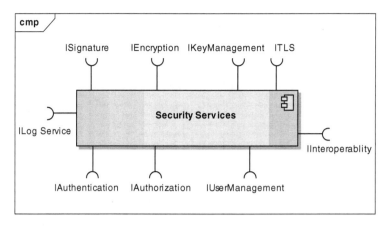

Fig. 5.9 Component model for Cloud security services

as performance, availability, reliability, security, integrity of both service as well as the data and maintainability of their data and services. The component model proposed in this chapter reflects such user requirements and flexibility of tuning the Cloud services by the users for their needs.

5.8.1 Component Model and Design Guidelines for Security in Cloud Computing

In any Cloud computing model (SaaS, PaaS, IaaS), security is an integral part of the Cloud applications, networks, services, servers, resources and architecture. Therefore, security architecture should not only address the infrastructure but also the application layer which shall reuse services wherever applicable. The UML component model shown in Fig. 5.9 provides a generic framework for Cloud security services. This is the basic software component for any Cloud services with software security built in. The required interfaces are shown with Isignature, Iencryption, Ikeymanagement, ITLS, Iinteroperability, Ilogservice, Iauthentication, Iauthorisation and Iusermanagement.

Security services allow customers to access the services, provide an easy way to manage the user life cycle (creation, modification, deletion), authorise access to the services, ensure confidentiality and integrity (encryption, signature, access control), manage cryptographic keys and provide mechanisms to establish a trusted tunnel scheme (TLS) between the client and service. Interoperability is a key characteristic in Cloud computing since a Cloud-based service can be accessed by other Cloud applications or from the client in a heterogeneous platform. Design for security in Cloud applications is paramount when designing Cloud services. The model shown in Fig. 5.9 is specifically designed for Cloud security.

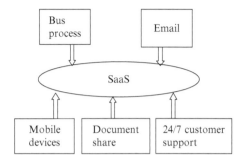

Fig. 5.10 SaaS architecture

5.8.2 Component Model and Design Guidelines for Software as a Service (SaaS)

SaaS is based on a bus process and open paradigm shift which can provide application on demand or Software as a Service without having to download the applications at the client site. An example of such software is Cobweb [7] system. Figure 5.10 shows a typical architecture and applications for a SaaS environment which consists of a bus process allowing various services to be plugged-in, email services (a common service for all types of organisations), mobile devices to be supported for all service requests, document share service which is gain a common service for all and 24/7 customer support service which can support all possible services. Taiyuan [26] considers a flexible framework support of customisation of SaaS business process by avoiding by orchestration caused by the use of BPEL (Business Process Execution Language).

Our aim is to use SaaS architecture environment to compose SaaS services as a set of software components. The main reason for designing SaaS as a set of software components is that we can see a clear link from our Cloud characteristics to design. UML component model notation provides a visual view of component services and their interfaces. There are two types of services that can be illustrated visually such as providers and requires services as shown in Fig. 5.11, a component model for Software as a Service (SaaS). As shown in the diagram, the SaaS component model provides a set of requires interfaces such as Icloud resources (this links to availability and resource effectiveness characteristics), Iservice connection, and Idiscover service. As shown in the diagram, the SaaS component model also provides a set of provider interfaces (a set of services offerered to other components) such as Ipublishable service, Iservice manager, Isubscribe service, Iautonomic service, and Isecurity service. We can see clearly that all the named interfaces refer and link to a best practice design that is based on a clear set of characteristics and design rationale which is highly efficient and flexible to configure services dynamically with data and service integrity which are the prime requirements of any Cloud service users.

This is a generic framework for service components where we can expect a set of services that are provided such as a set of functional (publishable) services, a service manager who can handle service-related issues, subscribe to a service and allocate resources, autonomic services, QoS services and security services. A set of requires

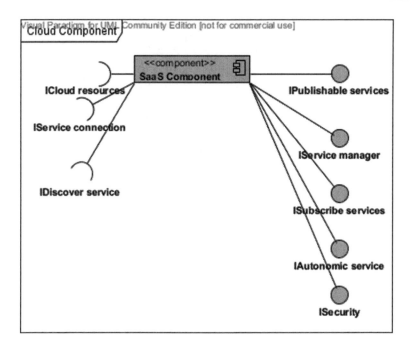

Fig. 5.11 Component model for a Cloud SaaS

services provides services such as resources and a set of secured service connection when a service is discovered. This model fits quite well with a list of characteristics that are identified for SoC earlier. Using this component model which is specifically designed for SaaS can support service level reuse and flexibility of business process customisation. According to this model, it provides interfaces such as Icloud resources, Iservice connection and Idiscover services. They are all part of requires services from other services and systems. The interfaces such as Ipublishable services through to Isecurity are all part of providers services which can be connected to other services and systems.

Best practice design guidelines include choosing appropriate design rationale between RESTful (Representational state transfer) and SOAP. Tyagi [27] discusses very interesting examples when choosing appropriate design styles for a web service. However, some common best practice guidelines should include:

1. Choose appropriate design method between RESTful and SOAP. This is the architectural design rules when building a SaaS as a web service.
2. RESTful is useful for limited profile devices such as PDAs and with limited bandwidth applications.
3. Ensure CRUD (create, read, update and delete) can be established using http put/get/post(update)/delete.
4. Ensure a web service interactions can be re-established/retained when a server is reset or re-started.

5. RESTful can be used with technologies such as AJAX (Asynchronous Java Script with XML) and a toolkit such as Direct Web Remoting (DWR) to utilise web services when building service applications.
6. SOAP-based design is appropriate when describing the formal contract for the SaaS interfaces. WSDL (Web Service Description Language) can be used to describe the details such as messages, operations, bindings and the location of the web service.
7. Hence, our main aim is to adopt software component design based on a set of best practice guidelines that are well known and have been successful in many other applications. Component-based design provides flexibility and reliability of services that are more efficient in the long term. This is mainly because software components support reuse, flexibility, extensibility and composition as its basic design criteria.

5.8.3   Component Model and Design Guidelines for Platform as a Service (PaaS)

Platform as a Service is hard to achieve but has a large potential for cost savings to be made. Therefore, component-based design offers a greater flexibility for resource management and service customisation. There are different types of PaaS [20] applications as follows. This categorisation will continue to grow in the near future:

1. Social applications like Facebook which provides APIs to write their own applications.
2. Raw compute platforms such as Amazon Cloud which provides storage, processors and bandwidth as service. Developers can upload their applications and run them as they need.
3. Web application platforms such as Google and YouTube which provide APIs and functionalities to develop their applications that leverage basic applications such as GPS-based maps and navigation, calendar, spreadsheets and sharing of multimedia assets (YouTube).
4. Business application platforms such as Force.com which provides application infrastructures specifically designed to support transactional business process applications such as database, integration, workflow and user interface services. Force.com is the clear choice for companies who are not prepared to accept compromise on scalability, reliability, flexible platform and manageability and security.

One of the main reason of cost savings comes from the reuse of platforms and hardware resources as part of the PaaS. Hence, this is the reason for designing PaaS as a component for which a model is shown in Fig. 5.12. As we discussed, PaaS provides a whole environment for developing, testing and hosting a complete SaaS services. Therefore, we need to make sure that the user platform integrity is maintained throughout. Each interface shown in the component model reflects a set of design criteria and a set of characteristics. This is reflected in the design of the

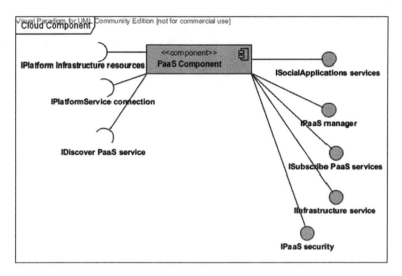

Fig. 5.12 Component model for a Cloud PaaS

component model and its interfaces. The set of providers interfaces are Isocial-Applications service, IPaaS manager interface that takes care of service and data integrity, Isubscribe PaaS service that supports connection to PaaS as a service and other related SaaS, Iinfrastructure service that looks after maintaining the platform infrastructure during the session and maintenance after the session is expired and IPaaS security that makes sure the security of the service and data is maintained. Similarly, this kind of discussion is applicable to all required interface (as shown with semi-arc).

As shown in the diagram designed using UML 2.2 version, Iplatform infrastructure resources through to Idiscover PaaS service are known as requires business services from other services and systems whereas IsocialApplications services through to IPaaS security interfaces are known as business services provided by this components to other services, users and systems which can be connected and customised. Interfaces can be designed in a way that can support interoperability and reusability of platform resource requirements, and resource manager interface can look for a required platform service and connect to on the fly.

5.8.4 Component Model and Design Guidelines for Infrastructure as a Service (IaaS)

The next highest level for cost saving to be achieved is through providing Infrastructure as a Service. Infrastructure as a Service (IaaS) is a model to provide computing Infrastructure as a Service such a complete network environment, data

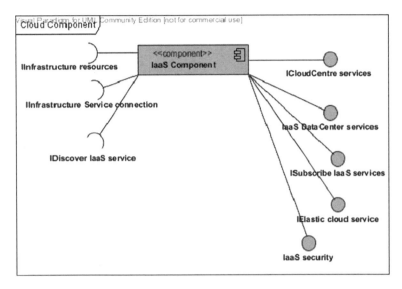

Fig. 5.13 Component model for a Cloud IaaS

centres, distributed databases, etc. It allows customers to buy those resources rather than purchasing them. According to IaaS [14], it supports:

- SLAs
- Utility computing
- Platform virtualisation
- Computer hardware
- Networks
- Requires web connectivity

Service level agreements are a set of business rules that can be represented as part of design rules. Utility computing offers potential for resource management that can be used to manage Cloud resources. Virtualisation technology offers Cloud services to be maintained efficiently. Some of the main characteristics are as described in IaaS [14] that it provides:

- Distributed resources as a service
- Dynamic scaling
- Variable costs
- Multiple tenants
- Enterprise grade infrastructure

Again, the reuse of infrastructures is paramount when designing IaaS service within the Cloud architecture. Therefore, designing them as components allows support for reuse and interoperability through components interfaces. Figure 5.13 shows a component model for a Cloud IaaS. IaaS service needs to be much more secured as the business model aims to provide the entire Infrastructure as a Service to customers. Therefore, our design models should reflect those design criteria and use expectations. The set of providers interface shown in the diagram reflects those characteristics. The providers services are Icloud centre service which aims to create a new infrastructure from a specific Cloud centre which may be located across the globe; IaaS data centre service which provides entire care for storage, servers and other data services; Ielastic Cloud service which provides support for elasticity; and IaaS security which provides support of both data and service level integrity, availability and maintainability.

As shown in the figure, interfaces such as Iinfrastructure resources through to Idiscover IaaS services are required business services from other services and systems whereas interfaces such as Icloud centre services through to IaaS security are known as business services that are provided by the component which can be connected to other services and systems.

5.8.5 Component Composition for Amazon Cloud Architecture

Cloud applications can be built by composing different Cloud services. This is the key difference to be considered when designing any Cloud applications and its services. Therefore, Cloud architectures are designed to build applications by using on-demand web services that are part of Cloud services. Zhang and Zhou [34] discuss the benefits of using Cloud Computing Open Architecture (CCOA) and provide four types of resources:

1. Infrastructure resources such as computing power, storage and machine provisioning example Amazon Cloud EC2 can provide web services which can configure and interface with online requests.
2. Software development and middleware resources. The middleware resources include Cloud-centric operating systems, application servers, distributed databases and other resources. The development resources include platform design and development tools, application development tools, testing and deployment tools and open-source and their reference projects.
3. Application resources and services. This includes Software as a Service (SaaS) model discussed in the earlier section.
4. Business process services such as business-driven applications that support resource sharing, reuse, composition and provisioning.

They have also proposed a seven-layer architecture model based on seven architectural principles for Cloud computing services which they believe to become a de facto standard for Cloud computing architectures. The seven principles are:

1. Integrated ecosystem management for Cloud
2. Virtualisation for Cloud infrastructure and its management
3. Service orientation for common reusable services

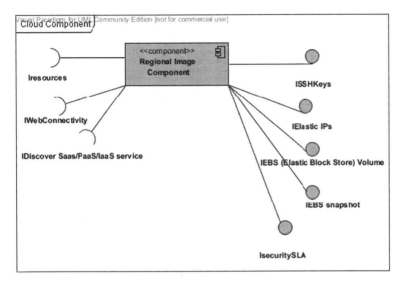

Fig. 5.14 Amazon regional component model

4. Extensible provisioning and subscription
5. Configurable enablement and compostable Cloud offerings
6. Unified Cloud information representation and exchange framework
7. Cloud quality and governance

Amazon web service (AWS) offers design flexibility and dynamic scalability with its elastic IPs (EIPs) and availability. Resilient applications can be built using AWS facilities. Best practice to design architecture using EC2 is to consider using failover and recoverability concepts built-in form the start. Availability zone (regional data centre) is the concept of using regional Amazon EC2 as and when required. Amazon EC2 offers three main centres such as US East, US West and EU regional centres. Each region consists of at least two sub-centres. Therefore, failover can be achieved using a mirror application running in another regional EC2 or in a sub-regional EC2. Figure 5.14 shows a component design for Amazon regional component which has supports requires' and providers' business service model. As shown in the diagram, component interfaces such as ISSHkeys, Ielastic ips, iebs volume, Iebs snapshot and IsecuritySLA all supports data and service level integrity and maintainability. In addition, these interfaces allow Amazon EC2 customers to connect and compose new services quickly.

This component model reflects Amazon EC2 regional level architecture and its services. A similar discussion applies to the set of requires interfaces such as Iresources, Iwebconnectivity and Idiscover SaaS, PaaS and IaaS services. Figure 5.15 shows a component model for Amazon AWS application which supports interfaces such as Iresources, Iwebconnectivity and Idiscover SaaS/PaaS/IaaS services that are requires services from other services and systems. The interfaces such as ISQS queues

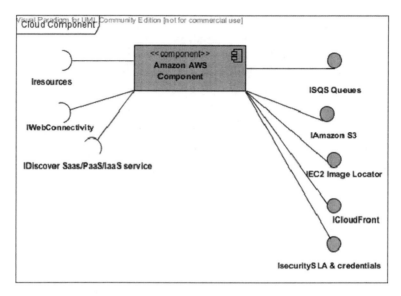

Fig. 5.15 Amazon AWS component model

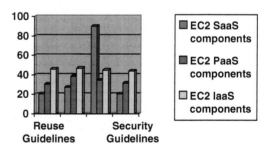

Chart 5.1 Component
guidelines satisfaction index

through to Isecurity, SLA, credentials are providers services to other services and systems. Similar design criteria based on our Cloud characteristics and user expectations are applicable to all the interfaces during the design.

Based on our research experiment, we collected those number of components for Amazon EC2 architecture and services that it aims to provide. We have also assessed our components against the set of good design characteristics and guidelines. The result shows a number of component guidelines *satisfaction index level* (we have introduced the notion of guidelines satisfaction level as the measure in percent of a number of good practice guidelines have been met by a component and its interfaces) as percent for Amazon EC2 components for SaaS, PaaS and IaaS based on our design guidelines and component models. This has been illustrated in Chart 5.1.

5.9   Conclusion

Cloud computing has emerged supporting cost-effective computing and IT systems. Designing Cloud services is complex and needs to be crafted systematically with good design principles that support Cloud criteria and characteristics. Componentisation of Cloud services offers software scalability and resiliency. This work has demonstrated a possibility of designing them systematically with specific process and components which can support effort and cost saving. Our previous work software components and best practice guidelines have led to the development of embedding best practice and reuse knowledge to be built-in rather than adding them at a later stage in the development. This work has also combined best practice design principles on object orientation, componentisation, design patterns for composing architectures, service-oriented design strategies and Cloud computing design strategies. All of which has lead to the development of various component architecture for Cloud services presented in this chapter. For Cloud computing, the characteristics such as security of services, failover and availability can only be achieved if the Cloud services are to be developed with those characteristics that can be built-in. Hence, the reason for a number of component-based framework and component-based development process for Cloud computing architectures has emerged in this project.

References

1. Wang, L., Laszewski, V.G.: Scientific cloud computing: early definition and experience. http:// cyberaide.googlecode.com/svn/trunk/papers/08-cloud/vonLaszewski-08-cloud.pdf (2008)
2. Creeger, M. Cloud computing: an overview, ACM Queue, June 1 (2009)
3. Aoyama, M., et al.: Web services engineering: promises and challenges. In: International Conference on Software Engineering 2002 (ICSE'02), Orlando, FL, 19–25 May 2002
4. Bertolino, A., et al.: Audition of web services for testing conformance to open specified protocols. In: Stafford, J., et al. (eds.) Architecting Systems with Trustworthy Components. Springer, Heidelberg (2006)
5. Bias, R.: Cloud expo article, cloud computing: understanding infrastructure as a service. Cloud Comput. J. http://cloudcomputing.sys-con.com/node/807481. Jan 2009
6. Chesbrough, H., Spohrer, J.: A research manifesto for services science. Special Issue on Services Science, Commun. ACM. **49**(7), 35–40 (2006)
7. Cobweb: http://www.cobweb.com/ (2009)
8. Curbera, F.: Component contracts in service-oriented architectures. Special Issue on Service-Oriented Computing, IEEE Comput. **40**(11), 74–80 (2007)
9. Clarke, R.: User requirements for cloud computing architecture. In: 10th IEEE/ACM International Conference on Cluster, Cloud and Grid Computing, Melbourne (2010)
10. Erl, T.: Service-Oriented Architecture: Concepts, Technology, and Design. Prentice Hall, Upper Saddle River (2005)
11. Farrell, J., Ferris, C.: What are web services? Special Issue, Commun. ACM **46**(6), 31 (2003)
12. Khaled, L.: Deriving architectural design through business goals. Int. J. Comput. Sci. Inf. Secur. (IJCSIS) **7**(3) (2010)
13. Helbig, J.: Creating business value through flexible IT architecture. Special Issue on Service-Oriented Computing, IEEE Comput. **40**(11), 80–89 (2007)

14. IaaS: Cloud computing world forum. http://www.cloudwf.com/iaas.html (2010)
15. IThound Video whitepaper: http://images.vnunet.com/video_WP/V4.htm. Accessed Feb 2010
16. Lakshminarayanan, S.: Interoperable security service standards for web services, IT Pro, IEEE CS Press, Dec 2010
17. Nano, O., Zisman, A.: Realizing service-centric software systems. Special Issue on Service-Oriented Counting, IEEE Software, Nov/Dec 2007
18. Naone, E.: Computer in the cloud, technology review. http://www.technologyreview.com/Infotech/19397/?a=f (2007)
19. NIST: http://csrc.nist.gov/groups/SNS/cloud-computing/index.html (2009)
20. PaaS: Types of PaaS solutions. http://www.salesforce.com/uk/paas/paas-solutions/ (2010)
21. Papazoglou, P.M., et al.: Service-oriented computing: state of the art and research challenges. Special Issue on Service-Oriented Computing, IEEE Comput. **40**(11), 38–45 (2007)
22. Ramachandran, M.: Software Components: Guidelines and Applications. Nova Publishers, New York (2008)
23. SaaS: SaaS. http://www.saas.co.uk/ (2009)
24. Science Group, 2020 Science Group: Toward 2020 science, Technical report, Microsoft. http://research.microsoft.com/towards2020science/downloads/T2020S_Report.pdf (2006)
25. Serugendo, G., et al.: Self-organisation: paradigms and applications. In: Engineering Self-Organising Systems: Nature-Inspired Approaches to Software Engineering. Springer, Berlin/Heidelberg (2004)
26. Taiyuan, S.: A flexible business process customization framework for SaaS. In: WASE International Conference on Information Engineering, Taiyuan, China July 2009
27. Tyagi, S.: RESTful web services. http://www.oracle.com/technetwork/articles/javase/index-137171.html (2006)
28. Venkataraman, T., et al.: A model of cloud based application environment. (IJCSIS) International Journal of Computer Science and Information Security **7**(3) (2010)
29. Verizon.: http://www.zdnet.co.uk/news/cloud/2010/10/08/the-cloud-lessons-from-history-40090471/. Oct 2010
30. Vouk, M.A.: Cloud computing – issues, research and implementations. J. Comput. Inf. Technol. (CIT) **16**, 235–246 (2008)
31. Wilson, C., Josephson, A.: Microsoft office as a platform for software + services. Architect. J. **13**. www.architecturejournal.net (2007)
32. Weiss, A.: Computing in the clouds. ACM networker **11**(4) (2007)
33. Yang, J.: Web service componentisation. Commun. ACM **46**(10), 35–40 (2003)
34. Zhang, L.-J., Zhou, Q.: CCOA: cloud computing open architecture. In: IEEE International Conference on Web Services, Los Angeles (2009)

Chapter 6
Identity and Access Management in Cloud Computing

Khandakar Entenam Unayes Ahmed and Vassil Alexandrov

Abstract With cloud computing, the latest addition in system architecture, consumers and companies can scale up to massive capacities in an instant without having any investment in new infrastructure or they can even shrink to a desktop within a second. But this service oriented computing is becoming controversial due to the lack of privacy and security issues. In a recent survey conducted by International Data Corporation (IDC), 87.5% of the participants suggested security as the main reason for reluctance on the part of enterprise IT to aggressively adopt cloud computing in future system deployments. This chapter discusses a possible solution for Identity and Access Management (IAM) to help enterprise IT organizations and cloud providers to improve their services. Managing access control and governance within IAM, to meet today's business needs in the cloud environment, remains one of the major hurdles for enterprises' adoption of cloud services. Today's aggressive adoption of immature cloud computing services by enterprises creates extreme thrust to have a strong cloud-based IAM system which provides support for business needs ranging from secure collaborations with global partners to secure access for global employees consuming sensitive information, from any location and using any device at any time. The motive of this chapter is to show readers a standard possible way to develop an IAM system. This idea can work as seed for someone or a development/research group to come up with a complete full solution.

K.E.U. Ahmed (✉)
School of Electrical & Computer Engineering, RMIT University,
Melbourne, Australia
e-mail: khandakar.ahmed@rmit.edu.au

V. Alexandrov
ICREA Research Professor in Computational Science at Barcelona
Supercomputing Centre, Barcelona, Spain
e-mail: vassil.alexandrov@bsc.es

Z. Mahmood and R. Hill (eds.), *Cloud Computing for Enterprise Architectures*,
Computer Communications and Networks, DOI 10.1007/978-1-4471-2236-4_6,
© Springer-Verlag London Limited 2011

6.1 Introduction

Consumers are required an access management interface to access to the Cloud service and also for managing resources. This feature of Cloud computing creates vulnerability which is much higher than traditional infrastructure where management functionality is limited to few administrator in a secured geographical location. For successful and effective management of authentication and identity in the Cloud, there are four essential functions: Identity Provisioning and De-provisioning, Authentication and Federation, Authorization and User Profile Management and Support for Compliance [1]. Some significant existing solutions have been investigated in this chapter in order to have a contrast between existing solutions and one that has been proposed here.

The chapter has been organized into six sections whereby Sect. 6.2 discusses reluctance of adoption despite having a huge Cloud computing market. Sect. 6.3 investigates different existing solutions for Identity and Access Management (IAM). Architecture and system design of a proposed prototype has been described briefly in Sect. 6.4 whilst Sect. 6.5 shows a deployment plan. Sect. 6.6 draws conclusion focusing of milestones that have been achieved through the new prototype to overcome hurdles that still exist in the current solutions.

6.2 Cloud Computing Market

Over the next 5 years, many companies will move individual or multiple applications and services out of their own IT departments into hosted, on-demand environments. In earlier quarter of previous year, survey on 200 European chief information officers conducted by networking and storage vendor Brocade found that more than 25% enterprise companies were planning to migrate a portion of their internal IT infrastructure to Cloud model within the next couple of years [2].

The global market is $37.8 billion in 2010 which is expected to grow to $121.1 billion in 2015 at a CAGR of 26.2% [3]. In this Cloud computing service market, Software as a Service (SaaS) is the largest segment accounting for 73% of the market's revenue in 2010. The major SaaS providers are Adobe Web Connect, Google Mail, Cisco WebEx and Yahoo Mail. 30% of the SaaS market revenues come from content, communications and collaboration (CCC) [4].

By 2014, the UK alone is expected to account for 29% of that investment, according to Gartner [2], with financial services, manufacturing industries, telecoms and public sector buyers at the forefront of Cloud adoption.

This enormous market is unstable with a number of issues including security which is the most primary concern. There are a few areas of concern that make enterprise IT reluctant in adopting Cloud computing. Though many enterprise IT organizations are aggressive, the survey conducted on them by International

Data Corporation (IDC) clearly shows how concerned they are on the following issues [5]:

• Security	87.5%
• Availability	83.3%
• Performance	82.9%
• On-demand model costs more	81.0%
• Lack of interoperability standards	80.2%

6.3   Related Work

Dancheng Li et al. [6] proposed a role-based access control (RBAC) model for SaaS systems which attempted to introduce a practical implementation of access control module for SaaS systems. They extended their model from the RBAC and ARBAC97 models and used layered structures to achieve system-level and tenant-level access control. By introducing RBAC, authors were able to overcome problems that existed with traditional access control method. These included role name conflicts, cross-level management and the isomerism of tenants' access control. The S-RBAC model which was proposed consisted of the following elements: General Permission, General Role, Admin Permission, Admin Role, GPRC, GURC, Admin Constraint, Tenant, Session, URC and PRC. The structure control method described in [6] is composed of the following components: ACS (Access Control Server), AFS (Access Filter Server), UDCS (User Dynamic Constraint Server) and PMS (Permission Management Center), AUC (Authentication Center), etc.

Dancheng Li et al. [6] applied S-RBAC model to the access control module of the community health services system based on SaaS. This provided some basic functions for small- or medium-sized community health organizations including registration management, medical record management, outpatient clinic, pharmacy management, etc. The system follows the SaaS patterns providing its services in the way of a single instance and multi-tenant structure.

The chapter also talks about the authentication process but totally skips how this is happening. Moreover, the authors left no sign of any implementation strategy. Though the model was named as S-RBAC and defined a few roles accordingly, it did not define how these roles would be assigned to different users. The model is incomplete in terms of using RBAC policies and implementation strategies.

Aiiad Albeshri and William Caelli [7] introduced a new approach named Mutual Protection for Cloud Computing (MPCC) whose underlying main concept is based on a philosophy of Reverse Access Control where customers control and attempt to enforce the means by which the Cloud providers control authorization and authentication within this dynamic environment. The Cloud provider ensures that the customer organization does not violate the security of the overall Cloud structure itself. The authors in [7] associated Policing Module with Cloud consisting of two MPCC functions (Initial Matching Function and Continuous Monitoring Function).

Table 6.1 Profile of organization

		AC	Geographic	Security requirements			
	Application	requirements	requirements	Confidentiality	Integrity	Availability	Cert.
Vector 1	Payroll	RBAC	Brisbane	Yes	Yes	Yes	IS15408
Vector 2	Inventory	DAC	Australia	Yes	Yes	No	IS15408
.....	.....	.....	...	...	...	...	...

Table 6.2 Profile of cloud provider

		AC	Geographic	Service requirements			
	Application	requirements	requirements	Confidentiality	Integrity	Availability	Cert.
Vector 1	Payroll	RBAC, DAC	Australia, China, USA	Yes	Yes	Yes	IS15408
Vector 2	Inventory	All	India	Yes	Yes	No	IS15408
...	...	...	....	...	...	...	...

Moreover, according to their architecture, Cloud provider and organization would have profile creation function allowing them to be able to provide their own profiles. These profiles would have to be matched by a profile matchmaker module to provide mutual protection to each other. The profile would be expressed as vector according to the proposal.

$$Profile_{org} = \left\{vector_1, vector_2, \ldots\ldots\ldots, vector_n\right\}$$

$$Profile_{cloud} = \left\{vector_1, vector_2, \ldots\ldots\ldots, vector_n\right\}$$

Tables 6.1 and 6.2 show the profile of organization and Cloud provider, respectively, which have to be matched to provide mutual protection to each other.

So, *Initial Matching Function* would match the profile whilst *Continuous Monitoring Function* would audit and watch the agreements and access control requirements. The contract should define how to police and who does the policing. The policing function might be a service provided by a third party or deployed within the organization. Apart from these two, there would be another two functions namely Customer Administration Function and Cloud Administration Function which would be responsible for administering corresponding parties.

The proposal is very hypothetical and superficial. In terms of implementation, authors have only mentioned different tools to use but did not explain or provide any plan. It was stated that for access control, RBAC or DAC would be used but no explanation was given of how to use them. Other security measurements suffered similar levels of confusion and no signs of implementation plans. In addition, vector

Fig. 6.1 The public-key
predicate encryption scheme [8]

1. Setup	PK,MSK
2. Encrypt(PK,PII)	CT
3. KeyGen (PK,MSK,p)	TK^p
4. Query (PK,CT,TK^p)	p(PII)

and profile standardization was not defined and was expected to be accomplished quickly by having an international standard to agree on notations for vectors and profiles. This lack of standard notations also put the future of the proposed architecture in danger.

Rohit Ranchal et al. [8] proposed an approach for building IDM systems using the active bundle scheme, computing predicate over encrypted data and multiparty computing without using Trusted Third Parties (TTPs). Authors heavily criticized all solutions using TTPs claiming that Personal Identifiable Information (PII) can be breached by man in middle attack or by compromising the third party. The proposed architecture in [8] has the following salient features: (1) ability to authenticate without disclosing unencrypted data, (2) ability to use identity data on un-trusted hosts and (3) independence of TTP. A sender (say Alice) uses a setup algorithm to generate a public key 'PK' and a secret key 'MSK'. Alice then uses PK to encrypt her *PII* using encrypt algorithm for generating ciphertext *CT*. Alice also has the function 'p' representing a predicate that she wishes to evaluate for her encrypted PII. She uses the KeyGen algorithm, PK, MSK and p to output the token TK^p (encoding p). She then gives TK^p to the host that evaluates the token (with p included in the token) for CT (the encrypted PII) and returns the result p(PII) to Alice (Fig. 6.1).

For negotiating use of a Cloud service, computing predicate has been combined over encrypted data with secure multiparty computing. The secret key MSK is split between n parties using the Shamir's [9] technique. The algorithm KeyGen is then provided to n parties and computed by them collaboratively using their shares of the secret key, function p representing a predicate, PK, and TK. This is done by the protocol defined by Ben-Or, Goldwasser and Wigderson for multiparty computing [10].

Though the researcher in [8] succeeded in devising a good approach in exchanging Personal Identifiable Information (PII) securely, they were not aware that details of PII can be limited down to such a stage that even if the PII was exchanged in plain text, it still would not be useful for intruders. Moreover, the approach was not simulated and was simply left as a plan, like many other proposals.

Subra Kumaraswamy et al. [11], powered by Cloud Security Alliance (CSA), provided a guidance for Identity and Access Management System. They discussed four major IAM functions: Identity Provisioning/De-provisioning, Authentication and Federation, Authorization and User Profile Management and Support for Compliance. They have discussed all these four major functions over three Cloud delivery models: Software as a Service (SaaS), Platform as a Service (PaaS) and Infrastructure as a Service (IaaS).

Contributors of *Guidance for Identity & Access Management V2.1* [11] recommended customers to use standard connectors provided by Cloud Service Providers (CSPs) as practically possible, preferably built on the SPML (Service Provisioning Markup Language) schema as it has been recognized as the industry standard specification in user access provisioning for multiple types of application. Any custom solution should leverage SPML so that it can be repurposed to suit a standard CSP-supported solution.

Technical solution for identity provisioning has been summarized as follows [11]:

Software as a Service/Platform as a Service:

1. Use native SPML adapters or connectors provided by the CSP.
2. Use SPML gateways to provision users in CSPs that do not have native support for SPML.
3. When supported, provision accounts dynamically using attributes in a Security Assertion Markup Language (SAML) authentication assertion.
4. Periodically audit users and their privileges; delete unauthorized users and minimize privileges by assigning the appropriate profiles for users. Automate processes to scale across providers.

Infrastructure as a Service:

1. Use native SPML adapters or connectors provided by the CSP.
2. Use SPML gateways to provision users in CSPs that do not have native support for SPML.
3. When supported, provision accounts dynamically using attributes in a Security Assertion Markup Language (SAML) authentication assertion.
4. Periodically audit users and their privileges; delete unauthorized users and minimize privileges by assigning the appropriate profiles for users. Automate processes to scale across providers.

According to the authors, authentication in SaaS and PaaS can be achieved by using enterprise's Identity Provider (IdP) for Enterprise. For individual user-centric authentication, Google, YahooID, OpenID, Live ID, etc., can be used. On the other hand, in IaaS, two sets of users need to be authenticated. The first set is enterprise IT personnel who will deploy applications and manage applications. The second set is application users who might be employees, customers or partner organizations. As a strong authentication method, they proposed to use Kerberos, token or smart card systems.

Control of access to transaction processing services is suggested to be best served by Role Based Access Control (RBAC) models, possibly complemented by data-centric policy (such as SQL views) implemented in underlying databases. Unstructured content may be best protected by an ACL model in many cases and a MAC/MLS model when it is necessary to make access control decisions based upon the classification of assets or information. Web service access to the Cloud is generally best supported by an ACL model. In addition to basic access control, Cloud environments may impose quota-based restrictions. Finally, large corporate customers will need to invest in designing a group or role model that maps user roles to their internal business functions in order to effectively manage the access model [11].

6.4   Proposed Identity and Access Management (IAM) Model

For maximizing security in enterprises, it is necessary to ensure a strong IAM systems and authentication process. IAM implementation in Cloud should have consistency with existing IAM and authentication implementation. Strong IAM should have standard to facilitate interoperability. According to IDC, an ideal IAM should have the following functions:

- Privileged user control
- Access management/single sign-on (SSO)
- User authentication/federation
- Identity management and role management
- Data loss protection/prevention
- Log management

In the following subsections, prototype of an IAM model is presented to overcome limitations of existing solutions that have been described in Sect. 6.3.

6.4.1   Analysis and Design

The primary purpose of this model is twofold: first to provide strong authentication between customer and provider, and second to provide a strong policy-based access control to the resources of Cloud. Clients will start communication with the provider through Access Control and Management Unit (ACMU) which will provide both authentication and access control. Figure 6.2 shows a schematic diagram of overall ACMU system consisting of two major units: Access Control Enforcement Unit (ACEU) and Access Control Decision Unit (ACDU). Here a slight modification has been brought in Kerberos[1] [12, 13] introducing a new unit called Edge Node which also implements Diffie-Hellman[2] algorithm [14–18].

6.4.1.1   Access Control Enforcement Unit (ACEU)

ACEU consists of Edge Node (EN) and three servers: Authentication Server (AS), Ticket Granting Server (TGS) and Service Server (SS). A request first comes to

---

[1] Kerberos is an authentication protocol for trusted hosts on un-trusted networks.

[2] First openly published public key or key-exchange mechanism.

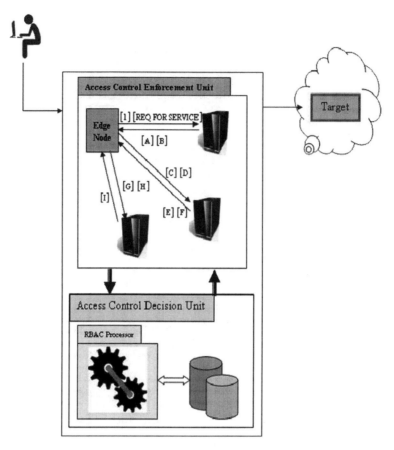

Fig. 6.2 Schematic diagram of overall ACMU system

Edge Node and then it goes to the Authentication Server. This is how one change is brought in the Kerberos Protocol bringing Edge Node (EN) between the client and the Authentication Server (AS).

6.4.1.2   Access Control Decision Unit (ACDU)

ACDU consists of RBAC processor written in Java and the storage for storing POLICIES written in XML. ACDU will communicate to the ACEU through Service Server (SS).

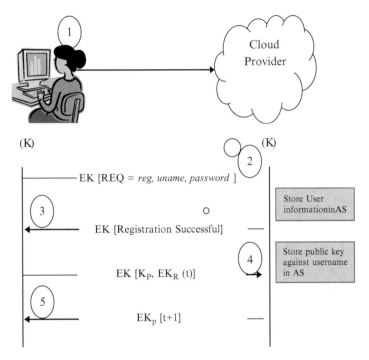

Fig. 6.3 User registration

6.4.1.3   User Registration

As described in Fig. 6.3, when a new user attempts to communicate with a Cloud provider, his/her request goes to Edge Node (EN) first. Both EN and user generate a common key using Diffie-Hellman algorithm. The following steps are involved:

1. After receiving first request from consumer, both parties generate a common secret key (K) using Diffie-Hellman algorithm.
2. On the basis of provider's query, consumer sends his/her details (reg, uname and password) which are encrypted by the secret key generated in step 1.
3. Login information is stored in the AS of ACEU, and an acknowledgement of successful registration is sent to the consumer.
4. Upon successful registration the user generates a public/private key pair and sends the following message which is encrypted by secret key:

   (a) K_p, public key of consumer and timestamp encrypted by private key of consumer ($EK_R(t)$)

   ACEU will decrypt the message and store the public key in the AS against the username.

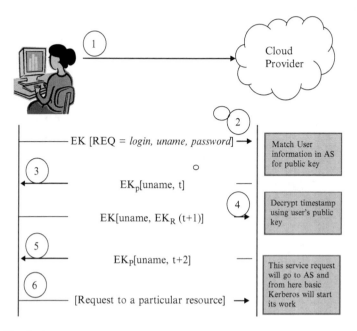

Fig. 6.4 User login

Encrypted message $(EK_R(t))$ received from consumer is decrypted using con-sumer's public key. The provider sends back a nonce $(t+1)$ to the consumer encrypted by public key which can be decrypted by consumer's own private key.

6.4.1.4 User Login

Also in the case of login, a user will first communicate with Edge Node [EN] (Fig. 6.4). Both EN and user will generate a common key using Diffie-Hellman algorithm and then will follow the following steps:

1. After receiving first request from consumer, both parties generate a common secret key (K) using Diffie-Hellman algorithm.
2. The Consumer then sends its login information (uname, password) encrypted by the key K generated in Step 1. The AS will match user information and look for the consumer's public key stored in the AS.
3. The Provider sends a nonce (t, uname) encrypted using consumer's public key.
4. The consumer sends another message encrypted by K [common secret key gen-erated in step 1]. The message contains uname and nonce $(t+1)$ which are encrypted using consumer's private key.
5. The provider then sends an acknowledgement containing 'uname' and nonce $(t+2)$ encrypted by consumer's public key.

Upon receiving acknowledgement from provider, consumer will send a request for a particular service. From this point Kerberos starts following basic algorithm which is illustrated in the next section.

6.4.1.5   Kerberos Authentication

According to Fig. 6.2, different messages that are exchanged amongst AS, TGS, SS and EN are numbered in third braces [...]. All the messages explained above through user registration and user login are indicated by message [1] between EN and AS in Fig. 6.2. Rest of the communication is explained through the following steps. All requests go via EN which is not mentioned here since it can be embedded in the AS instead of a separate node.

Authentication Steps

1. The Client sends a **[request to service]** message to the **AS** requesting services on behalf of the user. **Sample message**: 'User XYZ would like to request services'.
2. **Note**: Username and password is sent to the **AS**.
3. The **AS** checks to see if the client is in its database. If it is, the **AS** sends back the following two messages to the client:

   • **Message A: Client/TGS Session Key** encrypted using the public key of the client/user
   • **Message B: TGT** (which includes the client ID, client network address, ticket validity period and the **Client/TGS Session Key**) encrypted using the secret key of the **TGS**

4. Once the client receives messages A and B, it decrypts message A to obtain the **Client/TGS Session Key**. This session key is used for further communications with **TGS**. At this point, the client has enough information to authenticate itself to the **TGS**. **Note**: The client cannot decrypt message B, as it is encrypted using **TGS**'s secret key.

Client Service Authorization Steps

1. When requesting services, the client sends the following two messages to the **TGS**:

   • **Message C:** Composed of the **TGT** from message B and the ID of the requested service
   • **Message D:** Authenticator (which is composed of the client ID and the time-stamp) encrypted using the **Client/TGS Session Key**

2. Upon receiving messages C and D, the **TGS** retrieves message B out of message C. It decrypts message B using the **TGS** secret key. This gives it the **Client/TGS Session Key**. Using this key, the **TGS** decrypts message D (Authenticator) and sends the following two messages to the client:

   • **Message E: Client-to-Server ticket** (which includes the client ID, client network address, validity period and **Client/Server Session Key**) encrypted using the **SS** secret key
   • **Message F: Client/Server Session Key** encrypted with the Client/TGS Session Key

Client Service Request Steps

1. Upon receiving messages E and F from **TGS**, the client has enough information to authenticate itself to the **SS**. The client connects to the **SS** and sends the following two messages:

   - **Message G**: composed the message E received from the previous step (the **Client-to-Server ticket**, encrypted using the **SS** secret key)
   - **Message H:** a new Authenticator, which includes the client ID and timestamp and is encrypted using **Client/Server Session Key**

2. The **SS** decrypts the ticket using its own secret key to retrieve the **Client/Server Session Key**. Using the sessions key, **SS** decrypts the Authenticator and sends the following message to the client to confirm its true identity and willingness to serve the client:

   - **Message I:** the timestamp found in client's Authenticator plus 1, encrypted using the **Client/Server Session Key**

3. The client decrypts the confirmation using the **Client/Server Session Key** and checks whether the timestamp is correctly updated. If so, then the client can trust the server and can start issuing service requests to the server.

6.4.1.6   Access Granting

At this point every service request for a particular resource goes to the SS, which is forwarded to RBAC processor of ACDU. ACDU has all access policies written in XML and stored in databases. It should be noted that the database of ACDU unit will be connected to the AS because during registration of a user, all the relevant default policies will be written. However, RBAC processor reads the policies and takes decision accordingly. The decision is forwarded to the SS, and on the basis of this decision, the SS sends ACK/NACK to the user.

6.4.2   Defining Policies in XML

In this section, policy for access management is defined in XML through five XML sheets. Each time a user registers to the IAM by default, all XML files are updated by inserting corresponding default policies which can later be modified, inserted or deleted according to the user's preferences. In order to test the feasibility, it is decided to keep the system simple at the beginning. That is why instead of writing all policies, only sample policy for IaaS is written.

6.4.2.1   XML Permission Sheet

Figure 6.5 shows a few possible permissions relevant to IaaS storage written in XML. Permission is characterized by permi_id, target and operation. 'permi_id' is

```
XPS
<xps>
   <IaaS>
      <permission permi_id = P1>
                   <target id='S1'>storage</target>
                   <operation>insert</operation>
      </permission>
      <permission permi_id = P2>
                   <target id='S1'>storage</target>
                   <operation>update</operation>
      </permission>
      <permission permi_id = P3>
                   <target id='S1'>storage</target>
                   <operation>delete</operation>
      </permission>
      <permission permi_id = P4>
                   <target id='S1'>storage</target>
                   <operation name=delegation>
                      <sub-operation subpermi_id=P4.1>grant</sub-operation>
                      <sub-operation subpermi_id=P4.2>revoke</sub-operation>
                   </operation>
      </permission>
      <permission permi_id = P5>
                   <target id='S1'>storage</target>
                   <operation>move</operation>
      </permission>
      <permission permi_id = P6>
                   <target id='S1'>storage</target>
                   <operation>cancel</operation>
      </permission>
      <permission permi_id = P7>
                   <target id='S1'>storage</target>
                   <operation>destroy</operation>
      </permission>
      <permission permi_id = P8>
                   <target id='S1'>storage</target>
                   <operation>all</operation>
      </permission>
   </IaaS>
</xps>
```

Fig. 6.5 XML permission sheet

used to uniquely identify a particular permission, 'target' is used to refer the resource that the client/user want to use and 'operation' indicates the permission that a particular user can take on this target resource. For example, in Fig. 6.5, first permission for IaaS storage is identified by 'P1', targeted for 'storage' and the operation that a holder of this permission can do is 'insert'.

```
<XCredTypeDef>
<credential_type cred_type_id="C100">
      <type_name>AdminUser</type_name>
      <attribute_list>
             <attribute_nametype="string">service_model</attribute_name>
             <attribute_name type="string">resource</attribute_name>
             <attribute_name type="string">delegated</attribute_name>
      </attribute_list>
</credential_type>

<credential_type cred_type_id="C200">
      <type_name>DelegatedUser</type_name>
      <attribute_list>
             <attribute_nametype="string">service_model</attribute_name>
             <attribute_name type="string">resource</attribute_name>
             <attribute_name type="string">delegated</attribute_name>
      </attribute_list>
</credential_type>
</XCredTypeDef>
```

Fig. 6.6   XML credential type definition

6.4.2.2   XML Credential Type Definition (XCredTypeDef)

XCredTypeDef defines credentials that will be applied to different roles. Initially
two credentials are defined, namely, Admin User and Delegated User which are
applied to 'admin' and 'user' roles, respectively. When these credentials are imposed
on a rule, they must have few attributes defined in corresponding credentials, as
shown in Fig. 6.6.

6.4.2.3   XML Role Sheet (XRS)

XML Role Sheet defines different roles by two attributes, namely, 'role_name' and
'cred_type'. A credential defined in XCredTypeDef can be imposed on these roles,
and a role in that case should have the list of attributes defined by their corresponding credential. In Fig. 6.7, RI01 is an admin role for IaaS storage resource having
credential C100. It has sub-attributes: Service Model, Resource and Delegation as
defined by C100 in XCredTypeDef.

6.4.2.4   XML Permission Role Assignment (XPRA)

XML Permission Role Assignment (XPRA) assigns permissions to a role. In
Fig. 6.8, 'P8' has been assigned to role RI01. From Fig. 6.5 it is clear that a holder

Fig. 6.7 XML role sheet

```
<XRS>
  <ROLE role_id="RI01">
    <role_name>admin_iaas_storage</role_name>
    <cred_type cred_type_id="C100">
            <service_model>IaaS</service_model>
            <resource>Storage</resource>
            <delegated>No</delegated>
    </cred_type>
  </ROLE>

  <ROLE role_id="RI02">
    <role_name>Delegated_IaaS_User</role_name>
    <cred_type cred_type_id="C200">
            <service_model>IaaS</service_model>
            <resource>Storage</resource>
            <delegated>Yes</delegated>
    </cred_type>
  </ROLE>
</XRS>
```

Fig. 6.8 XML permission role assignment

```
<XPRA>
  <pa id=PA1>
        <role_name id="RI01">admin_iaas_storage</role_name>
        <permissions>
                <permi_id>P8</permi_id>
        </permissions>
        <cardinality>1</cardinality>
  </pa>
  <pa id=PA2>
        <role_name id="RI02">Delegated_IaaS_User </role_name>
        <permissions>
                <permi_id>P1</permi_id>
                <permi_id>P2</permi_id>
                <permi_id>P3</permi_id>
        </permissions>
        <cardinality>*</cardinality>
  </pa>
</XPRA>
```

of permission 'P8' can take any operation on 'storage' resource of IaaS. The value of attribute 'cardinality' is 1, which means this role can be assigned to only one user of a company/domain, whilst value of cardinality '*' means more than one user holding this role can exist in a domain/company.

Fig. 6.9 XML user role
assignment

```
<XURA>
  <ura ura_id="URA1">
    <users>
      <user user_id="john">
              <role_id>RI01</role_id>
              <domain>xx<domain>
              <delegation_authority>yes</delegation_authority>
              <delegated_by>NONE<delegated_by>
      </user>
    </users>
  </ura>
  <ura ura_id="URA2">
    <users>
      <user user_id="adam">
              <role_id>RI02</role_id>
              <domain>xx<domain>
              <delegation_authority>no</delegation_authority>
              <delegated_by>john<delegated_by>
      </user>
    </users>
  </ura>
</XURA>
```

6.4.2.5 XML User Role Assignment (XURA)

XURA sheet assigns role to a particular user. In Fig. 6.9, RI01 is assigned to 'john'.
Apart from role assignment it defines domain, delegation_authority and
delegated_by.

Let us see what *adam* can access once he logged in to the system.

From XURA it is clear that 'adam' is the member of role 'RI02'. Besides, he is
from 'xx' domain having no delegation authority and is created or delegated by
john.

On the basis of information found from XURA, RBAC processor will scan
XRS which describes what kind of role it is. After scanning XPRA, it is found
that permissions P1, P2 and P3 are assigned to role RI02, i.e. 'john' can
perform 'insert', 'update' and 'delete' operation on storage which belongs to
domain 'xx'.

6.5 Deployment Plan

Web services [19, 20] can be used to simulate the proposed prototype. In order
to do that, Axis2 should be configured in Apache Tomcat Web Server.
Figure 6.10 shows the schematic diagram of the deployment plan. According to
Fig. 6.10, it is clear that the system requires developing two sides: Consumer
and Provider.

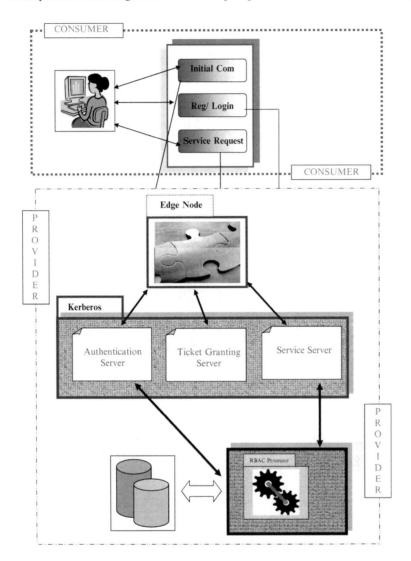

Fig. 6.10 Deploying design of IAM architecture in Axis2

Provider side will be deployed in Axis2 as different services. It must be noticed that though for the time being for simplicity all the services can be deployed in one Tomcat Web Server, but it has complete flexibility to deploy each services in separate web server to decentralize the load. So each server defined in Access Control Enforcement Unit of Fig. 6.2, Authentication Server (AS), Ticket Granting Server (TGS) and Service Server (SS), will be deployed as individual service. Apart from these servers, RBAC processor and Edge Node will also be deployed as two more services.

In consumer side, stub will be generated using wsdl2java tool from Web Service Definition Language (WSDL) of Edge Node service. Then a client program will be written in Java which will communicate with provider by accessing the generated stub and send/receive message in SOAP language. Implementation details have been described in [21].

6.6   Conclusion

A client from the beginning goes through secure communication and is later firmly authenticated by Kerberos whilst RBAC processor written in Java decides whether to give access to the user to a particular resource by reading RBAC policies written in XML.

All the access policies have been written in XML which kept the window open to expand, modify, create or delete. With the change of consumer's requirement, policies can be modified. For the time being, the chapter has only focused on storage resource of Infrastructure as a Service which can easily be expanded to any service levels.

The proposal is not hypothetical as it has been clearly shown how the whole plan can be deployed using Axis2 in Apache Tomcat [21]. Five services have been created, namely, Authentication Server Service, Ticket Granting Server Service, Service Server Service, RBAC Processor Service and Edge Node Service. Then a client has been written in Java which access the stubs generated from WSDL (Web Service Definition Language) of Edge Node Service using wsdl2java tool.

Many existing solutions use third party for identity management, whilst this prototype is independent of third party and uses its own Identity Management System (IMS). This avoidance of third party reduces extra protection of Personal Identity Information from *Man-in-the-middle attack* between CSP (Cloud Service Provider) and Trusted Third Party (TTP). Moreover, client even has no need to transfer any of its Private Personal Information in plain text, which ultimately makes it less prune to vulnerability during identity verification or management.

References

1. Kumaraswamy, S., Lakshminarayanan, L., Reiter, M., Stein, J., Wilson, Y.: Guidance for Identity & Access Management V2.1. Cloud Security Alliance (CSE), April 2010. Online: http://www.cloudsecurityalliance.org/guidance/csaguide-dom12-v2.10.pdf (2010). Last access 10 Oct 2010
2. Courtney M.: How mature cloud computing. Online: http://www.computing.co.uk/ctg/feature/1843193/how-mature-cloud-computing-market (2010). Last access 24 Dec 2010
3. Cloud Computing Market – Global Forecast (2010–2015): Online: http://www.marketsandmarkets.com/Market-Reports/cloud-computing-234.html (2010). Last access 1 Jan 2011

4. Cloud Computing Market – Global Forecast (2010–2015): Online: http://www.toadhillreviews. com/cloud-computing-market/ (2010). Last access 29 Dec 2010

5. Christiansen C., Kolodgy C., Hudson S., Pintal G.: Identity and access management for approaching clouds [white paper]. Online: https://community.jivesoftware.com/servlet/ JiveServlet/previewBody/29809-102-1-53773/cloud_secu rity_wp_236234.pdf (2010). Last access 22 Dec 2010

6. Li, D., Liu, C., Wei, Q., Liu, Z., Liu, B.: RBAC-based access control for SaaS systems. In: The proceedings of 2010 2nd International Conference on Information Engineering and Computer Science (ICIECS), Wuhan, pp. 1–4. doi:10.1109/ICIECS.2010.5 678213 (2010)

7. Albeshri., A., Caelli, W.: Mutual protection in cloud computing environment. In: The proceedings of 2010 12th IEEE International Conference on High Performance Computing and Communications, Melbourne, pp. 641–646. doi:10.1109/HPCC.2010.87 (2010)

8. Ranchal, R., Bhargava, B., Othmane, L., Lilien, L.: Protection of identity information in cloud computing without trusted third party. In: The proceedings of 2010 29th IEEE International Symposium on Reliable Distributed Systems, New Delhi, pp. 368–372 (2010)

9. Sharma, A.: Cloud computing and open source, May 2010. Online: http://ldn.linuxfoundation. org/article/cloud-computing-and-open-source (2010). Last access 11 Nov 2010

10. Ben-Or, M., Goldwasser, S., Wigderson, A.: Completeness theorems for on-cryptographic fault-tolerant distributed computation. In: Proceedings of the Twentieth Annual ACM Symposium on Theory of Computing, Chicago, IL, May 1988, pp 1–10 (1988)

11. Kumaraswamy, S., Lakshminarayanan, S., Reiter, M., Stein, J., Wilson, Y.: Domain 12: Guidance for Identity & Access Management V2.1. Cloud Security Alliance. Online: http:// www.cloudsecurityalliance.org/guidance/csaguide-dom12-v2.10.pdf (2010). Last access 2 Oct 2010

12. Harkins, D., Carrel, D.: The Internet Key Exchange (IKE), RFC 2409. IETF Network Working Group. Online: http://www.ietf.org/rfc/rfc2409.txt (1998). Last access 12 Jan 2011

13. Ricciardi, F., MIT Kerberos Consortium: Kerberos protocol tutorial. Online: http://www. kerberos.org/software/tutorial.html (2007). Last access 22 Dec 2010

14. SANS Institute InfoSec Reading Room: A review of the Diffie-Hellman algorithm and its use in secure internet protocols. Online: http://www.sans.org/reading_room/whitepapers/vpns/ review-diffie-hellman-algorithm-secure-internet-protocols_751 (2001). Last access 12 Jan 2011

15. Rescorla, E.: Diffie-Hellman key agreement method, RFC 2631. IETF Network Working Group. Online: http://www.ietf.org/rfc/rfc2631.txt (1999)

16. RSA Laboratories, RSA Laboratories': FAQ about today's cryptography, version 4.1. RSA Security Inc., 2000. Online: http://www.rsa.com/rsalabs/faq/index.html (2000). Last access 12 Dec 2010

17. Benjamin, L.: Diffie-Hellman method for key agreement. Online: http://apocalypse.org/pub/u/ seven/diffie.html (1997). Last access 22 Dec 2010

18. RSA Laboratories: PKCS #3: Diffie-Hellman key-agreement standard, version 1.4. Revised Nov 1, 1993. Online: http://www.rsalabs.com/pkcs/pkcs-3/index.html (1993). Last access 27 Jan 2011

19. Tutorial Point: Web Services behavioural characteristics. Online: http://www.tutorialspoint. com/webservices/web_services_characteristics.htm (2011). Last access 17 Jan 2011

20. Xuelei, W., Jia, C., Bilan, R.: Web Service architecture and application research. In: International Conference on E-Business and Information System Security, 2009 (EBISS '09), 23–24 May 2009, pp. 1–5. doi:10.1109/EBISS.2009.5138146 (2009)

21. Ahmed, K.E.U.: Developing a prototype of identity and access management. Research Project in ACET Center, University of Reading, Reading (2011). 28 Feb 2011

Chapter 7
A Cloud Architecture for Educational Enterprises: A Case Study in Robotics

Lucio A. Rocha, Leonardo R. Olivi, Fernando Paolieri, Guilherme Feliciano, Ricardo S. Souza, Diego Rodrigues, Fernando Pinho, Fábio Teixeira, Eliane G. Guimarães, and Eleri Cardozo

Abstract This work presents a Cloud Computing environment with support for educational robotics. The general purpose is to evaluate principles and methodologies to provide virtualized management architecture for educational enterprises in open source Cloud domains. These environments bring many advantages to its users as affordable cost of implementation and maintenance, large scale of resources integration, and others. We especially highlight its inherent low-level delays when performing remote experiments from outside enterprise's domain. In robotics, Internet overheads and delays have significant impact by reducing performance on experiments, and with a virtualized architecture in Cloud, this effect can be minimized. To achieve this, services and applications run on virtualized desktops in the Cloud with fast network connections. Users can log into their virtual machines hosted on local servers with common Internet. Once logged, users can benefit from fast local network to interact with the available resources. Cloud Computing is performed under these conditions to have its potentiality evaluated. Also, guidelines are described to reduce the effort to offer applications in these environments according to the proposed open source architecture. Many companies are focusing on this emergent paradigm seeking cost reductions, high availability of pre-configured computational infrastructures, billing proportional to demand, and others. In robotics, virtualization in Cloud is an alternate to keep collaborations between students and to promote safe and robust integration of geographically distant robotic resources. Implementations of remote experiments are discussed, showing how to make robotic Cloud domains possible with open source tools in these decentralized environments.

L.A. Rocha (✉) • L.R. Olivi • F. Paolieri • G. Feliciano • R.S. Souza • D. Rodrigues •
F. Pinho • F. Teixeira • E. Cardozo
School of Electrical and Computer Engineering, State University of Campinas – UNICAMP,
Campinas, Brazil
e-mail: outrosdiasvirao@yahoo.com.br

E.G. Guimarães
Information Technology Center Renato Archer, 13083-970 Campinas, SP, Brazil

Z. Mahmood and R. Hill (eds.), *Cloud Computing for Enterprise Architectures*, 135
Computer Communications and Networks, DOI 10.1007/978-1-4471-2236-4_7,
© Springer-Verlag London Limited 2011

7.1 Introduction

This work contemplates an educational robotic infrastructure to carry out applications in Cloud. The main contributions are (1) an explanation of how this infrastructure can be deployed in multiple domains using open source tools and (2) a systematic explanation of how this educational infrastructure can be used in robotic experiments. The educational theme is the interaction with robots by creating visual "building blocks" in a new workflow language.

In educational environments offer high-quality services is a challenge because depends of differents mechanisms of access. In order to achieve this goal, these companies need to offer a range of services and resources to their students, such as Internet access, internal institutional services, access to remote computing devices, and so forth. As a result, these factors increase the costs of deployment, management, security, and maintenance of such educational infrastructure. Emergent technologies such as Cloud Computing and virtualization can address these problems. For example, concerning reducing costs of hardware acquisition, a powerful server can be used to virtualize many users' desktops. Also, when these users are outside the local network, they can access their virtual environments by ordinary Internet connection and make use of the broadband of their institution. Using Cloud Computing techniques, these institutions go one step further, sharing resources and services safely among other collaborators in a federation. These considerations indicate that well-defined cloud architectures are good alternatives to simplify the maintenance and distribution of services in educational environments.

Virtualization is the basis of many Cloud approaches. However, this is a recent research area in robotic remote instrumentation. About this theme, three questions can be posed: (1) Why use virtualization in robotics? (2) How can it be done? (3) What are the consequences for network performance that justify its use? This relatively new approach is discussed in detail in this work.

For the last several years, the REAL project [1] has been developing infrastructure and applications to coordinate multiple robotic resources over the Internet. There have been recent advances [2] to integrate Cloud applications in post-graduation courses aided by experiments in Web Labs. Robotic resources are expensive, and prudence is necessary in robot manipulation. In the original approach, only one user can interact with these resources in time with previous scheduling in the Web Lab.

We extend this approach by using virtualization in Cloud with the purpose of reducing the complexity in remote manipulation. Students have their own Virtual Machine (VM) with the necessary applications, and manipulation occurs near the robot domain. As a consequence, network performance is increased, and results are more accurate.

Cloud nodes are instantiated as VMs, providing virtual organizations manageable by our REAL Cloud infrastructure. The notion that each VM is a node imposes the need of mapping to determine how to assign tasks to different nodes within the Cloud environment. This environment uses as its key strategy the automatic assignment of tasks generated by the mapping component, based in the features of Quality of Service (QoS). Considering the improvement of execution using non-Directed Acyclic Graph (non-DAG) Web workflows, based on repeatable sections of tasks within an iteration block, each application is represented as directed graph in which each vertex is a Grid application that interacts with virtual machines, and each edge represents the sequence of tasks between these applications.

Our approach extends the functionalities of Java Commodity Grid (CoG) Kit Karajan [3], using this workflow tool as Web workflow to dynamically schedule and map tasks according to several features of QoS in this Cloud domain. We intend to improve the execution of complex tasks respecting network features such as bandwidth, latency, jitter, and so on, as well as unavailability of virtual resources. Results are presented in REAL Cloud infrastructure with an example of an educational experiment: a Fuzzy workflow application. This article is organized as follows: Sect. 7.2 reports the background with related work; Sect. 7.3 describes the platform architecture; Sect. 7.4 explains the workflow management system architecture; Sect. 7.5 discusses the platform design and implementation; Sect. 7.6 brings the experiments and results; and Sect. 7.7 concludes the paper.

7.2   Overview of Virtualization

Virtualization is a technique for hiding the physical characteristics of computational resources [4, 5]. This means that a single physical resource, such as a server device storage or operating system (OS), is seen as multiple logical resources. In essence, this consists of the imitation of behavior of one resource by another. Virtualization can also be defined as a method for sharing multiple computational resources in isolated environments, known as virtual machines, by applying concepts of partitioning, timesharing, partial or full machine simulation, emulation, and QoS, among others.

Virtualization is recommended to consolidate multiple servers into one host; isolate different user applications in a single host; run/debug software and OS built for one architecture under another, while simplifying the installation of infrastructure software in different areas; and test applications in non-existing hardware.

Reductions in cost of hardware acquisition and information sharing led virtualization techniques to hibernate for a few years. Only in the mid-1990s, with the increase of computer processing power, did virtualization gain prominence with products like VMware [6], User Mode Linux (UML) [7], Xen [8], Kernel-based Virtual Machines (KVM) [9], and VirtualBox [10]. These products bring the concept of virtualization as an alternative to run multiple OSs without the need to increase the number of physical hosts. This reduces costs related to acquisition of hardware, physical infrastructure, energy consumption, cooling, support, and maintenance of multiple hosts.

The OS running the virtualization software is known as Host, and the virtualized OS, as Guest. Multiple Guests can be instantiated in the same Host, without interference among them. The kernel of Host provides the API to support multiple user spaces, known as Virtual Environments (VE), inside Guest. Each Guest has virtualization files, system libraries, users and groups, tree processes (with virtualized Process Identifiers (PIDs)), and virtualized network (with their own Internet Protocol (IP) addresses, routing tables, and other network attributes) [5].

With the advancement of hardware processing power, processor manufacturers such as AMD and Intel recently included virtualization support into their CPU hardware to improve performance of virtualized applications. The Intel CPU extension is called Intel VT (for Vanderpool Technology). AMD, in turn, developed the extension AMD-V (or Pacifica), also known as AMD Secure Virtual Machine (SVM). Theoretically, virtualization types can be grouped as follows [4]:

- Full Virtualization: A software layer provides a generic hardware abstraction without the need to modify the OS running on VM. Access control to system physical resources is managed by a hypervisor as soon as the translation of non-privileged instructions to access physical devices such as disk, memory, peripherals, and others is performed by the virtualized OS. VirtualBox is an example.
- Para-virtualization: The Guest OS is modified to interact directly with hypervisor drivers and gain direct access to hardware routines. Recent advances in CPU hardware have shown para-virtualization to be as efficient as full virtualization. Para-virtualization is an alternative to gain access to resources available in hardware, instead of using generic abstraction instructions provided by full virtualization. In para-virtualized systems, only the OS in domain 0 (zero) has access to devices in a privileged way. VMs in levels above zero field have access to devices through the VM from this domain 0. Xen and UML are examples.
- Hardware Virtualization: AMD-V and Intel VT processors support hardware virtualization for processors of the x86 architecture. Virtualization in hardware reduces the need to use a para-virtualized OS to provide direct access to hardware resources. Hardware virtualization is offered with a virtualized software environment modified to interact directly with the hardware, usually the processor. KVM is an example of extension of the Linux kernel to provide hardware virtualization.
- Virtualization in OS level: Implementation of multiple isolated execution environments within a single OS kernel. This approach allows a performance close to native and offers features of dynamic resources management; however, it is not possible to execute different kernels at the same time. LXC [11], OpenVZ [12], and Linux VServer [13] are examples.

7.3 The REAL Cloud Platform

The REAL Cloud software platform is an environment for educational robotics, as illustrated in Figs. 7.1, 7.2 and 7.3. This infrastructure is oriented to robotics in Cloud. Several open source approaches to Cloud applications are found in the

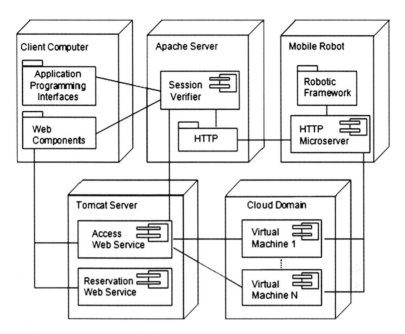

Fig. 7.1 Components of the REAL Cloud platform

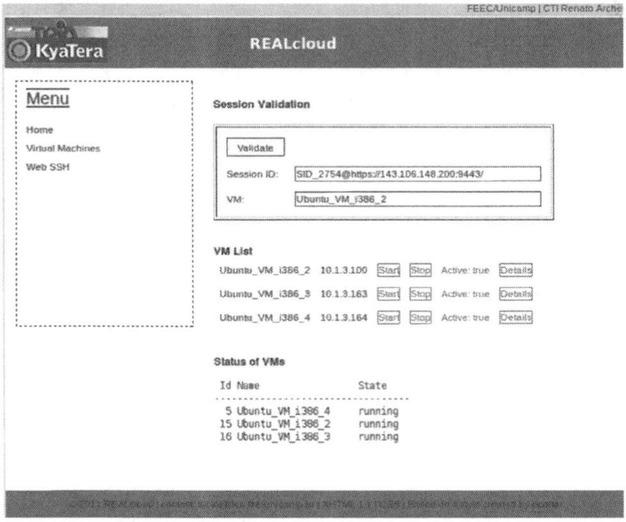

Fig. 7.2 REAL Cloud platform management interface

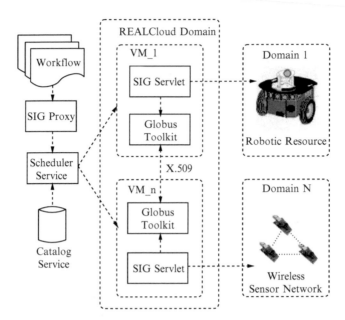

Fig. 7.3 Robotic model for Cloud Computing

literature, such as Xen XCP [8], Open Nebula [14], Nimbus [15], Eucalyptus [16], TPlatform [17], Apache VCL [18], and Enomaly ECP [19]. The integration of Cloud and robotics is relatively recent.

Considered in [20] to be a new proposal to the scientific community, Cloud Robotics is cloud computing applied to robots. This area has the potential of expanding queries in different data sources, i.e., distributed querying. Robots would be thin clients that perceive the environment and perform queries for data in clouds when necessary. This approach reduces the need to put information into robots and offers the possibility of consulting several remote data sources.

Robotics researchers have been working on this idea in projects such as Remote Brain [21] at Tokyo University, with teleoperated robots with AI systems. The robot system has separate brain and body, opening the possibility of using remote large-scale parallel computers. These robots could perform off-load computation-intensive tasks (such as image processing and voice recognition) remotely and download these new skills quickly. As a consequence, robots could decrease in size and keep only the minimum hardware required to consult the cloud and process real-time data locally, reducing power consumption.

Among other recent projects, Gostai [22] has built a cloud robotics infrastructure known as GostaiNet for the remote performance of operations such as video recording, and face and speech recognition. A technology known as Collaborative Cloud Robotics (CCR) [23] employs a software and hardware platform for human operators to control human-size robots doing remote tasks. In [24], a cloud computing infrastructure is used to perform computationally intensive algorithms simultaneously, such as mapping and localization (SLAM) using generated 3D models acquired from the environment. Another project, developed by Lamiraux and partners [25], is based on the creation of a set of object databases to reduce the complexity of robot task manipulation. In this context, robots would receive a set of minimal instructions to act in their environment, such as a workflow of tasks.

A project involving high schools [26] uses robotics and service-oriented robotics computing in a model of Robot as a Service (RaaS). It uses common service standards, development platforms, and execution infrastructure with open source code, especially for graphic composition.

Our original platform was extended to support virtualized applications running in Cloud, specifically in VMs accessed through the platform. Our experience suggests that virtualization is a good alternative to improve communication, optimizing performance of the remote instrumentation. In this scenario, access occurs in a virtualized environment, near the robotic resources (e.g., mobile robots, panoramic camera, Wireless Sensor Network, and others). On the client side, a Web graphical terminal with Secure Socket Layer (SSL) is sufficient for the interaction; our platform supplies other needs such as software updating, disk quota, RAM memory, CPU architecture, and Application Program Interfaces (APIs). This means that more accurate and precise experiments can be done by many users concurrently.

Performance of virtualized applications is limited by the hardware containing the VMs, network communication, and the mechanisms used by the emulation software managing these applications. In this approach, the hypervisor, known as Virtual Machine Monitor (VMM) or Virtual Machine System, is a software layer between the hardware and the virtual machine's OS. Access to resources in hardware is protected by this software layer that supports one or more VMs. The hypervisor must be instantiated whenever the VM is booted.

The virtualized OS is able to run in these VMs using the non-privileged instructions translated by the hypervisor. This software layer provides the features to share the computational resources as CPU cycles, RAM memory, storage devices, and I/O with multiple virtualized OSs.

Therefore, the hypervisor runs in supervisor mode and controls the access to resources shared by multiple VMs. Resource scheduling is similar to the usual scheduling process, with the allocation of processor cycles for each VM. As a VM runs in user mode, if an instruction is dispatched inside the VM, the OS in the Host machine would trigger an interrupt for subsequent treatment by an interruption handling routine. However, the hypervisor handles this interruption by emulating the execution of privileged instructions.

The main advantages of this approach are reducing the need for periodic software updating on the client side, reducing the latency of remote instrumentation, reducing the overhead of networking processing between client and server side, and improving access control to the robotic platform by multiple concurrent users. Figure 7.1 shows the REAL Cloud platform components, the software packages required, and the placement on processing nodes in Unified Modeling Language notation.

Robotic frameworks such as Player [27] and ARIA [28] employ distinct network protocols, restricting the integration of distributed applications; the client side must have an interface compatible with the robotic platform. In a robotic platform with virtualization, many APIs can be offered as shared services; updates to these services are immediately reflected to the users in a transparent way. Our approach uses virtualization to offer robotic services regardless of where they are hosted or how they are delivered. This model assumes that slices of computational resources must be offered only during the remote interaction.

Another consideration to employ virtualization is related with the way networks operate nowadays. Restrictions in packet forwarding using Hypertext Transfer Protocol (HTTP) are found in proxies, Network Address Translation (NAT), and firewalls along the network nodes. Besides, the amount of public IP address is generally reduced to a few hosts in administrative domains. In a virtualized environment, each user has a VM with services to access the platform, and each VM has a private IP address. The host machine that contains the VMs must perform Port Forwarding and NAT operations to secure connectivity with the Internet to each VM. Despite these assumptions, a more sophisticated access control by identifying the VM private IP source is possible by using Linux Iptables rules acting in Layer 3 of the TCP/IP model. These provisions make access more robust against external attacks over the Internet.

We highlight Cloud computing as a model of distributed computing that derives characteristics from Grid computing for on-demand provisioning of information [29]. In this arrangement, a domain offers applications in the Cloud regardless of where the services are hosted or how they are delivered. Slices of computational power within network nodes are offered, reducing the cost of supplying an internal infrastructure to provide the services. Cloud computing contrasts with traditional approaches. The resources in Cloud are rented only for the period of use, reducing energy consumption when resources are no longer necessary. Virtualization has provided the key technologies to improve Cloud computing. Common characteristics of Cloud environments are scalability, pay-per-use model, and virtualization. Furthermore, many solutions offer environments where developers are able to choose their virtualized resources such as programming languages, operating system, and other personalized services [19]. Since 2007, with the popularization of Cloud computing, many enterprises became Cloud computing providers. The following classification is suggested, and a solution can be assigned to more than one model:

(a) Infrastructure as a Service (IaaS): The service provider offers the infrastructure for the provision of services. This infrastructure is used for storage, processing, and other specific hardware and software needs. Xen Cloud Platform [8], Eucalyptus Ubuntu Enterprise Cloud (UEC) [16], Amazon with Elastic Compute Cloud (EC2) [49], and IBM Blue Cloud [30] offer IaaS to their users, among other services.

(b) Platform as a Service (PaaS): Keeps a framework for the provision of services. The framework offers a model for development, communication, and storage in the Cloud. This concept is an example of utility computing. Microsoft with Windows Azure Platform [31], Force.com [32], and Yahoo Pipes [33] are examples.

(c) Software as a Service (SaaS): Shared resources and applications are stored and provided by service providers. Google App Engine [34], Microsoft BPOS [35], Crownpeak [36], Eloqua [37], and Facebook [38] are examples.

7.4 REAL Cloud Implementation

The REAL Cloud Platform is implemented as a PaaS using open source tools and virtualization techniques to provide pre-configured virtual environments to many concurrent students. This infrastructure is able to manage many users' VMs in a transparent model by means of the browser: operations to start, finish, and query the VM status, as well as mechanisms to allow remote access to VMs are offered. As a consequence, only a visual SSL application with remote display [39, 40] is needed to interact with the VMs in the platform; each VM has a complete OS Linux to carry out the remote instrumentation.

Robotic experiments are done in this infrastructure offering two HTTP multi-threaded microservers running on Linux. These microservers have interfaces to the robotic frameworks Player and ARIA. Operations are performed through HTTP GET messages (e.g., sensor readings, laser scanning, and image capture). Operations that perform movements are done with HTTP POST messages.

A Extensible Markup Language (XML) document is returned for each operation, containing the requested data, an exception, or a notification that the operation was completed. This platform offers APIs in C++, Java, Python, and Matlab. Requests can be placed with HTTP/HTTPS using a front-end user interface that supports open standards such as Java Server Pages (JSP), Asynchronous JavaScript and XML (AJAX), and relational databases such as MySQL.

The platform is protected by the Apache Server that intercepts HTTP requests and uses proxy functions to communicate with HTTP intra-domain microservers. The component named Session Verifier is responsible for checking the session status. Iptables rules in Linux are used in the Host server to solve the problem of IP availability with NAT and Port Forwarding rules: the student has access to his or her VM in this platform with a public IP and a remote port. Only one public IP is used for this domain, and each remote port is mapped (Port Forwarding) to the respective VM. NAT rules are used to provide Internet communication from students' VMs, redirecting IP packets to the Host server interface.

A set of Web Services is kept in the Apache Tomcat application server. The Access Web Service component performs authorization and authentication operations to allow access to VMs. Usage reservation is controlled by the Reservation Web Service; this component offers an interface to schedule the usage of Cloud resources and other robotic resources. The session ends when the reservation time expires or when the user concludes the interaction.

VMs are an alternative to reduce the complexity of the pre-configurations needed to interact with robotic frameworks in different domains. This is a dynamic environment, and resources can be added by aggregating new students' VMs to the platform.

Figure 7.2 illustrates the resource management interface in browser view. Each student has an account in the system allowing usage of one or more virtualized resources. In this example, each horizontal line in the Resource List area shows the VM alias, a private IP, and options of Start, Shutdown, and status query. Interactions are done by submitting workflows in XML format. For this, the SIGFlow system, based on the Java CoG Kit Karajan, was developed. SIGFlow is a workflow engine and a language. The workflows are received by the SIG Proxy component that performs validation and upload of the XML files (Fig. 7.3).

Complex SIGFlow applications can be built modularly from less complex components. As these applications can be distributed and executed in many VMs in the Cloud, use of a scheduler is imperative. This function is performed in the environment by the SIG Scheduler. This component is a service that maps workflow tasks on VMs. The SIG Scheduler consults the Catalog service of registered domains to check the availability of VMs. Services are mapped by consulting the QoS parameters of each task. This mapping procedure performs a HTTP request to VMs listed in the Catalog service, querying the service status. The scheduling of tasks must guarantee QoS by allocating resources according to user demand and availability. The SIG Scheduler is able to consult the availability of resources in VMs located in other Cloud domains.

7.4.1 Workflow Management System Architecture

Experiments in workflows have the advantage of reducing the complexity of composition and interaction in the Cloud domain. Since many applications can be distributed in this environment, use of a management system is imperative.

The architecture of this Workflow Management System is shown in Fig. 7.4. It was conceived in a layered design pattern, in which services are grouped in layers, with the lower management layers providing services to higher management layers. This infrastructure was developed to fulfill the scheduling requirements of distributed services for the several VMs within this specific Cloud domain. Service scheduling is done by provisioning common interfaces in this Workflow Management System and in the VMs.

Services in VMs are Web Services in a Representational State Transfer (REST) approach, deployed in a Web Server Container. Web Service properties (e.g., required bandwidth, latency threshold, jitter threshold, CPU usage, CPU processing speed, free memory, storage amount, service cost, service availability, service authorization, service logs, and so on) can be queried through the Manager Service. This model allows interaction with the services by using Internet protocols.

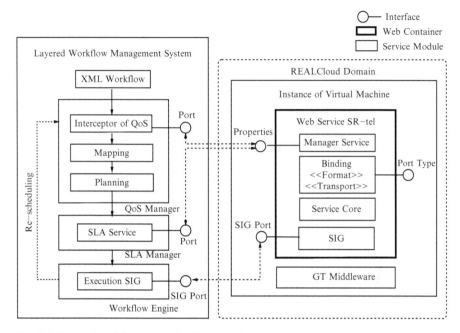

Fig. 7.4 Layered workflow system for Cloud services

7.4.2 Workflow Specifications

The infrastructure maintains QoS dependencies to Cloud services by submitting tasks in XML documents along with the previously presented workflow language. QoS constraints are related to non-functional requirements and do not change the relationship between nodes in the workflow. Each task incorporates optional QoS arguments that are mapped in classes of constraints. Each task is defined in a XML namespace that allows other customized tasks. Global QoS constraints are defined as tasks in the namespace. Global variables can be used by other local or global tasks as arguments. Local QoS constraints overwrite the global values.

Open Virtualization Format (OVF) [41] is a common packaging format to package and distribute virtual appliances, enabling cross-platform portability. Specifications in OVF format allow the distribution of virtual machines over many customers' virtualization platforms. In the REAL Cloud platform, each virtual machine offers an extended OVF that dynamically shows the many parameters of the current state of the virtual resource. This document is queried in the scheduling processing.

The scheduling process is done by the divide-and-conquer technique to group services that perform specialized functions, as in the methodology described below:

Step 1: Services of dynamic discovery recover available VMs registered in a Cloud domain catalog for tasks with QoS requirements. Recovery is done by querying the properties from the VM Manager Service.

Step 2: Services of Mapping perform the matching of VMs and QoS requirements.

Step 3: Services of Planning evaluate these correspondences in a rank matrix in which higher values have a better QoS matching.

Step 4: Services of Level Agreement (SLA) specify the minimum and maximum thresholds to query the properties of the VM Manager Service. Policies are applied when the contract is violated.

Step 5: Services of Execution in Workflow Engine perform the tasks with run-time monitoring. Re-scheduling is done when the SLA values are under provisioned.

7.4.3 SIG Scheduler Layer

Different tasks can be allocated to different services instantiated in VMs. The dynamic discovery process is efficiently performed by the Interceptor of the QoS layer that keeps querying services in the platform catalog. This layer selects the available virtual hosts, keeping the properties of the previous service. In a query, the Manager Service Layer returns the set of values of these properties in a XML document. The QoS parameters are evaluated with the matches in this document, and the same task can be offered in many VMs with different QoS properties.

The Mapping Layer sets the results of the Interceptor QoS related to the correspondence between virtual hosts and workflow services. The Planning Layer queries these correspondences in a rank where higher values have a better QoS matching.

7.4.4 SLA Manager Layer

Online requirements are allowed using forms aggregated as additional resources in tasks. The SLA Manager Layer recovers these additional values and queries the associated services, specifying the minimum and maximum thresholds for the task and the policies applied when the contract is violated.

7.4.5 Workflow Engine Layer

Cloud resources are provided in dynamic domains, with virtual resources that can be aggregated, removed, or updated in running time. A process of re-scheduling is initiated when the SLA contract is not respected, or in under provisioned QoS scenarios. This Layer holds monitoring services that periodically inform the higher layers when necessary.

Grid schedulers must deal with objective functions of the problem, concerning requirements that must be satisfied. Let $R = \{r_1, r_2, ..., r_n\}$ be the set of resources, $G = \{g_1, g_2, ... g_n\}$ the set of Grid application tasks, and $Q = \{q_1, q_2, ..., q_n\}$ the QoS requirements. The scheduling involves the dynamic mapping of elements $R \times G$ according to Q. A Grid application in G reserves at least one resource in R that can have one or more requirements in Q. A rank matrix is set to each match of r_i to g_j according to q_k, where $i, j \geq 1$ and $k \geq 0$, assigning a rank value to the resource. Resources with a higher sum of values have a better matching and are served in a round-robin–based scheduling process. When the task is executed in the workflow process, a new VM is allocated according to the current values queried in the dynamic OVF description.

Workflow tasks are composed of a set A of directed arcs (G_i, G_j), where child task G_j is only processed when parent tasks G_i are completed or, exceptionally, G_i are ignored by the user. The complete workflow specification is described as a tuple T (R, G, Q, A). The goal is to minimize workflow computation time according to the following rules (a simplified adaptation of [42]):

1. For each task, exactly one of the $G \times R \mid Q$ variables has to be equal to 1, implying a matching according to QoS requirements.
2. If there is a predecessor task G_i to G_j, then G_j cannot proceed before the execution of G_i is finished.
3. If there are constraints Q_i and Q_j for the same task G_k, then Q_j cannot be evaluated until Q_i be analyzed in G_k.
4. At any step in workflow execution, there is at least one running task in a given VM. This rule implies that parallelism can occur between VMs and inside VMs.

7.5   Platform Design and Implementation

This Cloud architecture for networked robotics was proposed in order to support resources between distinct domains with reliability and security, as shown in Fig. 7.5.

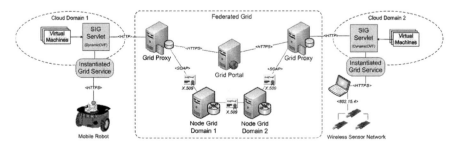

Fig. 7.5 Networked architecture to robotic Cloud Computing. This infrastructure supports interaction among heterogeneous resources in different domains. Authenticated users can use resources over a secure network with digital certificates assigned by Certificate Authority

The infrastructure allows visualization of VMs on Grid Portal node. To aggregate resources with portability, each virtual machine has the SIG Servlet component. This middleware simplifies the aggregation of robotic resources by implementing an abstraction to the Globus Toolkit (GT) middleware [43]. The Grid Proxy ensures that only digitally certified users interact with the resources intra-domain. To achieve this, each Grid Proxy and the Grid Portal uses the OpenAM platform [44] in order to authenticate and authorize users. In this identity management environment, each Grid Proxy acts as a service provider (SP).

A service provider, as the name implies, is an entity that offers clients a service of interest. The Grid Portal acts as the Identity Provider (IdP), serving Grid Proxies with local user identities. The Grid Proxies, the Grid Portal, and the Node Grid Domains 1 and 2 participate in the Federated Grid Circle of Trust (FG-CoT). The architecture shows only participating entities within the same domain environment, but due to the federation and the use of OpenAM platform, a multi-domain environment can be seamlessly built. New Grid nodes can be safely added with digital certificates signed by the same CA. Figure 7.5 shows this features at the Grid domain.

The implementation uses KVM with Ubuntu Linux. A N-tier approach with Java 2 Enterprise Edition is kept in the Grid Proxy. The Grid Proxies and the Grid Portal communicate security assertions based on Security Assertion Markup Language (SAML) version 2 [45] in an HTTPS tunnel.

The security assertion (AuthnRequest) is forwarded by a Grid Proxy (SP) after a policy agent intercepts a request to protect a resource and causes a redirection to the Grid Portal (IdP) for authentication. After user authentication, the Grid Portal sends an AuthnResponse to the Grid Proxy.

The Grid Proxy will deny or grant access to the service based on the current policy setting (user credentials). SIG Servlet has interfaces to Grid Proxy using HTTP, and an interface file to keep the abstraction about features being shared over the network by the resources. This testbed is composed of Dell Quad Core Grid nodes with gigabit Network Interface Cards (NICs), Pioneer P3-DX mobile robots, and Intel Imote2 sensors with TinyOS [45, 50].

This infrastructure is able to execute tasks by submitting XML documents as workflows at the Grid Portal node. VMs in the Cloud are allocated only by the necessary period of interaction, reducing energy consumption, and providing a more adequate management.

This infrastructure supports interaction among heterogeneous resources in different domains. Authenticated users can use resources over a secure network with digital certificates assigned by Certificate Authority. This is important to ensure communication over the Internet. Furthermore, using signed digital certificates ensures that the hosts in different domains are joined by Circles of Trust (CoT) in Virtual Organizations, as shown in Fig. 7.5.

7.6 Experiments and Results

This educational platform in Cloud was evaluated through robotic applications. We conducted a complete performance evaluation in [1] and [2]. We focused on Cloud experiments structuring applications developed by the Department of Computation and Automation. Tasks in the order of magnitude of million instructions to extract image borders from a robotic camera require adequate provision of QoS. To conduct the experiments in the REAL Cloud platform, the following features were taken into account:

- Performance evaluation: Data submitted are forwarded with reduced latency for accurate interaction with the distributed resources.
- Quality of submission: The infrastructure ensures data integrity and security among domains.
- Quality of tasks: Submitting workflows in XML format reduces the interaction complexity and offers traceability mechanisms.
- Evaluation with other approaches: This evaluation must offer a competitive network performance compared to well-known approaches that integrate workflow engines in Grid domains.

The execution engine uses an event model where elements in the workflow react to events. Each event is a status change notification process or an execution control mechanism. SIGFlow is initiated remotely in the user's browser as a Java Networking Launching Protocol (JNLP) process. Performance in this domain was evaluated with the following operations: (1) File transfer (Op1): fifty file transfer tests of 54 MB (Megabytes) using GSIFTP between VMs; (2) Sensor readings (Op2): data acquisition from 16 robot sonars between cloud domains; and (3) Real-time robot navigation (Op3): tasks of image detection from robotic camera, and robot navigation task with a Fuzzy controller. Measurements were conducted in the scenarios above, each one showing its overheads. Mean (ME), confidence interval (CI) of 95%, and standard deviation (SD) were calculated and are shown in seconds.

1. *Network Evaluation in Intra-domain Scenario*: In this scenario, the network overhead is evaluated by submitting a XML document at the Grid Portal with data for processing. Tasks are distributed between two VMs (cloud1 and cloud2) in the same host. Overhead is estimated by comparing the performances of GT, Karajan, and SIGFlow. The performance of GT, a common middleware, in transferring 54 MB intra-domain is better than that of SIGFlow and Karajan. SIGFlow had a better performance than Karajan in every metric in this evaluation. Figure 7.6 brings this analysis intra-domain and inter-domain. Examining these results, we conclude that students can share data and applications with a good performance. For our purposes, these performance results are sufficient to allow the remote conduction of experiments using open source tools with a remote graphical display.

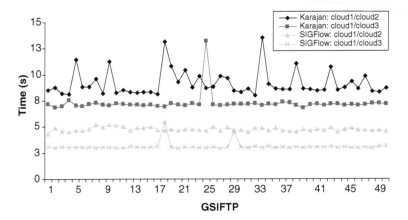

Fig. 7.6 Network performance evaluation for operation of GSIFTP intra-domain (cloud1/cloud2) and inter-domain (cloud1/cloud3) with Karajan and SIGFlow. The infrastructure supports transfer of large files between REAL Cloud domains

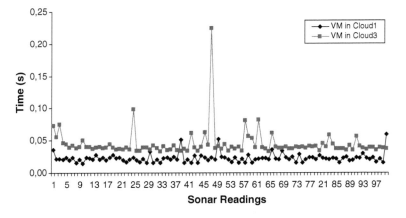

Fig. 7.7 Network performance evaluation for data acquisition from 16 robot sonars intra-domain (cloud1) and inter-domain (cloud3). Real-time experiments with telemetry are supported by the platform

2. *Network Evaluation in Inter-domain Scenario*: In this scenario, the overhead between two VMs (cloud1 and cloud3) in two REAL Cloud domains, with one hop of distance in the network, is evaluated. The gigabit network offers high performance, low latency, and reduced package loss. The GSIFTP between hosts in different Cloud domains has a better performance because of the memory and CPU overhead to keep and distribute tasks in the same host. In Fig. 7.7, the network performance evaluation of Op2 is done in different Cloud domains.

Tests were carried out with MobileSim [28], a mobile robot simulator. These tests were performed in the same host of cloud1, resulting in a better performance for it. Again, a better performance is obtained when less memory and

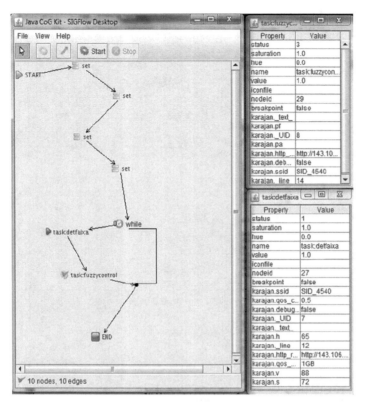

Fig. 7.8 Real-time robotic navigation in Cloud domain. The workflow in SIGFlow application is open in the users' browser. This example shows the main flow of line following tasks in VMs. Scheduling is performed in runtime to discover the available resource according to the SLA and QoS requirements described in XML submission

CPU usage is required to process tasks in the same host. These tests are important to conclude that applications in REAL Cloud can be conducted with reduced overhead between robotic resources and virtual machines; this is a consequence of both being in the same domain.

3. *Educational Robot Navigation in Cloud Domain*: This experiment evaluates the whole infrastructure of the REAL Cloud platform (Fig. 7.1). A description about the robot navigation includes two tasks: line detection (*DetFaixa*) and Fuzzy management (*fuzzyControl*). Figures 7.8 and 7.9 show the same experiment. Both tasks are distributed in the Cloud environment. Figure 7.10 shows the performance of the original task in comparison with the distributed execution. Results suggest that the platform is able to perform a set of robotic distributed experiments.

Fuzzy logic has been used with success for many years to design controllers for every kind of system. A clear advantage of Fuzzy logic over conventional control theory is that it can model any system, linear or nonlinear, without failing short

Fig. 7.9 Fuzzy line controller according to the described workflow. On the left side, the original image from the robot camera, and on the right, the same image converted to black and white (binary values) to reduce overhead in robot interpretation. The converted image will be sent to the next virtual machine according to QoS requirements

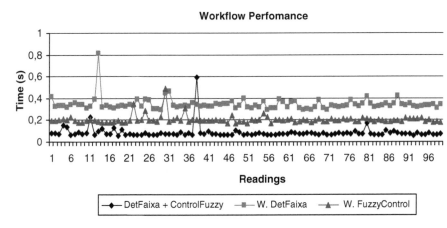

Fig. 7.10 Workflow performance of robot navigation using REAL Cloud infrastructure. The original algorithm was split in two tasks and distributed to VMs. The overhead using this infrastructure is low enough to allow the use of robotic applications in this Cloud domain

if there are disturbances, noise, or unmodeled nonlinearities. Another advantage is that Fuzzy controllers can integrate many control strategies that cannot be implemented in one single control law [46].

The experiment performed in this work uses computer vision. A camera centralized with the P3-DX robot sends images of the line that the robot must follow. Computer vision has many peculiarities related to the extraction of features from the scene, and these data represent the system to be controlled. Therefore, once the features have been extracted, they need control processing to provide inputs for the robot in order to complete the two tasks above. Data provided by computer vision can be highly nonlinear, and a classic control approach may not be functional.

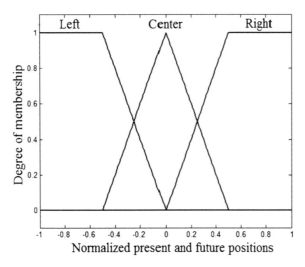

Fig. 7.11 Fuzzy present and future normalized pixels positions

Therefore, a Fuzzy controller was designed to process data acquired from the computer vision and guide the robot along the task, which is to follow a line with camera information only. The controller receives the position of the line in the image and returns velocities to the differential motors, keeping the line centralized on the image. For this application, the controller employs Mandani's Fuzzy inference method with MAX-MIN operators and centroid defuzzification [47].

The controller requests to the computer vision two pixel positions from the line on the scene, a lower and a higher one, relative to the horizontal axis of the picture. The lower pixel is relative to the robot's current position. The higher pixel is related to the situation along the line or to the robot's future position. With these two pixels, it is possible to say whether the robot is centralized with regard to the line and whether the line will bend or remain straight. Both present and future pixel positions were equally normalized and fuzzified, as shown in Fig. 7.11.

As shown in Fig. 7.11, the pixel position can be located to the left, center, or right, relative to the center of the image. The camera provided 640×480-pixel images. Thus, pixel positions are relative to the interval [0, 640] or normalized to [0,1]. Both the left and right motors of the robot need to be modeled as Fuzzy sets in order to be controlled. In this specific case, the robot does not need to move with negative velocities; therefore, only positive velocities were considered. Since the motors are identical, their normalized Fuzzy models, shown at Fig. 7.12, are also identical.

As shown in Fig. 7.12, the Fuzzy set for velocities assumed by the motors can be low, medium, or high, and they all have forward velocities. Motion control can turn the robot by applying different motor velocities at the same moment or keep the robot going straight by applying equal velocities. With the Fuzzy modeled system, nine rules were created to drive the robot along the line, keeping it in the picture center. Table 7.1 shows the rules with the AND operator between the left and right

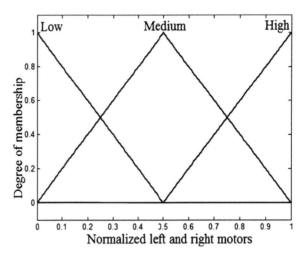

Fig. 7.12 Fuzzy left and right normalized robot motors velocities

Table 7.1 Interaction rules between pixels and motor Fuzzy sets

		Future position		
		Left	Center	Right
Actual position	Left	LM: M	LM: M	LM: H
		RM: L	RM: L	RM: L
	Center	LM: M	LM: H	LM: M
		RM: M	RM: H	RM: M
	Right	LM: L	LM: L	LM: L
		RM: H	RM: M	RM: M

motors. Abbreviations are LM and RM for left and right motor, and L, M, H for low, medium, and high motor Fuzzy set velocities.

The interaction among these rules predicts curves and straight lines, providing motor responses to negotiate the difficulties imposed by the line set. The rules create a control surface for the motors, shown in Fig. 7.13.

7.7 Conclusions

This paper shows guidelines to develop open source Cloud domains with support to educational robotic applications. The main contributions are systematic explanation about the educational Cloud infrastructure in robotic experiments, design of a new workflow language to support visual building blocks in Java Web Start, reduction of the complexity of remote instrumentation with robotic resources, and description of the implemented scheduling of virtual machines according to QoS features.

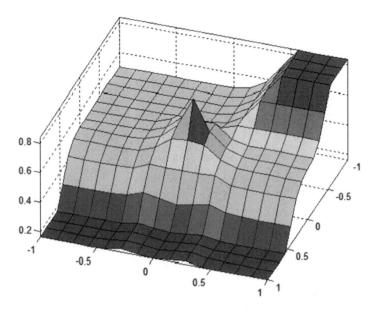

Fig. 7.13 Dynamic Fuzzy surface created by the rules in the environment

Cloud architectures simplify the distributed working in educational environments reducing the effort to keep virtual desktops to many concurrent users. These architectures are conceived with composition rules to guide the deployment of new services, avoiding a non-coherent combination of components and communication patterns. Building these architectures in a layered model is interesting because changes in one layer have lesser impact in the services of others. Also, Cloud architectures are neutral in terms of platform technology and implementation, and these features are important to promote interoperability among different Cloud domains.

An important fact underlying this research is that virtualization in robotics helps promote collaboration among students. This study shows the general procedures for the safe and reliable integration of geographically distant robotic resources. Pre-configured applications reduce the effort to interact with robotic resources in different domains.

The guidelines in this work show how Cloud domains can be implemented with open source tools. The management of VMs in REAL Cloud platform shows that it is necessary to avoid private network address conflicts by using the mechanisms of NAT and Port Forwarding.

We conducted a more complete performance evaluation in [1] and [2]. In the present work, we focus on evaluating how these results can be applied to robotic experiments in a Cloud model. This is important in experiments with QoS requirements, such as robotic visual line following experiments.

Cloud computing is a recent approach to provide on demand distributed services. In this environment, resource management is necessary to reduce energy consumption and offer QoS to users. Information sharing is supported by virtual pre-configured resources that can be forwarded inside the infrastructure, reducing the effort to keep the environment stable.

Additional research has been conducted to expand alternatives of collaboration, including federation over distinct administrative domains. OpenAM was shown to be suitable to drive this expansion. In comparison to Shibboleth [48], the OpenAM platform proved an easier and better documented solution. A class of experiments will bring up the interface standardization of resources from Web Lab in REAL Cloud platform, aided by a more detailed process of scheduling based on rules and heuristics.

Acknowledgment This research was supported by Coordination for the Improvement of Higher Level Personnel (CAPES) and Pró-Engenharias Project (918/2008).

References

1. Cardozo, E., Guimarães, E., Agostinho, L., Souza, R., Paolieri, F., Pinho, F.: A platform for Networked Robotics. In: IEEE/RSJ International Conference on Intelligent Robots and Systems, Taipei (2010)
2. Agostinho, L., Souza, R., Paolieri, F., Guimarães, E., Cardozo, E.: Uma Infraestrutura para Experimentos Robóticos Bio-Inspirados em Grades Colaborativas. In: XXIII Brazilian Symposium on Computer Networks and Distributed Systems, Gramado (2010)
3. Laszewski, G.v., Hategan, M., Kodeboyina, D.: Java CoG Kit. http://wiki.cogkit.org/wiki/JavaCoGKit (2010). Accessed Apr 2010
4. Carissimi, A.: Virtualização: da teoria a soluções. Mini-course. In: XXVI Brazilian Symposium on Computer Networks and Distributed Systems, Rio de Janeiro (2008)
5. Menascé, D.A.: Virtualization: concepts, applications, and performance modeling. In: International Computer Measurement Group Conference. Orlando, Florida, USA (2005)
6. VMware.: Virtualization software for desktops, servers & virtual machines for public and private Cloud solutions. Copyright VMware Inc. http://www.vmware.com. Accessed May 2010
7. The User –mode Linux Kernel.: http://user-mode-linux.sourceforge.net. Accessed May 2010
8. Xen Cloud Platform.: Advanced virtualization infrastructure for the Clouds. http://www.xen.org/products/cloudxen.html. Accessed May 2010
9. The Kernel Virtual Machine – Community Ubuntu Documentation: http://help.ubuntu.com/community/KVM. Accessed May 2010
10. VirtualBox: Oracle. http://www.virtualbox.org. Accessed June 2010
11. LXC – Linux Containers: Available at: http://lxc.sourceforge.net. Accessed June 2010
12. OpenVZ Wiki: Available at: http://www.wiki.openvz.org. Accessed June 2010
13. Linux VServer: Available at: http://www.linux-vserver.org. Accessed July 2010
14. OpenNebula: The Open Source Toolkit for Cloud Computing. http://opennebula.org. Accessed Aug 2010
15. Nimbus: Available at: www.nimbusproject.org. Accessed Aug 2010
16. Ubuntu Enterprise Cloud: Available at: http://www.ubuntu.com/cloud/private. Accessed Aug 2010
17. Peng, B., Cui, B., Li, X.: Implementation issues of a Cloud Computing Platform. IEEE Data Eng Bull **32**(1), 59–66 (2009)
18. VCL: Virtual Computing Lab. Available at: https://cwiki.apache.org/VCL. Accessed June 2010
19. Endo, T.P., Gonçalves, G.E., Kelner, J., Sadok, D.: A survey on open-source cloud computing solutions. In: XXVIII Brazilian Symposium on Computer Networks and Distributed Systems. Gramado, RS, Brazil (2010)

20. Guizzo, E.: Cloud Robotics: connected to the Cloud, Robots get smarter. http://spectrum.ieee. org/automaton/robotics/robotics-software/cloud-robotics (2011)
21. Inaba, M.: Remote-brained robots. In: Pollack, M.E. (ed.) Proceedings of the Fifteenth International Joint Conference on Artificial Intelligence – Volume 2 (IJCAI'97), vol. 2, pp. 1593–1606. Morgan Kaufmann Publishers Inc, San Francisco (1997)
22. Gostai – Robotics for everyone. http://www.gostai.com. Accessed Jan 2011
23. ReadyBot: Available at: www.readybot.com. Accessed Jan 2011
24. ASORO Laboratory: Available at: http://www.asoro.a-star.edu.sg. Accessed Jan 2011
25. Lamiraux, F.: Laboratoire d'Analyse et d'Architecture des Systèmes – LAAS. http://homepages. laas.fr/florent/. Accessed Jan 2011
26. Chen, Y., Du, Z., Garcia-Acosta, M.: Robot as a service in Cloud Com-puting. In: Proceedings of the Fifth IEEE International Symposium on Service Oriented System Engineering (SOSE '10), pp. 151–158. IEEE Computer Society, Washington, DC (2010)
27. The Player Project: http://playerstage.sourceforge.net. Accessed Jan 2011
28. MobileRobots, Inc.: Advanced Robot Interface for Applications (ARIA). Available at: http:// robots.mobilerobots.com/wiki/ARIA. Accessed Jan 2011
29. Buyya, R., et al.: Cloud computing and emerging IT platforms: Vision, hype, and reality for delivering computing as the 5th utility. Future Generation Computer Systems, 25(6), 599–616 (2009)
30. IBM: Cloud Computing. http://www.ibm.com/ibm/cloud. Accessed Jan 2011
31. Microsoft Windows Azure Platform: http://www.microsoft.com/windowsazure. Accessed Jan 2011
32. Application Development with Force.com: http://www.salesforce.com/platform/. Accessed Jan 2011
33. Yahoo Pipes: http://pipes.yahoo.com. Accessed Jan 2011
34. Google App Engine: http://code.google.com/appengine. Accessed Jan 2011
35. Microsoft Business Productivity Online: http://www.microsoft.com/online/business-productivity.aspx. Accessed Jan 2011
36. Crownpeak: http://www.crownpeak.com/. Accessed Jan 2011
37. Eloqua: http://www.eloqua.com. Accessed Jan 2011
38. Facebook: http://facebook.com. Accessed Jan 2011
39. FreeNX: Free Software (GPL) implementation of the NX Server. http://freenx.berlios.de. Accessed Jan 2010
40. RealVNC: VNC Remote Control Software. http://realvnc.com. Accessed Mar 2010
41. Open Virtualization Format (OVF): http://dmtf.org/standards/ovf. Accessed Jan 2011
42. Šůcha, P., Kutil, M., Sojka, M., Hanzálek, Z.: TORSCHE scheduling toolbox for Matlab. In: IEEE International Symposium on Computer-Aided Control Systems Design, Munich (2006)
43. The Globus Alliance: http://www.globus.org. Accessed Jan 2011
44. OpenAM: Available at: http://www.forgerock.com/openam.html (2010)
45. SAML V2.0 Technical Overview: http://www.oasis-open.org/committees/download. php/20645/sstc-saml-tech-overview-draft-10.pdf. Accessed Jan 2011
46. Novák, V., et al.: Mathematical Principles of Fuzzy Logic. Kluwer, Dordrecht (1999). ISBN 0-7923-8595-0
47. Zimmermann, H.: Fuzzy Set Theory and Its Applications. Kluwer, Boston (2001). ISBN 0-7923-7435-5
48. Shibboleth: http://shibboleth.internet2.edu. Accessed Mar 2010
49. Amazon Elastic Compute Cloud (Amazon EC2): http://aws.amazon.com/ec2. Accessed Apr 2010
50. TinyOS Community Forum: Available at: http://www.tinyos.net/. Accessed Mar 2010

Chapter 8
Cloud Computing: An Enabler in Developing Business Models for Global Enterprises

N. Raghavendra Rao

Abstract The advancements in information and communication technology (ICT) have resulted in new concepts being developed in this discipline. Cloud Computing is one among a number of other concepts resulting from ICT. Cloud Computing is providing a scope for radical changes in business processes in organizations. It would become a necessity for integrating businesses with this concept to face the new realities in business processes in organizations and the provision of customer services. Further to integrating businesses and business activities, the knowledge of domain experts and emerging technologies are the basic components for developing new and innovative business models. With this background, the organizations have started to realize the value of sharing resources such as human-centered assets, physical assets, and the components of information technology and systems to gain competitive advantage in the present globalization scenarios. This chapter presents and discusses a case study of Roa Motors Ltd., an India-based company which had a good share of the world market. In the course of time, they began losing their share when many other countries started following the globalization policy. As a consequence of this, the company decided to evolve an innovative approach in designing cars for the global market. With this objective, they hired the services of domain experts from Germany and Korea to design car models by making use of Cloud computing concepts. This chapter also explains how virtual reality concepts may be applied in Cloud Computing environments for developing a business model for the Roa Motors Ltd.

N.R. Rao (✉)
Advisor, FINAIT Consultancy Services, Chennai, India
e-mail: drrao_edu@hotmail.com

Z. Mahmood and R. Hill (eds.), *Cloud Computing for Enterprise Architectures*, 159
Computer Communications and Networks, DOI 10.1007/978-1-4471-2236-4_8,
© Springer-Verlag London Limited 2011

8.1 Introduction

The existing ways of doing business are constantly changing and opportunities in the present global markets have to be exploited at a rapid pace. The large centralized organizations which have established themselves over a considerable period of time may find it very difficult to introduce or diversify their product range in the present globalization scenario. They need to realize that managing technical knowledge as well as innovative process in conducting business in the way that is required to remain competitive in the global market is necessary. Every business enterprise has unique challenges to face in its sector. It is high time they take advantage of the opportunities available across the globe and make use of the expertise of global virtual teams. This chapter talks about a business model created by global virtual teams. They have made use of the concept of Cloud Computing in their development process of business models. The essence of Cloud Computing technology is computing resources and sharing among participants in virtualized organizations.

8.1.1 Benefits of Cloud Computing

Cloud Computing is one of the most promising concepts for an enterprise today. In the present ICT (Information and Communication Technology) scenario, new concepts appear as high space in the market place and at the same time they disappear. Cloud Computing is predicted to have more longevity. The analyst firm Gartner has predicted that Cloud Computing will be the top most technology area, and hence it should concentrate in the year 2010 [1]. The definition of Cloud Computing is in "Cloud" itself. In a simple example, the Cloud is a large group interconnected systems. These systems can be desktop or mobile systems or network services. Further there can be public or private Cloud Computing, supporting beyond a single enterprise. The application and data stored in the servers in the Cloud environment are available to a broad group of users, cross-enterprises and cross-platforms. Access is through the Internet only to any authorized users. This authorization facilitates the users to have access to the system in the Cloud environment from any devise which has an Internet feature. One of the important aspects of Cloud Computing is task centric. Instead of focusing on the application as what it can do, the focus is on what an end user needs and how the application can do it for them. Especially in this economy Cloud services can provide speed, efficiencies, and be cost effective for business enterprises. These benefits will enable enterprises to take advantage of the emerging concept. However data privacy and other concerns pose security threats. Access to Cloud Computing resources could be remote; enterprises need to consider measures such as encrypting data in the Cloud [2].

8.2 Cloud Computing from Enterprises' Perspective

Cloud Computing is a concept generally defined as a group of scalable and virtualized resources which make use of Internet to provide on demand services to end users. The National Institute of Standards and Technology (NIST) describes it as "a model for enabling convenient, on-demand network access to a shared pool of configurable computing resources that can be rapidly provisioned and released with minimal management effort or service provider interaction. This Cloud model promotes availability and is composed of five essential characteristics: on-demand self-service, broad network access, resource pooling, rapid elasticity, and measured service" [3].

The Cloud Computing has mainly five characteristics, which provide numerous advantages for enterprises, including:

- On demand service
- Ubiquitous network access
- Location independent pooling of resources
- Elasticity and scalability
- Pay-as-you-use approach

8.2.1 Cloud Development Models

There are different models available with different characteristics. Each model's characteristics are given below:

- *Private Cloud* – The Cloud infrastructure is owned or leased by a single enterprise and is operated solely for that organization.
- *Community Cloud* – The Cloud infrastructure is shared by several organizations and supports a specific community.
- *Public Cloud* – The Cloud infrastructure is owned by an organization selling Cloud services to the general public or to a large industry group.
- *Hybrid Cloud* – The Cloud infrastructure is composition of two or more Clouds such as internal, community, or public that remains unique entities [4]. They are bound together by standardized or proprietary technology that enables data and application portability.

8.3 What Is New in the Cloud?

In the early days of computing, many companies actually showed a single computer system that was located in a remote data center. The system personnel would allocate and manage resources for each user and each application. Users could request for more computing time or less by adjusting the amount of time they utilize for sharing the services. Similarly, Cloud Computing offers various components from deployment models and mix and match the solutions that are sought. One can make use of a component such as storage-as-a-service from one service provider, database-as-a-service from another and even a complete application development and deployment of platform from a third service provider [5]. One has to remember that Cloud Computing facilitates the use of different Cloud Computing deployment models over the Internet.

8.3.1 Cloud Computing as a Collaborative Technology

With the growing use of Internet, there is no need to limit group collaboration to a single enterprise's network environment. Users from multiple locations within an organization and from multiple organizations would like to collaborate on business processes across business organizations and geographic boundaries. Many leading manufactures in the area of infrastructure are offering the hardware necessary to build Cloud network. On the software side also, many software companies are developing Cloud-based applications and storage services. Cloud Computing concept facilitates users of any device which has an Internet feature, such as mobile phones, laptops, and other devices. Cloud architecture is reasonably simple [6]. It needs some intelligent management to connect all those devices together and assign task processing to multitudes of users.

The main use of Cloud Computing is the storage of data. Data is stored in multiple servers rather than in the dedicated servers used in network data storage. The user sees it as a virtual server. It is just a pseudo name used to refer virtual space carved out in the Cloud. In reality, the user's data could be stored in any one or more systems used to create the Cloud. Individual users will have their access to the Cloud environment through their devices, which have Internet features. At the same time they must be authorized users. The Cloud Environment shown in Fig. 8.1 gives an overview of an individual access to the Cloud.

The collaborative platform along with the communications network services and hardware provides the pipeline to enable the flow of knowledge, its context, and the medium for conversations. Besides this the collaborative platform provides a channel for defining, storing, moving, and linking to knowledge sources [7].

8.3.2 Data-Intensive Applications

Cloud Computing is more useful for data-intensive applications in the scientific and business domains. Research scholars require mechanisms to transfer, publish, replicate, discover, share, and analyze data across the globe [8]. Similarly business applications in the domains such as finance, production, marketing, and engineering

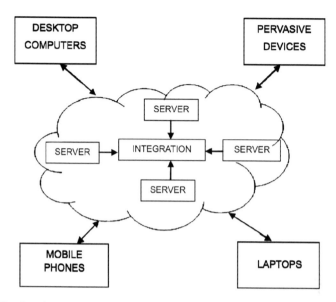

Fig. 8.1 Cloud environment

need to maintain database consisting regionally or worldwide. Further these applications have to manage data replication to facilitate data discovery and to respond dynamically to changes in the volume of data in databases.

8.3.3   Business Applications

Business generally covers many different sectors: sectors such as manufacturing, financial, hospitality, and health care. Every sector has different characteristics both on the use of data and data volumes [9]. Although the use of Cloud Computing technology in the business applications sector is just beginning to take hold, it is expected to emerge significantly [10].

8.3.4   Need for Business Models

Globalization which was initially viewed with fear and distrust has opened up huge new markets for many countries. This has been focusing on the need for an innovative approach in conducting business by enterprises. The world is poised to take a huge leap at the rate innovation is gaining importance. This is the result of use of enhanced sharing of information and collaborative possibilities provided by the convergence of information and communication technologies. Cloud Computing provides infrastructure for creation of virtual organizations.

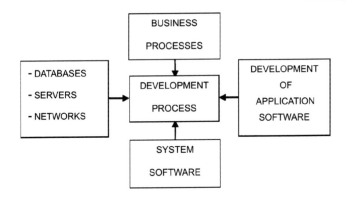

Fig. 8.2 Components in development process under Cloud Computing

8.3.5   Integration of Components in Cloud Computing

There are four components that need to be integrated under Cloud Computing for the development of business models for virtual organizations. They are business process, application, software, system software, and infrastructure such as servers, network and database. Figure 8.2 gives an overview of integration of components under Cloud Computing. Adding intelligence to the process of developing new models or to existing models and their management makes lots of sense because some business models need considerable expertise.

8.3.6   Storage of Data in Cloud Computing

The main use of Cloud Computing is the storage of data. Data is stored in multiple servers rather than in the dedicated servers used in traditional network data storage. The end user sees it as a virtual space carved out of the Cloud. In reality the user's data can be stored in any or more servers used to create a Cloud. There are many advantages in virtualization. Some of the advantages in relation to virtualization are given below:

- *Space and power* – Virtualization facilitates to consider infrastructure, thereby reducing the space and power requirements.
- *Utilization* – Virtualization helps in increasing utilization thereby resulting in decreasing capital investments.
- *Cost containment* – Virtualization concentrates on increasing utilization and consolidation of hardware thereby reducing capital costs, cabling operational costs such as power, and maintenance costs of hardware and software.
- *Business continuity* – Virtualization allows business process to run independent of the hardware thereby enabling to move the process to other systems at run time.

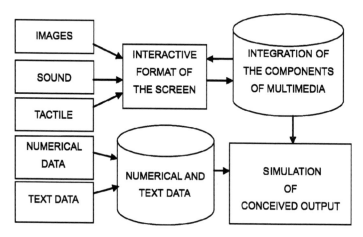

Fig. 8.3 Virtual reality application process

- *Data recovery* – The data may be replicated in multiple storage servers thereby enabling data to be recovered rapidly with a minimum loss of time. Virtualization sometimes is also seen as a low-cost alternative to disaster recovery [11].
- *Management* – Virtualization helps the system group to use the system with fewer problems.

8.3.7   Virtual Reality

Virtual reality is a way of creating a three-dimensional image of an object or scene [12]. It is possible for the user to move through or around the image. Virtual reality imitates the way the real object or scene looks and changes. Information system helps to use the information in data bases to simulate; the line dividing simulation tasks and their real world counterparts is very thin. The concept of multimedia is required in virtual reality application process. The components of multimedia are tactile (touch), visual (images), and auditory (sound). Developing a business process with virtual reality concept is explained in Fig. 8.3.

8.4   Case Study

An Indian-based Roa Motors Ltd. has been manufacturing motor cars for Indian and global markets. They have been in the market over a period of two decades. Their products are well received in both the markets. Their market share has been encouraging. Due to the globalization policy followed by many countries, the global market

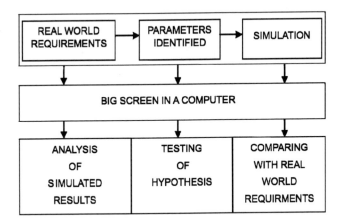

Fig. 8.4 Model used by domain experts

is now open to many players across the globe. Roa Motors Ltd. has started losing hold on the market due to globalization, and has decided to innovate new methods and business process in production of their motor cars.

They have decided to hire services of the domain experts who have rich experience in motor cars sector. They have identified the domain experts located in Germany and Korea. It has been agreed among them that domain experts and their team members will operate from their respective countries. Their role is to design car models and suggest the components with ISO standards required for manufacturing of the models suggested by them. The domain experts are expected to guide the employees of Roa Motors Ltd. in India for implementation of the design of the cars given by them. Furthermore, the vendors who will supply the components as per the standards will be given access to the bills of materials module for knowing the quantity of materials and date of supply by them. Engineering design of components will be made available through the system whenever it is needed. It has been decided to make use of the advanced concepts in information and collaboration technologies for developing their models.

8.4.1 Macro-level Design for Engineering Design and Bill of Materials Models

Figure 8.4 explains how the domain experts have made use of the resources of Roa Motors Ltd., in India from their respective countries. The software such as CAD/CAM, multimedia, and virtual reality are required to create a car model for engineering design and bills of materials module. The hardware and software resources from India are made available to domain experts. The domain experts have taken advantage of time differences in the respective countries. The time differences enabled minimizing of capital expenditure and operational expenditure through Cloud Computing.

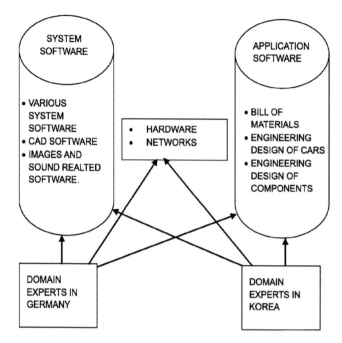

Fig. 8.5 ROA Auto model

Figure 8.5 explains the data and design created by the domain experts in Roa Auto Model; it will be made available to vendors across the globe and the employees of Roa Motor Cars Ltd., under Cloud Computing environments. Multimedia concepts are applied in the conceptual design of a car created by the domain experts. A car for the global market is simulated by domain experts is a virtual reality environment. A group of evaluators in the domain expert's team will test the functionalities and features in the simulated car. Once the simulated car meets the product specification, the next step will be to design the car by using Cad/Cam software. The devices such as mobile handsets and laptops would facilitate the end users to have access to the above model. The enormous competitive pressure in the automobile sector can get most engineering designs and the requirements of components for less turnaround time from the domain experts from any part of the world through Cloud Computing concepts.

8.4.2   Virtual Reality in Cloud Computing Environment

The domain experts have developed a model that considers real world requirements for which parameters are created on the basis of their requirements. Simulated version of a car has been designed, and experiments have been carried out in computer systems in Cloud Computing environment. The domain experts' team members have immersed themselves in every aspect of design and testing working in front of a large screen of a computer which has given a sense of actually testing a motor car in a real world situation. The concept of virtual reality has helped them to look from the real-world situation. Cloud Computing environment has made it possible for the domain experts to make use of virtual reality concept.

8.4.3 Vendors in Cloud Computing Environment

Besides the regular showing of information between Roa Motors Ltd. and their vendors, computer-aided design (CAD) software is made use of designing prototype items recommended by domain experts for vendors. Bill of material module in Roa Motors Cloud Computing environment provides the details of the items used in manufacturing of the cars. The drawings of these items generated by using CAD software are made available by giving an access to the system in the Cloud Computing environment.

8.4.4 Device Management

The need for device management is obvious in Cloud Computing environment [13]. Heterogeneous devices, applications, and users needed to be administrated. The core functionality of a pervasive device [14] is to perform a task with high speed. Memory management has to address spaces for each application and type of a devise. It has to support different kinds of user interfaces. The main requirement of device management is to take care of operating system structure, memory protection, security, and multitasking.

8.4.5 Cloud Computing in Roa Auto Model

Coordination of various resources such as computing power, data, hardware, devices, software, and applications are needed for Roa Auto model. In Cloud Computing environment, virtualization facilitates coordination in (1) application partitioning, (2) ascertaining and scheduling tasks, (3) distributing the data where and when it is required, and (4) providing and distributing codes to specific system device. Cloud Computing supports the above requirements and takes care in Roa Auto Model.

8.4.6 Development of a New Product in Roa Motors Ltd.

Roa Auto Model proves that a new product can be jointly designed by main experts in a global virtual team through a process of continuous exchange of ideas between members dispersed across the globe. This process helps in generating alternative ideas by taking inputs from different sources and structuring through virtual reality application. This model provides an idea for the creation of global innovation model. Further it helps to structure the work flow by visualizing the various phases of the development of a product. Customers' tastes are becoming more homogeneous around the globe. Consequently Roa Motors Ltd. can provide a significantly good product through the economies of scale with common design. Roa Auto Model can increase the chances of successfully diffusing knowledge, technology, and process. Advanced telecommunications technologies have drastically changed the business operations, providing new services and creating an interconnected worldwide community [15].

8.4.7   Summary of the Development of Roa Auto Model

Till recently the standard model of innovation has been a linear process from research through design, development and then manufacturing. In the case of Roa Auto Model many of these processes are carried out concurrently and collaborating through the concepts in information and communication technology in the private Cloud development model. The management of Roa Motors Ltd. could hire the services of the domain experts from Germany and Korea. The employees of Roa Motor and Domain experts with their team members have formed a virtual team to develop Roa Motor Model. It is because of Cloud Computing they could develop Roa Auto Model by making use of the virtual reality concept and the features in CAD software. At the same time, the bill of materials required for cars to be manufactured is made available to Roa Motor Ltd. and the vendors across the globe. Figure 8.6 illustrates developing a business model for Roa cars under the Cloud Computing concept.

8.5   Conclusion

In today's knowledge rich environment, enterprises can no longer afford to rely entirely on their ideas to advance their business, nor can they restrict their innovations to a single path to market. As a result, the traditional model for innovation, which has been largely internally focused or a "closed one," has become obsolete. Emerging in its place is a new paradigm "open innovation." This strategically leverages internal and external sources of ideas and takes them to market through multiple paths.

Global enterprises can take advantage of unique knowledge and resource wherever they are located. Information and communication technology has increased virtualization in business activities and ways of working. The term "virtual" is now appearing in many forms. Roa Auto Model explains how to adopt innovative approach in invoking global enterprises by applying the concept of "mind invoking."

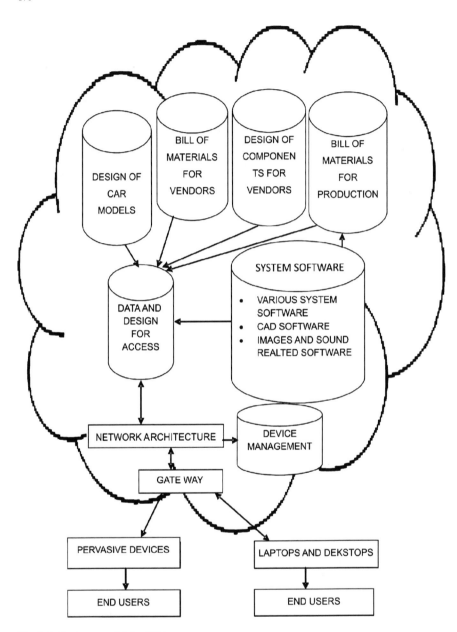

Fig. 8.6 Business model for ROA

It may be observed that Roa Motors Ltd. has made use of the services of the domain experts from Germany and Korea staying in their respective countries. The concepts of virtual reality and multimedia are made use of in their development process of designing cars for global market. At the same time, vendors are able to get the required information for the production of components. Designing of components is made easy by using CAD software. Cloud Computing concept facilitated innovation at Roa Motors Ltd.

Big business enterprises will find that private Cloud is a better solution for their organization in leveraging the benefits of Cloud Computing within their firewall. Even they can choose a mixture of public and private Clouds or a hybrid Cloud. Roa Motors Ltd. has taken advantage of making use of the Cloud deployment models.

Roa Motors Ltd. has proved that the concept of virtual organization is the key to Cloud Computing. All virtual organizations can share the common resources for computing power and accessing data across the globe.

References

1. http://www.clodave.com/link/Gartner-says-cloud-computing-is-the-top-technolohy-trend-in-2010
2. Mather, T., Kumarswamy, S., Latif, S.: Data security and storage. In: Cloud Security and Privacy. O'Reilly, Cambridge (2009)
3. http://www.princeton.edu/~ddix/cloud-computing.html
4. Hurwitz, J., Bloor, R., Kaufman, M., Halper, F.: Discovering private and hybrid clouds. In: Cloud Computing for Dummies. Wiley, Indianapolis (2010)
5. Linthicum, D.S.: The components of Cloud Computing. In: Cloud Computing and SoA Convergence in Your Enterprise. Pearson, New Delhi (2010)
6. Krutz, R.L., Vines, R.D.: Cloud computing architecture. In: Cloud Security A Comprehensive Guide to Secure Cloud Computing. Wiley, New Delhi (2010)
7. Tiwana, A.: Creating the knowledge management system blue print. In: The Knowledge Management Toolkit. Pearson, New Delhi (2005)
8. Dikaiakos, M.D., Pallis, G., Katsaros, D., Mehra, P., Vakali, A.: Cloud computing distributed internet computing for IT and Scientific Research. IEEE Internet Comput. **13**(5):10–13 (Sept/Oct 2009)
9. Miller, M.: Cloud computing for the corporation. In: Cloud Computing Web Based Applications That Change the Way You Work and Collaborate Online. Que, Indianapolis (2008)
10. Jennings, R.: Surveying the role of Cloud Computing. In: Cloud Computing with the Windows Azure Platform. Wiley, Indianapolis (2009)
11. Reese, G.: Disaster recovery. In: Cloud Application Architectures. O'Reilly, Cambridge (2009)
12. Chorafas, D.N., Steinhann, H.: An introduction to visualization. In: Virtual Reality Practical Applications in Business and Industry. Prentice Hall PTR, Englewood Cliffs (1995)
13. Burkhardt, J., Henn, H., Hepper, S., Rindtorff, K., Sahack, T.: Device management. In: Pervasive Computing Technology and Architecture of Mobile Internet Applications. Pearson Education, New Delhi (2002)
14. Schiller, J.: Telecommunication systems. In: Mobile Communications. Pearson Education, New Delhi (2004)
15. Dodd, A.Z.: Basic concepts. In: The Essential Guide to Telecommunications. Pearson, New Delhi (2003)

Chapter 9
Using Common Logic to Provide a Semantic Enterprise Architecture Framework for Cloud Computing

Jeffrey A. Schiffel and Shaun Bridges

Abstract We introduce OpenSEA, an architectural framework, to enable semantics in enterprise Cloud computing architectures to interoperate for information access and knowledge generation. The ISO 24707:2007 Common Logic Standards are designed to provide an abstract syntax for logic systems, the purpose of which is to provide a commonality for interaction between different systems. OpenSEA uses these open standards as the foundation of a framework for Semantic Enterprise Architectures by combining them with definitions for enterprise architecture provided by The Open Group Architecture Framework. By using abstract syntax and semantics based on standards that are free to extend and specialise, OpenSEA provides the possibility for systems to interact by providing common generalisations for all conceptual structures that adhere to the framework.

9.1 Introduction

This chapter introduces the architecture framework Open Semantic Enterprise Architecture (OpenSEA). It is intended to satisfy demands upon Cloud Computing (CC) architectures by enabling the semantics of enterprise architectures to interoperate for information access and knowledge generation. It uses tools that adhere to Common Logic (CL) [1] standards and unites the information through The Open Group Architecture Framework (TOGAF) [2]. CL provides the Meta-Ontology, and TOGAF provides the Upper-Ontology.

J.A. Schiffel
The Boeing Company – Wichita Division
e-mail: jeffrey.a.schiffel@boeing.com

S. Bridges (✉)
Open-SEA.org
e-mail: Shaun.Bridges@Open-Sea.org

Z. Mahmood and R. Hill (eds.), *Cloud Computing for Enterprise Architectures*,
Computer Communications and Networks, DOI 10.1007/978-1-4471-2236-4_9,
© Springer-Verlag London Limited 2011

Modern organisations must be adaptable in order to respond rapidly to competitive pressures with new or updated product and service offerings. Organisations must to find and consume data, processes and services from other dispersed organisations. These may be subsidiaries, outside organisations in the supply chain and publicly available competitor information. Whilst CC might be suggested as one 'solution', there is requirement for an enterprise architecture that defines protocols to enhance common understanding. New ontologies and technologies are being created to bring common semantics. These include modelling frameworks for the enterprise, service-oriented computing architectures and the protocols and programming paradigms like XaaS services providing Infrastructure as a Service (e.g. Amazon Web Services), Platform as a Service (e.g. Force.com) and Software as a Service (NetSuite, SalesForce, Business By Design) to tie the bundle together.

As early as 1992, Sowa and Zachman Sowa wrote:

> Dramatic improvements in the price-performance of information technology and the escalation of the rate of change show no signs of abatement. In the words of Alvin Toffler, "Knowledge is change…, and accelerating knowledge, fuelling the great engine of technology, means accelerating change." Gone are the days of computers for simple calculations. We are only now beginning to see the enormous complexity of integrating information technology into the very fabric of our enterprises. Soon, the enterprise of the information age will find itself immobilized if it does not have the ability to tap the information resources within and without its boundaries. [3]

Some 19 years later, the final prediction continues to hold true, yet a workable solution remains unrealised. In fact, data growth and information consumption is growing at an explosive pace. This makes it increasingly difficult to sort out useful information from a sea of data. Appliances are developed to analyse a company's data, but merging with other data and gaining knowledge is expensive, time consuming or both.

In addition to data access, solutions to the problems associated with accurate communication within and between enterprises are hampered by silos of knowledge within departments or industries. A team may understand a workflow yet cannot link it into another team or another organisation without complex business process modelling. The same team also understands how the interface of the IT system links to their physical processes yet cannot convey this knowledge to a data engineer or software engineer without calling on business process experts. Nor is it easy to restructure these 'hard-coded' practices to a corporate structure whose aims and objectives need to be agile in order to survive and thrive in the complex, fast moving information age.

Similarly, the concept of a Semantic Web of linked data continues to be discussed and developed but, at its heart, relies on a broad range of logic languages and systems that use different ontologies and knowledge bases. Communication between two logic systems using different languages, logic, ontologies and terminologies is difficult and remains an obstacle to the notion of a global pool of information from which knowledge can be generated.

In the last few years, two standards have been agreed upon that can be combined to address all these problems simultaneously into the OpenSea framework:

- Common Logic provides an abstract syntax for logic that can also be freely extended and adapted so that systems that have been built to the standards can agree on a common understanding and thus communicate without loss of information.

- TOGAF has become a widely accepted methodology for defining business processes, objectives, data structures, systems and interfaces that enterprises of all sizes and sectors can use. It provides the means to integrate vertically (from corporate aims through business processes, to systems, data and technology) and horizontally between teams and organisations. The abstract semantics and definitions have been designed to be freely extended and specialised so as not to attempt to provide a 'one size fits all' solution.

The purpose of OpenSEA is to capture the abstract semantics of enterprise architectures using tools that adhere to the Common Logic standards, using TOGAF to provide the Upper-Ontology and CL to provide the Meta-Ontology. This set of abstract definitions, rules and terminologies could be adapted to create different templates while retaining a chain of generalisations and specialisations that all adhering definitions could follow to agree a shared abstracted, common understanding.

9.2   Formalising the Enterprise Architecture

While tools such as online help are built specifically for users, and attempt to use the language of the user, these are relatively primitive, do not readily interface to other tools and do not promote enterprise modelling. Different tools exist for different types of developers, but all suffer from the lack of a common language required to pull a system model together. Without a coherent system model, an integrated, interoperating system is not possible. This is especially true of dispersed subsystems, whether separated geographically or by functionality. It is difficult, if not impossible, in the current state of the tools market to have one tool interoperate with another tool [2, 4].

Sowa and Zachman [3] noted that an enterprise will form a free market structure if the nature of the transaction between two organisation units is simple, well defined and universally understood. In this case, the organisation (or person) with work to assign would survey all possible workers to find one who is acceptable in terms of availability and cost. This method is much like a stock buyer who scans the pool of stockbrokers to find one who will execute a buy within an agreeable time and for a reasonable fee. They then identified the advantages offered by formalising Zachman's Information System Architecture with Conceptual Graphs, a means of capturing and expressing Peircian logic in a way that can be readily consumed by humans and predicate logic systems without compromising expression or logic [4]. Sowa is the driving force behind Common Logic; Zachman's Information System Architecture is often cited as being influential in developing or evolving enterprise architectures [5]. Their investigations and proposals are central to the ideas behind OpenSEA.

9.2.1   A Common Toolset and a Common Language

Conceptual Graphs allowed a common tool to capture and express information across the different sections of the model. For example, a process flow diagram

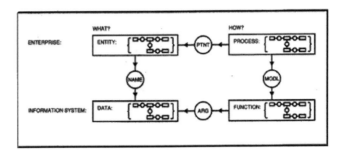

Fig. 9.1 Interconnecting different domains of an enterprise architecture to the supporting information systems

describes how an enterprise operates, a data flow diagram describes how a system captures this process and a master schedule document expresses when an enterprise undertakes the process. These are traditionally the domains of different experts using different tools. This erects a barrier to full, clear, meaningful interaction between subject domains. This can be avoided by using a common toolset and a common language. It is worth noting that The Open Group identified the same weakness.

Tools exist for both users and developers. Tools such as online help are there specifically for users and attempt to use the language of the user. Many different tools exist for different types of developers, but they suffer from the lack of a common language that is required to bring the system together. It is difficult, if not impossible, in the current state of the tools market to have one tool interoperate with another tool [2].

9.2.2   Gathering Knowledge Across the Enterprise

Building on this common toolset and language allows an enterprise architect to see how changes in one model could be seen to affect another. Previously observed is:

> It is worthwhile noting that if the nature of the dependency between cells could be understood and stored in the repository along with the cell models, it would constitute a very powerful capability for understanding the total impact of a change to any one of the models, if not a capability for managing the actual assimilation of the changes [3].

By way of an example, they showed how some of these different domains could be interconnected (Fig. 9.1):

The 'Entity' defines what an enterprise is, a 'Process' defines how an enterprise operates, and the two are connected by the PTNT (or 'Patient') relationship, that is, 'the patient of the process is the entity'. The model of the process is the function and thereby the physical world of the enterprise is mapped to the technical world of the information system.

One final quote from [3] shows how relevant their findings are today:

> an enterprise will form into a free market structure if the nature of the transaction between two organization units is simple, well defined, and universally understood. In this case, the

organization (or person) with work to assign would survey all possible workers to find one who is acceptable in terms of availability and cost. This method is much like a stock buyer who scans the pool of stockbrokers to find one who will execute a buy within an agreeable time and for a reasonable fee.

9.3 The Advantages of a Semantic Service-Oriented Architecture

In 2008, the International Research Forum (IRF) brought together leading thinkers and innovators from across the world to discuss the notion of an 'Internet of Services'. The Internet of Services is a vision of discrete, loosely coupled services that can be discovered and consumed by enterprises across the world in a global Service-Oriented Architecture [6].

9.3.1 Service Description and Discovery

Wahlster, Director and CEO of DFKI (German Research Centre for Artificial Intelligence), explained that services are currently described and discovered with metadata, keywords and ontology-based searches. This has its own challenges in a specific domain, but is unworkable in the Internet of Services.

The IRF looked beyond standard services by extending the definition to include the XaaS offerings, such as Software as a Service, Platform as a Service, Business Process Integration as a Service and Infrastructure as a Service. This extension introduces the need to offer and consume all levels of an enterprise and maps closely to the core structure of the TOGAF definitions.

The forum discussed the need to make semantically enriched service descriptions, and for services to become aware of both their environment and their role within it. 'If you want really to bring services on the Web, then you need to have this kind of Semantic Web' [6].

The advantages of semantically enabling web services include an improved opportunity for interoperation [7], a means of providing accurate, meaningful descriptions [8], better rates of discovery [9] and improved security [10]. The key factors behind the weaknesses of the current service discovery are the quality of the syntactic data and variations in meaning of the metadata.

9.3.2 Semantic Business Process Management

Business Process Management is 'the approach of managing the execution of IT-supported business operations from a managerial process view rather than from a technical perspective' [11]. Although business process modelling is widely used, it may be limited to simplified work-flows, paying little attention to capturing the

overriding reasons for modelling a process or the various models that may make a
process. Bridges [12] propose a Semantic Business Process Management to improve
the communication between the business requirements and the composite resources,
systems and labour:

> Current BPM does not overcome the underlying limitation that the business process space
> inside the organization as a whole is not accessible at a semantic level, especially because
> business process modelling languages like BPEL4WS are an insufficient means of captur-
> ing and representing such a domain of discourse. [13]

Creating a semantic enterprise architecture that bridges the business needs and
underpinning technology, the foundations for semantic Business Process Modelling
is inherent within OpenSEA.

9.4 TOGAF: The Upper-Ontology of OpenSEA

TOGAF has been designed to be used and specialised for different industries and
templates and is widely used and accepted already. The reasons for using it as the
foundation for OpenSEA have been covered in depth by [12]. Advantages are as
follows:

- It is vendor and industry neutral.
- It is designed to assist 'boundary-less' communication.
- It aims to integrate automated and manual processes in a manner that is quick to
  change and adapt.
- The Business, Data, Application and Technical architectures align with the new
  XaaS architecture and open the possibility of a distributed architecture.
- It provides an extensive and accepted language.
- It is compatible with SOA.

By using a language that is already widely used addresses one of the common
problems facing the ontology engineer: acceptance. OpenSEA utilises the widely
used language of TOGAF to provide a small vocabulary for a large number of users.
At the same time, it uses generalisation and specialisation relationships to extend
this upper-ontology whilst retaining a traceable link between all concepts that
adhere to the framework. Examples are provided later in the chapter to show how
this is done.

9.5 Common Logic: The Meta-Ontology of OpenSEA

Common Logic has been established with the following aim:

> The intent is that the content of any system using first-order logic can be represented in this
> International Standard. The purpose is to facilitate interchange of first-order logic-based
> information between systems.

It does not require a specific syntax; rather it provides an abstraction of syntaxes to allow languages to be developed independently but allows for them to retain the capacity to be expressed in other languages without compromise or confusion. In the same way that TOGAF provides a scalable language, CL provides a scalable logical standard to allow disparate data and knowledge bases to be combined within a distributed, boundary-less knowledge base.

9.6   The Extended Ontology

Central to OpenSEA is the notion of all definitions, facts and rules being specialised to suit a given enterprise architecture template, sector specific template, industry, organisation, team, process or individual. This is achieved using the generalisation/ specialisation relations to create a web of connected concepts where all artefacts that adhere to the framework can be traced back to a common generalisation. This simple approach is much the same way that the Internet can resolve host names across disparate domains, although in OpenSEA a concept or relation may be a specialisation of one or more generalisations.

Sowa provided the following example for how this may be expressed in the CL compliant CGIF format:

```
CLIF:
    (forall ((R1 MonadicRelation) (R2 MonadicRelation)
(x) (y))
        (if (and (GeneralizationOf R1 R2) (R2 x y)) (R1 x
y)))
    CGIF:
    [MonadicRelation   @every   *R1]   [MonadicRelation
@every *R2]
    [Entity: @every *x] [Entity: @every *y]
    [If (GeneralizationOf ?R1 ?R2) (#?R2 ?x ?y) [Then
(#?R1 ?x ?y)]]
```

That is, for all monadic relations R1 and R2 and any x and y, if R1 is a generalisation of R2 and R2(x,y), then R1(x,y). Once the GeneralisationOf statement is made, then the type hierarchy can be listed as a simple collection of assertions:

```
CLIF;
    (and (GeneralizationOf Architect Business_Analyst)
    (GeneralizationOf Architect Information_Analyst)
    (GeneralizationOf Information_Analyst Data_Analyst)
    (GeneralizationOf   Information_Analyst   Tech-
nical_Analyst))
```

Bridges, Schiffel and Polovina [15] built on this example to show how a doctor and patient could be seen to be specialisations of the same TOGAF definitions 'Agent', 'PerformsTaskIn' and 'Role':

```
TOGAF:
[Agent: @every *t]
  (PerformsTaskIn ?t [Role])
HealthCare
  (GeneralizationOf Agent Doctor)
  (GeneralizationOf Role Healthcare)
Sales
  (GeneralizationOf Agent Salesman)
  (GeneralizationOf Role Sales)
```

that we can translate to the CLIF form:

```
CLIF:
[Doctor: @every *t]
  (PerformsTaskIn ?t [Healthcare])
And
[Salesman: @every *t]
  (PerformsTaskIn ?t [Sales])
```

Bridges [12] drew on the TOGAF 'attributes' that are used to define and document all artefacts that are contained within a TOGAF-based architecture (specifically ID, Name, Description, Category, Source and Owner). Bridges proposed that these same attributes could be used to provide the information required to build the web of interlinks between the member concepts and relations (through 'Category' connecting each entry to its parent entries), maintaining unique URLs to identify the entry and locate the metadata (ID and Source) including Definition (a CL definition of the 'object', i.e. how it is defined by other relations and concepts), Name (a 'friendly' name), Description (a human readable free text) and Owner (the governing body to maintain the object). This metadata can be represented in CLIF as:

```
[Universal: @every *t]
  (chrc ?t [Category])
  (chrc ?t [Description])
  (chrc ?t [ID])
  (chrc ?t [Name])
  (chrc ?t [Owner])
  (chrc ?t [Source])
```

For example, the TOGAF definition of 'data-entity' is 'An encapsulation of data that is recognised by a business domain expert as a thing. Logical data entities can be tied to applications, repositories, and services and may be structured according to implementation considerations'. In OpenSEA this could be formalised in the upper ontology as:

```
CGIF:
[DEFINITION: "[DATA_ENTITY:*x1] [SERVICE:*x2]
    (isAccessedAndServicedThrough ?x1 ?x2) "]
      [NAME: Data Entity]
      [CATEGORY: OpenSEA.org/ENTITY]
      [SOURCE:
        "http://www.opengroup.org/architecture/togaf9-
        doc/arch/index2.html"]
      [ID: "OpenSEA.org/DATA_ENTITY"]
      [OWNER: OpenSEA]
      [DESCRIPTION: "AN ENCAPSULATION OF DATA..."]
      [DATA_ENTITY: *x1]
        (chrc ?x1 OpenSEA) (chrc ?x1 Universal) (chrc
?x1
        "http://www.opengroup.org/architecture/togaf9-
        doc/arch/index2.html")        (chrc      ?x1      "AN
ENCAPSULATION OF DATA")
        (chrc ?x1 "OpenSEA.org/DATA_ENTITY") (chrc ?x1
Data Entity)
        (chrc ?x1 ?x1] [SERVICE:*x2]
        (isAccessedAndServicedThrough ?x1 ?x2) ")
```

(from [14]).

In this example 'DATA_ENTITY' is related to 'SERVICE' with the 'IsAccessedAndServicedThrough' and is a specialisation of the 'ENTITY' concept ([CATEGORY: OpenSEA.org/ENTITY]); the source is maintained as the Open Group web page that contained the definition in this case as this; the ID (openSEA. org/DATA_ENTITY) is maintained by a body (OpenSEA in this case), and the TOGAF free text description is contained in the description.

9.6.1 Stability and Agility

Berners-Lee and Kagal [14] discussed how ontologies can be seen on a spectrum ranging from global ontologies that are massive and stable and involve significant effort to design to small, agile ontologies that are changed frequently yet relevant to very few. OpenSEA embraces this spectrum through the notion of the 'Owner' owning and governing the domain within which the specialisations are based. In this way, the upper ontology would remain static and provide the stability required, yet small teams could adapt their ontology rapidly, absorbing and extending other objects when required.

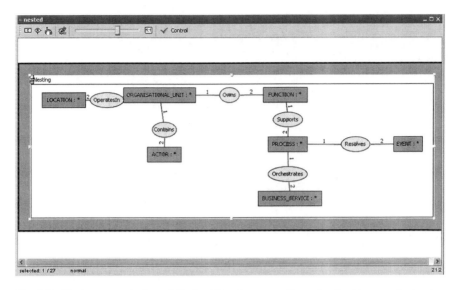

Fig. 9.2 'Business service' modelled within the perception of a business analyst using CoGui [12]

9.6.2 Formalising TOGAF

Conceptual Graphs have been used to show how the terms provided by TOGAF could be captured within a type hierarchy and basic definitions created from these concepts and relations [12, 15].

Bridges [12] used these terms to create basic, generic definitions for the upper ontology, an example of which is shown in Fig. 9.2.

9.7 Conclusion

In this chapter we introduced OpenSEA, an enterprise architecture framework intended to enable the semantics for interoperation in information access sharing. The goal is to increase competitiveness through shared knowledge, which promotes knowledge creation, in heterogeneous environments such as that found in CC. OpenSea permits the deployment of tools that adhere to Common Logic (CL) standards and unites the information through The Open Group Architecture Framework. CL provides the Meta-Ontology, and TOGAF provides the Upper-Ontology.

The OpenSEA framework seeks to formalise architectures that are aligned with TOGAF using CL compliant dialects that include CGIF in its linear and graphical representations. By formalising the links between the diverse system components (i.e. subsystems and federated systems), each may be represented with respect to the other components, and each could be represented using graphical CGs that have the power to embed the predicate calculus within an easily accessible form.

Further details can be found at http://www.open-sea.org/.

References

1. ISO/IEC 24707: Common Logic (CL): a framework for a family of logic-based languages. Retrieved Nov 1, 2009, from http://standards.iso.org/ittf/PubliclyAvailableStandards/index. html (2007)
2. The Open Group: TOGAF Version 9. Van Haren Publishing, Zaltbommel (2009)
3. Zachman, J., Sowa, J.: Extending and formalizing the framework for information systems architecture. IBM Syst. J. **31**(3), 590–617 (1992)
4. Sousa, P., Pereira, C., Vendeirinho, R., Caetano, A., Tribolet, J.: Applying the Zachman framework dimensions to support business process modelling. In: Digital Enterprise Technology. Session 3, pp. 359–366. Springer, Heidelberg (2007)
5. Emery, D., Hilliard, R.: Every architecture description needs a framework: expressing architecture frameworks using ISO/IEC 42010. In: Joint Working IEEE/IFIP Conference on Software Architecture 2009 and European Conference on Software Architecture, Cambridge, Sept 14–17: Proceedings, pp. 31–40. IEEEXplore (2009)
6. Heuser, L., Alsdorf, C., Woods, D.: International Research Forum 2008, 1st edn. Evolved Technologies Press, New York (2009)
7. Bussler, C., Fensel, D., Maedche, A.: A conceptual architecture for semantic web-enabled web services. ACM Sigmod Rec. **31**(4), 24–29 (2002)
8. Bell, D., et al.: A framework for deriving semantic web services. Inf. Syst. Front. **9**(1), 69–84 (2006)
9. Sabou, M., Pan, J.: Towards semantically enhanced Web service repositories. Web Semant. Sci. Serv. Agents World Wide Web **5**(2), 142–150 (2007)
10. Alam, A., et al.: Proceedings of the 3rd ACM Workshop on Secure Web Services, Alexandria, VA, pp. 69–76. ACM, New York. Retrieved Jan 12, 2011, from http://portal.acm.org.lcproxy. shu.ac.uk/citation.cfm?id=1180367.1180380&coll=ACM&dl=ACM&CFID=26721008&CF TOKEN=93552704 (2006)
11. Smith, H., Fingar, P.: Business Process Management: The Third Wave. Meghan-Kiffer Press, Tampa, Florida, USA (2003)
12. Bridges, S.: The extent and appropriateness of semantic enterprise interoperability with TOGAF9 and ISO Common Logic. Unpublished dissertation, Sheffield Hallam University, Sheffield, UK (2010)
13. Hepp, M., Roman, D.: An ontology framework for semantic business process management. In: Proceedings of Wirtschaftsinformatik, Karlsruhe (2007)
14. Berners-Lee, T., Kagal, L.: The fractal nature of the Semantic Web. AI Mag. **29**(3), 29 (2008)
15. Bridges, S., Schiffel, J., Polovina, S.: OpenSEA: a framework for semantic interoperation between enterprises. In: Bessis, N., Xhafa, F. (eds.) Next Generation Data Technologies for Collective Computational Intelligence. Springer, Heidelberg (2011)

Part III
Issues and Challenges

Chapter 10
The Cloud Challenges for Enterprise Architects

Pethuru Raj and Mohanavadivu Periasamy

Abstract Having understood the significant impact that cloud computing is having on the business sector, the enterprises and business houses are beginning to adopt the cloud paradigm. The business and technical advantages offered by the cloud provision are simply enormous, and so, its adoption and adaption are gaining unprecedented attention and acceleration. Market analysts and researchers have also come out with astronomical figures in order to indicate and insist on the exploding cloud market. Enterprises are formulating schemes and roadmaps for migration to the cloud environment. With the powerful emergence of cloud Computing, enterprises' thinking and planning have also drastically changed. The noteworthy impacts and insights of the cloud idea are being well articulated by cloud infrastructure, platform, software, and service providers. Enterprise architects, in charge of drawing and deciding about open and extensible Enterprise Architectures (EAs), need to relook their current architectures and to ponder about the viable means and mechanisms in order to deftly incorporate the emerging and evolving cloud aspects into their architectures. In this chapter, we have discussed this subject area wherein the architects need to focus more deeply and diligently in order to suggest cloud-inspired enterprise architectures to their executive management. There are also numerous cloud-induced challenges and constraints on EA. These are also described in detail to enable architects to tread carefully in their mission. This chapter is a definite eye-opener as far as clearly describing the cloud insights and implications on the hot domain of EA.

P. Raj (✉)
Enterprise Architect, Sify Software Ltd., 2nd Floor, Tidel Park, Taramani,
Chennai, Tamil Nadu 600113, India
e-mail: peterindia@gmail.com

M. Periasamy
Scientific Research Invision (SRI) Inc., Canada, 4872 Bourret Ave. Apt. # 407 Montreal,
QC H3W1L1, Canada
e-mail: sriinccanada@gmail.com

Z. Mahmood and R. Hill (eds.), *Cloud Computing for Enterprise Architectures*,
Computer Communications and Networks, DOI 10.1007/978-1-4471-2236-4_10,
© Springer-Verlag London Limited 2011

10.1 Introduction

The much-hyped and hoped cloud paradigm is seeing an unprecedented adoption
and adaption across the globe. The path-breaking cloud idea is actually a smart and
sensible combination of several proven and promising technologies such as consolidation, virtualization, optimization, Service Orientation (SO), and an array of computing
paradigms such as cluster, grid, on-demand, and utility computing. The complete and
compact automation of several complicated IT infrastructure management tasks such
as job scheduling, resource provisioning, expansion and contraction of cloud resources,
workload management, virtual machine creation and control, self-servicing, etc.,
remains the key for the upswing of the pioneering cloud technology.

The noteworthy aspect is that cloud infrastructures fulfill myriad quality attributes (nonfunctional requirements such as scalability/elasticity, availability, affordability, adaptability, amenability, alacrity, high performance, etc.). The cloud
paradigm has come as a boon and blessing for enterprise IT as it could introduce and
incorporate a series of innovations and improvisations there in order to realize the
target of business-IT alignment. As we all know, these are the days for business-
driven technologies, and hence, business agility and autonomy can be easily and
quickly attained. This extraordinary success of cloud computing is being spectacularly leveraged and replicated in the vast and varied embedded space. All kinds of
physical and embedded devices are being connected and linked up with clouds
inducing a kind of deeper and deft connectivity among disparate, distributed, and
decentralized devices enabling elegant and exotic applications.

Cloud, being a generic technology, is bound to raise a storm of advancements
and accomplishments across a variety of domains in the days to unfold. In other
words, the cloud space is all set to join as the third major force along with the enterprise and web spaces in accurately understanding peoples' needs, conceiving, con-
ceptualizing, and concretizing the identified requirements in the form of services
and applications that can be delivered unobtrusively to the right people at the right
time at the right place. Thus, there is a close linkup between cloud and the emerging
and evolving ideas and ideals of IT people. Cloud is bringing the much-needed
transition from the expensive IT to elastic, elegant, and finally exotic IT. The cloud
space is seeing much more value and verve as entrepreneurs, employees, and executives are on the know-how of the interruptive, disruptive, and transformative nature
of cloud technology.

10.2 Next-Generation Cloud Services

All kinds of enterprise services and applications are being modernized, migrated,
and managed in converged, dynamic, real-time, and adaptive cloud infrastructures
and platforms. In the recent past, we are being told that embedded services too are
being moved to clouds in order to reap the unique advantages being offered by cloud
infrastructures. There are several established as well as start-up companies in
offering lean, green, and self-manageable clouds. Platforms providers too are very

enthusiastically active in this space. Newer deployment and delivery models have erupted and are being consistently supported to reach greater heights. In a nutshell, it is all about distributed, decentralized, and disparate cloud centers taking care of growing array of different services, applications, and data (personal as well as professional). This induces and inspires the need for reflective and versatile cloud brokers (a kind of middleware for connecting, integrating, and composing people-centric and context-aware cloud services) and brokerage services firms. Primarily brokerage services involve discovery, negotiation, intermediation, arbitration, integration, and collaboration services in order to help cloud consumers as well as providers in enhancing the technical and business values.

As per the Gartner's latest market research and analysis report on the cloud Computing, there is a huge market out there for cloud brokerage services. Novel services and applications are being built by individuals, innovators, and institutions with the solitary goal of supplying them to the world from clouds. As the visibility, agility, availability, and acceptability of cloud services, platforms, and infrastructures are becoming prominent and dominant, there is a new group of companies and corporations emerging and establishing to act as connectors, brokers, mediators, arbitrators, and decision-makers of a variety of cloud resources.

10.2.1 Next-Generation Infrastructures for Cloud Enterprises

We need robust and resilient infrastructures and platforms for hosting, delivering, monitoring, regulating, and governing cloud services and applications. Cloud-empowered enterprises are the direct extension of Service-Oriented Enterprises (SOEs), and Service-Oriented Infrastructure (SOI) is the key for SOEs.

There are informative and inspiring literatures on service platforms and their features and functionalities. In the recent past, there is a new product called as Service Delivery Platform (SDP). The telecommunication industry first incorporated the SDP in the infrastructure kitty, and today there is a greater awareness and articulation across industries about SDP.

The Enterprise Service-Oriented Architecture (ESOA), which is a hybrid of Service-Oriented Architecture (SOA) and EA styles, is an abstraction of concrete enterprise service-oriented architectures, which includes SOA architectural elements, service design patterns as well as principles, and SOA quality attributes shown in Figs. 10.1.

It can be extended to a new style for realizing enterprise cloud computing. The principles of enterprise service-oriented computing facilitate the enterprise-wide adoption of cloud computing. The well-deliberated and defined ESOA style is to lead to a new hybrid architectural style, Enterprise Cloud Service Architecture (ECSA) [6]. ESOA introduces new challenges and issues to EA due to its on-premise characteristics.

- Enterprise owns a huge data center with ESOA services. However, the infrastructure is not dynamic such that it does not support auto scaling and elastic load balancing.
- Resources are dedicated to each workload and shared within the enterprise only.

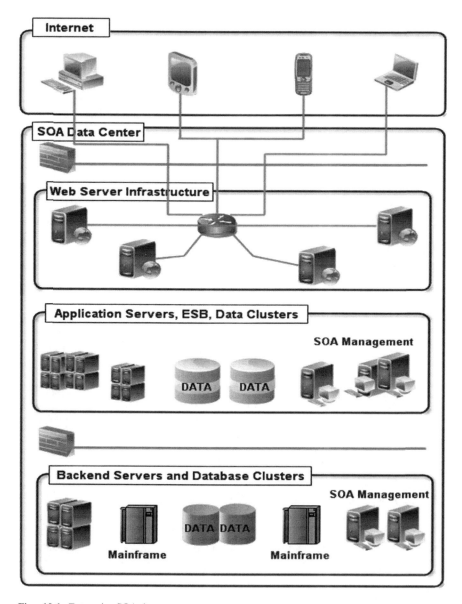

Figs. 10.1 Enterprise SOA data center

A traditional ESOA data center in Figs. 10.1 prominently comprises three-layer infrastructures.

- Web server infrastructure (Web Tier)
- Enterprise application server and service infrastructure which includes application database and SOA services, application monitors and SOA application management (Business Tier)

- Enterprise information storage and business service infrastructure (Storage Tier)

Further on, network connectivity tier comprises routers, security solutions, load balancers, switches, gateways, proxies, etc. As usual, enterprise services would run behind firewalls. Building a data center to support ESOA architecture is prohibitively expensive. It is impossible for small to medium enterprises. For large enterprise, it is still more difficult to develop and sustain data centers as its business processes are generally more complex, distributed, decentralized, etc., as it has to connect and collaborate dynamically with its business partners, retailers, suppliers, customers, and other stakeholders.

Moreover, many racks of servers in any large data center are sitting idle or passive especially during the non-peak hours, and resources are usually over-provisioned to meet up any unexpected spike or surge in resource usage. Thus, expensive resources are terribly wasted and more number of servers means more personnel for manning and managing data centers effectively. In short, higher energy consumption, heat dissipation and greenhouse gas emission, increased costs for operators, etc., insist on exploring, experimenting, and espousing cloud computing solutions. Also the present-day data centers are not enabling business agility, alacrity, and affordability.

Cloud computing is about sharing services, computation, and/or data off-site via an internal or external, location-transparent, centralized facility or contractor for lower cost and business benefits. Services and data, made available in the cloud, can be more easily and ubiquitously accessed, often at much lower cost, increase their value by creating opportunities for enhanced collaboration, integration, and analysis on a shared common platform. Therefore, adding cloud computing to ESOA takes it to the next level and expands it from on-premise to off-premise (Figs. 10.2).

10.2.2 Cloud Infrastructure Evaluation Parameters

Given the technological and organizational risks associated with the existing public cloud computing solutions, IT organizations evaluating these solutions need to determine if:

- Whether the cloud infrastructure is standardized, consolidated, virtualized, and optimized.
- Whether the infrastructure is modular, simplified, automated (automation of resource provisioning, virtual machine creation, expansion, contraction, retirement, etc., job scheduling and load balancing, change and configuration management, service governance, fault diagnosis, patch management)
- Whether the cloud migration is made simpler and quicker
- Whether disaster recovery, business continuity, cloud center security, data integrity and confidentiality, etc., are facilitated by the cloud infrastructure providers
- Whether service integration, composition, and provisioning, flexible offerings, etc., are enabled

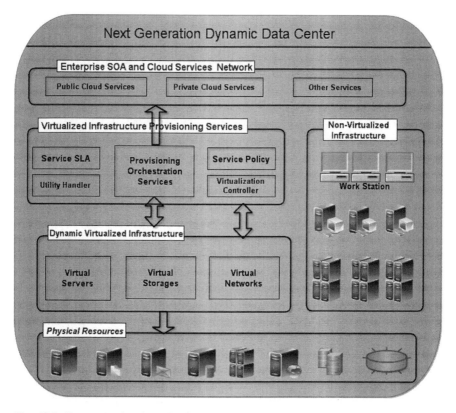

Figs. 10.2 Next-generation dynamic data center

10.2.3 Characteristics of Responsible Cloud Infrastructure

There is another twist and here comes responsible clouds. There are best practices
and key guidelines galore for carefully designing responsible clouds, which are well
managed to provide secure, compliant, and high-quality business service.
Responsible cloud environments [4] deliver more secure, reliable, and flexible IT
services to meet organizational requirements and reduce both capital and operational expenses. Whether building a responsible cloud infrastructure from existing
computing resources or an entirely new environment from the ground up, three
areas of focus should dominate design considerations: effectively size the infrastructure, ensure high availability, and minimize operating expenses.

The number of powerful servers in a Cloud center has a direct and distinct impact
on the cost (capital as well as operational). Additionally, the number of potential
security and failure points is proportionally decreased, improving overall reliability.
Consolidated servers are also more easily pooled and can better accommodate the
use of shared services, such as with commonly accessible storage and clustering.

This allows new resources to be more rapidly provisioned to meet service demands. Capacity planning is essential for effective infrastructure sizing. Systems that consolidate a large number of resources, such as blade servers and mainframes, are physically larger and more powerful than standard servers. Automated tools should be employed to track system and environmental resources availability so that instant and informed decisions can be made on the most effective ways to size and expand cloud services to meet an expected growth in service requirements.

Since cloud services are expected to be accessible all the time with high throughput, high availability is considered as a mandatory infrastructure requirement. Clustered servers have the requisite ability to be rapidly expanded, and the real differentiator is that they are able to load balance system resources instantaneously so that there would not be any breakdown and letdown. That is, they could provide uninterrupted fail-over services in the event an individual server experiences a catastrophic failure or requires downtime for maintenance. Clustered environments are typically contained within a single physical location so that they can share storage systems and do not have any performance latency due to WAN traffic.

Large cloud implementations typically have multiple clustered environments at multiple facilities at different locations. This allows failover of a Cloud service in the event of a site disaster due to a flood or fire. Individual cloud instances can be expanded to operate across multiple clustered environments, both local and remote, to create a "hub and spoke" architecture that ensures highly available and reliable compute services. Scores of automated tools should be employed to monitor the health of these systems as well as the availability of support services, such as power and network connectivity.

10.2.4 Key Resources in Cloud Infrastructure Management

As noted above, adept and assistive tools are very essential for the design and maintenance of a responsible Cloud infrastructure. They enable quick identification of the environmental health and status to facilitate effective capacity and environment planning, problem anticipation and instant resolution, and capacity expansion and contraction as needed to rapidly adjust to changing support requirements. Data center asset and configuration information is collected into a centralized repository that provides a holistic view of the cloud implementation. Not only does this provide a single point of access for viewing details about individual IT components but it also provides insight into how those components interact.

Modeling solutions can provide easily digestible and actionable infrastructure intelligence which is critical for enabling rapid cloud expansion to meet changing customer requirements. Intelligent modeling solutions go further to allow organizations to generate hypothetical scenarios so that quick and informed decisions can be made on infrastructure growth and improvement [3]. For instance, before adding a new server to an existing cluster, a modeling solution can identify if there is sufficient rack space, power, networking, and structural support for the new server. Since responsible cloud environments must rapidly adapt to support requirement changes without diminishing infrastructure reliability, a modeling solution can be an indispensable tool.

10.2.5   Identity Management Suite for Cloud Enterprises

Today's extended enterprises face the challenge of providing everywhere, every time, and every device access to business-critical applications and resources not just to employees but also to business partners, retailers, and suppliers and customers. The current setup is that these resources are available via web-based applications or network applications accessed through a Virtual Private Network (VPN). The task of managing which users can access which resources, both for security purposes and compliance requirements necessitating documentation of access privileges and actual usage, is often costly and time-consuming. This challenge has become even greater in recent years for organizations moving to cloud-based software solutions, which can be deployed more quickly than premises-based solutions.

The highly popular cloud applications getting deployed, managed, delivered, and billed are salesforce.com, the prominent online, on-demand, remote, off-premise Customer Relationship Management (CRM) suite, Ramco systems' Enterprise Resource Planning (ERP) package, etc. Security solutions too are being delivered from clouds these days.

The job of "managing the management" can be overwhelming for those who would rather have resources focused on strategic services – which is why many organizations have been moving key business applications, ranging from ERP to CRM, to the Cloud in a SaaS-based model. There are highly scalable directory services and identity management solutions in clouds. These cloud-based software modules offer compelling business efficiencies, less total cost of ownership (TCO), higher return on investment (ROI), etc. Other benefits include:

- *Centralized management for SaaS and enterprise applications* – Provides consistent application of policies across resources, reduces password management and authentication challenges, and helps strengthen security by providing secure sign-on to web applications, and VPN access to network resources.
- *Decreased implementation risks* – Eliminating the computer hardware and platform software components (such as relational databases, operating systems, security appliances, maintenance and management tools, etc.) and decreasing the overall implementation time help lower the probability for project delays and implementation failure risk.
- *Accelerated implementations fulfill business agility* – Without the incurred time and technical issues associated with the installation and configuration of data center appliances, hardware servers, platform software, and related computing hardware, Secure Access Services pre-configured deployment model offers a jump start and a decreased implementation period.

- *Cost control and affordability* – It is a well-known fact that the cloud principle has brought in a dramatic change from capital expense to operational expenditure. On-demand identity management that delivers enterprise-class identity capabilities without the investments required with software. It promises more predictable costs – no need to buy, install, configure, and operate expensive servers and software, or hire additional IT staff.
- *Demonstrable security* – Secure Access Services reside in SAS 70 Type II audited data centers with enterprise-class security monitoring and defenses that are designed to meet the stringent security requirements of financial services, health care, and government organizations.
- *Greater focus on core business activities* – Outsourcing the management of identity, security, and related business applications to experts allows internal IT resources to focus their time on core competencies, higher priority projects, and strategic services.

Now, with the opportunity to take advantage of hosted Identity and Access Management (IAM), we can deploy applications faster, control IAM operational and staffing costs, enjoy user-based and operational expense pricing models, and provide consistent, secure access to our resources. Smaller organizations can now take advantage of security technology that may have been previously beyond their reach, and larger organizations can upgrade and extend access control to the applications that were not brought under management due to resource constraints.

10.3   The Impact of Cloud Computing on the Service Industry

Service organizations are keenly watching the eruption and evolution of the cloud paradigm. There are significant disruptions and distractions for services companies. Cloud computing represents a golden opportunity to spend less on IT and instead to focus more on customers and to grow the service business. Customer satisfaction and delight are the direct output of the smart incorporation of cloud concepts. Modern and multi-tenant platforms allow thousands of customers to share the same IT resources. This leads to tremendous saving on IT spend. Agile services firms can grow quickly to meet new market demands. As indicated elsewhere, cloud computing facilitates IT agility by scaling up and down very rapidly to meet new requirements. Cloud technologies are making it extremely easy to configure services or to build fresh applications very quickly.

As a case study, take the case of Appirio [1]. What sort of growth it has achieved? It has built the business entirely on the cloud. From the beginning, the company has made the conscious decision to operate as a server-less enterprise. Professional Services Automation (PSA) is a software tool to help IT consultants, application approvers, and implementers for effective project and resource managements for clients' enterprise projects. PSA is accomplished by developing IT admin rules to quantify and qualify fledgling enterprise business processes to streamline and update to facilitate new addition.

They have run their communication and collaboration on Google Apps, their CRM on Salesforce.com, their marketing on Merketo, their financials on Intacct, the core operations of their services business on PS Enterprise, and the Professional Services Automation (PSA) application that they have built on Force.com. Besides achieving financial savings, a range of innovations have been elegantly enabled by cloud infrastructure. The cloud-based applications allow them to engage with their clients, customers, and consultants, and the broader community using next-generation sales and marketing techniques.

- *Client engagement* – Thanks to Force.com and Marketo, they have a single window and view of their multiple engagement points with clients: phone, email, etc.
- *Consultant engagement* – They have encouraged every consultant in their service business to contribute for their sales process. As both CRM and PSA are on the same platform, consultants have the chance to identify and influence newer opportunities with previously engaged customers.
- *Community engagement* – The cloud infrastructure allows engaging with potential customers, partners, and employees in the broader community through social networks.

It is presumed and predicted that over the years, most of the professional services organizations will run on catalytic and elastic cloud infrastructures. This is termed as cloudsourcing, which represents the transformative convergence of cloud and outsourcing. Cloudsourcing is an emerging trend and mechanism for managing IT across the enterprise that relies on partners to provide cloud-based IT applications and services necessary to support the business. It reflects a newer and better change in how IT is implemented, delivered, and consumed. The services industry is well positioned to continue leading the way in this transition. Services firms are people-centric businesses without complex supply chains or large amounts of physical assets that require on-premise IT management. This leads to greater agility and ability to sense and capture new business opportunities. Process modification becomes quicker and easier to implement any incoming and impending projects. Corporates and companies can spend their energy, resources, and money on core competencies and external experts on the rest. Establishing and running IT infrastructures, platforms, and applications to cloud service providers are the best strategy to grow and glow.

- *What next?* – The steps to be contemplated and completed are varying for different organizations. Here come some guiding principles to keep in mind while an enterprise architect sits for formulating a comprehensive enterprise strategy.
- *Start small* – We do not need a full-fledged roadmap and go-forward enterprise architecture to get started with cloud computing. Instead of setting up a spreadsheet or Lotus Notes application to track part of business, sign up for a Force.com account. Or sign up for a free Google Apps account and create a cloud-based spreadsheet with an online form.
- *Think big* – Once we are fully convinced with the business results due to the initial migration, then plunge into charting out a realistic path to move the core parts of the business to a cloud-based infrastructure. Consider and calculate the benefits of managing people, projects, customers, and transactions on Force.com

using a solution from the AppExchange or analyze how much is saved through the switching of the email and file sharing from Microsoft to Google Apps.

Modernization has been an ongoing process as legacy systems and services are being gradually replaced by modern technology-enabled solutions. With the arrival of cloud computing, server infrastructure undergoes through consolidation, virtualization, automation, and federation processes. That is, cloud enablement is the latest buzzword, and enterprises are very optimistic and opportunistic in recognizing and realizing cloud-compatible systems and solutions. Cloud has since then opened up newer avenues for fresh revenues for consulting organizations for providing cloud modernization, migration, and management strategy services.

10.3.1   Characteristics of Optimized Cloud Infrastructures

Given the technological [2] and organizational risks associated with public cloud offerings, organizations strategizing to move to cloud have to check those Cloud Service Providers (CSPs) to determine if:

- The IaaS services are optimized to support their applications.
- Their applications will run on the optimized cloud infrastructure.
- Organizational silos will impede the effective management of the overall solution.

10.3.1.1   Standardization, Simplification, and Modularization

The infrastructure should be strictly standards-based. The infrastructural components such as servers, switches, gateways, appliances, storage networks, etc., have to be highly modular in order to support flexibility and modifiability. Also the infrastructure has to be sensitive and simplified for configuration, customization, and consumption.

10.3.1.2   Virtualization

CSPs have to have extensive virtualization strategy as almost all IT resources such as server, storage, database, application, service, network, desktop, etc. Lately there are microvisors to enable virtualization of embedded devices.

10.3.1.3   Automated Management System

The CSPs must have automated as many of the data center processes as possible. This includes orchestration and provisioning, change and configuration management, resource reallocation, service monitoring, fault diagnosis, and software updates and maintenance.

10.3.1.4 Availability and Security

There must be an appropriate level of redundancy throughout the infrastructure, coupled with a fast failover capability to secondary or backup resources. There also must be a multilayer security architecture that provides full isolation of virtual data centers and also provides the option of screening all host-to-host traffic within each tenant's virtual data center.

Cloud infrastructures are technically advanced and are a pool of modular, consolidated, virtualized, and automated server systems. Service centricity is the base criterion.

10.4 Cloud Issues for Enterprise Architects

The much-proclaimed cloud approach is definitely a trendsetter and clearly represents a tremendous shift in the IT field. The cloud paradigm is fast maturing and stabilizing toward a comprehensive technology for not only service providers but also service consumers and brokers. The tactical and strategic implications are many. Data centers and server farms are being relooked, rekindled, and recognized as cloud centers. Every single IT resource is being transformed and exposed as virtual resource. A variety of automation tools are being introduced for effective leverage, monitor, and management of all kinds of virtual resources. Business applications, services, and data are being accordingly modernized as cloud ready and multi-tenant modules and exposed as virtualized entities. IT infrastructures and platforms too travel in that same route. It is not an exaggeration to say that the creation, sustenance, and usage of virtualized infrastructures are being announced as the spectacular and salient feature behind the cloud journey. It is being visualized that cloud computing model brings together four dimensions of complexity.

- Applications and services will further evolve from being monolithic and static toward composite and dynamic. This, in turn, increases the reliance on network performance as well as the separation from the traditional data center.
- IT infrastructure will continue to shift from physical to virtual dependence, complicating IT orchestration with more moving parts.
- Operational domains of control will move from single to dual toward multiple, which isolates operational decisions from management-based policy and complicates SLA and performance management.
- Business models move from per-instance licensing to pay-as-you-go licensing, which will require better project financial management and exploration into chargeback methods.

These evolving characteristics of dynamic applications, virtual IT infrastructure, multiple operational domains of control, and pay-as-you-go business models are in fact the common characteristics of cloud computing environments. Inherently, there is more to cloud services than just IT resources consumed on demand. However, it has brought forth a fresh set of ills and issues that cannot be taken lightly as their compact resolution leads to greater acceptance. Enterprise architect has to take extra care and pain toward analyzing and articulating the pros and cons of embarking the cloud method. As far as the third-party, external, commercial-grade, and public clouds are concerned, the major problem areas blocking the widespread adoption of the cloud style are listed below:

- Security and privacy
- Controllability and flexibility
- Visibility and availability
- Auditability and accountability
- Latency, performance/throughput
- Compliance

Private clouds are solving most of the pain areas of public clouds. However, the much-anticipated utility model gets missed out in private clouds, which are catering the needs of a limited set of users. For energy and cost efficiency and for vertical applications, community clouds are being recommended. All kinds of underutilized and unutilized compute machines are being networked, clustered, and virtualized to act as community clouds that are capable of effortlessly tackling the specific needs of a particular community. Then hybrid clouds are being suggested for enabling a seamless connectivity between private and public clouds in times of greater needs of computing. Further on, horizontally, there are several other advancements such as open cloud, inter-cloud, interoperable cloud, delta cloud, multi-cloud, etc. Vertically, there are data cloud, service cloud, application cloud, knowledge cloud, etc.

As overwhelming majority of users have voted and voiced that security is the main stumbling block and hence CSPs and academic researchers are working overtime in minimizing the malevolent security threats and risks in order to reinforce the sagging image of cloud computing, as virtual machines occupy higher value in the catalytic cloud arena, newer security holes via virtual machines have come to light. As the access for the public cloud is mainly through the Internet, which is being positioned as the cost-effective, common, and compact communication infrastructure, all kinds of cloud sources and resources are liable for intensive and intimidate hacking, intrusion, and transgression. Therefore, myriad intercontinental initiatives are being expedited to unearth impenetrable and unbreakable security algorithms and solutions. There are security-specific best practices, key guidelines, and metrics that can be very much suggested by enterprise architects while formulating the enterprise security strategy and framework. The currently used security mechanisms are also strengthened to be utilized for cloud systems. Infrastructure as a Service (IaaS) providers are lately open to provide more controllability, flexibility, modifiability, etc. Other drawbacks too are also being attended seriously.

10.4.1 Capabilities of Cloud Management Solutions

In the past, the underpinning of a business service was limited to IT resources that were wholly owned by the provider of that service. This invited silo-based approaches to management of services in areas such as system, network, security, and IT governance. But with cloud computing, the business service architecture will cross the organizational boundary and become a composition of diverse resources which are separately managed within different domains. Hence, it will not be enough for traditional IT management solutions to simply extend capabilities into this distributed and decentralized model. Cloud-centric IT management has to view the business service from the top-down, and provide capabilities in the following key areas:

• *Dynamic cloud service automation* – Automate control, update, and movement within the heterogeneous, multi-location IT infrastructure supporting our applications and data. This results in a more flexible environment which can support variable, up-to-the-minute business requirements, with an eye toward maintaining SLAs.
• *Cloud service quality and scalability* – Manage a composite transaction end-to-end, from the end-user's perspective through to the visible infrastructure. This assures that cloud service performance and availability meet expectations.
• *End-to-end cloud service visibility* – Visibility into the components of a composite application which may reside in multiple organizational domains. This will optimize our resource management and utilization, streamline IT processes, and reduce costs.
• *Security management and federation* – Manage the security and compliance of identities and information as they flow between organizational domains. This will unify identity and centralize policy access and control.

10.4.2 Service-Oriented Cloud Computing Architectures

There are some peculiar obstacles in the current cloud implementations. Migration to cloud is not an easy or rosy affair. Multi-tenancy is a key differentiator for the cloud style. There has to be a sharp improvisation in the cloud user interfaces in order to make more common and casual. Other pain areas are:

• *Vendor lock-in* – Applications developed and run in one platform could not deploy and run in another platform. The migration effort is enormous and time-consuming. Often, migration simply means redevelopment. For example, applications deployed on Amazon EC2 cannot be migrated easily due its particular storage framework. Applications developed on Google App Engine are not interoperable with other applications built on other platforms.
• *Computing components are tightly coupled* – This tight coupling between various cloud resources such as infrastructures, platforms, and software is clearly

hampering users' choices, comforts, and conveniences. This hurdle and hitch is definitely to affect the multidimensional and directional growth of the cloud ecosystem. The openness, transparency, flexibility, and modifiability are the direct damages of this tightness in coupling.

IBM considers current single providers cloud as limited resource, and the lack of interoperability among cloud providers prevents deployment across different clouds. A cloud computing architecture named Reservoir was proposed to create a federation from multiple cloud providers which acts as a global fabric of resources that can guarantee the required SLA. In Reservoir architecture, the computational resources within a site are partitioned by a virtualization layer into Virtual Execution Environments (VEEs). A service application is decomposed into a set of software components/services running on VEEs on the same or different VEEs within a site or across from different sites. However, Reservoir architecture does not allow a component/service to run on its duplicates on different VEEs. Moreover, computing resources are abstracted as hosting service which might not be necessarily true for all clouds.

SOA and cloud computing are related; specifically, SOA is an architectural pattern that guides business solutions to create, organize, and reuse its computing components, while cloud computing is a set of enabling technology that services a bigger, more flexible platform for enterprise to build their SOA solutions. In other words, SOA and cloud computing will coexist, complement, and support each other. There have been several initiatives at attempting bridging SOA and cloud computing.

10.4.3 SOCCA Layers

The service-oriented cloud computing architecture is layer centric, and the prominent layers are being described in detail below.

10.4.3.1 Individual Cloud Provider Layer

This layer resembles the current cloud implementations. Each cloud provider builds its own data centers that power the cloud services it provides. Each cloud may have its own proprietary virtualization technology or utilize open-source virtualization software. The distinction from current cloud implementations is that the cloud computing resources in SOCCA are componentized into independent services such as storage service, computing service, and communication service, with open-standardized interfaces, so they can be combined with services from other cloud providers to build a cross-platform virtual computer on the clouds. In order to achieve maximum interoperability, uniform standards need to be implemented.

10.4.3.2   Cloud Ontology Mapping Layer

Cloud providers might not conform to the standards rigidly, and they might also have to incorporate extra features to lure buyers. Cloud ontology mapping layer exists to mask the differences among the different individual cloud providers, and it can help the migration of cloud application from one cloud to another. Several important ontology systems are needed:

- *Storage ontology* – It defines the concepts and terms related to data manipulation on the clouds, such as data update, date insert, data delete, and data select, etc.
- *Computing ontology* – It defines the concepts and terms related to distribute computing on the clouds, such as map/reduce framework.
- *Communication ontology* – It defines the concepts and terms related to communication schema among the clouds, such as data encoding schema and message routing.

10.4.3.3   Cloud Broker Layer

Cloud brokers serve as the agents between individual cloud providers and SOA layer. Each major cloud service has an associated service broker type.

10.4.3.4   SOA Layer

This layer fully takes the advantages of the existing research and infrastructure from traditional SOA. Many existing SOA frameworks can be integrated into this layer. There are several concerns and challenges to be taken into consideration before deciding the best course of action for cloud-enabled enterprises.

10.5   Approaches for Cloud Enablement

Everyone is jumping into the cloud bandwagon in order to cut short their IT budget, to enable IT flexibility, to facilitate IT innovation, and to make IT people-friendly. With the faster stabilization of cloud technology, there is a renewed call to embrace it vigorously and rigorously. There are functioning applications that need to be modernized to be cloud compliant. Also there are mechanisms and methods being formulated for efficiently creating newer cloud applications from the scratch in a cloud-aware manner. In this section, we have given a potentially sound approach to move to cloud IT easily and quickly.

10.5.1   Bottom-Up Approach

The currently running services and applications can be appropriately amended before hosting them in private and/or public clouds. As the existing applications were not designed to be cloud-compliant, some refactoring and remedial steps need to be considered and performed. This approach is the starting point for most of the enterprises as legacy applications cannot be just thrown away. Also building, testing, and deploying newer applications in the place of existing applications are time-consuming and prohibitively expensive.

10.5.2   Top-Down Approach

This [5] is the most appropriate approach for future. Next-generation services and applications have to be analyzed, architected, and constructed for the cloud landscape from the ground up. Business conditions and constraints have to be taken into account while designing cloud-based applications. Primarily multi-tenancy is an important design feature not to be sidestepped. However, incorporation of multi-tenancy technique squarely depends on the application requirements and targets. There is a widespread view that all cloud services have to be multi-tenant as multi-tenancy puts a dampener for high performance, security, visibility, controllability, availability, etc. The overall system view too has to play a big role while designing and developing cloud applications. As articulated somewhere, there are some distinct qualities for the cloud environment. Applications and services ultimately move into a cloud infrastructure, which is highly converged, dynamic, virtualized, shared, and elastic. So the top-down approach to cloud enablement requires more involved and intensive application architecture like enterprise-scale applications.

10.5.3   TOGAF

The TOGAF framework provides a compact model and a process that is capable of incorporating both business and IT requirements into the Enterprise Architecture (EA) holistically and harmoniously. TOGAF Architecture Development Method (ADM) defines a vision, which aims to:

- Obtain the management commitment
- Validate business principles
- Define scope
- Identify stakeholders
- Define business requirements
- Describe appropriate solutions
- Obtain formal approval to proceed

These initial tasks are very much required for effective cloud empowerment. The prevailing trend is that business processes are increasingly tightly coupled with underlying cloud services. Various TOGAF architectural assessments are hence a natural fit for a top-down approach toward cloud enablement.

Tailoring of TOGAF architecture views for cloud applications – While TOGAF ADM is a good foundation to architect and design cloud applications from the top-down perspective, the architectural views defined in this framework need to be twisted and tweaked in order to simplify and streamline cloud enablement.

Business architecture – involves business goals, processes, and components. How the identified goals are being met by business processes and components is the main concern of business architecture. Also the architecture has to be very nimble and open for taking care of business changes and challenges quickly. Business architecture has a direct impact on business users.

Business applications are typically delivered from enterprise server machines. Now with the emergence of powerful and affordable cloud servers, business services and applications are to be deployed and delivered from the new environment. Applications to be cloud ready have to undergo some critical changes. The business architecture has to take care of security, privacy, and other quality attributes of cloud-based applications. Governance, visibility, and controllability are other important factors to be given a serious thought. There has to be a kind of synchronization between enterprise resources (services and data) and cloud-based applications.

Data architecture views – which address the concerns of database designers and database administrators, and system engineers responsible for developing and integrating the various database components of the system

Entity relationship to multi-tenancy for cloud applications – The core entity relationship (ER) modeling of a cloud application may match that of its traditional enterprise application counterpart. However, multi-tenancy aspect will introduce new variations to the logical data model. Also the process models for data security view will be totally different from a traditional enterprise application.

Applications architecture views – which address the concerns of system and software engineers responsible for developing and integrating the various application software components of the system. This includes custom-built shelf software to be converted into SaaS.

COTS to SaaS which addresses the concerns of acquirers (procurement personnel responsible for acquiring the commercial off-the-shelf (COTS) software and hardware to be included in the system), operations staff, systems administrators, and systems managers

Variation for cloud applications – The Platform as a Service (PaaS) will abstract several traditional components that are part of the application architecture view, and hence, this view will be different from a traditional enterprise application. Due to the tenants of cloud application like:

- Virtualized server environment
- PaaS platform
- On-demand instances

- Other virtual storage considerations, this view will be the one that will go through maximum changes for a cloud application when compared to a normal application.

The adoption of the cloud idea is to impact the enterprise architecture, and EA frameworks too have to go through a number of transformations in order to be directly usable for the on-demand world.

10.6   Conclusion

Bringing cloud capabilities to an enterprise is about more than just the latest technology; it is about changing the traditional business and collaboration model with partners, customers, and providers of services to the enterprise. It is much more important for companies to understand the changing trends in business and their impacts on enterprise architecture than to just implement the next "hot" technology product. The enterprise architect has a lot to do in helping enterprises define the best strategy to leverage the blooming and booming cloud method.

The key differentiation of cloud computing is to break the dependencies of applications on underlying hardware. This separation allows for more efficiency, easier management, better resiliency, and lower overall IT costs. The inference is that cloud computing can divide the data center into an application cloud, a hardware cloud, and a computing cloud. Rather than tying specific applications to hardware (such as servers, network ports, etc.), the applications can be separated and managed as independent clouds. As a result of this independence, applications can move from server to server, even data center to data center without performance degradation or data loss. Hosting applications that formerly resided on individual desktops further enable users to access necessary applications from anywhere. Cloud is a mixture of centralized and distributed architectures. Centralized management brings effectiveness for efficient service delivery where a distributed resource supports fault-tolerance, high availability, cost reduction, etc.

References

1. Appirio: Professional Services Cloud: What Cloud Computing Means for the Services Industry. White Paper: Appirio Inc., San Mateo, USA (2010)
2. Ashton, Metzler, & Associates: Optimizing the Cloud Infra-Structure for Enterprise Applications. White Paper: Ashton, Metzler, & Associates, Sanibel, Florida, USA (2010)
3. GAO: Organizational Transformation: A Framework for Assessing and Improving Enterprise Architecture Management (Version 2.0) (Supersedes GAO-03–584G). GAO, Washington, DC, USA (2010)
4. Steve, B.: Designing a Responsible Cloud Infrastructure. An Enterprise management associates® (EMA™). White Paper Prepared for Avocent® (2010)

5. Sundara Rajan, S.: Cloud Enterprise Architecture and TOGAF – A top-down approach to building new Cloud applications, SYS-CON Media, Inc. Nov 19 (2010)
6. Tang, L., Dong, J., Zhao, Y., Zhang, L.-J.: Enterprise cloud service architecture. In: IEEE 3rd International Conference on Cloud Computing (CLOUD), July 2010, vol. 5, pp. 27–34. doi:10.1109/CLOUD.2010.10, isbn:978–0–7695–4130–3

Chapter 11
Service Level Agreements in Cloud Computing: Perspectives of Private Consumers and Small-to-Medium Enterprises

G.R. Gangadharan and Davide Maria Parrilli

Abstract Service Level Agreements (SLAs) are the means through which the provision of infrastructure, platform, and software services in Cloud Computing is regulated, along with functional and non-functional specifications of services. SLAs are intended to set a framework for the provision of services and for the cooperation between service providers and service consumers. Currently, Cloud SLAs are usually drafted by Cloud providers and do not allow much negotiation. Therefore, it becomes critical to analyze and assess if, and to what extent, the rights and the expectations of Cloud users (in particular private consumers and small and medium-sized enterprises) are respected by these SLAs and by existing legal mechanisms. With this perspective, in this chapter, we analyze whether the current Cloud SLAs are sufficiently in accordance with rights (if any) and business expectations of users in protecting their data concerns and whether they are able to establish trust between Cloud consumers and Cloud providers.

11.1 Introduction

Service Level Agreements (SLAs) are one of the most common approaches for specifying some form of mutual understanding about business transactions between a provider (seller) and a consumer (buyer) in the software and telecommunications domain. An SLA is a representation of all features (including the functionality

G.R. Gangadharan (✉)
Institute for Development & Research in Banking Technology [IDRBT],
Castle Hills, Road No.1, Masab Tank, Hyderabad 500 057, India
e-mail: geeyaar@gmail.com

D.M. Parrilli
time.lex Information & Technology law firm, Congresstraat 35, 1000 Brussels, Belgium
e-mail: davide.parrilli@timelex.eu

Z. Mahmood and R. Hill (eds.), *Cloud Computing for Enterprise Architectures*,
Computer Communications and Networks, DOI 10.1007/978-1-4471-2236-4_11,
© Springer-Verlag London Limited 2011

delivered by the service and the quality that the buyer experiences) a consumer should expect to receive by a service [19]. Thus, an SLA represents functional and non-functional properties of services and serves as a way for controlling and managing these properties. Typically, an SLA is a bilateral binding statement signed between a service provider and a service consumer, over the agreed terms and conditions of the given service [27]. An SLA also sets out the remedial action and any penalties that could take effect if performance falls below the promised standard. SLAs play a pivotal role in Cloud Computing, the current technological evolution of information and communications technology. The revolutionary technology of Cloud Computing offers a scalable and flexible paradigm where infrastructure, platform, and software are offered to users in the form of "services," accessible anytime, anywhere. The provisioning of these computing services by Cloud providers are regulated by SLAs [20].

The basic assumption of this chapter is that SLAs applied in current Cloud-based business scenarios are usually not negotiated between the parties involved [23], at least in business to consumer (B2C) transactions and in business to business (B2B) operations where the client is a small and medium enterprise (SME) without a de facto notable power to negotiate the terms of the agreement with the Cloud provider. In case of an SME, the purchase of Cloud services is not likely to involve a notable amount of money (at least from the provider's perspective), and therefore, the SME in general cannot negotiate the terms of provisioning the services by the provider (at least when the transaction concerns common Cloud services that do not need to be tailored by the provider according to the user's needs).

The abovementioned lack of bargaining power may have several reasons: Basically, private individuals (consumers) and SMEs do not have the possibility to negotiate the content of the SLA simply because the provider does not have interest in doing so. In contrast, the Cloud provider intends to negotiate the content of the SLA with big clients where a large amount of money is involved. From a practical perspective, it is not feasible for a Cloud provider to negotiate the content of the SLAs with every user. The costs of negotiation would be huge, and this would impede the effective deployment and business exploitation of Cloud technologies.

According to the legal framework of the European Union[1] (that will be taken into consideration in this chapter), a consumer is a person acting outside his trade or profession, i.e., a natural (opposed to legal) person that uses Cloud services for his/her private goals. For example, if a professional such as an engineer buys Cloud services to store the photographs of his/her last holidays, he is deemed to be a consumer. If the same engineer buys the same Cloud services to store business records regarding his activities as self-employed or company, he will be considered as a business (and thus not a consumer).[2] In this chapter, we refer to users

---

[1] Inter alia by art. 15(1) of the Rome I Regulation, Regulation (EC) No 593/2008 of the European Parliament and of the Council of 17 June 2008 on the law applicable to contractual obligations (OJ L177, 4.7.2008, pp. 6–16).

[2] The European Court of Justice, in the case C-269/05 *Francesco Beniscasa v. Dentalkit S.r.l.* (ECR 1997, I-3767), decided that consumer contracts concern only agreements whose aim is to satisfy the private consumption needs of an individual, supposed to be the weakest party.

(including both consumers and SMEs) that usually de facto cannot negotiate the content of the SLA with the technology supplier. In other words, we analyze the risks and challenges faced by such typical users that buy Cloud services.

In the situations concerning consumers and small business clients, the user has only two possibilities: accept the SLA as it is, and therefore buy the Cloud services, or reject it. As there are no margins left for negotiation, this may impose several problems. In particular, from the perspective of consumers, it has to be assessed if, and to what extent, the rights and expectations of these specific users are respected. This chapter aims precisely inter alia at analyzing these issues (together with the matters relating to users' privacy and mechanisms to establish trust among users), starting from the typical contents of commercial Cloud SLAs and from a general assessment of consumers' rights.

The concept of "everything as services" heralded by the Cloud paradigm [3] has made ratifying SLAs more challenging and makes the relations among providers and users more complex. Cloud Computing is a way of delivering IT-enabled capabilities to users in the form of "services." Generally, Cloud delivery models describe the layer at which the user interacts with the services. Following are the three layers of delivery commonly seen in today's Cloud [21, 31]:

- Infrastructure as a Service (IaaS) refers to the capability of provision of raw computer infrastructure, such as servers and storage, by a provider to a buyer. The functions required to provide the infrastructure are abstracted. Users are not required to manage the infrastructure as they do not possess the ownership of the underlying Cloud infrastructure.
- Platform as a Service (PaaS) refers to the provision of the capability in which development platforms and middleware systems hosted by a vendor are offered to application developers, allowing developers to simply code and deploy without directly interacting with the underlying infrastructure.
- Software as a Service (SaaS) refers to the capability provided to the user to run and use applications on a Cloud infrastructure of the provider. Buyers are freed from the possession and maintenance issues of software and hardware. The capability can be accessed by users from various client devices.

One could argue that Business Process Outsourcing constitutes a fourth layer, providing "Business as a Service" [26]. Thus, the traditional way of accessing and consuming IT capabilities [2] is redefined by the service concept of Cloud Computing. This rather makes us rethink the terms and clauses of SLAs that represent expectations and obligations of the partners, given the characteristics of Cloud services.

Based on what we said above, one of the questions that need to be duly addressed is: do Cloud SLAs adequately protect private consumers and SMEs that buy Cloud services as they are, without negotiating the content of the SLA? In many cases, users (and especially consumers) are not familiar with Cloud Computing and do not have much experience in externalizing the storage of professional or personal data or in using applications and software that are stored in and accessed from external infrastructures [24]. In this chapter, assuming that we will investigate whether the currently adopted Cloud SLAs and the existing legal sources adequately protect users as defined above, we will assess as a consequence whether or not they contribute to building of trust between users and providers and to fulfillment of privacy compliance.

This chapter presents an extensive review of the SLAs usually adopted by international Cloud providers, like Amazon, Google, Microsoft, and other providers of Cloud-based services. The state-of-the-art literature review on the topic is used as a support tool when necessary. The detailed analysis of existing Cloud SLAs and the existing legal mechanisms intend to hypothesize following research questions:

- How do Cloud SLAs support the data concerns (including data security, privacy, and transparency) exploring the compliance obligations for service providers?
- How do Cloud SLAs act as a catalyst for establishing trust towards Cloud providers, by stimulating the adoption of Cloud by enterprises?
- To what extent rights and liabilities are shifted and balanced between the parties (service provider and users as defined above) in Cloud SLAs across legal jurisdictions?

This chapter is based on the solutions provided to the questions arisen in the context of the EU-funded FP6 IST project BEinGRID (IST5–034702).[3] The said research questions are addressed by extensive literature review of legal mechanisms and by analyzing the results of BEinGRID project. Based on our analysis of Cloud Computing technologies and existing legal frameworks, we present legal implications and proposals for each aspect of privacy, trust, and rights/liabilities for users in Cloud environment as well as possible solutions for the said research questions.

The reminder of the chapter is organized as follows: In Sect. 11.2, we describe the general structure of Cloud SLAs and analyze the existing Cloud SLAs (namely Amazon Web Services,[4] Amazon S3,[5] Amazon Elastic Compute Cloud,[6] Google Apps,[7] and Microsoft Windows Azure[8]) in the real world. Section 11.3 extends our discussions to invade the data concerns of users in the Cloud and discusses the way of protection mechanisms from the perspective of SLAs. Section 11.4 discusses how SLAs stimulate the adoption of Cloud by SMEs and private consumers by establishing trust towards Cloud providers by consumers and small and medium-sized enterprises. Following this, in Sect. 11.5, we describe how and to what extent consumers

---

[3] See http://www.beingrid.eu and http://www.it-tude.com

[4] Amazon Web Services™ Customer Agreement http://aws.amazon.com/agreement/ (Accessed on February, 2011).

[5] Amazon S3 Service Level Agreement http://aws.amazon.com/s3-sla/ (Accessed on February, 2011).

[6] Amazon Elastic Compute Cloud http://aws.amazon.com/ec2/ (Accessed on February, 2011).

[7] Google Apps Service Level Agreement http://www.google.com/apps/intl/en/terms/sla.html (Accessed on February, 2011).

[8] Microsoft Windows Azure Terms of Service http://www.microsoft.com/windowsazure/sla/ (Accessed on February, 2011).

and SMEs are protected in the Cloud environment. Furthermore, we describe the legal implications and proposals for each of the above issues and discuss some of the technological mechanisms to achieve a user-friendly Cloud environment.

11.2   Dissecting Cloud SLAs

A Cloud SLA specifies expectations and obligations of a provider and a user regarding the service characteristics in business-oriented terms, so that these characteristics can be measured, monitored, and managed. Furthermore, a Cloud SLA acts as a legally enforceable document that describes the minimum performance criteria a provider promises to meet while delivering a service. The terms that are agreed upon by the service user and the service provider are drafted in an SLA. Following are the key terms of a Cloud SLA[9] [11, 19, 34].

11.2.1   Subject Terms

The subject of an SLA relates to the definition of the IT capability that is being offered by the provider, and enables a service user to examine the service level that the provider is offering and thereby make good judgment about its function and value.

11.2.2   Scope of Rights

The Scope of Rights defines the rights the service provider authorizes the service user to exercise in a service. It defines the extent to which the Cloud capability may be used and accessed on the basis that any use outside the scope of this SLA would constitute an infringement. Understanding the Scope of Rights in an SLA helps users to know what they can and cannot do regarding the use of and access to a service [12]. An SLA clearly specifies whether a service can be used for commercial use and/or noncommercial use: in the former case, both consumers and small and medium-sized businesses can use the Cloud services, while in the latter situation, enterprises are excluded from the scope of the provision of the services that are intended only for consumers. SLAs reserve the right to control the service from being distorted, mutilated, or modified. Furthermore, most clauses deny the resale of services.

---

[9]The anatomy of Cloud SLAs is still evolving, and thus, it is almost impossible to generalize all the terms of an SLA. Furthermore, this paper is not intended as a substitute for legal advice. Therefore, we highly recommend that service providers and service consumers obtain appropriate legal counsel when making use of SLAs for their Cloud Computing initiatives.

Following are some of the clauses of the Scope of Rights (on allowing users to use software) of an Amazon Web Service customer agreement.

> Subject to your acceptance of this Agreement, ongoing compliance with its terms and conditions with respect to the subject Service, and payment if and as required for your right to use the subject Service, we hereby grant to you, without the right to sublicense, a limited, non-exclusive, non-transferable license during the Term, under our intellectual property or proprietary rights in the Amazon Properties, only to install, copy and use the Amazon Properties solely in connection with and as necessary for your use of such Services and solely to the extent in compliance with all the terms and conditions of this Agreement.
>
> We strive to keep Your Content secure, but cannot guarantee that we will be successful at doing so, given the nature of the Internet.

Analyzing the current SLAs, we can see that the following obligations are made by the SLAs to the providers:

- Providers own the infrastructures (platform and resource) and interfaces to software.
- Providers record events (depending on the requirements of users), and logs should be made available.
- Providers do not take full responsibility for security of data: in order to avoid infringement of users' (most notably, if not exclusively, consumers') legal rights, providers must assume some liability when users' data get lost or damaged (but this typically does not happen, since commercial Cloud providers tend to limit their liability as much as possible, and often their liability in case of security failures etc. is completely excluded).

11.2.3   Financial Terms

A provider determines the financial value as a return (profit) on investment in developing and providing the service. A consumer evaluates the financial value of a Cloud service by comparing the amount paid for the use of this service against the benefits that he/she is going to receive. The most commonly seen models for pricing of services are transaction-based models and subscription-based models [15, 32]. The pricing of Cloud services is associated with differentiated levels of service with varying capacity of memory, computing units, and platforms. The pricing also varies with respect to operating systems and geographical locations. The criteria for pricing of platform Cloud services can be based on the hour, CPU cycle, or otherwise. Pricing of infrastructural Cloud services depends upon levels of use, layers of service, or hybrids of these options. Software Cloud services are priced generally with a pay-per-use model.

The financial terms may not be a part of the SLAs in some cases. The costs of services are defined by a separate contract in these situations. Users should understand the cost structure and hidden costs (including taxes, add-on fees, and support fees) of Cloud capabilities. Also, users are required to clarify whether any kind of licensing fees are associated with the offered Cloud capabilities.

11.2.4   Representation

Representation clauses specify that the intellectual property rights (IPR) of the offered IT capability belong to the developer or provider who owns the IT capability. This avoids a situation where a third party (or the user of the Cloud services) claims later that he/she owns the IPR underlying the service and/or the software used to deliver the service.

11.2.5   Service Credits, Credit Requests, and Compensation Procedures

In case the provider fails to meet the agreed-upon service levels, a Cloud SLA offers a form of compensation to the users, such as service credits. However, the definition of service credits and requisition for credits by proving outage can vary among Cloud providers, based on what we see in different Cloud SLAs. In reality, a service user has to prove the outage (unavailability of the service beyond the service commitment and exceptions mentioned in the SLA), which is rather difficult. The currently available Cloud SLAs do not define mechanisms or ways to assist users in proving the outage. Furthermore, current SLAs define ridiculously low service credits for a suffering user.

In the Amazon S3 SLA, for example, credit request terms are stated as follows:

> To be eligible, the credit request must … (ii) include, in the body of the e-mail, the dates and times of each incident of non-zero Error Rates that you claim to have experienced; (iii) include your server request logs that document the errors and corroborate your claimed outage…

11.2.6   Evolution and Support Terms

Cloud capabilities are subject to evolution by the provider who can make changes in functional and/or non-functional specifications of a software service or any changes in physical infrastructures or changes in the operating systems. By evolution clauses, SLAs address the rights to future versions or releases of the service for a user. A buyer wants ideally to receive broader rights to new releases and enhancements of services. However, a provider wants to limit the commitments to the user for the sake of vitality of the business.

Support entitlements should be spelled out clearly in an SLA. SLAs should detail clear escalation processes in case a problem needs to be dealt with software development team. Cloud SLAs should offer fair support for new virtualization options.

11.2.7   Warranty

In commercial law, a warranty is seen as a promise that something sold is as factually stated or legally implied by the seller [14]. An SLA offers warranties that describe functional and non-functional properties of Cloud capabilities. Most of the measurable warranties [9] related to a Cloud service include response time, process time, throughput, availability, etc.

Following is a part of warranty disclaimer from Amazon Web Service customer agreement. (The clauses are written in capital letters as specified in the Amazon Web Services customer agreement.)

> EXCEPT TO THE EXTENT PROHIBITED BY APPLICABLE LAW, WE AND OUR LICENSORS DISCLAIM ALL WARRANTIES, INCLUDING, WITHOUT LIMITATION, ANY IMPLIED WARRANTIES OF MERCHANTABILITY, SATISFACTORY QUALITY, FITNESS FOR A PARTICULAR PURPOSE, NON-INFRINGEMENT, QUIET ENJOYMENT, AND ANY WARRANTIES ARISING OUT OF ANY COURSE OF DEALING OR USAGE OF TRADE. WE AND OUR LICENSORS DO NOT WARRANT THAT THE SERVICE OFFERINGS WILL FUNCTION AS DESCRIBED, WILL BE UNINTERRUPTED OR ERROR FREE, OR FREE OF HARMFUL COMPONENTS, OR THAT THE DATA YOU STORE WITHIN THE SERVICE OFFERINGS WILL BE SECURE OR NOT OTHERWISE LOST OR DAMAGED. WE AND OUR LICENSORS SHALL NOT BE RESPONSIBLE FOR ANY SERVICE INTERRUPTIONS, INCLUDING, WITHOUT LIMITATION, POWER OUTAGES, SYSTEM FAILURES OR OTHER INTERRUPTIONS, INCLUDING THOSE THAT AFFECT THE RECEIPT, PROCESSING, ACCEPTANCE, COMPLETION OR SETTLEMENT OF ANY PAYMENT SERVICES.

SLAs clearly specify that the services are not without errors. Typically, an SLA sets out the remedial action and any penalties that take effect if performance falls below the promised standard through a service credit system, and consumers (please be aware, as a principle only consumers) should realize that their legal rights are completely infringed if no remedies and penalties are set forth in the SLA and that, as pointed out above, service credits are not aimed at compensating clients for the damages arising from the use of the Cloud services.

11.2.8   Indemnification

SLAs specify indemnification clauses [8], a way of defense by the provider for the user if a third party sues the user, alleging that the user's use of the service infringes or violates the third party's intellectual property rights (IPRs). A service provider can indemnify the user for IPRs infringement, but only to the extent those infringement claims arise from the user's authorized use of the allowed service and if the infringement finally falls under the liability of the provider. However, the user is required to bear the cost of defending infringement claims to the extent those claims arise from the combination of the allowed service with user's own application/service, or from (not authorized) modifications of the allowed service by the user, or from user's misuse of the allowed service.

11.2.9   Limitation of Liability

Limitation of liability clauses [7] restrict the liability of each of the parties under the license agreement. Under this clause, both parties (service provider and service user) disclaim liability for unforeseeable damages (network errors or hosting server problems) or indirect damages.

Following are a compilation of clauses regarding limitation of liabilities from several service providers.

> Service providers shall not be liable to consumers for any direct, indirect, incidental, special, consequential, or exemplary damages, including but not limited to, damages for loss of profits, goodwill, use, data, or other intangible losses, resulting from:
>
> 1. The use or the inability to use the service;
> 2. The cost of procurement of substitute goods and services; or
> 3. Unauthorized access to or alteration of transmissions or data of consumers

Although the issues related to warranties, indemnities, and limitation of liabilities can be legally complex [34], these clauses identify the bearer of the financial risk of service failures and the bearer of the risk that a third party will bring a legal action claiming that the service violates his/her IPRs. Typically, providers want to be kept free from all liabilities and state this complete exclusion of liability in the SLA, thus infringing the legal rights of consumers. In other terms, the financial risk of service failures lies on the user's side, which is rather unfair and potentially inefficient, since it does not stimulate providers to improve the quality of the services they offer.

11.3   Data Concerns in Cloud SLAs: Co-existence and Balance

11.3.1   Data Security, Privacy, and Transparency Issues

The Cloud Computing paradigm usually involves the storing and processing of data. If these data involve an identified or identifiable physical person, then they are personal data. Personal data, according to the applicable European legal framework,[10] need to be processed according to well-defined procedural and substantial rules.

---

[10]We refer in particular to the Data Protection Directive (Directive 95/46/EC of the European Parliament and of the Council of 24 October 1995 on the protection of individuals with regard to the processing of personal data and on the free movement of such data – [OJ L281, 23.11.1995, pp. 31–50]) and to the Privacy and Electronic Communications Directive (Directive 2002/58/EC of the European Parliament and of the Council of 12 July 2002 concerning the processing of personal data and the protection of privacy in the electronic communications sector [OJ L201, 31.7.2002, pp. 37–47]).

The export of personal data[11] may require complex process of authorization by national privacy authorities and the drafting of agreements between the parties involving the exporter of personal data in the European Economic Area (EEA) and the importer of these data outside the EEA. Although the data are transferred from one country to another within one Cloud infrastructure (owned and managed by only one company), the said process can be complex due to a restrictive interpretation of data and privacy regulations.

Privacy issues are very important in Cloud Computing [5, 13]. Often, the nature and structure of Cloud Computing make it difficult for Cloud providers to respect existing data protection and privacy regulations [4]. One of the main reasons for this is due to the transnational nature of Cloud Computing [22] that has to face the national (and therefore local) nature of privacy regulations: one business, one Cloud, but several legislations.

It is pivotal (and compulsory) for Cloud providers that their users are informed about the way in which their data are processed [27]. In the case of enterprises, the personal data involved may concern names, addresses, e-mail addresses, health data of their employees, and consultants. As regards consumers, all data involving their identification and their personal characteristics may be qualified as personal data. Therefore, it is advisable to disclose about the processing of their data in a Cloud infrastructure.

Transparency towards clients must be the golden rule – too often the processing of data is opaque, in the sense that users do not know where and by whom their data are finally processed. Among the SLAs contemplated by this chapter, it has to be highlighted that the Amazon Web Services customer agreement states that the user "*may specify the AWS regions in which* [his] *Content will be stored and accessible by End Users.* [Amazon] *will not move* [his] *Content from* [his] *selected AWS regions without notifying* [him], *unless required to comply with the law or requests of governmental entities.* [The user] *consent*[s] *to the processing of* [his] *Content in, and the transfer of* [his] *Content into, the AWS regions* [he] *select*[s]." This provision takes into account the legitimate interests of the customers to know where the data are located and to prevent that they are transferred to other regions without authorization.

Transparency implies that the consent of the data owners shall be required every time these data are exchanged with other enterprises and every time such a consent is required by the law. Although the consent of the data owner to the processing of his/her personal data is mandatory, the applicable laws and regulations could relax this requirement of consent in some cases. The typical situation concerns the exchange of users' data between a SaaS provider and a Cloud provider, when the

---

[11]We refer to the export of data only if the data are sent outside the territory of the European Economic Area (EEA), comprising the territory of the member States of the European Union plus Iceland, Liechtenstein, and Norway. Thus, from the privacy point of view, 30 countries are seen as only one "jurisdiction."

data of the users of the SaaS provider are processed in the Cloud infrastructure owned and managed by a Cloud provider. In practice, the SaaS provider will need to set up a privacy policy for its clients disclosing all relevant information.

Amazon's privacy policy[12] has been drafted in accordance to US data protection laws. As Amazon participates in the Safe Harbor Program between the US Department of Commerce and the European Union, this provides a legal framework for transfer of data between the EEA countries and the United States. On the other side, the Microsoft Online Services Use Rights[13] state that "*Personal data collected through the online service may be transferred, stored and processed in the United States or any other country in which Microsoft or its service providers maintain facilities.*" This provision may pose problems of compatibility with the obligations arising under the European data protection framework, and it implies that the customer does not have any possibility to decide where his data are stored.

11.3.2   *Resolving Data Concerns in Cloud Computing*

In general, Cloud Computing is perfectly consistent with the necessary respect of data protection rights [24]. The chaotic management of data in the Cloud, of course, is not compatible with such respect. Therefore, Cloud providers are required to set up an efficient privacy policy that regulates all possible issues and problems, such as responsibilities, confidentiality, liabilities, scope of the processing, security, rules about data recording and storage, accessing and processing data, etc. [13].

The legal implications of data concerns of Cloud environment expect and require users to understand the following:

- Users solely own any kind of data, hosted and/or uploaded in the infrastructure (platform and resource) or created and/or modified by the software service based on the input from users themselves. In this way, it is the responsibility of users (data subject and employer of data subject) to make the data secure and to comply with privacy rules and regulatory laws, since the provider typically will not be contractually liable if the data infringe laws, their content is illegal, etc.
- Users should understand the nature of the data involved in the processing and the scope of their processing.
- Users are suggested to know the details of location of data hosted and transfer of data in Cloud environment.
- Users should host their data with those providers who have one of the following certifications: (1) International Safe Harbor Certification (which usually allows

---

[12] http://www.amazon.com/gp/help/customer/display.html/177–6089550–2338042?ie=UTF8&nodeId= 468496#share (Accessed on February, 2011).

[13] http://www.microsoftvolumelicensing.com/DocumentSearch.aspx?Mode=3&DocumentTypeId=31 (Accessed on February, 2011).

data transfer from the EEA to the United States and/or to other countries) (see Sect. 11.3.1 for more details), (2) adherence to model contracts drafted by the European Commission (which allow data transfer from the EEA to external countries when no safe harbor is applicable, but do not always work well with multi-tiered vendor relationships), or (3) Binding Corporate Rules (which are designed for a multinational company), in combination with an International Safe Harbor Certification or a contract based on the models drafted by the European Commission.

Following are some of the fundamental technological approaches that partially support data concerns of users in Cloud environments:

- *Privacy enhancing technologies*: using privacy enhancing technologies [18], a user can enclose individual privacy rights, conditions, and preferences directly to his/her own identity data. This approach is quite similar to digital rights management technologies.
- *Identity management*: the InterCloud [29] is a new perspective of Cloud Computing where Clouds cooperate with other federated ones with the purpose to enlarge their computing and storage capabilities. A high level of interoperability between different security technologies is required in the InterCloud. The InterCloud IdM, proposed by [6], is a distributed system for identity management based on the identity provider/service provider (IdP/SP) model, successfully applied to manage the authentication needed among Clouds for the federation establishment.
- *Data encryption technologies*: a homomorphic encryption scheme proposed by [30] allows cyphertext to be manipulated as easily as plaintext, making it perfect for modern Cloud Computing. In this way, operations of any complexity can be performed on encrypted data, with the condition that its noise level gets periodically refreshed. The algorithm enables queries and data to remain encrypted while searching, sorting, and processing, but in practice requires longer times to compute results since encrypted operations are much more complicated.
- *Design patterns*: design patterns provide a method for addressing maturity within the enterprise use of privacy policy and correspond to the control for privacy policy enforcement [10]. These patterns provide an intuitive way to engage with system architects and policy developers during Cloud service design.

11.4 Stimulating Cloud Adoption: SLAs as Catalyst for Trust

11.4.1 Trust and Legal Protective Measures

Trust is generally seen as a sliding scale of trade-offs and approaches, instead of discrete binary choices of policy enforcement [16]. For example, in using a payment processing application, users expect a high degree of trust. In the meanwhile, users do not expect a high degree of trust in using a weather forecast service. Generally, enterprises trust a service that is highly mature and commoditized whose data is deemed to be reliable and to have verifiable traits. Thus, for every scenario, the client determines the need for trust, while the provider should plan to offer the highest degree of trust.

The trust that businesses and consumers currently have towards Cloud providers is basically market-driven [23]. It is based on the reputation of existing providers and on the legitimate expectation that they will respect their promises [25]. This requires a certain level of availability and quality of services to be respected by an SLA. At the same time, providers tend to protect themselves, limiting as much as possible their liabilities.

Consumers and SMEs will be analyzed separately, due to the fact that the applicable legal framework provides for a set of protective rules for consumers, while this is not the case in point for SMEs.

The legal protection assured by the legislation of the European Union to consumers and SMEs is focused on the following pillars:

1. The SLA shall be regulated by the law of the country where the consumer has his habitual residence if the provider addresses this country through his website/portal.
2. Furthermore, the parties can state that another law (e.g., of a non-European State) will govern the contract, but consumer protection rules of the country of residence of the consumer apply. These principles are set forth by the Rome I Regulation.
3. Pursuant to other applicable legal sources (based on Directive 93/13/EC[14]), the provisions in the agreement that are too unbalanced in favor of the provider are invalid, i.e., clauses that exclude legal rights of the consumer in case of non-performance of the contractual obligations by the provider, clauses that allow the provider to unilaterally modify or terminate the agreement, etc.

In B2B transactions, according to the legislation of the European Union, if the SLA is unfair or unbalanced, the client could not be protected. In particular, the provider can limit his contractual liability, and it can be agreed that the competent court would be that of the place where the supplier is domiciled. In practice, the customer would not be able to get any compensation for the damages caused from the infringement of the contractual obligations of the Cloud provider and for the damages in case of security failures [33]. Therefore, many businesses are extremely reluctant to store data and information "in the Cloud." This also applies for services that are provided from remote locations and that require these data and information to be processed "in the Cloud."

---

[14]Council Directive 93/13/EEC of 5 April 1993 on unfair terms in consumer contracts (OJ L95, 21.4.1993, pp. 29–34).

From the legal point of view, it is not possible to say that these SMEs that prefer to act in "traditional" ways and to keep their data under their direct control are completely wrong and irrational. The risk may be more or less low, but the problematic issue is that there is no legal protection in case of problems, security failures, etc. It is therefore highly advisable that the (European) lawmakers should take into consideration this issue and analyze whether or not it is fair that SMEs do not have adequate protection when dealing with Cloud service providers. This point is even more urgent if one considers that very often the customer does not negotiate the content of the SLA he/she enters into, since this SLA is basically drafted unilaterally by the provider.

11.4.2 Understanding and Technological Approaches for Brokering Trust

The legal implications of trust aspects of Cloud environment expect and require clients to understand the following:

- Users should understand how the service levels and performance indicators are monitored and measured by the providers.
- Users can control access to Cloud applications and services and can mediate between different internal and external protocols and standards.
- Users can ensure that Cloud resources are performing as defined by SLAs.
- Users can ensure that Cloud resources meet internal governance policies.
- Users are allowed to monitor usage trends (both historical and current), and users are allowed to have third parties to perform an audit of the services on their behalf. Users can audit and report against logs and other artifacts created during the monitoring and management cycles.
- Users are allowed to sub-allocate sub-users, the service levels of whom will be provided and maintained by the users themselves.
- Users should look at the degree of lock-in (vendor, technology, and contract level) an SLA entails and have clear strategies for moving to alternative providers or services if required.

Following are some of the technological approaches for brokering trust among providers and users in Cloud environments [17]:

Remote access control: remote access control capabilities offer users proactive control over their data at the remote location and the ability to better specify and enforce policies. This method can give users more jurisdictions over their data, regardless of the Cloud provider's physical locations. Even when data is physically spread out and stored in various remote locations and processed by remote machines and software, the data owner could retain control of these activities by similar remote access mechanisms.

Certifications: a fully trusted Cloud model can be possible if an independent security certification authority could certify Cloud services in terms of their security properties and capabilities. This kind of certificates would act as a quality stamp, guaranteeing secure services with a given degree of confidence and ensuring the implementation of the service on compliance with the published security profiles.

Enclaves: similar to the enclaves in the defense industry, Cloud providers could form a security enclave for their users, providing a set of standard capabilities, such as incident detection and response, boundary defense, and monitoring. These enclaves could be specific to an enterprise or to a set of similar services that various enterprises consume. In enclaves, Cloud providers compartmentalize users' data, thus avoiding the mixing up of data with others.

11.5   Extent of Legal Mechanisms in Protecting Users

11.5.1   *Protection Ex Post and Practical Problems*

As pointed out in Sect. 11.4, legal mechanisms to protect Cloud users do exist in the European Union. This is based on the assumption that we live in a society where users' rights are perceived to be important and worthy to be protected [23]. As a consequence, Cloud providers cannot insert whatsoever content in the SLAs they sign off (usually through a click-wrap system) to their users.

These protections, however, work normally ex post. According to the existing applicable laws, each consumer typically has the possibility to sue the provider to stop using SLAs that violate consumers' protection legislation (usually a pecuniary sanction may be imposed too) [1]. However, the chance for a user (or an organization of user) suing against a provider is very low due to the costs involved for the proceedings, the necessary legal and technical competences, and the need for a specialized lawyer (with corresponding costs). Thus, it is not realistic that a user that buys Cloud services for a few Euros or dollars would sue the provider even if such consumers lose the money they spent. This statement is even more realistic for small and medium-sized enterprises that are required to sue the Cloud provider in their respective country of origin, with (potentially) very high costs. For these reasons, there are no notable judicial cases reported about Cloud SLAs disputes.

This kind of behavior of users and the lack of effective possibility for the user to sue the provider may be profitable for Cloud providers. The typical example narrates the clause of a standard SLA according to which a provider will not be obliged to compensate the user if the data stored/uploaded by the user get lost or damaged. This clause is against consumers' protection legislation and principles; however, in practice this provision is effective for the Cloud suppliers provided that it will reach its goal, i.e., preventing the user from claiming and obtaining financial compensation if users' data get lost or damaged.

The clause of limitation of liability by the Amazon Web Services customer agreement states that Amazon is never liable for any direct, indirect, etc., damage even if Amazon (or an affiliated party) has been advised of the possibility of such damages. In any case, the liability (if any) is limited to the amount paid by the customer under the agreement with Amazon for the services that gave rise to the claim during the last 12 months preceding the claim. Such clauses infringe the consumers' rights set forth by the legal framework of the European Union and are likely to be declared void by a judge, in case of dispute.

11.5.2   Enforcement of Decisions and Practical Proposals

Cloud Computing confronts users with the issue of the lack of substantial possibilities to enforce the decision of the competent court or government body after the users eventually sued the provider and won the case. In fact, there can be scenarios in which certain decisions are taken by a court or government body in one country (for instance in a European country) and must be implemented in another country (for instance in the USA or in Japan) where Cloud providers are usually located. In such scenarios, are providers legally obliged to change existing SLAs and make them more user or consumer-friendly, as decided by the court in a different jurisdiction?

The answer to the said question is "No," since there are no effective legal mechanisms of international enforcement of jurisdictional decisions. However, such mechanisms do exist only within the borders of the European Union. It is more profitable for Cloud providers to violate consumers' protection laws than respect them, since there are no effective systems to push them to respect these provisions [23]. As the legislation varies from country to country, it is difficult (and expensive) for Cloud providers to respect all existing consumers' protection legislations. Thus, existing legal mechanisms to combat violations of these regulations are ineffective.

In our opinion, one of the possible solutions could be as follows: providers can base their SLAs on the legislation that protects most of the consumers, and they can apply such SLAs also in the other countries where they sell their services. Generally, a user will not complain because the SLA he/she signed with a provider protects him/her more than it should do according to the local legislation! Actually, none of the SLAs or agreements taken into account in this Chapter takes into consideration this possibility.

Proposing other solutions that may solve these issues more radically is not easy. Since it is not actually realistic to have and to implement mechanisms of universal enforcement of judicial decisions and there is no real possibility to have a universally valid consumers' protection legislation [27], it is only possible and feasible to advocate changes on the social and business side, as we did immediately above. Through national campaigns, consumers understand their rights over Cloud providers and query about such rights when buying Cloud services. Awareness-raising campaigns can be a feasible solution as they push Cloud providers to modify the SLAs and to make them more compliant with legal requirements. The issue is partially similar for SMEs since there is no protective legislation that at least in theory shall be respected. However, it is objectively unfair that SMEs/users of Cloud services are completely unprotected in case of failure by the Cloud supplier to respect the SLA.

We believe that the solution should come from the Cloud providers themselves and that they should move to a more mature Cloud market where risks and liabilities are fairly balanced, since the actual "jungle" prevents the more careful users from moving their data and application to the Cloud. Ultimately, this is a loss of business opportunities for the providers themselves.

11.6 Conclusion

Cloud Computing is a way of delivering IT-enabled capabilities to users in the form of "services" with elasticity and scalability, where users can make use of resources, platform, or software without having to possess and manage the underlying complexity of the technology. Thus, the changing focus of computing paradigm brings the need for reflection of changes in SLAs for Cloud. In this chapter, we have described the different clauses that make a Cloud SLA and discussed the way in which Cloud service providers deal with these service level issues presently and their impacts on Cloud users, especially consumers and SMEs.

We have explicated the issue of data concerns faced by users in the Cloud together with possible viable solutions. Although Cloud Computing can be perfectly consistent with privacy, some precise privacy policies and agreements must be set up between the actors involved in the Cloud business. Following this, we have analyzed the factors that stimulate trust by users in adopting Cloud applications and services. Based on our analysis, we have seen that very often, standard SLA clauses are not compliant with European consumers' protection legislation and are prone to violate consumers' rights and do not stimulate, but rather impede, trust by consumers and SMEs toward Cloud providers.

The key rule is that it would be necessary to have more competition between Cloud providers so that they are pushed to propose better contractual terms to users in general (and not only to consumers but also to businesses), but this does not happen yet. So far, providers are basically completely free to set forth whatsoever contractual provision in the SLA with users (including consumers) since there are de facto no effective legal, social, or business systems to force providers to respect consumers' rights and users' expectations on a global scale and to offer viable and fait contractual arrangements to users.

References

1. Berliri, M.: Jurisdiction and the internet, and European regulation 44 of 2001. In: Woodley, S. (ed.) E-Commerce: Law and Jurisdiction, pp. 1–12. Kluwer Law International, The Hague (2002)
2. Buchanan, S.: Cloud Computing Changes IT Asset Acquisition and Ownership. Gartner Inc, Stamford (2008)
3. Buyya, R., Yeo, C., Venugopal, S., Broberg, J., Brandic, I.: Cloud computing and emerging IT platforms: vision, hype, and reality for delivering computing as the 5th utility. Future Gener. Comput. Syst. 25(6), 599–616 (2009)

4. Casassa-Mont, M., Pearson, S., Novoa, M.: Securing information transfer in distributed computing environments. IEEE Secur. Priv., Nov/Dec, **6**(1), 34–42 (2007)
5. Cavoukian, A.: Privacy in the Clouds. Identity in the Information Society. **1**(1), Springer Netherlands. pp. 89–108 (2008)
6. Celesti, A., Tusa, F., M. Villari, M., Puliafito, A.: Security and Cloud Computing: intercloud identity management infrastructure. In: Proceedings of the 19th IEEE International Workshops on Enabling Technologies: Infrastructures for Collaborative Enterprises (WETICE 2010), Tei of Larissa, Greece, pp. 263–265 (2010)
7. Chavez, A., Tornabene, C., Wiederhold, G.: Software component licensing: a primer. IEEE Softw. **15**(5), 47–53 (1998)
8. Classen, W.: Fundamentals of software licensing. IDEA J. Law Technol. **37**, 1 (1996)
9. Colling, D., Ferrari, T., Hassoun, Y., Huang, C., Kotsokalis, C., McGough, A.S., Ronchieri, E., Patel, Y., Tsanakas, P.: On Quality of Service Support for Grid Computing. Grid Enabled Remote Instrumentation. Springer, New York (2009)
10. Creese, S., Hopkins, P., Pearson, S., Shen, Y.: Data Protection-Aware Design for Cloud Computing. Proceedings of Cloud Computing. Springer LNCS, Berlin/New York (2009)
11. Eliadis, H., Rand, A.: Setting Expectations in SAAS. Technical White Paper. Software & Information Industry Association (SIIA), Washington, DC (2007)
12. Gangadharan, G.R.: Service licensing. PhD thesis. International Doctorate School in Information and Communication Technology, University of Trento, Trento, Italy (2008)
13. Gellman, R.: Privacy in the clouds: risks to privacy and confidentiality from Cloud Computing. Technical Report, World Privacy Forum (2009)
14. Goode, R.: Commercial Law. Penguin Books Limited, London (2006)
15. Gunther, O., Tamm, G., Leymann, F.: Pricing web services. Int. J. Bus. Process Integr. Manage. **2**(2), 132–140 (2007)
16. Kenney, F., Plummer, D., Thompson, J.: What's between you and the cloud? Gartner Report ID Number G00163985 (2009)
17. Khan, K., Malluhi, Q.: Establishing trust in cloud computing. IT Prof. **12**(5), 20–27 (2010)
18. Koorn, R., et al.: Privacy-Enhancing Technologies. White Paper for Decision-Makers. Ministry of Interior and Kingdom Relations, The Hague (2004)
19. Kotsokalis, C., et al.: SLA Foundations and Management, *SLA@SOI EU FP7 Project Deliverable D.A5.a* (2009)
20. Leff, A., Rayfield, J., Dias, D.M.: Service-level agreements and commercial grids. IEEE Internet Comput. **7**(4), 44–50 (2003)
21. Maximilien, E.M., Ranabahu, A., Engehausen, R., Anderson, L.C.: Toward cloud-agnostic middleware. In: Proceedings of ACM International Conference on Object-Oriented Programming, Systems, Languages, and Applications (OOPSLA), Orlando, FL (2009)
22. Navetta, D.: Data breach in the clouds. Hiscox Global Technology News. January, 2011 (2011)
23. Parrilli, D.M.: Service level agreements in grid and cloud computing environment: real protection for customers? In: e-challenges 2009 Conference Proceedings, Istanbul (2009a)
24. Parrilli, D.M.: Grid and cloud computing as a tool to transform European economy: legal considerations. In: Proceedings of the FITCE 2009, Prague (2009b)
25. Perez, S.: In cloud we trust? www.readwriteweb.com/enterprise/2009/01/inCloud-we-trust.php (2009). Accessed Oct 2010
26. Reynolds, E., Bess, C.: Clearing up the cloud: adoption strategies for cloud computing. Cutter IT J. **22**(June/July), 14–20 (2009)
27. Stanoevska-Slabeva, K., Wozniak, T., Ristol, S.: Grid and Cloud Computing. A Business Perspective on Technology and Applications. Springer, Berlin/Heidelberg (2010)
28. Stantchev, V., Schröpfer, C.: Negotiating and enforcing QoS and SLAs in grid and cloud computing. In: Proceedings of the 4th International Conference on Advances in Grid and Pervasive Computing (GPC). Lecture Notes in Computer Science. Springer, Berlin (2009)

29. Sun Microsystems: Take your business to a Higher Level – Sun Cloud Computing technology scales your infrastructure to take advantage of new business opportunities. Technical Report (2009)

30. van Dijk, M., Gentry, C., Halevi, S., Vaikuntanathan, V.: Fully homomorphic encryption over the integers. In: Proceedings of EUROCRYPT, LNCS, vol. 6110, pp. 24–43 (2010)

31. Vaquero, L.M., Rodero-Merino, L., Caceres, J., Lindner, M.: A break in the clouds: toward a cloud definition. ACM SIGCOMM Comp. Commun. Rev. **39**(1), 50–55 (2009)

32. Weinhardt, C., Anandasivam, A., Blau, B., Borissov, N., Meinl, T., Michalk, W., Stößer, J.: Cloud computing – a classification, business models, and research directions. Bus. Inf. Sys. Eng. **1**(5), 391–399 (2009)

33. Wild, C., Weinstein, S., Riefa, C.: Council regulation (EC) 44/2001 and internet consumer contracts: some thoughts on article 15 and the futility of applying "in the box" conflict of law rules to the "out of box" borderless world. Int. Rev. Law Comput. Technol. **19**(1), 13–21 (2005)

34. World Intellectual Property Organization (WIPO): Successful Technology Licensing. WIPO Publishers, Geneva (2004)

Chapter 12
Enterprise HPC on the Clouds

Ioannis A. Moschakis and Helen D. Karatza

Abstract In the past few decades, the use of high-performance computing (HPC) has become more and more relevant in the enterprise. From aeronautics to the car industry, and from large computer manufacturers to Internet start-ups, everybody has the need to process enormous amounts of data in order to reduce costs and cope with the speed that technology is evolving today. Companies know that the need for an HPC solution is paramount to their success and the viability of their business in the future. While large enterprises have the required funds for an in-house HPC system, many smaller companies do not have the budget to deploy such solutions, although their needs for data processing may be equally high. Through commoditization of hardware, the need for supercomputers in HPC has evaporated; clusters of servers can nowadays provide the same functionality and performance, at a much lower cost. The latter has led to the advent of "cloud computing" which constitutes a major paradigm shift in how we, as users, can have access to large-scale computing infrastructure. "Clouds" offer virtually limitless resources, on-demand, at a relatively low cost. In the future, this can lead to a complete outsourcing of enterprise HPC and demolish the need for in-house solutions. In this chapter, we are going to discuss the major issues that must be addressed in order to make clouds viable for enterprise HPC, and review research, based on existing or simulated cloud systems, that hints as to how the problems can be solved.

I.A. Moschakis (✉) • H.D. Karatza
Department of Informatics, Aristotle University of Thessaloniki, 54124 Thessaloniki, Greece
e-mail: imoschak@csd.auth.gr; karatza@csd.auth.gr

Z. Mahmood and R. Hill (eds.), *Cloud Computing for Enterprise Architectures*,
Computer Communications and Networks, DOI 10.1007/978-1-4471-2236-4_12,
© Springer-Verlag London Limited 2011

12.1 Introduction

The term "cloud computing" can be described as a combination of varying technologies, architectures, and services, but its main purpose can be summarized as *"processing on the web."* Though there are various "cloud" platforms, and each of them offers a different level of programming abstraction, their purpose is essentially to provide web-based processing of data in remote data centers. This "outsourcing" of data processing has obvious benefits for users since they do not need to provide for the maintenance and administration of the data centers. Thus, a user with a simple credit card can have access to virtually infinite amounts of computing infrastructure.

It quickly becomes obvious that all of this processing power can easily be used for enterprise HPC requirements. Enterprises will no longer have the need to build in-house systems that, apart from the initial cost for construction, need routine maintenance and administration. The cloud provider will provide the virtualized resources, administer the underlying hardware, and provide for upgrades and maintenance. Even for companies with already deployed infrastructure, the cloud can be used as an extension to local solutions when the present infrastructure is not enough. Furthermore, the cloud has the added benefits of failover backup systems and data redundancy across different sites. Even in extreme cases, such as a natural disaster, data stored on the cloud are safe.

The use of the cloud can be particularly beneficial to new enterprises and web companies. For example, up until now, a web start-up would have needed to invest in hardware before starting a web service. If the service fell short, then all those funds would have gone to waste. Even worse, if the service had unexpected demand and was not adequately provisioned to meet that demand, outages would occur. These outages would have dire consequences for the future of the service. By using the cloud, the same start-up would have avoided the initial capital expenditure (CapEx) [3], for infrastructure, and gained time to develop its service, by using all the funds for operating costs alone. In addition, lest the service met high demand, it could have scaled quickly to meet that demand since the addition of cloud servers is a process that can be done in minutes not days.

However, despite all of the above, cloud computing is still a relatively young concept and has not yet gained momentum in, or trust of the enterprise, for HPC applications. Many obstacles have to be overcome in order for the cloud to be considered as a capable replacement to private HPC solutions. In this chapter, we are going to analyze the issues involved in this process and review research that pertains to these specific problems.

We must clarify here that throughout this chapter, the term cloud, unless stated otherwise, refers to Infrastructure-as-a-Service (IaaS) clouds, which usually provide virtualized resources in the form of virtual machines (VMs). Current characteristics of cloud computing environments suggest that IaaS clouds are a suitable solution for HPC-as-a-Service and provide the flexibility required by enterprise customers [13].

This chapter is structured as follows: in Sect. 12.2, we provide a descriptive analysis of the obstacles that hinder the use of the cloud as a reliable enterprise HPC platform; in Sect. 12.3, we review current research on areas related to HPC, with application on cloud platforms, like parallel job scheduling, performance case studies, resource brokering, and more; Sect. 12.4 provides a brief overview of currently available cloud HPC implementations; and finally, Sect. 12.5 provides our conclusive remarks and thoughts about future research on the subject.

12.2   Adoption Issues

As stated above, before the "cloud" becomes a solution for enterprise HPC, cloud providers have to address multiple problems. The following figure depicts some of the issues that we are going to analyze in the following sections (Fig. 12.1).

12.2.1   Security

As is expected, large enterprises are not very forthcoming about their data. In fact, for most of them, the security of their data is paramount, and loss of data could be, potentially, catastrophic. Furthermore, they also require protection from third parties since for many companies their survival may be dependent on keeping their research or client data confidential.

Thus, when considering the outsourcing of data, enterprises must be certain that the cloud will retain a high level of confidentiality and security, equal to or better than an in-house solution. Multiple reasons are the cause of mistrust towards the cloud; some of them are addressed below:

- **Location of Data**. We know that cloud data centers are deployed in a multitude of places, across different continents, with location selection based on multiple factors like electricity prices, network connection prices, etc. We do not know however where exactly our data is stored. For enterprise applications, this feature is particularly important since companies need to have a perspective on who has access to their data and what laws apply in the area. For example, if a US weapons manufacturer uses the cloud for data processing and storage, and the cloud provider stores the data in its data center in China, then that may become a serious security issue. Enterprise clients need to know who has access to their data and what laws regulate the data center where their data is stored. Furthermore, companies may require that their data do not migrate to cloud sites outside their country of origin.
- **Data Security**. As happens with in-house systems, unless they are disconnected, clouds are prone to malicious attacks with the intent to steal data or bring down the system. While no system can be 100% secure and though the sophistication of hackers and botnets is growing, cloud manufacturers must provide increased

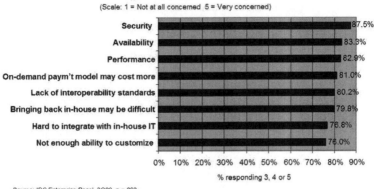

Fig. 12.1 Cloud issues (Source: IDC Survey, 3Q09) [12]

security measures for their deployments in order to attract enterprise customers [9]. The application of virtual machines as infrastructure from Amazon EC2 is a viable solution since VMs can be configured to run in a sand-boxed environment that minimizes security risks, which stem from resource sharing with other VMs. Furthermore, the same model allows the customer to build his own software stack and thus incorporate his own specific security solution and configure it according to his needs.

- **Auditing of Data**. Enterprise customers may also require that mechanisms be put in place, by the provider, that allow the data to be audited, in regular intervals, in order to reassure the customer that they are secure and unaltered. Since the human factor exists, the client must be trustful of the people that manage the data center.

Recently, Amazon EC2 has introduced a service called Virtual Private Cloud (VPC).[1] This service aims to provide the security required by the enterprise while maintaining all the features of EC2. VPC allows companies to create a private cloud, consisting of isolated virtual machine instances connected in a virtual private network (VPN). While this feature is currently in beta, future development may provide an adequately safe platform for enterprise cloud computing.

12.2.2 Performance

High-performance computing solutions are performance-critical systems, which up until now have consisted of supercomputers, or computer clusters. These systems can be carefully tuned to provide high and homogeneous performance, required by

---

[1] Amazon Virtual Private Cloud (Amazon VPC) – http://aws.amazon.com/vpc/

HPC applications. The cloud regrettably does not provide fine-grained resource tuning to the user; the provider, though, can customize the way VMs work and share the underlying hardware.

The problem with virtualized systems is that multiple VMs compete for the same resources. The virtual machine monitor (VMM) is responsible for the allocation of resources to the VMs running on a system and can be configured to share these resources in specific ways. For example, the VMM can allocate a specific amount of CPU cycles to a VM along with a part of real memory [20]. Apparently, this can be used by the cloud provider to provide guarantees related to VM performance in the form of Service Level Agreements (SLAs), which are formal documents and have repercussions for the provider if they are not followed to the letter.

The initial aim of cloud providers were business applications and web services. This lead to a perception that clouds are not suited for HPC applications. In fact, studies have concluded that clouds may not yet be ready for large-scale HPC [15]. Nevertheless, as the need for high-performance solutions is rising in the enterprise, cloud services are beginning to provide HPC solutions like Amazon's Cluster Compute and Penguin Computing's Penguin on Demand (POD) service, which we are going to describe at a later section. These solutions try to maintain all the beneficial features of clouds while providing performance on par with in-house HPC systems.

Another problem that is related to performance issues and needs to be addressed by cloud providers is the scalability of their service. As cloud services become more and more popular, providers need to upgrade their infrastructure in order to maintain the level of performance offered by their service. Since adding hardware infrastructure involves a nontrivial delay, temporal performance differences may constitute a problem, if the provider finds his service underprovisioned to handle the increasing load.[2]

12.2.3   Availability

Another very important issue is the availability of service. Most enterprises require continuous access to their systems, and while the cloud has shown tremendous resilience to downtime, problems may still arise.

First, the high level of sophistication of the cloud management software makes it prone to bugs, and thus, there is always the chance that it can fail [8]. In addition, other technical issues such as networking hardware malfunctions or overloading of authentication and I/O systems may still occur. Although cloud vendors strive to deliver high availability and reliability of service through specialized software and hardware technologies, they still constitute "a single point of failure" [3].

---

[2]Visual evidence of Amazon EC2 network issues – https://www.cloudkick.com/blog/2010/jan/12/visual-ec2-latency/

Therefore, users should replicate their services across multiple clouds in order to achieve maximum availability. Replication, of course, is a problem in itself since clouds are not directly compatible with each other. Therefore, a cloud-middleware platform, like RightScale,[3] is required to allow interoperation between different cloud computing environments.

Another possible failure point, on the user side, is loss of connection to the cloud. This problem can be addressed by implementing connection redundancy using multiple network connections and through local caching of transactions in case all other backup systems fail.

12.2.4 Integration and Interoperability

As mentioned above, clouds can also be considered as an extension to in-house infrastructure for handling data processing and number-crunching operations. Therefore, integration and interoperability between private systems and the cloud becomes a concern.

This problem is twofold and must be addressed from both sides:

- **Cloud Provider**. The cloud provider must provide adequate programming interfaces through APIs, libraries, and development tools, in order to facilitate the creation of control systems by the cloud users, for the virtualized infrastructure. The level of abstraction of these interfaces depends on the cloud platform. For example, IaaS providers like Amazon EC2[4] provide extensive APIs that handle the creation, booting, management, and deletion of EC2 instances. Others like Google's AppEngine[5] platform-as-a-Service (PaaS) implementation do not provide any control over infrastructure. On the other hand, AppEngine incorporates mechanisms for automatic backup, scaling, and fallback in case of failure.
- **Cloud User**. Given that the cloud provider provides all the appropriate tools for managing the cloud, the user, or in our case the enterprise, must utilize those APIs and integrate them with its in-house system. Moreover, if the user has replicated his service across different cloud environments, as proposed in Sect. 12.2.3, he has to implement mechanisms for interoperation between the utilized platforms. Obviously, this is not an automatic procedure and problems may arise due to software incompatibilities between the different cloud environments.

While this issue is very important, it can also be rather easy to solve as long as both parties are willing to dedicate time to the process. As will be shown in Sect. 12.3.2, private HPC systems can benefit a lot by delegating jobs to the cloud.

---

[3] RightScale Cloud Management Platform – http://www.rightscale.com/

[4] Amazon Elastic Compute Cloud (Amazon EC2) – http://aws.amazon.com/ec2/

[5] Google AppEngine – http://code.google.com/appengine/

12.2.5   Customization

The level of customization that is provided to the cloud user depends on the cloud platform, for example, if the IaaS cloud services like Rackspace and Amazon EC2 allow the user to customize his implementation, relatively, at will [7]. In fact, Amazon provides the ability to create specialized images for VM instances called Amazon Machine Instances or AMIs. The user can create his own AMI containing his applications, libraries, data, and associated configuration settings. The same AMI can then be deployed across multiple virtual machines forming a customized cluster.

On the other hand, if the cloud is a Software-as-a-Service (SaaS) or PaaS implementation, then the ability to customize the system is significantly lower. Usually, these types of cloud implementations provide a very specific toolset, in the form of software development kits or SDKs. These SDKs cannot provide the functionality of APIs since they set some hard limits within which the user can operate. Furthermore, the user cannot customize the software stack of the underlying system.

Conclusively, only IaaS implementations seem viable for enterprise HPC in the cloud since they provide fine-grained control over the infrastructure. Also, in-house applications can be easily ported to the cloud if the user mirrors his configuration in VM instances.

12.3   Related Research

In this section, we are going to review current research on the application of cloud computing as an HPC platform. While most of these case studies and benchmarks relate to scientific HPC applications, the same basic rules apply for enterprise HPC.

12.3.1   Performance Studies

Since the introduction of EC2 from Amazon, multiple studies have been conducted to assess the performance of the virtualized resources that it offers. While there are other IaaS clouds, EC2 is one of the first solutions to be offered and has a broad perspective offering a multitude of services that include storage, content delivery, database systems, and a large selection of computational units. Therefore, it constitutes a "de facto" platform for cloud research; consequently, most of the research presented here is done using either EC2, or systems based on technologies applied on EC2 such as the Xen virtual machine hypervisor.

12.3.1.1 Performance Studies on the Xen Hypervisor

We mentioned above that there exists a general perception that virtualized systems introduce high overheads, and thus are not suitable for HPC environments. However, studies [26, 27] have shown that the use of paravirtualization, through the Xen hypervisor, provides results on par with modern, nonvirtualized systems. These studies have evaluated the performance of Xen against popular Linux kernels, namely RHEL 2.6.9 and 2.6.12, and the specialized CHAOS Linux HPC kernel on the same cluster system. Furthermore, these benchmarks extended to multiple subsystems in order to provide a fine-grained view of the results.

In the first study [27], Youseff et al. benchmarked network communication performance and computational performance:

- Network bandwidth performance of Xen was lower than the nonvirtualized competitors, but only for small message sizes due to the implementation of Xen's communication subsystem, which uses two I/O rings of buffer descriptors for guest–host operations. For unidirectional and bidirectional messages, this overhead can be amortized when messages get larger. The study concludes that advances in I/O rings and descriptor management are needed to improve the network efficiency of Xen. Network latency on the other hand was better than most other contestants, for up to 32 MPI Processes. This is due to the use of page flipping, which optimizes the guest–host data transfer by avoiding copying. This optimization however offers diminishing returns when we get past 32 processes.
- Computational performance of Xen was about 2% lower than that of CHAOS, but better than other contestants. Although this may seem counterintuitive for a virtualized system, Xen incorporates a very efficient implementation of the borrowed virtual time scheduler (BVT) [10].

In the second study [26], Youseff et al. benchmarked memory access with the Stream benchmark[6] and disk I/O performance with the Bonnie I/O benchmark,[7] and applied two known macrobenchmarks for parallel systems, NAS Parallel Benchmarks,[8] and MIT General Circulation Model[9]:

- Memory Access Performance for Xen was lower than CHAOS since the latter is heavily optimized for memory-intensive workloads. Against RHEL 2.6.12, Xen provided consistently better memory bandwidth due to the asynchronous I/O data transfer between guest and host that we mentioned above. On the contrary, these differences were not as apparent between Xen and RHEL 2.6.9.
- Disk I/O performance is particularly important for applications that require heavy disk usage, like enterprise database-driven applications. The Bonnie benchmark showed that Xen did manage to attain on par I/O performance with

---

[6]http://www.streambench.org/

[7]http://www.textuality.com/bonnie/

[8]http://www.nas.nasa.gov/Resources/Software/npb.html

[9]http://mitgcm.org/

other systems for smaller files. Larger files though pose a problem since Xen tries to reorder requests in order to achieve highly efficient disk access for all guests, and thus makes sequential access of large files inefficient. Since HPC applications may require high-speed I/O, this research proposes that tuning of default I/O buffer rings may help to alleviate this performance degradation.

- NPB and GCM benchmarks combine all of the above microbenchmarks and test the system under computational, communicational, and data I/O workloads. Both tests showed promising results. Researchers argued that Xen can satisfy requirements of HPC applications since, in the overall performance, statistical differences between Xen and CHAOS or RHEL kernels were negligible under the combined workloads provided by NPB and GCM.

12.3.1.2 Performance Benchmarks on Amazon EC2

Research on Xen has proved that virtualized systems do not suffer any significant performance difference and can be effectively used as HPC systems. We must keep in mind though that these benchmarks were applied to dedicated virtualized systems. Clouds are shared between thousands of users, and multiple VMs run on the same hardware, sharing the same resources. The question that arises therefore is whether existing implementations can be used for HPC. In order to answer this question, we have to review case studies on real cloud implementations. Most of the related research utilizes the Amazon EC2 implementation, which uses the above-mentioned Xen hypervisor.

In [22], Ostermann et al. studied the performance of various EC2 cloud resources by applying multiple HPC benchmarks, designed to test both single instances and multiple instances working in collaboration. Initially, they tested EC2 for provision and release times; long-term results showed that while waiting times for provisioning of new instances of VMs may fluctuate, by a small margin, the overall waiting time is unaffected by high system loads.

In terms of compute performance per EC2 instance type, all of which are summarized in Table 12.1, the LMbench benchmark[10] showed that high-cpu instances c1.medium and c1.xlarge underperformed in multiplication while having excellent addition performance. These operations are particularly important for HPC applications, and thus current cpu-intensive instances are suboptimal for the job.

Using the Bonnie benchmark, EC2 instances were tested for disk I/O. Results for sequential operations, which are more typical for HPC, looked promising. In fact, all instance types from m1.small to c1.xlarge performed better than modern commodity systems. Since disk I/O is usually the operation that costs more in terms of time, it is very promising to observe such performance output from virtualized systems.

---

[10]http://www.bitmover.com/lmbench/

Table 12.1 Amazon EC2 instance types – US N.Virginia – UNIX/Linux OS

Name	ECUs[a]	RAM	Arch(bit)	Storage(GB)	Net I/O	Cost($/h)[b]
m1.small	1	1.7	32	160	Moderate	0.085
m1.large	4	7.5	64	850	High	0.34
m1.xlarge	8	15	64	1,690	High	0.68
m2.xlarge	6.5	17.1	64	420	Moderate	0.50
m2.2xlarge	13	34.2	64	850	High	1.00
m2.4xlarge	26	68.4	64	1,690	High	2.00
c1.medium	5	1.7	32	350	Moderate	0.17
c1.xlarge	20	7	64	1,690	High	0.68
cc1.4xlarge	33.5	23	64	1,690	Very high[c]	1.60
cg1.4xlarge	33.5[d]	22	64	1,690	Very high[c]	2.10

[a]EC2 compute units
[b]Prices for February 2011
[c]10 gigabit Ethernet
[d]Also 2×Nvidia Tesla "Fermi" M2050 GPUs

Table 12.2 HPCC benchmarks used in [22]

Benchmark	Description
HPL	The Linpack TPP benchmark measures the floating point rate of execution for solving a linear system of equations
DGEMM	Measures the floating point rate of execution of double precision real matrix–matrix multiplication
STREAM	A simple synthetic benchmark program that measures sustainable memory bandwidth (in GB/s) and the corresponding computation rate for simple vector kernel
RandomAccess	Measures the rate of integer random updates of memory (GUPS)

Memory performance was evaluated through the CacheBench benchmark.[11] Results showed that instances were subject to large performance losses when working sets got near or past the CPU's L2 memory size. This drove researchers to speculate that Amazon has integrated a throttling mechanism into EC2 in order to limit resource consumption.

This study also used the HPC Challenge benchmark[12] in order to assess the capabilities of multiple EC2 instances while serving a single job. Researchers used four of the seven benchmarks of HPCC, namely HPL, DGEMM, STREAM, and RandomAccess all of which are summarized, along with their purpose, in Table 12.2.

The HPL benchmark showed that most of the instance types of EC2 provide performance far below their theoretical peak, as advertised by Amazon. In fact, most of them do not even get close to 50% of their peak performance. The only exception is c1.xlarge, which overcomes 50%.

---

[11] http://icl.cs.utk.edu/projects/llcbench/cachebench.html

[12] http://icl.cs.utk.edu/hpcc/

Table 12.3 NAS parallel benchmarks used in [1]

Benchmark	Description
EP	An "embarrassingly parallel" kernel, which evaluates an integral by means of pseudorandom trials. This kernel, in contrast to others in the list, requires virtually no interprocessor communication
MG	A simplified multigrid kernel. This requires highly structured long-distance communication and tests both short- and long-distance data communication
CG	A conjugate gradient method is used to compute an approximation to the smallest eigenvalue of a large, sparse, symmetric positive definite matrix. This kernel is typical of unstructured grid computations in that it tests irregular long-distance communication, employing unstructured matrix vector multiplication
FT	A 3-D partial differential equation solution using FFTs. This kernel performs the essence of many "spectral" codes. It is a rigorous test of long-distance communication performance
BT	Solution of multiple, independent systems of non-diagonally-dominant, block tridiagonal equations with a (5×5) block size. This benchmark also serves as an I/O benchmark

For HPL only c1.xlarge instances are comparable with HPC clusters. Nevertheless, performance of EC2 clusters for DGEMM, STREAM, and RandomAccess is either close to, or better than modern HPC clusters. Researchers attributed this counter-intuitive behavior to the network latency of the EC2 platform, which can have a negative impact on the HPL benchmark. Amazon uses 1-gigabit Ethernet for all instances except cc1.4xlarge and cg1.4xlarge, that use 10-gigabit, and were not yet available. Modern HPC clusters use either 10-gigabit Ethernet or Infiniband; therefore, it is quite reasonable that such a difference should be present. This makes scalability of EC2 clusters problematic and thus not a suitable option for HPC systems that depend heavily on network performance.

This study concluded that HPC applications need tuning before being deployed to the EC2 cloud. The gains in performance of hand-tuned applications can be quite significant. In addition, results showed that some HPC applications could not be efficiently deployed on clouds unless cloud providers improve the network latency by upgrading their network interconnections.

Another relevant study is [1]. In this, Akioka and Muraoka evaluated the performance of EC2 nodes through the HPL and NPB benchmarks mentioned above. Results of HPL in this study agree with [22] that, while increasing the number of cores available to the system did provide performance benefits, the scaling of the system offered diminishing returns, and measured results were far below their theoretical peak limits.

For the NPB benchmarks, which are summarized in Table 12.3, results again agree with the previous study in that scalability for HPC on EC2 maybe an issue since we cannot control how nodes are scattered, and thus, significant network performance variability may occur. Furthermore, no guarantees are given for performance, and therefore the user cannot be certain if the node will perform in the same fashion during the time that it is leased. The resource broker may allocate many virtual nodes onto the same hardware node, causing an overload that will result in decreased performance.

12.3.1.3 HPC Workflow Performance Evaluation on Amazon EC2

In [17], Juve et al. took a different approach. Instead of applying HPC benchmarks on EC2 nodes, they used scientific workflows that consist of loosely coupled parallel applications of computational tasks connected by data and control flow dependencies. The workflows applied were Montage, Broadband, and Epigenomics. Montage[13] is a low memory and cpu, but high I/O workflow. Broadband[14] is a medium I/O and cpu, but high memory workflow. Finally, Epigenomics[15] is a low I/O, medium memory, and high cpu workflow. The importance of this study lies in the use of real scientific HPC applications. Benchmarks, in previous studies, are like stress tests to the systems they are applied. They try to test a single resource of a system under heavy workload, whereas workflows provide a more all-around view of the system by stressing multiple resources simultaneously.

Experimental results came from execution of these workflows on EC2 nodes and NCSA's Abe cluster. The workflows were applied on all EC2 instance types. Results for Montage showed that m1.xlarge instances were better suited for this workflow. In fact, m1.xlarge managed to surpass the Abe node with local disk. The other Abe node though, equipped with a Lustre[16] file system, achieved more than two times faster performance. The overall virtualization overhead between c1.xlarge and Abe local was less than 8% indicating relatively good I/O performance.

For the Broadband workflow, which is memory intensive, Abe Lustre again provided better performance, although by a much smaller margin compared to c1.xlarge. The I/O performance of the Lustre file system was not as apparent due to the medium I/O of this workflow. The virtualization overhead for this workflow was only 1%.

Finally, for Epigenomics, which is almost entirely CPU bound, the Abe nodes provided better performance than c1.xlarge. The overhead of virtualization this time was about 10%. Researchers suggested that this result might mean that virtualization incurs larger overheads for CPU-bound applications in general.

Conclusively, the researchers assessed that the overall performance of EC2 for HPC workflows is quite reasonable in comparison to a modern cluster. In fact, EC2 nodes were less powerful than the cluster nodes so a difference in performance was expected. Results showed that for memory-intensive and CPU-intensive applications, the virtualization overheads are small, and in the future with the improvement of relative technologies, they will become even smaller. For I/O intensive applications, EC2 stands at a disadvantage compared to modern clusters since it lacks a distributed file system like Lustre. Allowing multiple EC2 nodes to use one Elastic Block Storage (EBS)[17] volume may help to alleviate this problem. Although these results are promising, this study did not consider the application of workflows across

---

[13] http://montage.ipac.caltech.edu/

[14] http://scec.usc.edu/research/cme/

[15] http://epigenome.usc.edu/

[16] http://en.wikipedia.org/wiki/Lustre_(file_system)

[17] http://aws.amazon.com/ebs/

multiple interconnected nodes. That application may have held different results, due to the low-speed connectivity between EC2 instances.

Many more studies on the subject of performance provide comparable results to the studies mentioned above. For further research, readers can also refer to [5, 14, 18, 24, 25].

We must note here that all of the above research was conducted before the introduction of Cluster Compute and Cluster GPU instances,[18] which are the HPC-as-a-Service implementation of Amazon and will be described in detail in Sect. 4.1.

12.3.2   Scheduling Studies

Given the important characteristics of cloud computing, like the ability to dynamically scale infrastructure or the usage-based billing model, it becomes obvious that new methods of scheduling must be implemented in order to take advantage of these features. This is in the interests of both the cloud provider and the cloud consumer. Scheduling methods must be aware of the scalability capabilities of the environment in which they are deployed. In addition, they must seek to minimize costs for the consumer, while maintaining a good performance. This is particularly important for enterprise HPC since enterprises need to be convinced that maintaining their resources in the cloud is not only better but also less costly. Furthermore, scheduling methods implemented by the cloud provider must be aware of the SLA terms that exist between the provider and the consumer in order to maintain the availability and performance of the user's application, at a desired state.

12.3.2.1   Hybrid Cloud Scheduling Studies

Though the term "hybrid cloud"[19,20] is still under discussion, the use of a public cloud as an extension to a private cloud or cluster naturally falls under this category.

In [23], Salehi and Buyya considered two market-oriented scheduling policies aimed at the evaluation of EC2 resources as an extension to a private cluster. They implemented an extension for the Gridbus[21] broker, which allows it to lease resources from the EC2 cloud. They implemented two scheduling policies: Time Optimization, which aimed for the minimization of time, within time and budget constraints, and Cost Optimization, which aimed to minimize cost within the same constraints.

---

[18] http://aws.typepad.com/aws/2010/07/the-new-amazon-ec2-instance-type-the-cluster-compute-instance.html

[19] http://en.wikipedia.org/wiki/Cloud_computing#Hybrid_cloud

[20] http://csrc.nist.gov/groups/SNS/cloud-computing/

[21] http://www.cloudbus.org/broker/

They applied the two policies and found that for time optimization, the completion time scales almost linearly with the budget. This was an expected result since by increasing the budget, the broker was able to lease more instances to serve uncompleted tasks. On the other hand, cost optimization policy does not improve performance over a certain budget. This result is also intuitive since this policy would not lease more resources than those absolutely required to finish within deadline, even if there is still budget available.

They also measured the efficiency of the methods and came up with interesting results. Since EC2 charges per hour, the optimal time to release a resource would be close to the end of the hour in order to avoid being charged for the next hour. In this manner, efficiency, for the time optimization policy, dived sharply when the available budget was not enough for the system to complete work before the next charging cycle. Therefore, resource brokers should bear in mind that significant gains are to be expected if unneeded resources are released right before the next charging cycle.

Finally, they conducted experiments with different workload types in order to assess the applicability of their policies and concluded that these policies are indeed applicable to various workloads while not breaching the set deadlines.

In another study [4], Assunção et al. used discrete event simulation in order to evaluate the performance and cost of a cluster system that used cloud computing as an extension to in-house resources. The implemented simulator considered the Amazon EC2 as the cloud platform. The job scheduler was split in two parts: the Site scheduler, which was responsible for the scheduling of jobs in the in-house cluster, and the cloud scheduler, responsible for the scheduling of cloud resources. The system was studied under multiple strategy sets involving conservative, aggressive, and selective backfilling. These strategies sets were paired with multiple different redirection policies that determined whether a job should be sent to the cloud or be executed on the cluster. Redirection was considered a one-way process, and the usage of reservations for jobs was considered in multiple strategies.

Furthermore, user-submitted applications fell under two categories. Deadline constrained applications, which required service within a specified time frame, and Best-Effort applications, which were not strict about the time of execution. All strategy sets used are summarized in Table 12.4.

A metric, termed performance cost, was used to evaluate the gain in response time relative to the cost incurred by each strategy, in comparison to the cluster without the cloud extension. Another metric, termed nonviolation cost, was used to assess the cost of reducing deadlines to meet SLAs provided to consumers.

The workloads for experiments involving performance cost were generated using the Lublin99 [19] model. The model was tuned by modifying three of the parameters specified by this model, namely the mean number of virtual machines for each request, the parameter affecting the interarrival time of requests at rush hours, and a third parameter that affects the computation of requests runtimes.

Results showed that the naive strategy was the most costly strategy under all workload configurations. They also found that performance cost scaled linearly, as the number of VMs increased, under all strategies but naive; the latter was very

Table 12.4 Scheduling strategy sets used in [4]

Strategy set	Description
Naïve	Conservative backfilling in conjunction with the redirection algorithm executing upon arrival of a job. If the job cannot be scheduled for execution immediately, on-site, the cloud scheduler checks for adequate cloud resources and schedules it on the cloud. Otherwise, it is queued on-site
Shortest queue	FCFS with aggressive backfilling. Redirection executes upon arrivals and completions. It computes the ratio of VMs required by waiting jobs to VMs available for both site and cloud and tries to balance the two ratios by redirecting to the cloud
Weighted queue	An extension of the previous strategy. Redirection again upon arrival or completion of a task. This strategy assesses the number of VMs that can be started on the cloud and redirects waiting requests to the cloud until either the VM limit is reached or all requests are redirected
Selective	Selective backfilling; uses ratios of site's and cloud's queues as with shortest queue, assesses where jobs with expansion factor over the threshold can have the earliest start time, and makes a reservation for them accordingly
Conservative	Conservative backfilling for both sites; the scheduler selects the site or the cloud depending on which can meet the deadline. If it cannot be met, the scheduler selects best site according to the earliest start time
Aggressive	Aggressive backfilling with earliest deadline first (EDF). Scheduler builds a schedule upon each arrival for the currently waiting requests sorting them according to EDF. If a request can be scheduled without violating its deadline locally, then it does so; if not, then a schedule is build for the cloud. If the request can be served by the cloud without violating deadlines of other requests, then it is redirected to the cloud. If the deadline cannot be met under any circumstances, then the best site is selected according to the earliest start time
Conservative with reservation support	Both sites use conservative backfilling and support in-advance reservation. Arriving best effort requests are scheduled locally. Reservation requests are also scheduled locally, if it is possible within the required period; if not, then available cloud resources are checked. Finally, if no site can service the request under the reservation conditions, then the request if rejected

expensive even for small requests. For the second parameter, results showed that for small interarrival times, all methods provided similar performance except for naive which had a high performance cost again. As the interarrival times increased, requests arrived at a slower rate, and thus relying on the cloud became more costly for all strategies. For the last parameter, all strategies provided similar performance under all configurations, with naive having consistently higher performance cost, but by a smaller margin this time.

For experiments involving the nonviolation metric, real workloads were used. Researchers used a Bernoulli distribution for the selection of jobs with deadlines from the trace and used the method described in [16] to generate the deadlines for requests. They evaluated their model for tight, normal, and relaxed deadlines.

Results depicted the amounts spent to reduce violations of deadlines; conservative and aggressive deadline strategies provided better results since they were significantly less costly than other strategies. These results were expected since only these strategies do consider deadlines in their operation. All other strategies, except for naive, sort requests according to deadlines, but redirect requests by evaluating other performance characteristics. For all types of deadlines, both strategies provided similar results on average, although for high percentages of requests with deadlines, the aggressive method was more costly than the conservative method.

12.3.2.2 Public Cloud Scheduling Studies

In [21], Moschakis and Karatza studied a model of a public cloud computing system with Gang Scheduling and evaluated both the performance and cost of two scheduling algorithms, namely Adaptive First Come Fist Serve (AFCFS) and Largest Job First Served (LJFS) under various workloads and job size characteristics.

This model considered an elastic cluster of VMs built on Amazon EC2. The number of VMs leased by the system scaled dynamically while serving jobs. The job entry point, a dispatcher VM (DVM), implemented a Shortest Queue First (SQF) algorithm for the allocation of jobs to VMs. The maximum number of VMs allowed was 120 since EC2 allows up to 20 regular plus up to 100 "spot" VMs. The VMs were considered to belong in the same instance type, and thus the system was considered homogeneous in terms of performance. Job arrival and service times were exponentially distributed, while job sizes fell under two uniformly distributed categories, namely lowly parallel with 1–16 parallel tasks per job and highly parallel with 17–32 tasks per job. The job size coefficient q determined what percentage of jobs belonged to the first category. The system was examined under a q of 0.25, 0.50, and 0.75.

In gang scheduling, tasks of jobs are scheduled for simultaneous execution, and therefore, each one must be mapped to a different VM. The gang scheduling algorithms examined were two of the most commonly used in the field. AFCFS usually shows preference to smaller jobs, while LJFS prioritizes larger jobs.

Apart from scheduling, algorithms related to the leasing and releasing of VMs were also implemented. The system leased VMs under either of two conditions:

- VM inadequacy. This condition happened when a job with more tasks than available VMs arrived.
- VM overload. A metric termed Average Load Factor was applied to assess the load of VM waiting queues. If this metric breached a certain threshold, the system provisioned for a number of VMs equal to the degree of parallelism of the next arriving job. Jobs waiting for VM lease were queued at the DVM's queue.

The release system required that a VM is idle, with no waiting jobs, and that its release would not lead to a new shortage of VMs for jobs waiting at the DVM.

Multiple metrics were used to assess the performance of the model. Average and Weighted, Response, and Waiting Time, in conjunction with Slowdown metrics described in [11], were applied. Moreover, a metric termed Cost-Performance Efficiency (CPE) was devised to evaluate the gain in response time in relation to the cost for both scheduling algorithms.

Results concluded that LJFS was better equipped to handle heavier workloads even more so when there was a plethora of large jobs. It provided better response times than AFCFS for faster arrival rates and on par average slowdowns. Cost–performance wise, LJFS again achieved better overall cost efficiency than AFCFS even when the latter provided better response times.

For further studies on the subject of scheduling, readers can also refer to [2, 6].

12.4   Implementations

To the best of our knowledge, currently, there are two existing implementations offering HPC-as-a-Service. In this section, we are going to provide a brief description of the characteristics of both services.

12.4.1   Amazon EC2 Cluster Compute and Cluster GPU

As we mentioned above, the Amazon EC2 cloud now provides HPC-targeted instances termed "Cluster Compute and Cluster GPU."[22] These instances are designed to provide high-performance computing resources for HPC applications, and faster interconnect between the instances in order to reduce the networking latencies that performance benchmarks described above have found.

Furthermore, enterprises can benefit from this for their HPC applications since no costly hardware infrastructure is needed, no maintenance, and no problems stemming from insufficient provisioning of resources. Cluster compute instances are scalable and flexible by providing hourly operating costs just like normal instances.

Cluster Compute and Cluster GPU instances, according to Amazon, provide low latency with 10 Gbps bandwidth between nodes and allow for cluster sizes up to 128 instances. In addition, in contrast to normal instances, which are deployed on Intel or AMD CPUs, Cluster instances are deployed on specific architectures, namely Intel Nehalem, in order to allow developers to tune their applications by using compilers designed for those architectures, and thus achieving better performance.

The specifications for Cluster Compute and Cluster GPU instances are summarized in Table 12.1.

Amazon has gone one step further and provides two more web services for HPC. The first is Amazon Elastic MapReduce, which utilizes the Hadoop Framework[23] to process data through EC2 and therefore is scalable on demand. The second is the Public Data Sets web service that provides a central repository of public data sets, which can be seamlessly integrated into applications running on the EC2 cloud.

---

[22] http://aws.amazon.com/ec2/hpc-applications/

[23] http://hadoop.apache.org/

12.4.2   Penguin on Demand

Penguin Computing is a company providing HPC hardware in form of custom build servers and HPC middleware. Scyld ClusterWare[24] is a cluster management solution, which allows multiple servers to provide their combined computing resources as one entity. The Penguin on Demand (POD)[25] service provides a scalable on-demand HPC platform with high-density nodes and directly attached storage; POD does not make use of any virtualization technology; instead, it provides direct access to physical nodes, which are interconnected with a 10 Gigabit network, either Ethernet or Infiniband.

The service provides access to users through SSH, or through a web interface. In addition, Scyld ClusterWare is used to provide rapid provision of additional resources. The system incorporates two scheduling managers, TORQUE[26] and Oracle Grid Engine.[27] Data transfers to POD happen through either the Internet or an overnight disk transfer service. Submitted jobs are queued and then scheduled by the POD job scheduler according to a "Fair Share" policy. Users are able though to inquire for the status of the waiting queue.

The difference between the two solutions described above is that Amazon provides a completely customizable solution offering developer APIs for almost everything in their service. Users can build, customize, and contribute their own AMIs completely up to their specification. On the other hand, POD is like an HPC platform as a service solution since it limits developer access by providing only specific compilers and libraries with which programmers can work.

12.5   Conclusion

Our perception of computing is changing constantly. Two decades ago, HPC applications run only on mainframe supercomputers, while PCs were able to perform only trivial tasks. Ten years ago, the grid and clusters of commodity computers replaced supercomputers and took the lead in the HPC market. The rise of cloud computing presents a new opportunity for the evolution of computing. Maybe, 10 years from now, computers will be nothing more than thin clients, and all our processing will be done on the clouds. Until then though, multiple issues have to be addressed before clouds become viable for large-scale processing like HPC. Problems like integration and customization can be handled by existing technologies, while others like security and availability will need the improvement of existing technologies, or the introduction of new ones, in order to achieve scalability that

---

[24] http://www.penguincomputing.com/software/scyld_clusterware

[25] http://www.penguincomputing.com/POD/PODEnvironment

[26] http://www.clusterresources.com/products/torque-resource-manager.php

[27] http://www.oracle.com/us/products/tools/oracle-grid-engine-075549.html

spans thousands of nodes. In addition, for issues like performance, scientific research has begun studying the characteristics of cloud systems in order to assess the status of the technological improvements needed to achieve optimal results. While initial studies showed that clouds might not be suitable for this application, newer HPC-targeted offerings show that HPC is within the goals of major cloud providers. Thus, the first steps towards an HPC cloud have been taken, but only the future will show if clouds are up to the task.

References

1. Akioka, S., Muraoka, Y.: HPC benchmarks on Amazon EC2. In: Proceedings of the 24th IEEE International Conference on Advanced Information Networking and Application Workshops (WAINA), IEEE Computer Society, Washington, DC, pp. 1029–1034 (2010). doi:10.1109/WAINA.2010.166
2. Andrzejak, A., Kondo, D., Yi, S.: Decision model for cloud computing under SLA constraints. Research Report INRIA. http://hal.inria.fr/inria-00474849/en/ (2010). Accessed 23 Feb 2011
3. Armbrust, M., Fox, A., Griffith, R., Joseph, A.D., Katz, R.H., Konwinski, A., Lee, G., Patterson, D.A., Rabkin, A., Stoica, I., Zaharia, M.: Above the clouds: a Berkeley view of cloud computing. Technical Report, UC Berkeley. http://radlab.cs.berkeley.edu/publication/285 (2009). Accessed 23 Feb 2011
4. Assunção, M.D., Costanzo, A., Buyya, R.: A cost-benefit analysis of using cloud computing to extend the capacity of clusters. Cluster Comput. **13**, 335–347 (2010). doi: 10.1007/s10586-010-0131-x
5. Bientinesi, P., Iakymchuk, R., Napper, J.: HPC on competitive cloud resources. In: Furht, B., Escalante, A. (eds.) Handbook of Cloud Computing. Springer, Boston (2010). doi:10.1007/978-1-4419-6524-0_21
6. Buyya, R., Ranjan, R., Calheiros, R.N.: Modeling and simulation of scalable cloud computing environments and the cloudSim toolkit: challenges and opportunities. In: Proceedings of the 7th High Performance Computing and Simulation Conference (HPCS), Leipzig, Germany (2009). doi:10.1109/HPCSIM.2009.5192685
7. Buyya, R., Yeo, C.S., Venugopal, S., Broberg, J., Brandic, I.: Cloud computing and emerging IT platforms: vision, hype, and reality for delivering computing as the 5th utility. Future Gener. Comput. Syst. **25**(6), 599–616 (2009). Elsevier B.V. doi:10.1016/j.future.2008.12.001
8. Clarke, E.M., Grumberg, O., Peled, D.: Model Checking. MIT Press, Cambridge (2000)
9. Dillon, T., Wu, C., Chang, E.: Cloud computing: issues and challenges. In: Proceedings of the 24th IEEE International Conference on Advanced Information Networking and Application (AINA), Perth, Australia, pp. 27–33 (2010). doi:10.1109/AINA.2010.187
10. Duda, K.J., Cheriton, D.R.: Borrowed-virtual-time (BVT) scheduling: supporting latency sensitive threads in a general-purpose scheduler, ACM SIGOPS. Oper. Syst. Rev. **33**(5), 261–276 (1999). doi:10.1145/319344.319169
11. Feitelson, D.: Metrics for parallel job scheduling and their convergence. In: Feitelson, D., Rudolph, L. (eds.) Job Scheduling Strategies for Parallel Processing. Lecture Notes in Computer Science, vol. 2221, pp. 188–205. Springer, Berlin/Heidelberg (2001)
12. Gens, F.: New IDC IT cloud services survey: top benefits and challenges. IDC exchange. http://blogs.idc.com/ie/?p=730 (2009). Accessed 23 Feb 2011
13. Goyal, P.: Enterprise usability of cloud computing environments: issues and challenges. In: 19th IEEE International Workshops on Enabling Technology: Infrastructure for Collaboration Enterprise, pp. 54–59 (2010). doi:10.1109/WETICE.2010.15

14. Hazelhurst, S.: Scientific computing using virtual high-performance computing: a case study using the Amazon elastic computing cloud. In: Proceedings of the 2008 Annual Research Conference of the South African Institute of Computer Science and Information Technology on IT Research in Developing Countries: Riding the Wave of Technology, SAICSIT'08, ACM, New York, NY, pp. 94–103 (2008). doi:10.1145/1456659.1456671 (2008)
15. He, Q., Zhou, S., Kobler, B., Duffy, D., McGlynn, T.: Case study for running HPC applications in public clouds. In: Proceedings of the 19th ACM International Symposium on High Performance Distributed Computing, ACM, New York, NY, pp. 395–401 (2010). doi:10.1145/1851476.1851535 (2010)
16. Islam, M., Balaji, P., Sadayappan, P., Panda, D.: QoPS: a QoS based scheme for parallel job scheduling. In: Feitelson, D., Rudolph, L., Schwiegelshohn, U. (eds.) Job Scheduling Strategies for Parallel Processing. Lecture Notes in Computer Science, vol. 2862, pp. 252–268. Springer, Berlin/Heidelberg (2003). doi:10.1007/10968987_13
17. Juve, G., Deelman, E., Vahi, K., Mehta, G., Berriman, B., Berman, B.P., Maechling, P.: Scientific workflow applications on Amazon EC2. In: 5th IEEE International Conference on E-Science Workshops, Oxford, UK, pp. 59–66 (2009). doi:10.1109/ESCIW.2009.5408002 (2009)
18. Kim, H., el Khamra, Y., Jha, S., Parashar, M.: An autonomic approach to integrated HPC grid and cloud usage. In: Proceedings of the 5th IEEE International Conference on e-Sci'09, Oxford, UK, pp. 366–373 (2009). doi:10.1109/e-Science.2009.58
19. Lublin U, Feitelson, D.G.: (2003) The workload on parallel supercomputers: modeling the characteristics of rigid jobs. J. Parallel Distrib. Comput. **63**, 1105–1122. Elsevier. doi:10.1016/S0743-7315(03)00108-4
20. Mergen, M.F., Uhlig, V., Krieger, O., Xenidis, J.: Virtualization for high-performance computing SIGOPS. Oper. Syst. Rev. **40**(2), 8–11 (2006). doi:10.1145/1131322.1131328
21. Moschakis, I., Karatza, H.: Evaluation of gang scheduling performance and cost in a cloud computing system. J. Supercomput. (2010). Online First. doi:10.1007/s11227–010–0481–4
22. Ostermann, S., Iosup, A., Yigitbasi, N., Prodan, R., Fahringer, T., Epema, D.: A performance analysis of EC2 cloud computing services for scientific computing. In: Diaz, M., Avresky, D., Bode, A., Bruno, C., Dekel, E. (eds.) Cloud Computing: First International Conference, CloudComp 2009, Munich, Germany, 19–21 Oct 2009, Revised Selected Papers LNICST, vol. 34, pp. 115–131 (2010). doi:10.1007/978–3–642–12636–9
23. Salehi, M., Buyya, R.: Adapting market-oriented scheduling policies for cloud computing. In: Hsu, C.H., Yang, L.T., Park, J.H., Yeo, S.S. (eds.) Algorithms and Architectures for Parallel Processing. Lecture Notes in Computer Science, vol. 6081, pp. 351–362. Springer, Berlin/Heidelberg (2010). doi:10.1007/978-3-642-13119-6_31
24. Vecchiola, C., Pandey, S., Buyya, R.: High-performance cloud computing: a view of scientific applications. In: Proceedings of the 10th International Symposium, on Pervasive Systems, Algorithms, and Networks, Kaohsiung, ISPAN'09, pp. 4–16. IEEE Computer Society, Washington, DC (2009). doi:10.1109/I-SPAN.2009.150
25. Wang, G., Ng, T.S.E.: The impact of virtualization on network performance of Amazon EC2 Data Center. In: Proceedings of the 29th Conference on Information Communications, INFOCOM'10, pp. 1163–1171. IEEE Press, Piscataway, NJ (2010). doi:10.1109/INFCOM.2010.5461931
26. Youseff, L., Wolski, R., Gorda, B., Krintz, C.: Paravirtualization for HPC systems. In: Min, G., Di Martino, B., Yang, L., Guo, M., Ruenger, G. (eds.) Frontiers of High Performance Computing and Networking – ISPA 2006 Workshops. Lecture Notes in Computer Science, vol. 4331, pp. 474–486. Springer, Berlin/Heidelberg (2006). doi:10.1007/11942634_49
27. Youseff, L., Wolski, R., Gorda, B., Krintz, C.: Evaluating the performance impact of Xen on MPI and process execution for HPC systems. In: Proceedings of the 2nd International Workshop on Virtualization Technology in Distributed Computing, VTDC 06', Guilin, IEEE Computer Society, Washington, DC (2006). doi:10.1109/VTDC.2006.4

Part IV
Further Research and Studies

Chapter 13
Cloud Computing and the Emerging Market

J. Doug Thomson

Abstract The aim of this chapter is to review the range of emerging 'cloud' marketing alternatives from dedicated private communication solutions to multi-tenanted public solutions. Cloud computing is a global trend which promises to be the single biggest growth area in ICT. Current estimates are that by 2020, approximately 14% of all digital information will be stored in the cloud. Organizations look at cloud computing as a utility to lower ICT costs and boost effectiveness and are seek to move from fixed capital expenditure investments to variable operating expenses, using these resources to withstand seasonal peaks and for improved shareholder value.

Cloud vendor organizations are developing, so they are well placed to take advantage of this technology trend and the anticipated market growth. This requires investing in leading software and virtualised hardware so as to offer customers security, speed, lower costs and service reliability over high-performance networks. Cloud computing is an evolving market opportunity for both customer and cloud vendor alike. However, in the development of cloud-marketing strategies and campaigns, there are significant risks for both vendor and consumer. These are discussed in this chapter.

13.1 Background

Cloud computing can be defined as a scalable and flexible share computing solution in which third party suppliers use virtualization technology to create and distribute computing resources to client organizations on demand via the internet browser [20]. In many ways, cloud computing attempts to copy the functional and structural

J.D. Thomson (✉)
Graduate School of Business and Law, RMIT University, Melbourne, Australia
e-mail: doug.thomson@rmit.edu.au

Z. Mahmood and R. Hill (eds.), *Cloud Computing for Enterprise Architectures*,
Computer Communications and Networks, DOI 10.1007/978-1-4471-2236-4_13,
© Springer-Verlag London Limited 2011

aspects of a living being. In the human body, the autonomic system facilitates and regulates a variety of functions including respiration, blood pressure, circulation and emotive response. The autonomic nervous system is the interconnecting fabric that supports feedback loops between internal states and various sources by which internal and external conditions are monitored. It comprises self configuration, self healing, self optimization and self protection [17]. Autognostics or self knowledge provides the autonomic system with a basis for response and validation. It includes a range of self discovery, awareness and analysis capabilities that provide the autonomic system with a view on a high-level state, and interoperation with configuration and policy management, and automatic defence. This represents the human perceptual subsystems that gather, analyze and report on internal and external states and conditions. The aim of human autonomic networking is to create self managing networks and to enable their continuous growth. Future communication systems such as cloud computing may be designed in a similar way to the human autonomic nervous system, with inputs from individual network elements, traffic flows, end hosts, application performance data, logic diagrams and performance specifications [15, 17]. The twenty-first century vision of computing promises to deliver computing as a utility [5].

13.1.1   The Aim of This Chapter

The aim of this chapter is to review the range of emerging cloud-marketing options and their associated risks from dedicated private cloud solutions to multi-tenanted public cloud solutions.

13.2   Introduction

Cloud computing is being heralded as an important trend in information technology throughout the world with suggested benefits for business including reduced costs and increased productivity – however, many organizations may be moving too quickly to the cloud without making sure their information is secure [24]. Cloud computing is a model for enabling organizations to access ubiquitous computing resources though a utility network [5]. The cloud is no more nor less than an integrated service offering organizations the opportunity to rent software and virtual hardware applications on demand at a cost less than that of individually owning, servicing and maintaining the same service [1, 2, 32]. Cloud computing uses a collection of distributed services, applications, information and infrastructure comprising pools of computer, network, information and storage resources – such components can be rapidly orchestrated, provisioned, implemented and decommissioned using an on-demand utility [24]. It has become a global trend that is offering software services in a different way through marketing of the cloud concept.

Gantz and Reinsel [10] estimate that by 2020, approximately 14% of all digital information will be stored in the cloud. Cloud computing is the single biggest growth area in ICT, and the industry globally is expected to be worth more than US $150b by 2014 [11]. Organizations anticipate cloud computing will lower their ICT costs and boost ICT effectiveness. They are seeking to move from capital investment to variable operational expense and using this to cope with seasonal peaks and for processing software intensive tasks [8]. Such resources need to be planned to be made available from a nominated but not dedicated resource pool which can be released with minimal management effort [1]. Web hosting is rapidly converging with cloud system infrastructure services. For the last several years, the market has been evolving towards on-demand infrastructure provided on a flexible, pay-as-you-go basis. But the introduction of cloud computing offerings has radically accelerated innovation in this market. The 2008 economic downturn has accelerated adoption of these offerings, thanks to the cost savings that can be achieved by the move from physical to virtual services and from purchasing for peak capacity to obtaining what is needed only when it is needed. The majority of organizations now obtain at least some of their IT infrastructure on demand. This evolution has quickly changed the vendor landscape, bringing in new entrants.

13.3   Delivery Models

There are commonly recognized delivery models (Fig. 13.1) – software as a service (SaaS), where the client organization has an application deployed from the network and does not configure or manage the software, operating system, platform or any

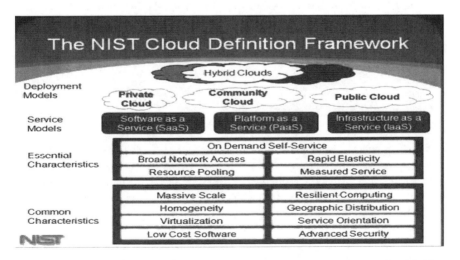

Fig. 13.1 National Institute of Standards and Technology (NIST) cloud computing definition framework (Source: Grance [13])

aspect of the network; platform as a service (PaaS), where the client organization uses the hosting environment for applications; infrastructure as a service (IaaS), where the client organization accesses the core computing resources and can configure and manage the operating system, storage, middleware and networking components, sometimes also referred to as utility computing; and communications as a service (CaaS), where collaboration and communication technologies are hosted in the 'cloud' [1, 13]. There are a range of alternatives from dedicated private cloud communication solutions through to multi-tenant public cloud solutions. This applies to services such as video conferencing, collaboration solutions and voice over internet protocol (VoIP).

The cloud computing suite of goods and services are at different stages of the product life cycle [33], and when combined, they offer an organization flexibility to manage costs and leverage the benefits offered by an on-demand utility computing service together with managed security and platforms [9].

While software as a service has been established for more than 5 years, with few exceptions, it has not truly delivered the expected benefits. This has been so because on-demand capacity based on virtualized computing was not commercially available to most client organizations. But the market segments of cloud computing are now entering maturity and so are in the product growth stage (excluding communications as a service).

Competitors in the provision of cloud computing can be grouped into global service providers, system integrators, online specialists and hosting providers. Global software service providers are establishing their cloud computing service offerings and offer whole of business contracts to multinational corporations. System integrators have the potential to extend existing relationships into outsourced or offshore cloud computing services [20, 28]. In the longer term, online specialists are likely to develop competing organization offerings globally [20, 28]. Hosting providers offer hosting and data centre services which will expand into the cloud computing market. The best opportunity for cloud vendors is to maximize their relationship with client organizations at the beginning of their cloud journey based on a marketing vision and strategy which emphasizes the ability to execute [5, 10, 22].

13.4   Marketing Strategy

Cloud computing has a direct marketing opportunity and is core to underpinning broader indirect revenues for cloud computing vendors. Marketing strategies need to demonstrate vision, smart network capabilities, skilled staff, global monitoring, service assurance and security methodologies. Vendors will need to differentiate their offerings, probably by highlighting future possibilities and improved extended network-based services. Marketing campaigns will need to address the software vendor's organization strategy to grow new wave revenues that leverage next generation Internet Protocols.

It is suggested that a cloud-marketing strategy emphasizes three specific phases: awareness, experience and value. The awareness phase aims to generate recognition that a particular vendor has an appropriate cloud computing offer. This is an advertising and direct marketing campaign aimed at a potential client's decision-makers. Such advertising is likely to be in IT publications, e.g. CIO magazine and online news sites. Other awareness options include public affairs programs, interviews and speeches.

The experience phase invites client organizations to experience cloud technology which will give them an opportunity to understand the technology, security, scalability and to witness smart and skilled staff in action. The value phase should establish relationships with key IT decision-makers, understand their business requirements and demonstrate market leading capability in a way that is targeted to meet their organization's needs. Cloud computing is an evolving opportunity particularly for retail software vendors directly targeting organizations, particularly small to medium business, public and not for profit organizations [18, 34].

13.5   Target Markets

In a recent survey of IT professionals by IDC, it was found that the demand for cloud computing is moving significantly beyond collaboration applications and web hosting into a range of emerging cloud-based opportunities [11]. This could indicate that cloud computing has established a broad appeal to IT professionals regardless of their specific industry. The opportunities range from simple backup and storage options through comprehensive services such as collaboration and organization application suites. The value that client organizations put on cloud computing services, such as providing IT support for new ventures and data intensive applications, will help identify market opportunities and, in due course, establish brand dominance [1, 2, 23]. Demand for cloud computing has now progressed beyond the early adopters and the visionaries and is attracting mainstream market client organizations [22]. Like any innovation, the competitive value will depend upon the client organization's ability to evaluate future opportunities, risk and costs. As a result, there will be some who will be slower to take up the service [12, 14]. The strongest opportunities for cloud vendors may be to attract organizations looking for one of the following cloud solutions: event related, where organizations need additional bandwidth capacity and computer power to supplement their existing hosting or application computing capability for a specific event on demand as extra capacity is required; redundancy, where dual site is a significant cost for most organizations and one that previously has been an acceptable cost to ignore but which cloud computing now may provide a way to mitigate such costs.

13.6   Major Risk: Security

Lack of information security is a major risk issue for both parties, vendor and client organizations. Security involves authentication, authorization and access. This requires contractual definition of vendor and client organization roles and their relationship to resources, processes and to each other. High-level concepts such as privacy, anonymity and verification need to be embedded in the form of role definition derived from the vendor and client organization's strategic policies. Security mediates between competing demands to achieve maximum performance at minimum risk, with automatic defence recovering the balance when inevitable risk translates to threat. It is necessary for security subsystems to interoperate with policy management, configuration management and automatic defence mechanisms. The latter should maintain the assigned roles in balance with performance [15, 17]. A Ponemon [24] study suggests that organizations using cloud computing resources may be at risk as a consequence of insecure cloud computing applications, infrastructure and platforms since deployment decisions are frequently made by executives or end users who may not have the knowledge or expertise to properly evaluate security risks. Without vetting procedures that involve IT security practitioners or other experts, organizations may find mission critical applications are operating in insecure environments. Organizations need to evaluate vendor proposed security technologies and control practices, and whether these are best deployed either on-premise or in the cloud, and rate the types of sensitive or confidential information too risky to be moved to the cloud [24]. Organizations with high security requirements such as banks are unlikely to consider public or multi-tenanted infrastructure, but may prefer private cloud or dedicated virtual infrastructure to meet a range of potential needs [27].

Security in the cloud is a shared responsibility between the vendor and the client organization. IT security experts may be needed to advise the appropriate levels of cloud security. It will be necessary for organizations to develop policies requiring knowledgeable people to evaluate the security posture of potential cloud vendors together with procedures that will enable mission critical applications to be vetted as a priority before moving to a 'secure' cloud environment [24]. After migrating to the cloud, organizations will need to ensure access rights are effectively managed and continuously identify sensitive, mission critical or confidential data to ensure such data are kept on premise. For this to be effective, defined contractual responsibility and liability is needed to ensure vendors carry accountability to ensure a safe IT environment for their client organization. But enhancing security practices is likely to increase the cost of cloud computing, so diminishing is one of the main reasons for choosing the cloud. Ponemon [24] study suggests that mitigation of security risks may be achieved by taking an inventory of all cloud computing resources and assessing the risks they pose to the organization's security posture. For all high risk cloud applications, there is a need to consider whether to discontinue their use or to allocate more resources to make them more secure. In case of disastrous migration to the cloud, there is a need to have plans for business continuity, disaster recovery and e-rediscovery. Security and other risk allocation must be clearly defined and determined in all contracts between the vendor and the client organization, with risk allocated to the party best able to carry the risk.

13.7 Value Proposition

There are a number of aspects which make up a value proposition for each organization contemplating cloud computing – and each will have different requirements. These may include the illusion of infinite computing resources on demand so eliminating the need for complex resource planning and significant capital investment and the elimination of complete commitment to one arrangement so starting small and growing into future requirements without the need for re-architecture or complex and expensive platform migrations [5]. The option of paying for the use of the cloud computing resources on a short term or on an as needed basis is likely to be attractive.

The vendor needs to demonstrate high performing connectivity with increased bandwidth options, improved application performance and increased reliability for mission critical requirements [6]. Client organizations will expect increased business productivity through improved effectiveness and flexibility of business applications, especially ERP and CRM [27]. Previous poor experiences with software vendors may make some organizations reluctant starters [29]. Client organizations will anticipate a lower cost of ownership and an operations expense model with dynamic scale to meet peak business or seasonal capacity demands [26, 34]. Vendors will need to demonstrate a depth of network centric people, applications, service capabilities and network operational facilities, together with a large fully integrated Internet Protocol network – that is, a virtual network interface implemented in software only and not connected to any hardware, but which is fully integrated. Further value will be expected by client organizations to be delivered by reputable, not rent seeking [30] vendors in the strategic follow-up phase.

13.8 Clients and Vendors

Strengths of cloud computing include 24/7 global operations, monitoring assurance, network integration and world class integration. Weaknesses include performance unpredictability since these are emerging platforms with resources shared across public/private networks [25]. Opportunities for vendors include low cost, low performance initial offers for network security, security monitoring and mitigation and software licensing. Follow on arrangements for the anticipated growth in the volume of digital information going into the cloud [10] and improved security, self healing and hybrid diagnostic tools may be expensive [7]. Threats for vendors include their OEM partners selling dedicated virtualization as private cloud infrastructure directly to larger organizations, and global vendors establishing offerings taking top end market share with entry level hosting vendors picking up the SME sector.

Client organizations have market choice, so vendors will have competitors with similar offerings trying to differentiate themselves. Vendors have significant power in relationships as they have the potential to conduct individual deals with SMEs and organizations who wish to self host. At this early stage of cloud development, the threat of new entrants is medium, as existing global telecommunications competitors already provide network services to global multinational corporations based on whole of business contracts. The option of self hosting will remain. This may act as a step towards migrating to private cloud or shared public cloud infrastructure. Dedicated data centres will continue to evolve, and new substitutes will probably arise. The key dynamics may be flexibility and depth of computing capacity on demand, existing and future contractual commitments and security capability.

13.9 Quality of Service

The traffic engineering term quality of service (QoS) refers to resource reservation control mechanisms rather than achieved service quality [16]. QoS is the ability to provide different priority for different application, users or data flows or to guarantee a certain level of performance to a data flow. QoS guarantees are important if the network capacity is insufficient, especially for real-time streaming multimedia application such as VoIP, as this often requires fixed bit rate and is delay sensitive in networks where the capacity is a limited resource.

QoS sometimes refers to the level of quality of the service, i.e. guaranteed service quality. High QoS is often confused with a high level of performance or achieved service quality. QoS is affected by various factors, human and technical. Human factors include stability and availability of service, delays and user information. Technical factors include reliability, scalability, effectiveness, maintainability and grade of service. As packets of information travel from origin to destination, there may occur packet throughput difficulties, dropped packets, packet corruption, packet delays and queues, packets from the source reaching the destination with different delays and out-of-order delivery problems [3, 16]. When the expense of the mechanisms to provide QoS is justified, network client organizations and providers typically enter into the key aspect of a contractual agreement termed a Service Level Agreement (SLA). This specifies guarantees for the ability of a network/protocol to give guaranteed performance or throughput delivery boundaries based on mutually agreed measures, usually by prioritizing traffic. Resources are reserved at each step on the network as it is set up. This approach is simple and economical for networks with predictable and light traffic loads. Performance could be expected to be reasonable for many applications. This might include demanding applications that can compensate for variations in bandwidth and delays [31]. The amount of over-provisioning in interior links required to replace QoS depends on the number of users and their traffic demands. This is an important factor that limits usability of over-provisioning. Newer more bandwidth intensive applications and the addition of more users results in the loss of over-provisioned networks. This then requires a physical update of the relevant network links which is an expensive process. Over-provisioning cannot be assumed on the Internet. A compelling reason of the need for QoS on the

Internet relates to congestion collapse. The Internet relies on congestion avoidance protocols to reduce traffic load under conditions that would otherwise lead to Internet meltdown. QoS contracts limit traffic that can be offered to the Internet and thereby enforce traffic shaping that can prevent it from becoming overloaded. They are an indispensable part of the internet's ability to handle a mix of real-time and non-real-time traffic without meltdown [16].

An alternative to complex QoS control mechanisms is to provide high quality communication over a 'best effort' network by over-provisioning the capacity so that it is sufficient for the expected peak traffic load. The resulting absence of network congestion eliminates the need for QoS mechanisms.

Another approach is differentiated services, in which packets are marked according to the type of service they need. In response to these markings, routers and switches use various queuing strategies to tailor performance to requirement. Routers supporting differentiated services use multiple queues for packets awaiting transmission from bandwidth constrained interfaces. Router vendors provide different capabilities for configuring this behaviour, including the number of off queue supports, the relative priorities of queues and the bandwidth reserved for each queue.

13.10 Marketing Campaign

A vendor's marketing campaign may be based on key themes such as being scalable for rapid growth, reducing complexity, controlling costs, more efficient use of resources and single point of accountability. Elements to the campaign may include direct marketing to CIOs and IT decision-makers, creating an awareness of cloud product offerings, advertising in trade journals, online websites and the demonstration cloud experience. Establishing a joint 'go to market' with key system integrators may well provide a more extensive sales pipeline that broadens reach in global opportunities. The 'go to market' partner can identify, define, qualify, develop and close the proposal with potential organization client organizations in establishing significant opportunities for further growth.

The learning, use and reassessment stages for client organizations should include undertaking trials before introduction, understanding the benefits and desirability of the applications. Thus, a vendor framework for cloud computing could emphasise introductory pricing. Such a pricing strategy would need to be attractive to the specific client organization following an examination of the viability of cloud computing for reasons of redundancy, additional capacity or development. Such market penetration pricing is aimed to establish the offer [19]. The second element of a vendor's marketing campaign could be to wrap the base service in offerings such as managed services, guaranteed quality of service, enhanced service level agreements, application aware networking, managed security and 24/7 monitoring and assurance. For larger client organizations who might find the step to shared infrastructure initially too large, a private cloud offer could be made that utilizes all the virtualization and infrastructure models but is hosted in a secure dedicated environment. The goal is to have client organizations trial and commit to new products and services. Introductory pricing is more effective when it mirrors the organization client's stages of understanding and product experience [19].

13.11 Implementation

Planning for product life cycles [33] necessitates an implementation strategy. Migration of computer systems has evolved from the process of a complete rebuild and then copying over the data files to transferring the settings of a particular system and then the data files. Once completed, a computer system administrator wants to have confidence that the equipment and operating system are going to function normally, and not be a disaster. Visualizing the product map of the software an organization uses and planning major equipment purchases will help a client organization structure a hardware and software retirement strategy. By synchronizing hardware purchases with software investment, organizations may minimize the impact of large capital expenditures by staging purchases, with software purchases on alternate years from hardware purchases.

Thought needs to be given as well to the settings and other customization client organizations have on their workstations. Some users are allowed to have a number of rights over their computer and can thus customize software installations, default file locations to alternative locations or can have a number of programs that are unknown to the IT department. This can make a unilateral migration unsuccessful because of all of the unique user settings. The after-effect is a disaster with users having missing software and data files, lost productivity and overwritten or lost files.

Deployment test labs are a must for migration preparation. A test lab should include a domain controller, one or two sample production file servers and enough workstations, sample data and users to simulate a user environment. Virtualization software can assist with testing automated upgrades and migrations. The software tools to do the actual migration are varied – some are from operating system software vendors, others may be third-party applications or enterprise software suites that provide other archiving functions.

The success of a migration rests on analysis, planning and testing before rolling out changes. For example, Barry [4] reports one company with over 28,000 employees had a very detailed migration plan for its users. The IT department used a lab, separate from the corporate network infrastructure, to test deployments and had a team working specifically on migration. The team completed the test-lab phase of the plan, and the migration was successful in that controlled environment. The next phase was to roll out a test case on some of the smaller departments within the company. The test case migration was scheduled to run automatically when the users logged in. The migration of the user computers to a new operating system started as planned. After the migration, the user computers automatically started downloading and installing software updates (a domain policy). Unfortunately, one of these updates had not been tested. The unexpected result was that user computers in the test case departments were inoperable. Some of the users in the test case contacted the IT help desk for assistance. IT immediately started troubleshooting the operational issues of the problem without realizing that this was caused by a migration test case error. Other users in the department who felt technically savvy tried solving the problem themselves. This made matters worse when one user reformatted and reinstalled the operating system and overwrote a large portion of original data files. Fortunately for this company, the plan was built in phases and had breakpoints along the way so that the success of the migration could be measured. The failure in this case was twofold in that there were some domain policies that had not been implemented on test lab servers, and the effect of a migration plus the application of software updates had not been fully tested. The losses were serious for some users, yet minimal for the entire organization.

For other migration rollouts, the losses can be much more serious. Kroll Ontrack [21] describes one company's IT department creating a logon script to apply software updates. However, an untested line of the script started a reinstall of the operating system. So as users were logging into their computers at the start of the week, most noticed that the start-up was taking longer than usual. When they finally were able to access their computer desktop, they noticed that all of their user files and settings were gone. The scripting problem was not seen during the test lab phase. Over 300 users were affected, and nearly 100 computers required data recovery services. This illustrates the importance of the planning and testing phases of a migration. Creating a test environment that mirrors the IT infrastructure will go a long way towards anticipating and fixing problems.

But despite the most thought-out migration, experienced data professionals know to expect the unexpected. Even the best planning for any deployment can result in disaster for users and critical data loss. In order to be prepared, client organizations should include data recovery planning. Considerations include handling an unexpected event during the deployment process, having enough break points within the automation to capture errors, performing a backup before cloud deployment, estimating how much time or resources would be necessary to recover from migration disaster, the alternatives if there is a hardware failure during the migration, and data recovery vendor relationships for timely data recovery. Responsibility for such risks should be included in the organization client/cloud contracts and be carried by the party best able to carry the various risks.

13.12   Conclusion

The cloud computing emerging market is the single biggest growth area in ICT. The industry globally is expected to be worth more that US $150bn by 2014. Cloud vendors need to place themselves to take advantage of this market growth and invest in leading software and virtualized hardware so that the organization client offer is safe, is secure and provides speedy service and reliability over high-performance networks. In the Ponemon [24] security study, only 14% of respondents believed that cloud computing would actually improve their organization's security posture. This low percentage means that there is reluctance on the part of potential client organizations, but significant opportunities for reputable cloud vendors to demonstrate that cloud infrastructure are equal or superior to on premise computing environments. While on premise, computing is also not without inherent security risks, cloud computing poses new threats and challenges that need to be seriously considered before adoption. Because of the dynamic nature of the emerging cloud market, continuous monitoring of the quality of service and security requirements of client organizations and appropriate risk allocation in Service Level Agreement contracts is vital to avoid unexpected cost increases, insecurity and poor quality service which may lead to souring of relationships and even litigation.

References

1. Amrhein, D.: The Effect of PaaS on Cloud Delivery Models, SYS-CON Media, Inc., Montvale, NJ, USA, 7 July (2010)
2. Armbrust, M., Fox, A., Griffith, R., Joseph, A.D., Katz, R., Konwinski, A., Lee, G., Patterson, D., Rabkin, A., Stoica, I., Zaharia, M.: Clearing the clouds away from the true potential and obstacles posed by this computing capability. Commun. ACM 53(4), 50–58 (2010)
3. Ash, G.: Traffic Engineering and QoS Optimization of Integrated Voice & Data Networks. Elsevier, Amsterdam (2006)
4. Barry, S.: Computer Life Cycle Management and Migration, The Data Administration Newsletter. Robert S Seiner publisher, Pittsburg, Pennsylvania (2008)
5. Buyyaa, R., Yeoa, C.S., Venugopala, S., Broberg, J., Brandic, I.: Cloud computing and emerging IT platforms: vision, hype, and reality for delivering computing as the 5th utility. Future Gener. Comput. Syst. 25(6), 599–616 (2009). Elsevier
6. Candela, L., Castelli, D., Pagano, P.: Making virtual research environments in the cloud a reality: the gCube approach. In: European Research Consortium for Informatics and Mathematics (ERCIM) News 8,3 Special Theme: Cloud Computing, Oct 2010, p. 46
7. Dai, Y., Xiang, Y., Zhang, G.: Self-healing and Hybrid Diagnosis in Cloud Computing. Lecture Notes in Computer Science, vol. 5931, pp. 45–56. Springer, New York (2009). doi:10.1007/978-3-642-10665-1_5
8. Datamonitor: Trends to watch: cloud computing 2010, Datamonitor North Adams, MA, USA (2009)
9. Fabbi, M., Skorupa, J.: Citrix Positioned in the Leaders Quadrant for 2010 Application Delivery Controllers Magic Quadrant, Gartner, 22 Nov 2010
10. Gantz, J.F., Reinsel, D.: A forecast of worldwide information growth through 2010. The Expanding Digital Universe, An IDC White Paper, EMC, USA; White Paper. Sponsored by EMC (2007)
11. Gens, F., Mahowald, R., Villars, R.L., Bradshaw, D., Morris, C.: Cloud Computing 2010: An IDC Update. Springer, New York (2010)
12. Golden, B.: How Cloud Computing Can Transform Business, Harvard Business Review, Boston, MA, USA, June (2010)
13. Grance, T.: The NIST Cloud Definition Framework, National Institute of Standards and Technology, Gaithersburg, MA, USA (2010)
14. Hagel, J., Brown, J.S.: Cloud Computing's Stormy Future, Harvard business Review, MA, USA, Sept (2010)

15. IBM: Autonomic Vision and Manifesto, IBM, New York (2001)
16. Iversen, V.B.: Teletraffic Engineering and Network Planning, Technical University of Denmark, Copenhagen, 20 May (2010)
17. Kephart, J.O., Chess, D.M.: The vision of autonomic computing. IEEE Comput. **31**(1), 41–50 (2003)
18. King, S.: Dangers of Cloud Computing, Computer Weekly.com, 14 July (2008)
19. Kotler, P., Adam, S., Denize, S., Armstrong, G.: Principles of Marketing, 4th edn. Pearson Education Frenchs Forest, Frenchs Forest, Sydney, Australia (2009)
20. Krikos, A.: Disruptive Technology Business Models in Cloud Computing, MIT, Cambridge, MA, USA, Jan (2010)
21. Kroll Ontrack.: Computer Life Cycle Management and Migration, Kroll Ontrack, Minneapolis, Minnesota, USA (2008)
22. Leong, L., Chamberlain, T.: Web Hosting and Cloud Infrastructure Services (On-Demand). Gartner, Stamford, CT, USA, 2 July (2009)
23. McAfee, A.: 2010: The Year the Cloud Rolled In, Harvard Business Review, Boston, MA, USA, 15 Dec (2010)
24. Ponemon, L.: Security of Cloud Computing Users, Ponemon Institute, Islander, NY, USA, 12 May (2010)
25. Püschel, T., Anandasivam, A., Buschek, S., Neumann, D.: Making money with clouds: revenue optimization through automated policy decisions. Journal: 17th Eur. Conf. Info. Syst. Verona, Italy (2009)
26. Somashekar, S.: White Paper: Opportunities for the Cloud in the Enterprise, CA, Islandia, NY, Jan (2010)
27. Staten, J.: Justifying Your Cloud Investment: Web Sites Web Sites Are Great First Candidates for Cloud Deployment, 2 Nov, Forrester Research (2010)
28. Tata: Tata Communications: The Making of a Global Data Center Leader, Stratecast Perspectives & Insight for Executives SPIE No. 12, 27 March (2009)
29. Thomson, J.D.: Enterprise resource planning – an E-entrepreneurial challenge. In: Kollman, T., Kuckertz, A., Stockmann, C. (eds.) E- Entrepreneurship and ICT Ventures: Strategy, Organization and Technology (Business Science Reference). IGI Global, Hershey (2010)
30. Tullock, G.: The welfare costs of tariffs, monopolies, and theft. West. Econ. J. **5**(3), 224–232 (1967)
31. Vael, M.: Cloud Computing: Business Benefits with Security, Governance and Assurance Perspectives, Information Systems Audit and Control Association (IACA), Brussels, Belgium (2009)
32. Vaquero, L.M., Rodera-Merino, L., Caceres, J., Lindner, M.: A break in the clouds: towards a cloud definition. ACM SIGCOMM Comput. Commun. Rev. **39**(1), 50–55 (2009)
33. Vernon, R.: International investment and international trade in the product cycle. Q. J. Econ. **80**(2), 190–207 (1966)
34. Xia, T., Li, Z., Yu, N.: Research on Cloud Computing Based on Deep Analysis to Typical Platforms, First International Conference, Cloud Computing Proceedings, pp. 601–608. Springer, Berlin/New York (2009)

Chapter 14
Fair Non-repudiation Framework
for Cloud Storage: Part I

Jun Feng, Yu Chen, Douglas H. Summerville, and Kai Hwang

Abstract Data storage is one of the most profitable applications on the cloud computing platforms. Although a transparent service model provides more flexibility and convenience, it also brings new challenges with respect to data security. For example, existing vulnerabilities in some commercial cloud storage services can potentially lead to repudiation problems. In this chapter, we first analyze potential integrity vulnerabilities existing in today's commercial cloud storage platforms. Then, we present an overview of security issues and introduce a framework that supports a fair data transmission procedure without the risk of dispute. More specifically, a basic two-party non-repudiation (TPNR) protocol has been proposed. This chapter addresses the scenario in which a consumer may be reluctant to move his private data to the cloud because of existing vulnerabilities. To eliminate concerns between the consumer and the provider, the solution needs to bridge the two sessions with an integrity link based on a new TPNR. A multiparty non-repudiation (MPNR) protocol and more comprehensive analysis of its security properties are discussed in the next chapter.

14.1 Introduction

The accelerated development in networking technology and the increasing need for computing resources have led to a new economic and computing model that is referred to as cloud computing. Under a different context, cloud computing has been referred to as "Infrastructure as a Service" (IaaS), where a customer makes use

J. Feng • Y. Chen (✉) • D.H. Summerville
Department of Electrical and Computer Engineering,
Binghamton University, SUNY, Binghamton, NY 13902
e-mail: ychen@binghamton.edu

K. Hwang
Department of Electrical Engineering – Systems,
University of Southern California, Los Angeles, CA 90089

Z. Mahmood and R. Hill (eds.), *Cloud Computing for Enterprise Architectures*,
Computer Communications and Networks, DOI 10.1007/978-1-4471-2236-4_14,
© Springer-Verlag London Limited 2011

of a service provider's computing, storage, or networking infrastructure; "Platform as a Service" (PaaS), where a customer leverages the provider's resources to run custom applications; and "Software as a Service" (SaaS), where customers use software that is run on the provider's infrastructure [17].

Cloud storage has been recognized as potentially one of the most profitable applications that cloud computing platforms can support. Due to its low cost and flexible services [14], cloud storage will, hopefully, benefit users significantly in the near future. Cloud storage providers typically try to persuade their users to migrate their important and sensitive data to the cloud in order to generate additional revenue. They advertise that this new business model can make it more convenient for users to access their data. A major advantage of cloud storage is data loss prevention. In recent years, there have been many reported instances in which large companies or financial institutions have lost important customer information as a result of various cyber attacks [31]. The probability of lost data is expected to decrease if the information is maintained in cloud storage services under professional management. In addition, flexibility, low cost, high confidentiality, robust integrity, and easy access have been selling points that today's cloud computing service providers use to attract potential clients. Commercial cloud service providers, such as Amazon's AWS [1] and Microsoft's Azure [26], have elected to outsource their storage services for profit. Examples of services provided by cloud storage platforms include online data backup, email exchange, picture sharing, and video hosting.

The uniqueness of secure cloud storage still has not been recognized. One of the cloud storage's characteristics is mass storage. Data is not only communicated through the Internet but also shipped by FedEx or other methods if the data size is huge (e.g., more than one TB). Potential users may question whether the confidentiality, integrity, and availability of their data are guaranteed in cloud storage. Users are reluctant to move important and sensitive data to the cloud unless these challenges have been well addressed. Therefore, security is ranked as the greatest challenge and concern regarding cloud computing [13]. A survey conducted by IDC [13] implies that the expected benefits are not enough to persuade executives to outsource their information to the cloud. This is due to the fact that research in cloud computing security is in its infancy, and negative experiences have shown that none of the large-scale storage services is completely reliable and any of them may lose or corrupt customer data [5, 32].

In this chapter, we introduce today's commercial cloud storage platforms [1] and some proposed architectures and approaches [17, 29] for secure cloud storage. As discussed in detail in Sect. 14.2, there still exist vulnerabilities that may potentially lead to a dispute, which would not be acceptable to a customer. To address such weaknesses, we propose a new fair TPNR scheme for secure cloud storage systems. We focus on how to maintain integrity with fair non-repudiation, not how to calculate it, since the current integrity algorithm is sufficient for the data. The idea of an integrity check and non-repudiation is not new. To date, however, there is little reported effort that integrates them to solve problems on cloud storage systems.

The remainder of this chapter is structured as follows:

- Section 14.2 gives a brief introduction to related background knowledge required for secure cloud storage.
- Section 14.3 summarizes the potential security challenges in today's storage cloud platforms.
- Section 14.4 introduces a basic TPNR protocol.
- Section 14.5 concludes this chapter.

14.2   Background

Cloud Storage applications involve three entities: the data owner, the service provider, and the user group. The owner moves important or sensitive data to the cloud and pays for the service. The service provider provides secure storage services and earns a profit. The users fetch data from the cloud storage and pay for the service. Only the owner can decide and change the access control polices for his data. We also suppose that no one is trustworthy in cloud. The data owner, service provider, and users are willing to deny their actions or attack the other parties if it is in their best interest to do so. To date, there has been no reported research done on fair non-repudiation for cloud storage.

We analyze the vulnerabilities in today's commercial cloud storage systems first. Such weaknesses open the door for potential data integrity tampering and disputes. Then, several secure architectures proposed for cloud storage are discussed.

As illustrated in Fig. 14.1, cloud storage is an application that covers a number of services (SaaS, PaaS, IaaS, etc.). The life cycle of data in cloud storage can be divided into three phases: uploading, maintenance, and downloading. While data integrity in the uploading and downloading phases is achieved by cryptographic

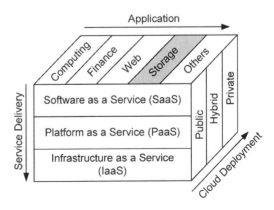

Fig. 14.1 View of cloud storage [24]

Fig. 14.2 Integrity in platforms

protocols such as SSL (Secure Sockets Layer) protocol or TLS (Transport Layer Security) protocol, it is more complicated for users to monitor integrity and availability of remote data.

14.2.1 Existing Platforms for Cloud Storage

Several commercial cloud storage platforms, such as Amazon S3 and Microsoft Azure, have been developed in recent years. For large blocks of data (greater than 1 TB), service providers such as Amazon AWS [1] require that the data be shipped on a storage medium (e.g., a hard drive), while additional authentication or authorization information is delivered through email. Smaller blocks of data (≤50 GB) can more easily be uploaded or downloaded via the Internet, just as Microsoft Azure [26] does.

Although the software may be different, a similar strategy has been taken to provide data integrity. As shown in Fig. 14.2, when the owner uploads data into cloud storage space, it can ship or send data to service providers with a digital digest, MD5_1. If the data is transferred through the Internet, a signed non-repudiation request could be used to ensure that data has not been tampered with.

When the service provider receives the data with a signed MD5, it stores the data with the corresponding MD5_1. When the service provider gets a verified request to retrieve data from users, it will send/ship the data with an MD5 to that user. On the Azure platform, the original MD5_1 is sent by the owner when uploading, and a re-computed MD5_2 is sent by Amazon's AWS when downloading. In contrast, to provide data integrity, Azure storage service stores the uploaded data MD5_1 in a database and returns it to the user when he wants to retrieve the data [26].

The procedure is secure in each individual session. Integrity and confidentiality of data during transmission are guaranteed by SSL protocol. However, from the perspective of cloud storage, data security depends not only on uploading and downloading sessions but also on the maintaining session. The uploading phase ensures that data received by cloud providers is the same as the owner uploads. The downloading phase guarantees that what the user retrieves is the same data as the cloud provider sends. Unfortunately, there is one critical link missing to protect or track data stored in cloud storage [11]. It is maintaining data integrity with non-repudiation.

14.2.2   Other Architectures for Secure Cloud Storage

Being considered as a service delivered over the Internet using hardware and systems software, traditional distributed storage can be treated as a specific case of cloud storage. Security requirements, such as authentication, authorization, availability, confidentiality, integrity, key sharing and key management, auditing and intrusion detection, usability, and performance, in distributed storage systems also should be considered in cloud storage. Kher and Kim [18] presented a survey of existing secure storage systems and listed some solutions. However, cloud storage systems have their own features. The Cloud Security Alliance report [33] lists 15 different issues, and Chow et al. [10] have grouped them into three categories, namely, traditional, availability, and third-party control. Cachin et al. [8] presented a brief survey of solutions to secure cloud storage. They use a "provable data possession model" (PDP) [3] or a "proof of retrievability model" (POR) [15] for ensuring possession of a file during the maintenance phase. Such models and their derivatives can efficiently and sufficiently find gross omissions such as a 1% data loss and have proved to be effective. They also use some protocols, such as SUNDR [19], to realize fork-consistent storage.

Based on recent and non-standard approaches, Kamara and Lauter [17] described a secure cloud storage architecture. They believe confidentiality, integrity, availability, reliability, efficient retrieval, and data sharing services should be provided. In their architecture, there are four components: a token generator (TG) to generate indices that enable the provider to search data, a data processor (DP) to encrypt the data by various methods such as AES, a data credential generator (CG) for an access control policy, and a data verifier (DV) to check integrity. In their architecture, cloud storage providers are responsible for availability and reliability. DP is responsible for confidentiality as well as for integrity. CG is responsible for data sharing. TG is responsible for data retrieval. POR/PDP is responsible for proof of storage.

Kamara's work is useful for proving the integrity of data, but it is not perfect for a holistic cloud solution. Popa et al. [29] presented an architecture for secure cloud storage. They divided the security properties of cloud storage into four categories: confidentiality, integrity, write-serializability, and read freshness. With signed messages and chain hash, the architecture can provide non-disputable and write-serializability property. Freshness is guaranteed by periodically auditing the data.

14.2.3   Related Non-repudiation Protocols

This subsection describes existing research work in two related areas, the TPNR protocol and MPNR protocol design. Before introducing the NR protocols, the notations and definitions of terms are provided. In this chapter, we abbreviate the owner and users as "O" and "U" and the cloud service provider as "C".

14.2.3.1 Notation and Definitions

For a description of the fair non-repudiation protocol, some notation and definitions used are as follows:

- EOO: Evidence of origin, which is generated by the originator and will be transferred to the recipient [34, 35].
- EOR: Evidence of receipt, which is generated by the recipient and will be transferred to the originator [34, 35].
- On-line TTP (trusted third party): TTP intervenes in each transaction session between two peers but not in each message transmission between them [25].
- Off-line TTP: TTP is initiated only in case of a dispute (incorrect behavior of a dishonest party or a network error). TTP does not intervene in the session in regular cases. It is also called the optimistic or efficient TTP [25].
- NRO: Non-repudiation of origin, which is held by the provider and intended to protect against the sender's false denial of having originated the message. NRO is presented to an arbitrator, who can unambiguously decide whether the sender is the author of a given message or not [34, 35]. It is usually further denoted as NRO_{OU}, NRO_{OC}, etc. where "OU" means the evidence is produced by the owner and will be stored by the user and "OC" has a similar meaning.
- NRR: Non-repudiation of receipt, which is held by the sender and is intended to protect against a recipient's false denial of having received the message. It is presented to an arbitrator [34, 35] who can unambiguously decide whether the recipient received a given message or not. Usually, it is noted as NRR_{OU}, NRR_{OC}, etc.
- Timeliness: Timeliness is achieved if and only if all honest parties always have the ability to reach, in a finite amount of time, a point in the protocol where they can stop the protocol while preserving fairness. Timeliness avoids situations where a party does not know whether it can stop the protocol without losing fairness. A multiparty protocol is said to respect timeliness if all honest entities are able to terminate the protocol in a finite amount of time without losing fairness. In each round, T1 is the time limit for the sender to wait for the NRR from the recipient. T2 is the time limit for the recipient to wait for the time limit [21].
- L: A unique label throughout the session. Here, we suppose L is a set of data hash and the version number.
- Seq: In general, Seq represents the unique sequence number of each step. Each step must be unique throughout the entire transaction in order to prevent replay attacks. For this reason, the Seq field is added, and each party must increment the Seq value after receiving the previous message. It is denoted as Seq1, Seq2,..., etc.
- Flag: The flag indicates the purpose of this step. For example, it could be "Version 1, upload request from Alice." In the traditional protocol, it is noted as f1, f2,..., etc.
- Tg, Ts: The timestamp indicating when the message is generated or stored or sent should be authenticated.

Fig. 14.3 Non-repudiation
model

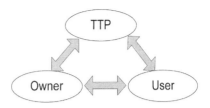

- EGU{ }: any group encryption scheme that only the user Ui∈ U can decrypt [9].
  NRO is encrypted with a group encryption scheme. We do not imply that this is
  the only option. Different schemes can be used under different scenarios. For
  example, if there are fewer recipients, we can encrypt the NRO with each recipient's public key, add a label for location and concatenate them together. If there
  are many recipients, we can use other group encryption methods. When a user Ui
  downloads the data from cloud, he will decipher it using K (here, K is the key list
  for Ui to decipher the data).
- EX(M): asymmetric encryption of message M with party X's public key.
- DX(M): asymmetric decryption of message M with party X's private key.
- SX(M): signature of the message by party X, normally with X's private Key.
- H(M): one-way hash function over the message M.
- X→Y: party X sends a message M to party Y.
- X↔Y: party X fetches a message M from party Y.

14.2.3.2   Non-repudiation Protocols

ISO/IEC 13888 has defined the non-repudiation model as shown in Fig. 14.3. This
model consists of three parties, the owner (Alice), the user (Bob), and TTP. These
parties exchange messages with each other.

Actually, it is a straightforward to design a non-repudiation protocol if every
party involved in a transaction is honest and willing to cooperate. For example,
Alice signs the message using her private key, sends it to Bob, and vice visa.
However, this is obviously impractical in Internet-based applications such as
message exchange, certified email, and contract-signing since the recipients have an
advantage over the other party. Fairness should be introduced into the applications.
Normally, there are two methods to achieve fair non-repudiation, one is gradual
exchange and another is through the TTP [34, 35].

There have been a number of reported efforts of non-repudiation (NR) protocols
under the standard framework [34, 35]. It is still an active research field [7, 20, 28, 30].
In this section, we analyze two typical NR protocols on traditional Internet plat-

forms. The difference lies in the detailed specifications for different applications. The frameworks proposed in the literature are very similar.

TPNR Protocol

Assume that the communication channels between the TTP and each transacting entity (the owner and the user) are resilient and the communication channel between the owner and the user is confidential. If the two parties want to exchange messages secretly, the exchange protocol is as follows [36].

Exchange sub-protocol

$O \rightarrow U$: f1;f5;U;L;C;TTP;ETTP(K); EOO_C;SUB_ K

If U gives up

THEN

   quit

ELSE

   $U \rightarrow O$: f2;O;L;EOR_C

IF O gives up

THEN

 abort

ELSE

   $O \rightarrow U$:   f3;U;L;K;EOO_K

IF U gives up

THEN

 resolve

ELSE

   $U \rightarrow O$:   f4;O;L;EOR K

IF O gives up

THEN

   resolve

In the protocol, L is equal to H(M,K), and EEO_C = S_O(f1, U, L, C) as evidence of the origin of C, EOO_K = S_O(f3, U, L, K) as evidence of the submission of K to the TTP, EOR_C = S_U(f2, O, L, EOO_C) as evidence of receipt of C, EOR_K = S_U(f4, O, L, EOO_K), SUB_K = S_O(f5, U, L, K, TTP, EOO_C) as evidence of submission of K to the TTP, CON_K = S_{TTP}(f6, O, U, L, K), and as evidence of confirmation of K by the TTP, abort = S_{TTP}(f8, O, U, L).

Abort and *resolve* protocols provide evidence of abort or completion. In the middle of a transaction, when O or U sends a request to TTP to abort or resolve, TTP will check the status of the transaction. If it is in the "resolve/abort" status already, TTP will return the status; otherwise, TTP will deliver the abort/resolve result to the requestor after the identity of the requestor has been verified. The abort and resolve protocols are as follows:

Abort sub-protocol, performed only by Originator

$O \to TTP$: f7;U;L;S_A(f7;B;L)

IF resolved

THEN

   $TTP \to O$: f2;f6;O;U;L;K;CON_K;EOR_C

ELSE

   $TTP \to O$: f8;O;U;L; abort

Resolve sub-protocol

$X \to TTP$: f2;f5;O;U;L;TTP;E_{TTP}(K);

      SUB_K; EOO_C; EOR_C

IF aborted

THEN

   $TTP \to X$: f8;O;U;L; abort

ELSE

   $TTP \to X$: f2;f6;O;U;L;K; CON_K;EOR_C

Once a dispute occurs, O can submit (EOR_C, EOR_K/CON_K) as NRR to prove that U has received the message M. Meanwhile, U can use (EOO_C, EOO_K/CON_K) as NRO to prove that O has sent the message M.

MPNR Protocol

Markowitch proposed an MPNR protocol based on the above TPNR protocol [22]. Actually, the MPNR protocol is very similar to Zhou's TPNR protocol except for the number of the recipients. It can be seen as an extension of TPNR.

The *message exchange* protocol serves as the main protocol for the entire process, which consists of two sub-protocols that are described as follows:

Exchange sub-protocol

$O \to U$: f_{EOO};f_{SUB};U;L;T;C;TTP; E_{TTP}(K);EOO; SUB_K

$U_i \to O$: f_{EOR};O;L;EOR_i

$O \to U'$: f_{EOOK};U;L;$E_{U'K}$;EOO_K

$U'_i \to O$: f_{EORK};O;L;EOR_{ik} where $U'_i \in U'$

Where $EOO = S_O(f_{EOO}$, U, L, T, H(C)) as evidence of the origin of C, $SUB\_K = S_O(f_{SUB}$, U, L, E_{TTP}(K)), $EOR_i = S_{Ui}(f_{EOR}$, O, L, H(C)), $EOO\_K = S_O(f_{EOOk}$, U', L, H(K)), $EOR_{ik} = S_{Ui}(f_{EORk}$, O, L, H(K)).

In the message exchange protocol, the owner first sends the message to all recipients who include the label, and the cipher with the key K ciphered using the public key of the TTP (this information is used by the TTP in the case of a resolve). The owner also sends a time-out T to assure that the resolve procedure is only to be performed after T. If one of the recipients does not accept the time-out, it can quit the protocol. The owner also designates a time limit. All responses arriving after this moment are not considered. Afterwards, when the owner receives the response, it will group the recipients who respond into U' and forward them with the deciphering key. In order to cipher only once and to use multicasting, the owner uses a group encryption scheme. The idea is that the key can be ciphered in such a way that only recipients in U'_i can decipher it.

Resolve sub-protocol

$X \rightarrow TTP$: f_{Recx};f_{SUB};O;U;L;T, $H(C)$,$E_{TTP}(K)$; RecX; SUB_K; EOO
If resolved
then
    $TTP \rightarrow X$: f_{Conk}; O; U'; $E_{U'}(K, S_{TTP}(K))$; Con_k
Else
  if before T
    then
        $TTP \rightarrow X$: f_{Early}; Early
    Else
        Resolved = true
$TTP \leftrightarrow X$: f_{Set};U';L; Set
$TTP \rightarrow O$: f_{Conk}; O; U'; L; Con_K
$TTP \rightarrow U'\{X\}$ f_{Conk}; O; U'; L; $E_{U'}(K, S_{TTP}(K))$; ConK

If there is a dispute, O can submit (EOR_i, EOR_{ik}, or Con_K, L, M, K, and U' EOR_K/CON_K) as NRR to prove that U has received the message M, and U can use (EOO, EOO_K or Con_K, L, M, K, U and U') as NRO to prove that O has sent the message M.

Although, these non-repudiation protocols may be applicable to cloud storage, their efficiency is low. It takes four steps to achieve fair non-repudiation in one session. If we apply it to the model in Fig. 14.4, it will take eight steps to finish the upload and download sessions, which at least doubles the burden on the provider.

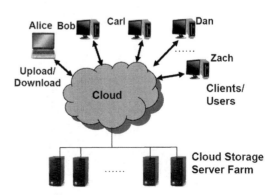

Fig. 14.4 Cloud storage application example

In addition, cloud storage differs from traditional Internet-based applications in two ways. First is that in most cloud storage applications, the machines belonging to the service provider merely function as the storage medium. The client usually does not want the service provider to interpret the information the data carries. In fact, for this purpose, the data stored in the cloud is usually encrypted, and it is unnecessary to share the key with the service provider. Therefore, although it is possible to adopt the non-repudiation protocol developed earlier, an optimal protocol can achieve higher efficiency and more convenience for cloud storage.

The other difference, which is more critical, is that in cloud storage, the data is transferred to three entities: the owner, the provider, and the users. The TPNR and MPNR can only be designed to be implemented on two peers, not three. Therefore, even if we apply the traditional TPNR and MPNR to cloud storage, there are still vulnerabilities as illustrated in Sect. 14.2.1.

14.3   Overview of Security Issues in Cloud Storage

In order to illustrate the potential security threats in more detail, consider the scenario shown in Fig. 14.4. Assume that the owner, a company's CFO, stores the company's financial data and data processing software in a cloud storage space. The company employees, Bob, Carl, Dan, and Zach will share the data on the cloud. Each of them has a different level of authority to access the data. There are several important concerns to consider regarding data safety during the procedure:

- Confidentiality: The service provider is assumed to be an untrustworthy third party, and the owner does not want to reveal the data to the provider.
- Provenance: The users or the owner can verify the data stored in the provider.
- Availability: The service provider should guarantee that the data is available when users send a request from anywhere and at any time.
- Space Consistency: Since the data is moved from the owner's space to the user's space through the provider, the user cannot ensure that the data received is the same as that uploaded earlier by the owner. It may have been tampered with while stored in the cloud.
- Collusion Problem: The owner encrypts the data with a symmetric key, uploads the encrypted data onto the cloud, and distributes the key and permission access to the employees. The service provider cannot reveal the data without the key. Any one of the employees is able to access only that portion of the data that he has authorization for. None of the employees has access to the entire data set due to their limited access authorization. However, if the service provider colludes with one of the employees by exchanging the key and data, both of them can obtain the entire data set.
- Roll-back Problem: Assume that the owner has uploaded 1 TB of data, and a user, Bob, downloaded it. Later, the owner updates 1 GB, and Bob wants to download the updated 1 GB of data. At this time, Bob needs certain evidence to help ensure that the data is updated and that the downloaded 1 GB of data is

up-to-date. If a malicious cloud service provider deletes the updated content and delivers outdated data, Bob should be able to detect the inconsistency based on the evidence. This is also defined as "user's freshness."

- Scalability Problem: "Enterprises are important customers for the cloud. They have many employees that require highly scalable access control and have large amounts of data." [29].
- Write-serializability Problem: "The Cloud provider must make sure that every 'put' advances the version number of the most recently stored block by exactly one." [29].
- Multiple Writer Multiple Reader (MWMR) Problem: What happens when multiple users want to write a block of storage at the same time.
- Repudiation Case #1: Assume the owner is honest, and the provider is malicious. The owner finds that the data has been tampered with. The provider needs evidence to demonstrate that it is the provider who is at fault as well as to prove his innocence.
- Repudiation Case #2: The repudiation problem can open the door for black-mailers. For example, the owner stores some data in the cloud and later downloads that data. Then, he reports that his data was compromised and that it is the fault of the storage provider. If the owner seeks compensation for his so-called loss, the provider needs proof to demonstrate his innocence.
- Repudiation Case #3: The repudiation issue also exists between the owner and the users. A user gets business data through the cloud service. If the user finds that the data is not the same as what the owner uploaded, the party responsible for the fault should be identifiable and provable.

Obviously, current cloud storage platforms can meet basic requirements of mass storage at a low cost. As previously noted, the security of cloud storage can be enhanced by applying some of the methods listed in the architectures mentioned in Sect. 14.2.2. Confidentiality can be guaranteed by encryption, integrity by message digest, non-repudiation by the exchange of signed message digests [12], freshness by periodic audit [29], and write-serializability by chain hash [19] or persistent authenticated dictionary (PAD) [2]. SUNDR [19] can be used to detect "fork consistency attack" and "write serializability."

Majuntke proposed two "lock-free" protocols, namely linear and simultaneous, to deal with the problem of SWMR [23]. However, SWMR is a case-dependent problem and is beyond the scope of this chapter. Broadcast encryption [6] and key rotation [16] are used to improve scalability. Reddy has proposed technologies to handle the provenance issues [27]. Data availability can be improved through POR or PDP methods with high probability [3, 15]. For a collusion attack, if the users are not willing to exchange their private keys, a policy-based encryption system (PBES) can be implemented to guarantee a collusion-free environment [4]. If the users are willing to exchange their private keys but do not want to exchange the decrypted content, a mediated decryption system can be used to avoid collusion attacks. If the users are willing to exchange the decrypted contents, digital rights management can be used to avoid the collusion attacks. Recently, we have proposed TPNR protocols to address disputes resulting from the integrity issues [12].

While it may seem that the security problems in cloud storage systems have been covered, a crucial aspect of cloud storage that has not been addressed is that none of the three entities may always be trusted. Any one of them could be malicious. That is why non-repudiation is a key mechanism [29] for secure cloud storage.

As cited in prior references [12, 29], signed digests were used for non-repudiation in cloud storage. However, "fairness" was not extensively considered. In this context, fairness means: *"no party gains an advantage over another at any moment during the running of the protocol. The protocol would not be fair, for example, if one of the parties obtained the signed contract without the other being able to do likewise"* [30].

It is obvious that "non-repudiation" in both references [12, 29] cited in this paragraph is not "fair" since any party can refuse to send his/her own certification after receiving the sender's certification.

Although PAD can be used to solve the roll-back and consistency problem, it contains an assumption that users need to know the correct element in cloud. SUNDR can also detect a consistency problem. However, it still makes two assumptions. One is that at least one user has the correct updated data. The other is that other users can communicate with the user, and each user can be trusted.

Actually, for the solutions to the concerns related to problems of "provenance, space consistency, roll-back problem, write-serializability, and SWMR," there is an assumption that the users have the correct data or version. Otherwise, the provider can easily gain an advantage over the users through a "fork consistency attack" or a "roll-back attack." For example, suppose the owner updates the data in the cloud ten times. The data has ten versions. The owner can put a chained version hash into the data, periodically audit the data freshness, and use POR to check the integrity of that data. The provider knows that it has the correct data. Suppose Bob and Carl do not know each other, and the provider can keep all versions to himself. The provider can give the two users different versions of the data. If Bob and Carl then want to check the consistency, integrity, or freshness, they cannot detect an attack since all data and all signatures come from the original owner himself and will pass all the tests. Even if Bob and Carl know each other and can compare data, the provider can give them both the same older version and not the most up-to-date version. Bob and Carl are unable to know that their version is out of date. How can they ensure that they are getting the correct data?

We introduce a novel fair non-repudiation framework to address the problems listed above and enhance the security of cloud storage. Section 14.4 introduces a basic TPNR protocol, which can be applied to the personal peer-to-peer cloud storage application. An MPNR protocol introduced in the next chapter can also be implemented to serve this purpose in multiuser environments.

14.4   A Basic TPNR Protocol

Consider the following scenario: A consumer may be reluctant to move his private data to the cloud because of the vulnerabilities described in Sect. 14.2.1. To eliminate concerns between the consumer and the provider, the solution needs to bridge the two sessions with an integrity link based on a new fair non-repudiation protocol. It also must cover the uploading session and downloading session. In addition to the normal process, a "Resolve" mode is included to allow the owner to complete or abort an execution, without waiting for a response from the other potentially malicious party.

14.4.1 Normal Mode

Figure 14.5a shows that there are four roles in the NR protocol: an owner, a provider, a TTP, and an arbitrator. Assuming that, in most cases, the owner and provider are honest and willing to complete the transactions by themselves and the TTP is only initiated as a last resort, none of the parties is going to act against its own interests.

In each transmission, the entity must attach certain extra information to the message, collectively called *evidence*, since its function is to settle repudiation when it appears. For the owner, it is NRO; for the provider, it is NRR.

To maintain confidentiality, the sender encrypts the evidence with the recipient's public key. To prevent replay attacks, a random number and a sequence number are included. The sequence number increases incrementally by one. In case someone refuses to accept the message, we add a time limit and a sub-protocol to resolve this. Besides a flag to label the process, we also include the IDs for the sender, the recipient, and the TTP in the plaintext message. The evidence consists of the hash results of these IDs and the hash of the data.

To achieve non-repudiation, we require the sender to sign the hash value with her/his private key. Then, the evidence is *encrypt{Sign(HashofData), Sign(Plaintext)}*. After one transaction is completed, the owner will get an NRR from the provider; the provider will get an NRO from the owner. The peers should first check the consistency between the hash of the plaintext and the plaintext.

The NR protocol utilizes the signed integrity checking of the data in the evidence, not only to facilitate the detection of data tampering and the signature of the sender but also to make it impossible for the sender to deny his activity. Meanwhile, being encrypted with the public key of the recipient, the evidence guarantees the consistency of the hash with the plaintext.

For instance, the owner owns the NRR signed by the provider, and it can send it to him when he downloads the data. This is helpful to avoid repudiation when the downloaded data has been tampered with. When there is an inconsistency, they have to submit a signed integrity receipt to the arbitrator. When the owner and the provider are honest and the network functions well, they can exchange messages in the Normal mode which works with an off-line TTP as shown in Fig. 14.5b.

The requirement of evidence can guarantee non-repudiation. However, in practice, not all users or service providers are willing to completely obey the rules set by the protocol. The honest party will suffer the consequences if there is no mechanism to protect him. In order to ensure fairness, it is expected that once a user/service

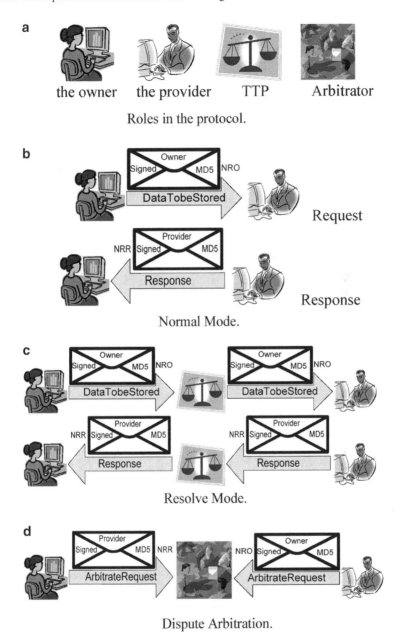

Fig. 14.5 Illustration of the two-party non-repudiation (TPNR) protocol work flows

provider has sent his evidence to this peer, there must be some mechanism to guarantee that he will receive the evidence. For instance, if the provider does not respond after it has received the NRO from the owner, the owner will be at a disadvantage while doing business with the provider.

There is a special case that occurs in the normal process when the owner wants to terminate an ongoing data transfer procedure and quit an undesired situation. He can initiate the "Abort" mode. He only needs to send the provider the transaction ID with an NRO. A TTP is not necessary to finish the abort process. This is different from the traditional non-repudiation protocol. Only when the message cannot be delivered is the TTP needed.

On receiving an abort request from the owner, the provider should verify the data consistency first. If the request is valid, the provider will respond with "Accept" or "Reject" along with an NRR. Otherwise, the provider will send an "Error" message that requests that the owner double check the parameters included in the abort request, regenerate it, and re-submit the request.

To provide a fair working environment, the Resolve mode is implemented in the NR protocol.

14.4.2   Resolve Mode

More complicated scenarios, in which the data transaction agreement cannot be achieved without interference from a trusted third party, are possible in either the normal data backup procedure or in an abort operation. For instance, when in the middle of a data transaction, the owner does not receive a response from the provider within the pre-set time-out limit. There are multiple reasons that may lead to such an anomaly (e.g., the link between the owner and the provider may be broken, the request was dropped and never received), or the provider is malicious and it did not respond to the requests. It is beyond the owner's capability to solve the problem and requires a reliable third party who plays the role of arbitrator.

Figure 14.5c illustrates the functionality of the Resolve mode, which works as an in-line TTP. In this scheme, the TTP could be a reliable server or a reliable service provider other than the main provider. The owner sends the transaction ID, the NRO, and a report of any anomalies to the TTP and requests the TTP's help to resume the disrupted data transfer process. Once the TTP verifies the genuineness and the consistency of the transaction, the TTP will send the resolve request to the recipient along with a time stamp.

Assume the communication channels among the TTP, the owner, and the provider are reliable. The owner sends the provider a resolve message to initiate the resolve procedure. The resolve message carries the query along with the information such as the transaction ID, the owner's user ID, etc. After checking the contents of the query and verifying its consistency, the provider will respond to the owner through a TTP with the NRR including the actions it will take according to the status. For example, the provider may agree to continue the transaction, or it may require the owner to restart the session. If the provider does not reply to the resolve query from the TTP before time out, the TTP will respond to the owner by telling him/her that this session failed since the provider did not respond.

The Resolve mode functions as the kernel of our non-repudiation protocol. When the owner has to stop the transaction, he needs evidence to protect himself in case of repudiation. For this purpose, the NRR from the provider and information from the TTP are critical. At the same time, the provider cannot get any benefit if it refuses to reply. In this design, we do not consider the data exchanged through the TTP in the context of cloud storage services. Normally, the size of the data set is very large, which is not feasible to be stored and/or forwarded by the TTP.

Meanwhile, if the owner has sent the NRO and has not received the NRR before the time out, he can initiate the Resolve mode. Here, the owner hopes that the TTP will help to make the transaction continue and expects to get the NRR from the provider by triggering the resolve procedure.

If the provider sends an NRR to the owner and has not received the response from the owner directly before time out or has not received a resolve from the TTP, the provider may assume that the owner has agreed to the NRR or the provider can send a resolve procedure to the TTP.

14.4.3   Summary

There are two modes in the basic TPNR protocol, Normal mode and Resolve mode. The Normal mode works in an off-line TTP mode as shown in Fig. 14.5b. The Resolve mode works in an in-line TTP mode as shown in Fig. 14.5c. If a dispute happens, the arbitrator can ask the owner and the provider to provide evidence to be considered as shown in Fig. 14.5d.

When the owner cannot get the non-repudiation evidence from the provider, a TTP will be invoked in the Resolve mode. From the perspective of the provider, the situation is simpler. If it did not receive the NRO, it is not required to take any action since most of the transactions are initiated by the owner. Only when there is no further response or specified activities after it has sent the NRR does the provider need to initiate the resolve procedure in case a dispute occurs.

The TPNR protocol in this section can be applied to the personal basic cloud storage application. There is no need to consider a "roll-back" attack since the owner has the correct data. However, if the owner wants to distribute his data to other users, the protocol is not enough. More considerations are needed.

14.5   Conclusions

This chapter has revealed some existing vulnerabilities in cloud storage platforms due to the missing connection between the otherwise robust uploading and down-loading phases. The potential security issues have been summarized systematically and a new basic TPNR framework has been introduced specifically for cloud storage. This method can enhance the security of cloud storage, make cloud storage more trusted, and attract more potential consumers. However, in practice, a cloud-based storage system is required to support data sharing among multiple clients concurrently. In the next chapter, an advanced MPNR protocol will be presented. Also, additional security properties will be discussed.

References

1. Amazon Inc.: Amazon import/export developer guide version 1.2. http://aws.amazon.com/decumentation (2009). Accessed Aug 2009
2. Anagnostopoulos, A., Goodrich, M.T., Tamassia, R.: Persistent authenticated dictionaries and their applications. In: Proceedings of the 4th International Conference on Information Security, pp. 379–393, Springer, London, UK (2001)
3. Ateniese, G., Burns, R., Curtmola, R., et al.: Provable data possession at untrusted stores. In: Proceedings of the 14th ACM Conference on Computer and Communications Security (CCS'07), pp. 598–609. ACM, New York, NY (2007)
4. Bagga, W., Molva, R.: Collusion-free policy-based encryption. In: Katsikas, S., et al. (eds.) Information Security. LNCS, vol. 4176, pp. 233–245. Springer, Berlin/Heidelberg (2006)
5. Bairavasundaram, L.N., Goodson, G.R., Schroeder, B., Arpaci-Dusseau, A.C., Arpaci-Dusseau, R.H.: An analysis of data corruption in the storage stack. In: USENIX Conference on File and Storage Technologies, San Jose, CA, pp. 223–238 (2008)
6. Boneh, D., Gentry, C., Waters, B.: Collusion Resistant Broadcast Encryption with Short Ciphertexts and Private Keys. LNCS, vol. 3621, pp. 258–275. Springer, Berlin/Heidelberg (2005)
7. Carbonell, M., Sierra, J.M., Lopez, J.: Secure multi-party payment with an intermediary entity. Comput. Secur. **28**(5), 289–300 (2009)
8. Cachin, C., Keidar, I., Shraer, A.: Trusting the cloud. ACM SIGACT News **20**(4), 81–86 (2009)
9. Chiou, G., Chen, W.: Secure broadcasting using the secure lock. IEEE Trans. Softw. Eng. **15**(8), 929–934 (1989)
10. Chow, R., Golle, P., Jakobsson, M., et al.: Controlling data in the cloud: outsourcing computation without outsourcing control. In: Proceedings of the 2009 ACM Workshop on Cloud Computing Security (CCSW 2009), pp. 85–90. ACM, Chicago, IL (2009)
11. Feng, J., Chen, Y., Liu, P.: Bridging the missing link of cloud data storage security in AWS. In: The 7th IEEE Consumer Communications and Networking Conference Security for CE Communications (CCNC'10, Short Position Paper), Las Vegas, NV (2010)
12. Feng, J., Chen, Y., Ku, W.S., Liu, P.: Analysis of integrity vulnerabilities and a non-repudiation protocol for cloud data storage platforms. In: The 2nd International Workshop on Security in Cloud Computing (SCC 2010), in conjunction with ICPP 2010, San Diego, CA (2010)
13. Gens, F.: IDC on "the cloud": get ready for expanded research. http://blogs.idc.com/ie/?p=189 (2008). Accessed Sept 2008
14. Gibson, A., Meter, R.V.: Network attached storage architecture. Commun. ACM **43**(11), 37–45 (2000)
15. Juels, A., Kaliski, B.S. Jr.: Pors: proofs of retrievability for large files. In: Proceedings of the 14th ACM Conference on Computer and Communications Security (CCS'07), pp. 584–597. ACM, New York, NY (2007)
16. Kallahalla, M., Riedel, E., Swaminathan, R., et al.: Plutus: scalable secure file sharing on untrusted storage. In: USENIX Conference on File and Storage Technologies (FAST), San Francisco, CA, pp. 29–42 (2003)
17. Kamara, S., Lauter, K.: Cryptographic cloud storage. In: Sion, R., et al. (eds.) Financial Cryptography and Data Security. LNCS, vol. 6054, pp. 136–149. Springer, Berlin/Heidelberg (2009)

18. Kher, V., Kim, Y.: Securing distributed storage: challenges, techniques, and systems. In: Proceedings of the 2005 ACM Workshop on Storage, Fairfax, VA, pp. 9–25 (2005)
19. Li, J., Krohn, M., Mazieres, D., Shasha, D.: Secure untrusted data repository (SUNDR). In: Proceedings of the 6th Conference on Symposium on Operating Systems Design & Implementation. 6. USENIX Association, Berkeley, CA, pp. 9–9 (2004)
20. Li, S., Wang, G., Zhou, J., Chen, K.: Fair and secure mobile billing systems. Wirel. Pers. Commun. **51**(1), 81–93 (2009)
21. Louridas, P.: Some guidelines for non-repudiation protocols. SIGCOMM Comput. Commun. Rev. **30**(5), 29–38 (2000)
22. Markowitch, O., Kremer, S.: A multi-party optimistic non-repudiation protocol. In: Proceedings of 2000 International Conference on Information Security and Cryptology, Seoul, Korea, pp. 109–122 (2000)
23. Majuntke, M., Dobre, D., Serafini, M., Suri, N.: Abortable fork-linearizable storage. In: Abdelzaher, T., Raynal, M., Santoro, N. (eds.) Proceedings of the 13th International Conference on Principles of Distributed Systems (OPODIS'09). LNCS, vol. 5923, pp. 255–269. Springer, Berlin/Heidelberg (2009)
24. Mather, T., Kumaraswamy, S., LatifCloud, S.: Security & Privacy. O'Reilly, Sebastopol (2009)
25. Menezes, A.J., van Oorschot, P.C., Vanstone, S.A.: Handbook of Applied Cryptography. CRC Press, Boca Raton (1996)
26. Microsoft Azure Services Platform: http://www.microsoft.com/azure/default.mspx (2009). Accessed 2009
27. Muniswamy-Reddy, K.K., Macko, P., Seltzer, M.: Provenance for the cloud. In: Proceedings of the 8th USENIX Conference on File and Storage Technologies (FAST'10). USENIX Association, Berkeley, CA, pp. 15–24 (2010)
28. Onieva, J., Lopez, J., Zhou, J.: Advances in Information Security Series. Springer, Berlin/Heidelberg (2009). ISBN 978–0–387–75629–5
29. Popa, R.A., Lorch, J., Molnar, D., et al.: Enabling security in cloud storage SLAs with CloudProof. Microsoft TechReport MSR-TR-2010–46. http://research.microsoft.com/apps/pubs/default.aspx?id=131137 (2010). Accessed May 2010
30. Ruiz-Martinez, A., Marin-Lopez, I., Bano-Lopez, L., Gomez-Skarmeta, A.F.: A new fair non-repudiation protocol for secure negotiation and contract signing. J. Univ. Comput. Sci. **15**(3), 555–583 (2009)
31. SANS News: Growing concern about cyber attacks in US, UK and EU. http://www.sans.org/newsletters/newsbites/newsbites.php?vol=12&issue=19 (2010). Accessed Mar 2010
32. Schroeder, B., Gibson, G.A.: Disk failures in the real world: what does an MTTF of 1,000,000 hours mean to you? In: USENIX Conference on File and Storage Technologies (FAST 2007), San Jose, CA, pp. 1–16 (2007)
33. Security Guidance for Critical Areas of Focus in Cloud Computing: https://cloudsecurityalliance.org/research/initiatives/security-guidance (2009). Accessed Dec 2009
34. Zhou, J., Gollmann, D.: A fair non-repudiation protocol. In: Proceedings of 1996 IEEE Symposium on Security and Privacy, Oakland, CA, pp. 55–61 (1996)
35. Zhou, J., Gollmann, D.: An efficient non-repudiation protocol. In: Proceedings of the 10th Computer Security Foundations Workshop. IEEE Computer, Oakland, CA, pp. 126–132 (1996)
36. Zhou, J., Deng, R., Bao, F.: Evolution of fair non-repudiation with TTP. In: Proceedings of 1999 Australasian Conference on Information Security and Privacy, Wollongong, Australia, pp. 258–269 (1999)

Chapter 15
Fair Non-repudiation Framework for Cloud Storage: Part II

Jun Feng, Yu Chen, Douglas H. Summerville, and Kai Hwang

Abstract Data storage is one of the most profitable applications on cloud computing platforms. Although a transparent service model provides flexibility and convenience, it also brings new challenges with respect to data security. For example, the existing vulnerabilities in some commercial cloud storage services can potentially lead to repudiation problems. In part I of this two-part chapter, a basic TPNR protocol is introduced that addresses disputes between an individual user and a service provider. In this chapter, we introduce a framework that supports a fair data transmission procedure without the risk of disputes in environments where data sharing among multiple users is required. An advanced MPNR protocol is presented. Fairness is achieved with the help of a TTP. Both parties can get evidence at the end of a round. In addition, taking advantage of the Merkle hash tree, the MPNR protocol can prevent rollback attacks by limiting the data access priorities of individual users. The rationale behind the new protocol's design and its working modes are analyzed in detail. We also discuss its robustness under typical malicious network attacks.

15.1 Introduction

In part I, we have revealed potential vulnerabilities existing in today's commercial cloud storage platforms [1, 2] and discussed some proposed architectures and approaches [3, 4] for secure cloud storage. To address such weaknesses, we

J. Feng • Y. Chen (✉) • D.H. Summerville
Department of Electrical and Computer Engineering,
Binghamton University, SUNY, Binghamton, NY 13902
e-mail: ychen@binghamton.edu

K. Hwang
Department of Electrical Engineering – Systems,
University of Southern California, Los Angeles, CA 90089

Z. Mahmood and R. Hill (eds.), *Cloud Computing for Enterprise Architectures*,
Computer Communications and Networks, DOI 10.1007/978-1-4471-2236-4_15,
© Springer-Verlag London Limited 2011

introduced a TPNR protocol to eliminate potential dispute between a single client and a service provider. We focused on how to maintain integrity with fair non-repudiation, not on how to calculate it since the current integrity algorithm is sufficient for data storage. However, in practice, a cloud-based storage system is required to support data sharing among multiple clients concurrently. It is important to have a framework that can resolve disputes when multiple users and/or service provides are involved.

In this chapter, new MPNR schemes for secure cloud storage systems are presented. While eliminating disputes and integrity risks among users, this new scheme is able to prevent collusion attacks and rollback attacks.

The rest of this chapter is structured as follows:

- Sections 15.2 and 15.3 present an advanced MPNR framework for single-write-multiple-read (SWMR) and a multiple-write-multiple-read (MWMR).
- Sections 15.4 and 15.5 discuss performance considerations and the robustness of how our scheme functions to prevent typical malicious attacks.
- Section 15.6 offers a brief summary and conclusions.

15.2 SWMR MPNR Protocol

This section presents a new advanced MPNR protocol. Figure 15.1 illustrates the framework under which our MPNR protocol is proposed. The owner uploads data to cloud and other users, (such as Bob and Carl) download data from cloud.

If there is only one client, a TPNR procedure can be added between API and SSL, and data integrity is supported as part of NRR and NRO. The integrity NRO can be integrated into a ticket that is encrypted by Bob's public key and delivered to Bob through the cloud. Then Bob deciphers the ticket and checks the integrity when he downloads the data from cloud by TPNR. Furthermore, the data can be divided into blocks and encrypted with different keys, and each individual user can only get the permitted keys for their cipher text block.

This MPNR protocol enables the storage cloud to defend against collusion attacks and rollback attacks. In this section, we will start with a defense against these two attacks before discussing the message exchange sessions among data owner, service provider, and users.

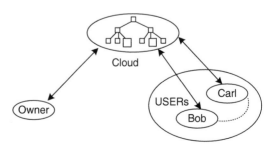

Fig. 15.1 System framework of MPNR protocol

15.2.1 Defense Against Collusion Attacks

There are many reported efforts on how to protect critical information from collusion attacks.

Consider a passive collusion attack that targets an encrypted file or protected sensitive data launched on cloud-based storage as shown in Fig. 14.4 of part I. Since each individual user such as Bob and Carl owns part of the sensitive data, they can combine them together to get the entire file. To date, there is no effective solution for this type of attack except for digital rights management.

Figure 15.1 shows the framework we propose to deal with this collusion attack problem. In our architecture, we use a collusion-free policy-based encryption [5], which assumes that no end-user is willing to share his private key with others. However, another collusion-free scheme could be implemented such as mediated encryption [6].

Basically, the owner breaks the data into multiple blocks and encrypts each of them with a different key. Then the owner creates a ticket for each user, which includes a list of accessible blocks and corresponding keys. The ticket is encrypted with the users' public keys and is uploaded to the cloud with the data and hash tree value by TPNR. Then the owner distributes the root hash to each user (Bob, Carl, etc.) by MPNR using group encryption. When a user (e.g., Bob) gets the root hash, he can download the data from cloud and check its integrity. We also assume that the users do not want to exchange their keys.

This approach consists of three NR rounds:

- Round 1: Between the owner and the cloud service provider. (Operations in this session are specified by a TPNR protocol)
- Round 2: Among the owner and the users. (Operations are specified by an MPNR protocol)
- Round 3: Among the users (insiders such as Bob and Carl) and the cloud service provider. (The rules and access controls are set based on a TPNR protocol)

15.2.2 Rollback Attack Solution Based on Merkle Hash Tree

Yun et al. [7] proposed a solution to deal with rollback attacks based on a universal hash scheme. Figure 15.2 illustrates an example of their solution.

Assume that there is a fixed size for each file of public and trusted storage, which is designed specifically to protect against "rollback" of content to its previous versions. A nonrepeated counter is adopted to generate a pseudorandom sequence. The sequence is used for the nonce-based authenticated encryption scheme for each data block. The operation is as shown in Fig. 15.2a. The counter itself is hashed and authenticated by its ancestor counter, which is shown as the dotted line in Fig. 15.2b.

When some data is updated, all the counters and tags on the path leading to the root counter should be fetched to check for integrity, then the leaf counter and its ancestor are increased and an authentication tag (tag) is recalculated again.

Fig. 15.2 Merkle hash tree
for rollback attack defense [7].
(**a**) Authentication tag
construction for data and
(**b**) MAC tree construction
for counter

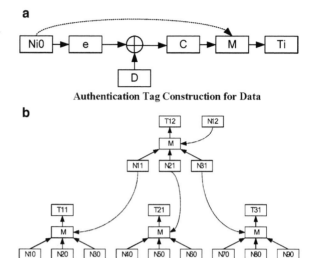

Finally, the number of the data blocks n, the number of active leaf counters m, the depth of the MAC tree k, and the root counter N_{1k} are stored in trusted storage. The other information, such as the remaining counters, the tags, and the encrypted data blocks can be stored anywhere. The idea behind this method is that the trust in the root counter can be transferred to its children by checking the integrity of the tag and also the data blocks.

Yun's scheme is feasible for preventing rollback attacks. However, there is a prerequisite that is not satisfied in the cloud storage application. It needs a trusted storage for the root counter that guarantees that the trust can be transferred from the root to the leaf. Most of the similar solutions make use of such methods.

In our architecture, the untrustworthy relationship can be handled by a non-repudiation protocol, which is discussed in more detail in Chap. 14.4.2. The hash tree is introduced purely to generate and maintain the evidence of integrity of the data.

Because the size of the data is huge in cloud, we need a tree structure to compute and store hash. There are many candidates such as the Merkle hash tree, balanced binary tree, and the red-black tree. The key concern in our protocol is how to transfer the root hash from the owner to the users.

Therefore, it does not matter which construction algorithm is used. Here we give an example of tree construction and some notations, which will be used in the protocol description. Figure 15.3 shows the construction. The root hash value H_R is the evidence of integrity.

Assume H_R is the root hash value, H_H is the history of the H_Rs, and H_Chain D is the influenced hash value adjacent to the data and the root hash when one data block has been updated. We also define H_Chain_G as the union of H_Chain with more data blocks.

For example, if the data block D2 in Fig. 15.3 has been updated, we have

- H_Chain(D2) = {H_R, H00, H10, H20, H11, H21, H31}, and
- H_Chain_G (D2, D3) = {H_R, H00, H10, H40, H50, H21, H31}.

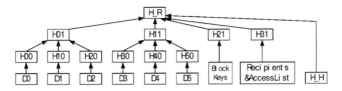

Fig. 15.3 Merkle hash tree for data integrity evidence

Each data block is encrypted using a different key. Assume $K(i)$ is the group of keys for the data that user i has the right to fetch. Then, if user U_i can fetch data blocks {D0, D2, D3}, $K(i)$ is the set of {K0, K2, K3} encrypted by U_i's public key. For convenience, the set of all keys and all recipients are considered as two blocks.

The evidence makes it easy for any user to detect rollback attacks launched by a malicious storage service provider. For instance, once the owner has updated data blocks D2 and D3, he just needs to recalculate H_Chain_G (D2, D3).

Then, when a user, Bob, downloads the updated data from cloud, if cloud gives him the old version, since Bob has the H_R from the owner through a broadcast session, he can verify the consistency easily by comparing the two H_Rs from the owner and the provider. This integrity evidence prevents the service provider from obtaining any benefit by launching a rollback attack.

For convenience, in the following sections when we talk about data, we mean that it includes the H_H, the key lists, the user list, and the access control list (ACL).

15.2.3   Multiparty Non-repudiation Framework

15.2.3.1   Overview

To date, there are only two approaches for fair non-repudiation [8, 9]. One is gradual exchange, which is not practical. Another is TTP, which is used in nearly all non-repudiation protocols. In traditional non-repudiation applications, the following five steps are needed to finish the fair non-repudiation protocol:

- A sender forwards an encrypted message EK(M) to a recipient with an NRO.
- The recipient responds with an NRR.
- After the sender gets an NRR, he will send the key to the recipient with an NRO.
- The recipient responds with an NRR.
- An entity can initiate a Resolve mode if it is needed.

We assume that communication channels between the peers and TTP are resilient and reliable. "Resilient" means messages will be eventually received. We also assume that generally all the parties are willing to complete the transactions by themselves, and the TTP is only required as a last resort. None of the parties is going to act against its own interests.

Fig. 15.4 Consistency

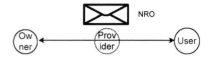

Fig. 15.5 Rollback

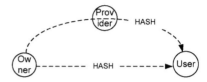

Fig. 15.6 MPNR frame
for cloud storage

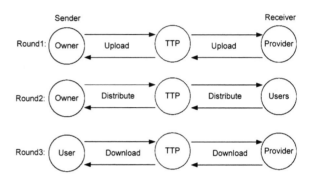

For "consistency," in our MPNR protocol, the provider is just like a hollow man-in-the-middle. Data and its hash from the owner to users is packed and encrypted. The provider can only check the integrity of the packed data and decide whether users can access the data according to an access list managed by the owner. The provider cannot know the content of the message and cannot tamper with the message inside, as illustrated in Fig. 15.4. When a user downloads the data, he can check the integrity for consistency.

Based on this "consistency" strategy, we add one more channel to defend the "rollback attack." Since the owner himself has the correct data, only the users should defend against such attack. The key idea is that in the MPNR protocol, a user downloads the data from the provider and gets two hashes of the data. One is from the provider as shown in Fig. 15.5 and the other is from the owner.

Therefore, it is impossible for the provider to implement a "rollback attack" unless the provider and the owner can collude together. For example, although the data has been updated to Version 10, both the owner and the provider can give Version 9 information to the users. However, the owner and the provider cannot get any profit from such process.

The MPNR needs three rounds. The rounds are between owner and provider, users and TTP, and owner and users. They include the upload, broadcast, and download sessions, which are shown in Fig. 15.6. Each round has two steps and two modes, normal mode and resolve mode.

The normal mode is similar to that in [10, 11] and does not need the TTP. It supposes that the two peers are willing to exchange messages and non-repudiation evidence, and messages are not lost during transmission. When the sender cannot obtain non-repudiation evidence, the resolve mode is invoked through the TTP as illustrated by a dotted circle.

In the new MPNR protocol, we still use a TTP to guarantee "fairness" as illustrated in Fig. 15.6. In addition to the normal upload/download processes, we provide a resolve mode to guarantee that every party is able to complete or abort the execution of a protocol without being forced to wait for responses from other parties, who are potentially malicious or irresponsible.

15.2.3.2   Normal Mode

- Owner$<=>$Provider (Round 1)
  A sender wants to upload data to cloud and update it later.

  In this step, the owner encrypts data blocks with a key list and generates two proofs of non-repudiation, NRO_{OU} and NRO_{OC}, for the users and the cloud provider, respectively. NRO_{OU} is critical for multiparty communication. Different users will get different key lists to decipher the different data blocks.

  Users will verify the data integrity $S_O(H(Data_{Upload}))$ after they download data. The sender uses the group encryption scheme to guarantee that only the users in the ACL can decipher the signed NRO_{OU}.

  This signed hash is very critical since it is the missing link between the uploading and downloading sessions. The owner encrypts the NRO_{OC} and delivers it to cloud as the non-repudiation evidence. The step is described as follows:

Procedures:
Step 1: O=>C; Request$_{OC}$=L, O, C, TTP, Data$_{Upload}$, H_Chain_G$_{Upload}$, Seq1, flag, Tg, T1, $\quad$ E$_C$\{NRO$_{OC}$\}, EG$_U$\{NRO$_{OU}$\}
Step 2: C=>O; Response$_{CO}$=L, O, C, TTP, H_Chain_G$_{Store}$, Seq2, f2, Tg, T2, Ts, E$_O$\{NRR$_{CO}$\},

where

$NRO_{OC}:=S_O\{(H\_Chain\_G_{Upload})\}, S_O\{H(L, Seq1, flag, Tg, T1)\}$.
$NRO_{OU}:=S_O(H\_Chain\_G_{Upload})$
$NRR_{CO}:=S_C\{ H\_Chain\_G_{Store}\} S_C\{H(L, Seq2, flag, Tg, T2, Ts, NRO_{OC}, NRO_{OU})\}$.

Once the message is received from the owner in step 1, the provider verifies the validity of L with O, C, TTP, and H. If it is valid, the service provider decrypts the message with his private key and conducts further verification of the integrity of the parameters in the request. Then, the integrity of the data will be checked. When all procedures are done without any anomalies detected, the service provider sends NRR_{CO} back to the sender before time is up. Otherwise, the service provider will respond with an ERROR message.

On receiving the NRR_{CO}, the owner verifies whether the hash of data $H(Data_{Store})$ is the same as what he has sent and validates the NRR_{CO}. Then, the owner stores the NRR_{CO} for future use. Otherwise, he initiates the resolve process.

After the provider sends an NRR_{CO} to the owner, there are two possibilities. One is that the message is lost and the owner cannot get the NRR_{CO}. In such case, the provider will get a request from the TTP through the resolve mode. Otherwise, it means that the owner gets and agrees to the NRR_{CO}. The uploading session ends.

- Owner<=>Users (Round 2)
  After the upload session is completed, if the owner wants the users to get the data, he should deliver the root hash to the users through a broadcast session. When a user receives the message, he will decipher the NRO_{OU}, obtain the hash, and check the message integrity. The user will also check the validity of the NRO.

  If the owner does not receive the NRR_{UiO} before the time limit after sending NRO to B_i, he can initiate a resolve mode.

  If Ui has not received a response after the time limit T2 or Ui has not received a request from TTP, Ui concludes that the owner has received the response, and there is no dispute. The broadcast session ends. Otherwise, the response means something is wrong with the NRR_{UiO}, Ui will respond according to the request.

Procedures:

Step1: $O => U$: $Request_{OU} = L, O, U, TTP, H\_Chain\_G_{Upload}, S_C(H\_Chain\_G_{Store}), Seq1, flag,$
Tg, T1, $EG_U\{NRO_{OU}\}$,

Step2: $U_i => O$: $Response_{UiO} = L, A, U_i, TTP, H\_Chain\_G_{Upload}, Seq2, flag, T2, E_O\{NRR_{UiO}\}$,

---

where

$NRO_{OU} := S_O\{S_C(H\_Chain\_G_{Store})\}, S_O\{H(L, Seq1, flag, Tg, T1)\}.$
$NRR_{UiO} := S_{Ui}\{S_O\{S_C(H\_Chain\_G_{Store})\}\}, S_{Ui}\{H(L, Seq2, flag, T2)\}.$

- Users<=>Provider (Round 3)
  When any user wants to download data, he should send a request with non-repudiation evidence NRO_{UiC} to the cloud provider. The request includes the user's identity. The provider will validate the request and verify whether the user is on the B list that was previously forwarded by the sender. If it is matched, the data along with $EG_U\{NRO_{OU}\}$ will be sent to the user with the provider's non-repudiation evidence.

  When the user gets the data and EG_U, he can obtain the key list and $H(data)$ by decrypting $EG_U\{NRO_{OU}\}$, and then, he should compare the hash from the provider and from the owner. Meanwhile, the user will also check the validity of the NRR_{CUi}.

Procedures:

Step 1: $U_i => C$; $Request = L, O, C, U_i, TTP, Seq1, flag, Tg, T1, E_C\{NRO_{UiC}\}$

Step 2: $C => U_i$: $Response = L, O, C, U_i, TTP, Data_{Download}, H\_Chain\_G_{Download}, Seq2, flag, T2,$
$EG_U\{NRO_{OU}\}, E_C\{NRR_{CUi}\}$,

---

where

$NRO_{UiC} := S_{Bi}\{H(L, O, C, U_i, Seq1, flag, Tg, T1)\}$

$NRR_{CUi} := S_C\{H\_Chain\_G_{Download}\}$ $S_C\{H(L, O, C, U_i, Seq2, flag, Tg, T2),$
$EG_U\{NRO_{OU}\}\}.$

After the provider responds by sending an NRR_{UC} to the users, there are two possibilities. One is that the message is lost and the owner cannot get the NRR_{UC}. In such case, the provider will get a request from the TTP through the resolve mode. Otherwise, it means that the owner gets and agrees to the NRR_{CU}. The downloading session ends. T4 should not be shorter than T3.

Now, the user has two root hashes, one from the provider and the other from the owner. He can compare the two hashes to avoid a rollback attack.

15.2.3.3   Resolve Mode

Anomalies do not necessarily lead to the termination of a transaction. The owner or users need fair non-repudiation evidence. Therefore, a process of error correction and/or anomaly resolution is required in this protocol.

The sender (owner or users) transmits the message identification and evidence to the TTP to start a resolve process. TTP will transfer the request to the recipient along with a time limit. If the recipient agrees to continue the process, he will return a message to the TTP with an NRR before time is out. He also will restart the lost step 2 unless the channel is broken. In that case, he should inform the TTP by message.

There are two possibilities for the sender. One is that the recipient refuses to respond. In such case, after time is out, the TTP will generate an evidence of NRR to the sender. The resolve session is done. Since the channel in resolve mode is resilient and the TTP is reliable, the arbitrator would look at the NRR as the evidence. Another case is when the sender can receive an NRR from the recipient. In this case, the sender will inform the TTP and the resolve session is done. The flow chart is shown in Fig. 15.7.

For SWMR, there is a problem when multiple users want to read a block of storage. We can use a parallel process, mutex, and timeliness to deal with the problem. However, the problem is condition-dependent and beyond the scope of this chapter.

15.3   MWMR MPNR Protocol

In the multi-write multi-read (MWMR) case, every user has the authority to modify the data in the cloud storage. Therefore, the provider needs to sort the write sequence list according to stated policies. The solution is condition-dependent.

For example, if there are a few users, they can communicate with each other first to determine an update sequence list. If there are hundreds of users, they can use

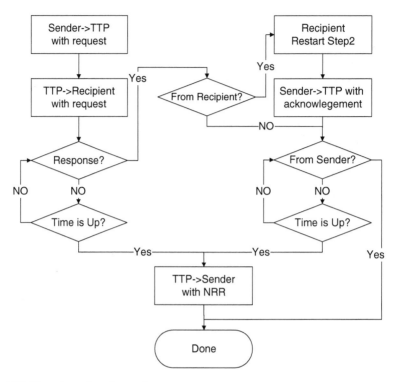

Fig. 15.7 Flow chart of resolve mode

methods similar to carrier sense multiple accesses with collision detection or collision avoidance (CSMA/CD/CA) protocol or ALOHA protocol in the wireless system. If there are millions of users, these solutions will not work well.

Other methods could be taken into consideration. For example, the owner can assign the cloud provider the right to arbitrate. Then the provider can decide what to do when a collision happens according to an agreed upon policy and priority list. Similar methods can be found in [4].

Sometimes the modified data is huge (GB, TB), and it is impractical to send the data. In such cases, a negotiation process is needed. However, no matter which solution is selected, there is only one SWMR MPNR operation at a time. Therefore, the MWMR MPNR protocol can be an extension framework of SWMR MPNR. The MWMR MPNR protocol is described in the following steps:

- The users should send a "request to write" negotiation message.
- The users should apply the MWMR algorithm to decide the write sequence list.
- Then the first one chosen starts the SWMR MPNR protocol to update the data.
- Step 3 is repeated according to the sequence list or go back to step 1.

Since the negotiation algorithm is condition-dependent, we cannot proceed further and again, it is beyond the scope of this chapter.

15.4   Performance Discussion

The proposed non-repudiation protocol is like the TCP/IP three-phase handshaking protocol. It is designed to exchange the evidence in the data transaction which removes any ambiguities that may lead to repudiations or disputes among users or between the user and the service provider. Actually, while all of the papers on non-repudiation focus on the design of protocol, there are no such experiments in them [12–14].

Moreover, cloud storage is different from the traditional distributed storage. In traditional distributed storage applications, data is normally exchanged through the Internet, which requires an implementation and quantitative evaluation to find the transaction bottleneck to test performance.

For cloud storage, however, since the data volume is often very large, the bottleneck definitely lies in either the uploading or downloading processes. Therefore, the current cloud storage services, such as S3, normally use the ship method (Fedex, etc.) to solve the problem. The time required for executing the proposed protocol is then trivial compared to the time consumed in data transfer via Fedex etc.

For the problem of overhead, let us consider an example. We define overhead simply as the extra time needed by the protocol. The overhead is less than 512 bytes if only considering the root hash, (<128 bytes for MD5 or <384 bytes for SHA-512, occupy one sector for disk). Even including other overhead, it is less than 32KB [4]. The signature generation time is about 100 ms (ECDSA, Platform ARM7TDMI 50 MHz; curve: secp384r1) [15], the total DSA that needs three DSA is about 300 ms.

The computational time depends on the data size. Table 15.1 summarizes the time needed for a large data set.

If we upload and download 2GB via the Internet, it will take at least half an hour. For data at the TB level or above, it would take more time when shipping by Fedex or other methods.

Therefore, compared to shipping time, the overhead cost of computation is relatively small. Additionally, there are various factors that influence performance including disk type, system architecture, and algorithm. Thus, we will leave the experimental study of performance evaluation for the future due to the complexity involved.

On the other hand, consider each entity's extra overhead burden when applying the MPNR protocol.

- The cloud provider: The MPNR does not add any additional burden when compared with the existing platform since both of them need to provide the hash and the signature. This means, a provider can expect similar performance when implementing the MPNR.

Table 15.1 Time (s) (Intel E8400, 3G RAM)

Data size	2G	200M	20M	2M
MD5	28.42	2.79	0.264	0.028
SHA-512	94.00	9.00	1.00	0.140
AES	184.17	14.41	0.844	0.125

- The owner: The MPNR needs one broadcast session to communicate with the users. It will increase the owner's burden if there are millions of users and it runs in "resolve" mode. However, such broadcast sessions can be outsourced to other cloud providers since they do not leak any information of plaintext.
- The user: The user needs one extra integrity check task because of the broadcast session. However, it does not consume much time for an individual. Therefore, the influence on the original performance caused by our MPNR is negligible.

15.5 Security Analysis

To date, there have been few methods proposed to verify the robustness of non-repudiation protocols [16, 17]. They are not adopted here for two reasons. On the one hand, they are not well accepted or mature test platforms. On the other hand, the test logic is based on a user-defined test vector. This means they cannot run random test cases. However, from the perspective of testing, most weak points are found through random testing.

Therefore, in this section, we will analyze the robustness of the MPNR protocol from three aspects. We first discuss the non-repudiation process. The provider must convince the customers that its service will be reliable under the MPNR protocol. Then we will talk about some desirable security properties: confidentiality, integrity, scalability, write-serializability, and freshness.

We also analyze robustness against some general malicious attacks, some of which are difficult to defeat in other related systems. Finally, we analyze the robustness of the MPNR protocol for some specific attacks which are found in other previous non-repudiation protocols.

15.5.1 Disputes

Here, a typical example is illustrated to explain the resolution of disputes. The traditional secure file and data storage system can uncover an entity's misbehavior, but they cannot find the reason for that misbehavior. The existing platforms and some architectures provide proof, but they are not always fair. Customers may hesitate to try such an application. We provide fair non-repudiation through a "resolve" mode.

Suppose the owner uploads data to the cloud provider and exchanges evidence, then he distributes the evidence to two users, U1 and U2. U1 and U2 download the data. Now the owner updates some data to the provider and informs the users. U1 and U2 download the updated data from the provider. The owner can also download data if it is needed.

Having studied the behaviors of each party in the MPNR protocol, there are six typical possible cases.

- Case 1: If the channels among the entities are broken or the recipient does not want to give the evidence, the sender cannot receive the NRR. He can start the resolve mode to get the NRR evidence. This is very critical for each entity in the cloud since no entity can be trusted and each can only defend its innocence with evidence. This is different from that proposed in reference [3, 4] since they suppose that the entities are trusted and do not mean to cause the disputes.
- Case 2: The owner uploads the data. At a future time, he downloads it from the provider. This is a typical cloud storage application for the individual user. However, he finds some data to be corrupted [18]. If there is a dispute, both the owner and the provider can provide their NRO and NRR to the arbitrator to defend their innocence.
- Case 3: The owner and users collude to blackmail the service provider. The owner first stores some data in the cloud, and the user subsequently downloads that data. They claim that the data has been tampered with and ask the service provider to pay for the so-called loss. The service provider can easily prove his innocence by presenting the NROOC from the owner.
- Case 4: Consider the scenario where the provider wants to charge more service fees. The owner stores 500GB data. However, after several weeks, the provider claims that the owner stored 1TB. The owner can provide the NRRCO, and the NROCO would not support the provider's claim. Similarly, such evidence also helps the provider if the client tries to deny the service fees.
- Case 5: There is also the possibility that disputes can happen between the owner and users. In the case that the owner claims that a user has received the data but the user denies it, the arbitrator can easily figure out the truth by referencing the NROUiC.
- Case 6: Our MPNR protocol is also helpful to deny access to unauthorized users. For instance, a client, Bob, claims that he has permission to access the data. The Cloud provider can easily verify this by checking the list of recipients with his NROOC.

15.5.2   Some Desirable Secure Properties

Here, we consider confidentiality, integrity, scalability, write-serializability, and freshness [4].

As mentioned earlier, the cloud provider is only responsible for access control. It can decide whether a user can access the data according to the ACL from the owner.

The owner is responsible for data confidentiality. He should encrypt the data and guarantee that the data cannot be decrypted without the key even if the data is leaked.

Integrity is guaranteed by each entity. The owner and the provider generate the hash value of the data using well-recognized algorithms such as MD5 or SHA. The owner, the provider, and the users should check the integrity of the data when they receive messages.

We use broadcast encryption and key rotation techniques to achieve a "scalability" property similar to that used in reference [4].

"Write-serializability" means that every update operation "advances the version number of the most recently stored block by exactly one" [4]. "Freshness" means the data received must be up-to-date. Popa uses a chain of attestations to avoid the serializability violation and periodically audits to guarantee freshness. However, they are still vulnerable to a rollback attack since there is no direct link between the owner and the users. Based on his idea, one more channel is added, as shown in Fig. 15.5, to defend against such attack.

This MPNR can easily guarantee the serializability since it is a "one-write-multi-read" mechanism. The freshness can also be guaranteed by the broadcast session. Even if we need a multi-write-multi-read mechanism, we can use the chain hash (similar to [4, 13]) to avoid a serializability violation and use the broadcast session to guarantee the freshness and avoid attacks.

15.5.3 General Attacks

- Man-in-the-middle (MITM) attack
  The MITM attack [19] is a form of active eavesdropping in which the attacker makes an independent connection with its victims and relays messages between them. The attacker can intercept all messages being exchanged between the two victims and inject new ones.

  However, an MITM attack can succeed only when the attacker can impersonate the end party. It can be prevented by authentication. In our MPNR protocol, authentication and digital signature are required for the purpose of eliminating disputes. Automatically, when the parties get the other's public key, they should authenticate the validity against the MITM.
- Reflection Attack
  A reflection attack [19] is a method that attacks a challenge-response authentication system that uses the same protocol in both directions. The protocol in this paper is not a challenge-response authentication system. However, since each message contains a unique identifier, the reflection attack can be avoided.
- Interleaving Attack
  The interleaving attack [19] is similar to the man-in-the-middle attack, but it can attack the protocol in which all parties have authentic copies of all others' public keys.

An interleaving attack can possibly succeed when there are several rounds that exchange the key, and the to-and-from messages are symmetrical or the symmetric key establishment is on a shared session key. In this protocol, the message is not symmetrical and binding with a unique sequence number, and each session is finished in only one round. Therefore, the interleaving attack cannot threaten the MPNR protocol.

• Replay Attack
A replay attack [19] is a form of network attack in which a valid data transmission is maliciously or fraudulently repeated or delayed. This is carried out either by the sender or by an adversary who intercepts the data and retransmits it.

A replay attack can be defended by the use of challenge-response techniques and by embedding the target ID party in the response or the timestamp. In this protocol, we use a unique sequence number with the sender signature to avoid the attack. For example, an adversary, Eve, has intercepted the message and replayed it to the TTP. Even though he can modify the SeqN in the plain text, the hash value that has been encrypted by the sender's private key cannot be changed without being detected.

15.5.4 Specific Attack

• Timeline attack
Timeline attacks are typical in non-repudiation protocols. In fairness, each party can stop the execution after a fixed time out. In this protocol, the Tx field is used in each message to limit the reception time of a message. Thus, when a party receives a message, it will check the validity of the Tx with the actual time. If it is invalid, the party discards the message and initiates the resolve mode. However, simply grafting some note of expiry may also cause troubles. Let us consider the following protocol [20]:

Step	Acts	Parameters
1	A=>B	B,L,T,C,NRO
2	B=>A	A,L,NRR
3	A=>TTP	B,L,T,K,sub'_K
4	A<=>TTP	A,B,L,T0,K,con_K
5	B<=>TTP	A,B,L,T0,K,con_K

Step 4 and step 5 can be conducted concurrently. Since T is the time limit on the TTP clock and T0 is the time that the confirmed key has been made available to the public, it remains so until time T. However, party A can delay step 3 up to the last moment before T, so that he can perform step 4 so that there is a good chance that B might subsequently miss step 5 [21].

Another example is shown below by adding a time limit. Where B adds a time limit T1 in step 2, where T1 < T. B wants A to perform step 3 before T1 to avoid

the problem above. When there is repudiation, the adjudicator checks that
T0<T1<T. However, since the TTP does not know T1, B can give the time limit
T1<T0. After B gets K and the decrypted message, he is able to claim that the
protocol execution is invalid [22].

Step	Acts	Parameters
1	A=>B	B,L,T,C,NRO
2	B=>A	A,L,T1, NRR
3	A=>TTP	B,L,T,K,sub'_K
4	A<=>TTP	A,B,L,T0,K,con_K
5	B<=>TTP	A,B,L,T0,K,con_K

In our MPNR protocol, this attack is not possible since there is only one round
in one session, and party can get an advantage over another. Furthermore, in each
step, the party tracks the time limit clearly.
• Reuse of ETTP(K)
In one non-repudiation protocol [23], sub'_K contains only items sent as part of
the first message. In particular, it contains E_{TTP} (K). Thus, B can reuse E_{TTP} (K) in
a different protocol run with B' and produce a valid sub'_K that consists of
$S_B(f_{sub}$, B',L',E_{TTP}(K)), where L' is a new random label. By using this sub'_K
together with appropriate EOO'_C and EOR'_C values in the resolve sub-protocol, B gains K and thus learns message M.
A cannot receive any evidence of receipt for this message, as A has only
enough information to run the abort sub-protocol. But as B executes the resolve
sub-protocol under a different label L', the attack always succeeds. Thus, the
protocol is unfair for A (assuming that knowledge of M is valuable information
for B) [24]. This type of attack would have no impact on this MPNR protocol
since there is no need to generate a valid sub'_K.
• Reuse of Labels and Keys
In some protocols, labels are equivalent to H(Data, K) and are unique. However,
B cannot know the Data until the last step. This property implies that B can only
check the validity of L in the last step. Under certain situations, the TTP also
cannot check the validity of L since the TTP never gets the message for
confidence.
For example, A can initiate the protocol with data M' but using the wrong
label L=H(M, K). B cannot verify its validity until the last step. Therefore A can
receive evidence of receipt for K from B if B forgets to check the label or from
the TTP since the TTP cannot check the label at all. When B detects the error and
initiates the resolve process, the TTP may reject its request since A has aborted
the transaction already [24].
Such an attack cannot threaten the MPNR protocol since each party can check
the validity of the Label in every step. The TTP can also check the validity of the
Label of each step.
• Wrong sub'_k Attack

This attack is special to certain NR protocols. Let's consider the NR protocol proposed in [25]. If A sends a wrong $E_{TTP}(K)$, the resolve protocol has to stop with an error when it is initiated by B. Then, it prevents B from terminating the transaction. However, A can construct a resolve request with the correct encryption of the key and then A can complete the protocol at any time [24].

In our MPNR protocol, the attack is not feasible since the TTP only checks the consistency in the resolve mode, and it is the responsibility of A and B to decide the result of the resolve procedure. If the sender sends a wrong message, the message cannot reach the other party and the sender cannot take any advantage.

15.6 Conclusions

Data storage has been considered as one of the major applications in cloud computing. However, security is the most critical concern that prevents commercial applications from being accepted widely. Although traditional non-repudiation protocols can be applied to cloud storage, more steps are required to complete the entire transaction, which places a heavy burden on the TTP with large data. In addition, since a cloud service provider plays a role of man-in-the-middle, more security requests should be considered during transaction.

This chapter introduced new MPNR frameworks specifically for the environments in which multiple clients and service providers are involved. Then, the performance and related security properties of the fair non-repudiation framework for cloud storage platforms were discussed. This approach is based on the non-repudiation according to the special conditions in cloud computing platform with efficient and light burden. The ideas of integrity check and non-repudiation are not new, but the idea of integrating them to solve the problem in cloud storage is novel. The research on security in cloud computing is far from mature. We hope the discussions in these two chapters will inspire more interest in this area.

References

1. Amazon Inc.: Amazon import/export developer guide version 1.2. http://aws.amazon.com/documentation (2009). Accessed Aug 2009
2. Microsoft Azure Services Platform: http://www.microsoft.com/azure/default.mspx (2009). Accessed 2009
3. Kamara, S., Lauter, K.: Cryptographic cloud storage. In: Sion, R., et al. (eds.) Financial Cryptography and Data Security. LNCS6054, pp. 136–149. Springer, Berlin/Heidelberg (2009)
4. Popa, R.A., Lorch, J., Molnar, D., et al.: Enabling security in cloud storage SLAs with CloudProof. Microsoft TechReport MSR-TR-2010–46. http://research.microsoft.com/apps/pubs/default.aspx?id=131137 (2010). Accessed May 2010
5. Bagga, W., Molva, R.: Collusion-free policy-based encryption. In: Katsikas, S., et al. (eds.) Information Security, LNCS 4176, pp. 233–245. Springer, Berlin/Heidelberg (2006)

6. Bairavasundaram, L.N., Goodson, G.R., Schroeder, B., Arpaci-Dusseau, A.C., Arpaci-Dusseau, R.H.: An analysis of data corruption in the storage stack. In: USENIX conference on File and Storage Technologies, pp. 223–238. USENIX Association, San Jose, CA (2008)

7. Yun, A., Shi, C., Kim, Y.: On protecting integrity and confidentiality of cryptographic file system for outsourced storage. In: Proceedings of the 2009 ACM Workshop on Cloud Computing Security (CCSW '09), pp. 67–76. ACM, New York, NY (2009)

8. Zhou, J., Gollmann, D.: A fair non-repudiation protocol. In: Proceedings of 1996 IEEE Symposium on Security and Privacy, pp. 55–61. IEEE Computer Society, Oakland (1996)

9. Zhou, J., Gollmann, D.: An efficient non-repudiation protocol. In: Proceedings of the 10th Computer Security Foundations Workshop, pp. 126–132. IEEE Computer, Oakland (1996)

10. Feng, J., Chen, Y., Liu, P.: Bridging the missing link of cloud data storage security in AWS. In: The 7th IEEE Consumer Communications and Networking Conference Security for CE Communications (CCNC'10, Short Position Paper), IEEE Press, Las Vegas, Nevada (2010)

11. Feng, J., Chen, Y., Ku, W.S., Liu, P.: Analysis of integrity vulnerabilities and a non-repudiation protocol for cloud data storage platforms. In: The 2nd International Workshop on Security in Cloud Computing (SCC 2010), in Conjunction with ICPP 2010, IEEE Computer Society, San Diego, CA (2010)

12. Carbonell, M., Sierra, J.M., Lopez, J.: Secure multiparty payment with an intermediary entity. Comput. Secur **28**(5), 289–300 (2009)

13. Li, S., Wang, G., Zhou, J., Chen, K.: Fair and secure mobile billing systems. Wirel. Pers. Commun. **51**(1), 81–93 (2009)

14. Onieva, J., Lopez, J., Zhou, J.: Secure Multi-party Non-repudiation Protocols and Applications. Springer, Boston (2009)

15. Certicom Inc.: ECDSA fast verify. http://www.certicom.com/index.php/software-security-solutions (2005). Accessed 2005

16. Bella, G., Paulson, L.C.: Mechanical proofs about a non-repudiation protocol. In: TPHOL01, vol. 2152 of LNCS, pp. 91–104. Springer, Heidelberg (2001)

17. Bruso, M., Cortesi, A.: Non-repudiation analysis with LYSA with annotations. Comput. Lang. Syst. Struct. **36**, 352–377 (2010)

18. Amazon Developer Forum: S3 data corruption? http://developer.amazonwebservices.com/connect/thread.jspa?threadID=22709 (2008). Accessed 2008

19. Menezes, A.J., van Oorschot, P.C., Vanstone, S.A.: Handbook of Applied Cryptography. CRC Press, Boca Raton (1996)

20. Zhou, J., Gollmann, D.: Towards verification of non-repudiation protocols. In: Proceedings of International Refinement Workshop and Formal Methods Pacific, pp. 370–380. Springer, Canberra (1998)

21. Louridas, P.: Some guidelines for non-repudiation protocols. SIGCOMM Comput. Commun. Rev. **30**(5), 29–38 (2000)

22. Kim, K., Park, S., Baek, J.: Improving fairness and privacy of Zhou-Gollmann's fair non-repudiation protocol. In: Proceedings of 1999 ICPP Workshop on Security, pp. 140–145. IEEE Computer Society, Aizu, Japan (1999)

23. Markowitch, O., Kremer, S.: A multi-party optimistic non-repudiation protocol. In: Proceedings of 2000 International Conference on Information Security and Cryptology, pp. 109–122. Spinger, Seoul, Korea (2000)

24. Gurgens, S., Rudolph, C., Vogt, H.: On the security of fair non-repudiation protocols. Int. J. Inf. Secur. **4**(4), 253–262 (2005)

25. Boyd, C., Kearney, P.: Exploring fair exchange protocols using specification animation, lecture notes in computer science 1975. In: Proceedings of 2000 Information Security Workshop, pp. 209–223. Springer, Wollongong, Australia (2000)

Chapter 16
Clowns, Crowds, and Clouds: A Cross-Enterprise Approach to Detecting Information Leakage Without Leaking Information

Neil Cooke and Lee Gillam

Abstract In this paper we elaborate a near-duplicate and plagiarism detection service that combines both Crowd and Cloud computing in searching for and evaluating matching documents. We believe that our approach could be used across collaborating or competing Enterprises, or against the web, without any Enterprise needing to reveal the contents of its corporate (confidential) documents. The Cloud service involves a novel document fingerprinting approach which derives grammatical patterns but does not require grammatical knowledge and does not rely on hash-based approaches. Our approach generates a lossy and highly compressed document signature from which it is possible to generate fixed-length patterns as fingerprints or shingles. Fingerprint sizes are established by estimating likely random hit rates resulting from the size of the pattern and target search. Our Cloud service is geared towards enabling detection of Clowns, those who may attempt to, or have, leaked confidential or sensitive information, or have otherwise plagiarized, without needing to provide a copy of the original information. Crowds are to be used to validate results emerging from systematic evaluation of the service, ensuring that service modifications continue to act effectively and enabling continuous scaling-up. We discuss the formulation of the service and assess the efficacy of the fingerprinting approach by reference to an international benchmarking competition where we believe our system achieves top 5 performance (Precision=0.96 Recall=0.39).

N. Cooke • L. Gillam (✉)
Department of Computing, University of Surrey, Guildford, Surrey, UK
e-mail: N.Cooke@surrey.ac.uk; L.Gillam@surrey.ac.uk

Z. Mahmood and R. Hill (eds.), *Cloud Computing for Enterprise Architectures*, 301
Computer Communications and Networks, DOI 10.1007/978-1-4471-2236-4_16,
© Springer-Verlag London Limited 2011

16.1   Introduction

Cloud computing has become a topic of substantial investigation [1], with a number
of enterprises exploring how to make most effective use of cloud systems [2]. A key
challenge for providers of cloud computing is to convince potential users that such
environments are secure. This relates in particular to having private and/or confidential data stored in and processed by such systems. Some would suggest that
cloud providers can offer higher-strength security, continuously available, contractually obliged, and certifiable according to internationally acknowledged frameworks. Meanwhile, enterprises may merely be getting the best efforts of moderately
paid, moderately motivated, and moderately knowledgeable people during typical
working hours. External-facing information security technologies, virus detectors,
firewalls, and so on are able to fend off various attack attempts, provided they have
been correctly installed and are appropriately maintained and, hopefully, regularly
tested. There is always the opportunity for significant zero-day attacks to occur, so
hopefully enterprises can also ensure that vulnerabilities are fixed as rapidly as fixes
become available. It is vital, and perhaps more so, that cloud providers cater for
such fixes in inherently timely ways. Those who believe that a cloud provider's
system is less secure than their own, simply because of the apparent security at the
physical perimeter, may be underestimating the risk on their own systems. Further,
there is evidence that some organizations are quite prepared to use third party companies as, for example, email scanners – so can already be putting some very private
and confidential material through such external, implicitly cloud companies – and
yet some of these very organizations will be reluctant to make use of similar services
for which the cloud label is explicit. The cloud providers, for whom information
security must be a cornerstone of their business – or will rapidly lose their business –
must be able to handle distributed denial of service (DDoS) attacks to assure
companies that they are able to withstand such attacks and offer business continuity.
Enterprises subjected to DDoS attacks, and who cut costs by only employing the
moderately paid, may find it more difficult to cope; reputation and customer relations may suffer.

Most enterprise efforts on information security focus on inbound security
threats such as those identified above. In this chapter, we are considering how to
deal with issues of outbound security, in particular relating to information leakage
and data breaches. In part, we are searching for leaked information "in the wild",
but do not wish others to know what we are searching for. Consider this for an
email system: We'd like to block certain outgoing emails but without the sender
being able to test the words and phrases upon which these were being blocked in
order to discern the contents of the confidential repository. One suggestion is
"making encrypted queries to search engines" and "searching over encrypted
data" Gentry in [3, 4]. We wish to show how to allow for such searching without
revealing the contents of the query or, necessarily, the data being queried. Our
approach avoids the use of cryptographic techniques, thus alleviating us from the
difficulties and complexities that arise from the use of such techniques. For

information leak detection, we essentially need to describe a near-duplicate and plagiarism detection service. The service we describe combines both crowd[1] and cloud computing with an efficient and novel document fingerprinting approach. Each document fingerprint is a bit pattern produced using a lossy compression approach. Variation of both the range of recognized patterns and the length of these patterns can be used to reduce the likely number of false positives. Our approach does not require grammatical knowledge, nor does it require part-of-speech information.The compression algorithm must be linear and, if convolutional, must decay within an acceptable synchronization period and ideally not introduce error extension, else the robustness performance against minor changes will be compromised. The lossy compression properties we are referring to in cryptographic terms are the familiar synchronization and error extension properties of Counter Mode Encryption (CTR) and Cipher Feedback Mode Encryption (CBF). Being linear, it retains a homomorphic relationship with the original text – the compression is not cryptographic but is sufficiently lossy such that it is a one way function like a hash – but it is not a cryptographic signature like a hash. Hence, this technique does not rely on cryptographic, hash, or Rabin's methods, but is compatible for content computation purposes with them at a given grain.

Typical plagiarism detection relies on chunked hash-based methods and similar approaches. Our approach is compatible with these at a given grain, but we have a much lower overhead of computation with a higher collision rate, making brute force attacks more challenging. Unfortunately, for reasons of intellectual property protection, we are unable to disclose details of the approach used.

We have used the cloud to trial the service and intend to make further use of it to support efficient scaling of such a system, demonstrate the cross-enterprise approach, and be able to offer both the fingerprinting and matching services on demand. The document fingerprints could either be entrusted to a secure cloud service or created using internally hosted software.

The crowd is to be used to establish match efficacy by evaluating the generation of false positives for relationships between public documents, and as the document (fingerprint) collection continues to increase in size – whereby longer bit patterns may become necessary. The crowd may also be used for authorship attribution and to track the evolution of documents – in both cases, looking for the true original and deriving paths of derivation.

Such a system is aimed at detecting clowns, persons who have leaked confidential or sensitive information, or otherwise plagiarized, for whatever reason and however obtained. How clowns gain access to this information in the first place is out of

---

[1]Crowd computing entails the use of a number of people who are offering human intellect and their computers to solve problems which are at present unsuitable for computational approaches. Financial rewards may be available but are often of limited value.

scope. Generically, it is not a given that to obtain information from a cloud system, one must first find and exploit a cloud computing vulnerability.

The novelty of our proposal is that it should be possible for multiple competing enterprises to be able to search for such leakage in each others' corporate repositories. In principle, the document fingerprints could be shared openly without necessarily revealing the content of any individual document, particularly if shorter bit patterns were used to generate likely external hits for subsequent testing.

The cloud would offer up a subscription-based plagiarism detection service. The approach we have already informally demonstrated is:

1. Efficient, in being able to produce results of analysis rather faster and on lower performance hardware than internationally leading systems
2. Effective, in being able to achieve top 5 performance based on competition benchmarks
3. Readily scalable to the number of users

The cloud service will offer cross-enterprise matching and provide for access to public documents, which may have certain articles cached to cloud storage. In a sense, this becomes a community cloud with each participant needing to contribute derivatives of their data and paying for the running services. In this system, corporate documents can be matched against public documents or documents of other corporates through the cloud service. An enterprise would create the document fingerprints we require and would use them to match against both the public data and the fingerprints of other subscribers. Matches would be of likely interest to both of the parties involved, particularly if these are indicative of intellectual property (IP) issues, though the content of the matches would still remain to be revealed.

Using cloud technology, our system has performed near-duplicate and plagiarism detection against large benchmark corpora, with top 5 scoring precision and recall, and speeds 150 times faster than some top-performing competitors. Part of our motivation is to provide a cloud/crowd-based service for real-time protection of intellectual property against those who ether leak, steal, or plagiarize (clowns), and also to register and search intellectual property without revealing content.

In Sect. 16.2, we review the background relating to such information leaks, mishaps, the thefts that arise, and the clowns that attempt to hide their theft through obscuration. We also review existing systems, research, and approaches for detection of said clowns. Section 16.3 describes how such a full-scale public/private cloud/crowd system would operate. Section 16.4 describes and assesses the efficacy of our approach by estimating likely false or random hit rates and hence the pattern lengths required for confirmation. Section 16.5 provides a short review of results obtained from our prototype cloud system and benchmarks. Section 16.6 concludes the work to date and indicates how to validate the novel fingerprinting approach at Internet scale.

16.2 Background

Despite increasingly strong security technologies, it is still possible to propagate specifically targeted attacks against enterprises. A targeted email attack, for example, uses convincingly formed emails sent to employees who may have a desire to know more about others in their environs – authority of the source can be crafted through inclusion as a signature of footer of the name, position, and using the (spoofed) email address of a relevant internal employee who would be able to distribute information about the "salaries of all employees" [5]; name and position information may be readily available on the web via the corporate website or professional/social networking sites, making such attacks easy to formulate. Such content can appear sufficiently like standard business communications to avoid being blocked by spam filters. Furthermore, with large proportions of spam emails now blocked, spam can exist and malware be propagated via other means including through spamming the web, with datasets of such efforts readily available [6]. Such threats rely on naïve employees requesting content and being misled by the results of a search engine. Equally, naïve employees can also deal inappropriately with outgoing communications in various forms. This is demonstrated amply by the UBS bankers' email to over 100 people disclosing the flotation price of General Motors, thought to have cost the UBS Bank some $10m in fees, and also by the UK county council being one of the first to be fined for data breaches – £100,000 for sending two separate and very sensitive *faxes* to the wrong numbers. While both such events were apparently accidental, a particularly potent threat is posed by the determined insider. A raft of controversy currently surrounds the Wikileaks website which is making available the contents of some 251,287 US embassy cables captured by such a determined individual using a rewritable CD. This follows on from a previous Wikileaks release of some 90,000 classified US military documents. Such releases may damage public confidence and trust. Each of these information leakage incidents demonstrates the relative ease with which confidential and/or sensitive information can find its way to unintended recipients and become problematic or costly for the controlling organization.

In all such cases as those above, we would expect the relative strength of technical and organizational measures in place for information security at these organizations to be quite strong. Clearly there are failings: (1) in ensuring employees are aware of the importance and risk of certain kinds of information; (2) in ensuring careful use of a familiar old technology, probably not considered to be a risk, where the employee or employees were likely attempting to propagate information expediently to the right parties; and (3) in removable media governance which appears to have failed through the actions of a determined person. However, it is highly likely that such leaks would have occurred irrespective of whether the data were stored in a cloud system.

The predicament for any enterprise is the extent to which to be paranoid over which kinds of information security. An enterprise could strongly encrypt all of its information, but will need it decrypted at point of use unless such information can be usefully processed without revealing its contents, the promise of homomorphic encryption [4]. Still, those with valid decryption keys who may want to read such information or do something more with the information "in clear" pose a potent threat. The issue for any computer system, cloud systems included, is that the decrypt key must become accessible alongside the data, wheresoever the data are hosted, and perhaps in an already compromised system.

Information leakages should always lead enterprises to reappraise their approaches to dealing with private and/or confidential information. Although it is not possible to prevent all kinds of human errors, it should be possible to reduce occurrences of certain kinds of mistakes. In previous work, we have demonstrated how to reduce false positives in outbound email filters in order to spot accidental propagation of confidential information, and also how executable Acceptable Use Policies (execAUPs) might be formulated instead of relying on policies that are written and infrequently read and understood [7].

We approach the problem by considering how techniques for data deduplication and plagiarism detection could be adapted. Near duplication and plagiarism takes many forms and may have a variety of legal and moral consequences. Near duplicates can be an issue for efficient storage [8] and for version control for written documents, computer programs, and system configuration. Within a centralized system, such issues can be readily addressed by assessing document-to-document similarities, finding best matches and showing differences. When using decentralized systems, where we may only expect eventual consistency, there may be multiple possible current versions. Detection is similar, but resolving the version to retain may be problematic. In such situations, we assume that there is no intention to disguise the origins of the document and that all documents are available within the network perimeter of an organization. A greater challenge exists when attempting to identify material duplicated from multiple, distinct, sources and, in particular, when deliberate efforts have been made to try to disguise the duplication in order to prevent detection. Such kinds of disguised duplication can occur for reasons of:

1. *Political posturing*: a prime example being the so-called "dodgy dossier" which contained material lifted, with minor modifications, from the MERIA journal.
2. *Grade enhancement*: plagiarism of material from websites and other reference materials by students attempting to gain credit with minimal effort. Collusion or copying from other students or purchasing essays from others are also common. Examples of the scale and impact for student reports can be found in [9, 10].
3. *Career enhancement*: plagiarism may occur even in members of the academic faculty, where publications are target-driven, rather than research-driven. If detected, the employing organization may be unduly protective.
4. *Commercial advantage*: relative costs and time taken in proving, for example, patent infringement, may entice companies toward using the Intellectual Property of one or more other organizations in the knowledge that the value attained is greater than the costs that would be incurred and the risk of detection.

5. *Syndication*: using source material without permission from the producers, where the material originates from a (trusted) agency such as Reuters.
6. *Website reputation*: lifting material from other reputable sources in order to improve the hits on, and reputation of, a new website with a low search ranking.
7. *Lazy reporting*: routinely duplicated, revised, and/or re-spun news articles, often within a provider, resulting in vast numbers of similar copies of a current or old story.
8. *Self-plagiarism*: reuse of own published material in order to tell a similar, or related, story to another audience.
9. *Opinion suppression*: strategic duplication of material can dominate the discourse and give the impression of an absence of debate. For example, in political lobbying through pre-written email and near-duplicate mass email campaigns, the voice of individuals is effectively reduced [11]; politicians simply "switch off" or get their aid to refine their SPAM filters.

These various issues of duplication, near duplication, unintentional versioning, copy look-alike, and so forth, often arise because of the nature and scale of modern electronic media and reference material, and the perception of risk. The perpetrator either believes they won't get caught or that it is acceptable because everybody does it. Indeed, the scale of the web makes it difficult for search engine crawlers to index efficiently, and material plagiarized from the "deep web" [10] may indeed go undetected. In scientific papers, potential plagiarism of references can lead to problems of attribution which can be difficult to resolve and can even escalate as follow-on citations increase [12, 13]. An example of this problem is the often-cited Salton paper that does not exist – "A Vector Space Model for Information Retrieval," JASIS 1975; [13]. One anticipates that a requirement of referencing is reading, yet we still find the number of citations to this 1975 paper increasing.

16.2.1 State-of-the-Art Detection Systems

In recent years, many plagiarism and duplication detectors have been devised. Free Internet-based detectors of varied quality are widely available, some of which appear make to use search engines (such as Google) to check short strings against web content; others appear on sites that also advertise essays for sale.[2] There are numerous commercial tools available, though their capability and cost models vary wildly. Some claim not to save a *copy* of your work on their site, which may only be true in principle; others charge high fees for relatively small word counts ($50 for 40,000 words in 6 months).

Most plagiarism detection tools appear to be web dependent, i.e., only check that which is openly available (alongside that which has been submitted and stored).

---

[2]http://www.degree-essays.com/plagiarism-checker.php, Accessed 18 February 2011.

These detectors are not suitable for plagiarism that occurs within a company, especially where this may concern:

- Material stolen from an organization
- Material accidentally released from an organization's private system
- Potential self-plagiarism (accidental or deliberate), for example, through simultaneous submission to publishers of, say, journals and conferences, both trade and academic

To try to address plagiarism issues, there are some commercial detectors which also store previously submitted work, from all subscribing sites, as an additional reference. These are targeted at schools and universities and have caused some interesting ethical and legal debates because of copyright relating to submitted work, which becomes an inherent part of the system being sold, and issues of privacy. Consider, for example, legal actions[3] in 2006 against Turnitin™, which were dismissed[4] in 2008, following a defense relating to the use of clickwrap licenses as part of the registration process required of each student. Finding a good plagiarism detector on the Internet can be difficult as there is little material regarding comparisons and little in the way of independent benchmarks. There are, however, active research competitions aiming to provide benchmarks and test corpora for such a task, in addition to generally seeking improved detection performance for participating systems [14].

16.2.2 Leak Detection at Internet Scale

In 2005, Google CEO Eric Schmidt[5] estimated the "deep web" at five million terabytes ($5 \times 10^6 \times 10^{12}$). Not all this data is readable text, and the estimate assumes 8-bit words (bytes), so this could offer an upper bound of 10^{17} text words for an Internet corpus consisting of all languages. This is a useful approximation for evaluating system performance, and particularly the length of bit pattern needed, to truly operate at Internet scale.

The Web1T 5-gram corpus[6] is a Google dataset from 2006, derived from approximately 1 trillion (1,024,908,267,229) words (10^{12}) of the web. This is of interest to detection systems that either use Google search for detection, or bag of words methods. The dataset contains frequency lists for individual words (1-grams; minimum

---

[3] http://en.wikipedia.org/wiki/Turnitin, with court proceedings outlined in http://www.dontturnitin. com/images/iParadigms_Amended_Complaint.pdf. Accessed 18 February 2011.

[4] The court judgment http://www.iparadigms.com/iParadigms_03-11-08_Opinion.pdf. Accessed 18 February 2011.

[5] http://www.zdnetasia.com/google-eta-300-years-to-index-the-world-s-info-39276458.htm. Accessed 18 February 2011.

[6] Available from http://www.ldc.upenn.edu/Catalog/CatalogEntry.jsp?catalogId=LDC2006T13. Accessed 18 February 2011.

Table 16.1 Details of the various elements of the Web1T collection[7]

n-Gram	Vocabulary	Est. average frequency
1-gram	13,588,391	75,425
2-grams	314,843,401	3,255
3-grams	977,069,902	1,049
4-grams	1,313,818,354	780
5-grams	1,176,470,663	871

frequency = 200) and frequency lists for patterns using sliding windows of length 2–5 (2-grams to n-grams; minimum frequency = 40). Figures for the lengths of these lists are given in Table 16.1. The estimated average frequency assumes no overlapping and is based on the 10^{12} sample (not the 10^{17} text words) and does not take into account Zipfian behaviors.

Using the estimated average frequency for a *whole* Internet hit count requires a multiplier of 10^5 with appropriate considerations for a Zipfian distribution and Heaps law on vocabulary. Web1T provides useful insights into bag of words permutations and the number of hits one might expect on average if the whole Internet were indexed. A 41-bit (Rabin or hash) code (2,199,023,255,552) would cater for all individual tokens and hence the space for all n-grams. However, a 32-bit (Rabin or hash) code, giving 4,294,967,296 possible combinations, would easily represent all the grams due to the above cutoffs. However, such cutoffs would imply that a plagiarism detector would only detect already well-plagiarized materials. The implied five million terabytes would require 59 bits – leaving headroom for modern 64-bit systems.

As these figures represent 2005–2006 data, present Internet scale may exceed a 64-bit index. An elastic cloud infrastructure, combined with crowd computing for human intelligence resourcing, is almost certainly required in order to keep pace with such scaling.

16.2.3   Approaches to Plagiarism Detection

Plagiarism detection tools rely on simple measures of document similarities ascertained by the number of shared normalized strings which are either sampled (fingerprints) or overlapping (shingles). Searches are made for pattern matches (shingles) against the index database, or a heuristic assessment is made of similarities (fingerprints) against feature-classified document sets. The text parts which provide best returns are then brought to the checker's attention, and a more detailed human analysis usually occurs. Shingling, an analogy to overlapping tiles on a roof, can allow for word deletions, insertions, and minor changes. Such document fragments are converted to a fixed-length value. Shingling is an exhaustive approach used for identifying documents containing specific copied segments, with the extent of plagiarism given by the quantity of sequences of word-for-word matches (pairwise) [15]. Computing the

---

[7] Source: http://www.ldc.upenn.edu/Catalog/docs/LDC2006T13/readme.txt, Accessed 18 February 2011.

fixed-length values is usually achieved using a hash or Rabin's method [16, 17]. The important characteristic is the flattening to give every resultant bit a 0.5 probability of change for a single input bit change. This makes every code in the full output range equally probable for any single bit change to the input. This preserves the document's fingerprinting structure without coloring with the flattening function's bias and allows indexing, random models, and statistical assumptions to be applied to the near-duplication problem. Rabin's method [17] is credited as the first approach in this field and was initially used for a physical fingerprinting application. Rabin's method is computationally simpler than hash-based flattening approaches: the result is roughly similar in flatness to hash, i.e., a fixed-length number with a predictable collision probability, but Rabin's does not have the cryptographic "security" properties of a hash.

The fingerprinting approach finds similar documents by means of combination of techniques such as the following:

- Resemblance and containment [18, 19]
- Pairwise matching [15]
- Content sensitive hashing:

  - Spot signature hashing [20]
  - Inverse document frequency (IDF) feature selection for Rabins signature [8]

- Feature similarity:

  - Sentence length features [21]
  - Syntactical POS features [22]

- Cosine or Jaccard similarity measures or other similarity measures [23]
- Clustering analysis [8, 16, 23, 24]

Exhaustive shingling approaches require one n-bit hash or Rabin's calculation for every step, and the index has to operate using the resulting fixed-length pattern, typically 32, 48, or 64 bits in length, depending on the application. As a result, creating a document's shingle set is expensive both in memory and computation, and indexing singles is equally expensive. Non-exhaustive, i.e., heuristic-based or sampled, approaches have advantages in reducing total processing as compared to the exhaustive techniques and should scale better over the Internet. These are best suited to cases where whole document plagiarism or duplication is suspected and perform best with "in subject" material, hence their use with many web search engines to check for similarities with the search terms.

16.2.4   Defeating Plagiarism Detection Systems

Clowns will often attempt to obscure their plagiarism or their source material for their own benefit. The flatness characteristic required for these approaches causes brittleness in the detection; single character or bit changes produce a completely new code for the shingle or fingerprint. Clowns can perform simple, yet deliberate,

Table 16.2 A segment of the Marashi article with and without character substitutions

Marashi (original)	Marashi (with substitutions)
Part Two gives up to date details of Iraq's network of intelligence and security organisations whose job it is to keep Saddam and his regime in power, and to prevent the international community from disarming Iraq.	Part Two gives up to date details of Iraq's network of intelligence and security organisations whose job it is to keep Saddam and his regime in power, and to prevent the international community from disarming Iraq.

obscuration attacks such as making "speeling" errors and using thesaural substitutions. We have previously demonstrated how seven plagiarism detection systems, including Essayrater, Seesources, PlagiarismDetector, and the popular Turnitin, can be defeated and so may be unsuitable for such a task [25]. These systems were susceptible to sufficient numbers of small alterations to characters or words in the text. Our results suggested that, at minimum, at least two such systems should be used in combination to reduce the likelihood of failed detection and increase the difficulty for the determined, and yet somehow lazy, plagiarist.

Defeats are possible because of the ways that these systems select the (set of) strings for comparison from a source document with some set of target documents. Typically, such strings are either a fixed number of characters or a fixed number of words in length, and so alterations within any such strings in a source document will have an effect on matching. These strings are often hashed, and hash collisions are used to indicate similarities; low probability of collision is required to avoid false positives. Hashes may be efficient where large strings are involved and reduce pa tterns of variant length to a single bit-space. However, while hash collision has beneficial outcomes in matching, similarity of hashes tends not to indicate similarity of strings.

To demonstrate such a defeat, four character changes have been applied to a segment of the Marashi article that was modified to become part of the dodgy dossier. There are 16 replacements of "e," 2 of "h," 2 of "v," and 4 of "l" (Table 16.2). Visually, these remain highly similar, so are likely to pass human checking, and these changes are also likely to pass detection by most of the systems tested.

Various attempts have been made to reduce brittleness, including input options such as the "bag of characters," and robust hash approaches [15]. More specifically, for SPAM hash identification where there are high obscuration issues, systems are proposed to prevent random characters and other variations from defeating the hash signature using chunked or sliding hash codes [26]. These chunked or sliding hashes are a special application of the hash computations – only small fragments or whole words are hashed, and special algorithms for mixing, overlaying, and stepping are used to reduce fragility to minor textual changes. This is not necessarily how the designers intended hash algorithms to be used, and they require especially intensive mathematical processing capacity. Detection is achieved through pattern matching the hashed output, hence small chunks of text with short hashes and small steps in text provide a finer output for better detection, but this is at the cost of increased computation.

When creating the fingerprint or shingle, the precision and robustness performance of a detector is impacted by:

- The size and stepping of the "bag of words" – large bags are more specific and longer steps are more coarse and more brittle.
- The bit length, which affects precision – too short, and false hits due to random noise increase as the library increases in size; too long, and the benefits of length compared to the costs of handling long index codes are not necessarily achieved. This is because the entropy becomes significantly less than the bit length. Words tend to follow a Zipfian distribution, and doubling the corpus size does not double the vocabulary.

For both exhaustive and non-exhaustive approaches, pre-processing is required to remove document formatting, surplus white space, and minor character variation and resolve uppercase/ lowercase, use of hyphens, etc. Some approaches also filter certain words before shingling/fingerprinting Kasprzak et al. [27].

With existing approaches to near-duplicate detection, there are two main strands of research: reducing the computing resource required and reducing sensitivity to minor changes in text – often referred to as either reducing fragility or improving robustness. Both strands are rooted in the use of Rabin's method or hash approaches for fingerprinting or shingling the text.

For our cloud and crowd approach, these detectors of plagiarism and near duplicates are not well suited because of the computing resource required or the lack of robustness. For a *crowd* system, tools should have light computing resource requirements, be fast, and be naturally robust to minor variations. To be robust, this also implies that false returns will be higher, and so the tool should also provide a means to scale and optimize the detection criteria for the task.

16.3 Crowds and Clouds

Our plagiarism detection system is envisaged as making use of both crowd computing and cloud computing. In our considerations of cloud, we make reference to specific kinds of cloud as elaborated in the Cloud Computing Use Cases White Paper.[8] Our cloud component involves a core plagiarism detection service that scales to meet demand, around which is formed a dynamic community cloud. The core service provides for access to public documents, which may have certain articles cached to cloud storage. Matching services against public documents are then available on demand in the public cloud by submission of one or more texts. This would match the approach of extant systems.

---

[8] Available via http://cloud-computing-use-cases.googlegroups.com/web/Cloud_Computing_Use_Cases_Whitepaper-2_0.pdf, Accessed 18 February 2011

However, we aim to go beyond the state of the art by using our detection method to support trustworthy communities. At minimum, there need be no retention of source documents – only of derived bit patterns and association to the versions of certain information, the reference data, used in its production – which should help to resolve fair use discussions. However, asking for documents "in cleartext" and assuring organizations that there is no retention are likely to prove challenging. Here, we can offer a novel service for bespoke detection. Using the same method, an organization would be able to produce its own bit patterns and use these to match against both the public data and the bit patterns created using the same version of the reference data for data of the other organizations within the community cloud; matches would be of likely interest to the parties involved, particularly if these are indicative of intellectual property (IP) issues. At higher computational cost, which would need to be paid by the requester, an organization could also generate its own reference data – providing that it meets specific criteria – and trigger other members of the community cloud to recode their collections against this reference data. Then, either the bit pattern for search would be run against this recoded collection inside the other organization, or the collection patterns and bit pattern could be submitted to the public cloud detection service for matching purposes, or to a private cloud equivalent.

Our use of the crowd is formulated similarly – a public crowd and a community crowd. A public crowd can be joined by anybody on the Internet and is likely to require monitoring for quality in a similar manner to that required for large public contributory resources such as Wikipedia. A community crowd is a membership-based group, potentially bounded by some arrangement such as a non-disclosure agreement (NDA), or comprising a federation of university employees or "subject expert" volunteers, and so on. The public crowd will be used to establish match efficacy by evaluating the rates of false positives for relationships between public documents. This is a relatively bursty service that becomes necessary at intervals when the document collection increases in size beyond a specific threshold – whereby longer bit patterns may become necessary. The crowd would also be used for authorship attribution and to track the evolution of documents. The community crowd would be engaged in relation to determining the nature of the problem at hand in the event of a potential hit on a private collection. For example, university crowds would collaborate to minimize plagiarism among students (and staff) and be able to exchange processed versions of documents among an academic crowd and into the public, if suitable, or community, if access should be limited, cloud. Each university crowd member would provide a server with an index of their own data and a *published* fair use policy relating to students reports and papers. Community crowd or cloud index owners would set hit rates in accordance with their published policy and only respond to an enquiry should they believe that there are sufficient contiguous hits to merit an investigation by both parties, bearing in mind that neither can see each other's original work.

Consider an example in which the public crowd has been tasked to trace the evolution of the Hansel and Gretel fairy story (Fig. 16.1). Source data exists on the web, and cloud storage is used for the search engine indexes. Members of the public crowd can use the detection service to rapidly locate reasonable number of texts containing Hansel and Gretel. The public crowd investigates the resulting hits,

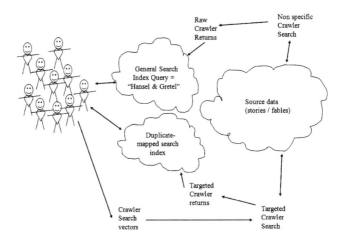

Fig. 16.1 Crowds and cloud system

removes false positives, and researches remaining differences. The public crowd is only concerned with detection; the community crowd will ascertain a course of action. Perhaps they will find copies of the fairy story where Hansel and Gretel have been replaced with Pete and Tracy and the Witch by a Clown?

We believe, but need to establish, that the document fingerprints could be readily shared in the open without revealing the content of any individual document. Thorough evaluation would be required before such a system could be deployed. Many of the mechanisms discussed above are geared toward providing for additional assurance in relation to detecting *clowns* who have leaked confidential or sensitive information, or otherwise plagiarized, for whatever reason.

16.4 Detecting Clowns

Our approach does not use hashes, language models, or keywords. It is based on a fingerprinting approach using patterns composed in a proprietary way. We undertake some pre-processing and word filtering, and use a fingerprint/shingle generator which has a standardized output format and an indexer. Each word is represented by a single bit, and we believe this compression to be sufficiently lossy to be private.[9]

Document fingerprints, of any given length with respect to the number of likely hits generated, can be selected from this bit-string. The fingerprint can be used for

---

[9]To address the issues outlined in footnote 3, when student or other IP owned work is submitted for checking, instead of retaining the "in clear" text, we would retain the reference data and the 0/1 representation. When a pattern match of length greater than "fair use" occurs, the submitter/supervisor and author/owner can both be contacted to verify the hit or to seek/offer permissions for use.

Table 16.3 Frequency variation of 3-bit long sequences

3-bit pattern	x00	x01	x10	x11
0xx	82,608	129,648	167,240	135,664
1xx	129,648	173,256	135,664	69,513

indexing, and related to information about documents and locations within documents. A shingling approach would be similar but exhaustive. An advantage of our method is that the computational overhead involved with this indexing is considerably smaller than for Rabin's method or a hashing approach: Rabin and hash typically use a 32-bit number to represent each "bag" of words. A one word step size would produce a 32-bit number for every word in the file, while our method uses slightly more than 1 bit per word.

Our system uses an index keyed to a linked list, and we can readily assess shingles-based pairwise matching. We initially assume the use of a fixed-length (sliding) window, set at 32 bits and with a step size of one,[10] against each document to create an index that uses the contents of the window as an address to a linked list which holds document source and position data. Both window size and step size can be configured appropriately – indeed, it may be possible to have the window size automatically tuned to hit rate at a gross level or according to each n-bit pattern since documents and locations are indexed.

In searching, a nil response suggests that there is not a plagiarism issue, at least in respect of the materials indexed. Thresholds need to be set in relation to the number of matching fingerprints for a document, or the number of reasonably contiguous shingles, given the length of the bit pattern. The values for such thresholds may also vary according to document length and step size. Here, large-scale fuzzy match, to which human intelligence is well tuned, suggests that the crowd would be able to undertake this with reasonable effectiveness.

To demonstrate the remaining information after lossy compression to which fingerprinting or shingling may be applied, we consider the hit rates of small patterns and their frequency variation. 3-bit sequences from the Brown corpus using our approach are demonstrated in Table 16.3. There is considerable frequency variation and also a large number of possible solutions – hence making reverse engineering a document that makes using such information quite a challenge. Fingerprinting using frequency counts of sliding window patterns of sufficient length and number should be a good heuristic for near-duplicate detection.

We consider patterns of n-bits generated using our method. The opening lines of a well-known nursery rhyme are encoded by our approach as 21 bits. This 21-bit pattern would be readily reversible with prior knowledge of the key words, and their order would be encoded since we are using a linear compression technique, but might also indicate other phrases. In addition to exact matching, we can also look for similar patterns in case "minor" editing has occurred and use multiple pattern

---

[10] A prime number, or a number not divisible into the window length, may also be used.

Table 16.4 Closed/open pattern search results: brown corpus

Pattern	Number of hits sliding/(sentence cut)
01110	25162/(2230)
1001010	13369/(301)
101	131385/(11431)
101111	10155/(557)
Cumulative pattern	Cumulative hits sliding/(sentence cut)
01110	25162/(2230)
011101001010	357/(18)
011101001010101	62/(3)
011101001010101101111	2/(0)

matches to build up confidence. Short patterns will create larger numbers of hits, which would require some subsequent form of disambiguation. We consider the impact of this with respect to the Brown corpus in which two of the words in the nursery rhyme occur 97 times and 7 times, respectively, but the 20-word rhyme does not occur and nor do any of its component lines. The number of hits for each encoded line of the rhyme, as well as for the cumulative assembly, is shown below (Table 16.4). As expected, short patterns produce a significant number of (false) returns; however, the final search using the whole pattern, based on a sentence start point, produces two sliding hits and zero sentence bounded hits. Visual inspection confirms that these do not flag instances of the rhyme, as expected.

As another example, the Brown corpus contains seven proclamations of a particular form with minor variations to dates and days. These produce a 42-bit pattern:

100110010101011011010010110110100010111010110100. Against the Brown corpus, the 42-bit pattern reveals 6 exact matches and 1 match with 1 bit difference.

At one million words, the Brown corpus is short by modern standards and negligible in comparison to the shallow web and especially to the deep web. As discussed previously, to detect plagiarism – and hence leaked information – at such scales requires longer patterns than used for these examples. To this end, we must also consider what plagiarism is and what constitutes fair use or fair dealing. We do not suggest "random" as text does not behave randomly – there are many common phrases in repeated use, and certain text characteristics are relatively predictable. For an estimate, we look to the PAN-09 Workshop where the smallest block of plagiarism in the test data is 50 words – roughly a paragraph in length.

Our approach also demonstrates a degree of natural robustness. In particular, it is largely unaffected by spelling errors or simple substitutions. A downside is that document segments composed in certain ways can produce long patterns of zeros which may require special handling. In general, our robustness is at the cost of false hits.

To establish false hit rates for pairwise matching, we use an imaginary 200-million-word corpus with random characteristics such that Zipfian frequency distribution and

Table 16.5 False hit prediction and actual false hits

Pattern	Pattern length	Predicted false hits	Actual false hits
101	3	125,000	173,256
01110	5	31,250	26,561
101111	6	15,625	9,819
1001010	7	7,812	**13,948**
011101001010	12	244	**357**
011101001010101101111	21	0.47	**2**

Heaps vocabulary conditions hold. We assume this corpus exists as one contiguous file to avoid need to consider the additional per-document stepping. We expect a single 2-bit pattern, when single bit stepped, to occur 100 million times in this example, likewise a single 3-bit pattern 50 million times. The random hit formula is:

$$\text{Random Hits} = (\text{Corpus size in words})/2^n$$

where n is the search pattern length

For the Brown corpus, the expected number of random hits against pattern length is shown in Table 16.5 and is compared to our previous example where we know the text strings do not occur. It shows that, for these short patterns, we are close to the false hit rates that we would expect assuming randomness. However, for longer patterns, we appear to be getting more than we expect shown in bold in the table.

Using this information, we can set the length of pattern in relation to the size of corpus to match our hit rate requirements. For a 200-million-word corpus, a 32-bit pattern representing 32 words of text will occur by chance about 0.05 times. Hence, we would expect a 32-bit indexed linked instance of this corpus to contain 5% noise. For a deep web of 5×10^{17} words, a 32-bit pattern would return approximately 232,000,000 hits; a 50-bit pattern representing 50 words of text (a small paragraph) would give approximately 450 hits and thus still require further filtering to find the source data. To obtain similar direct access performance as for our 200-million-word example, the pattern would have to be extended toward 64 bits. The larger the corpus, the longer the search pattern needed to reduce false hits; this approach suggests 64 words of text to uniquely identify near duplicates or plagiarism at Internet scale. To definitively confirm for 50–64 words requires Human Intelligence Tasking (HIT) to optimize the pattern match parameters, identify false hits and reasons, and collate document evolution metadata.

16.5 Experiments

A prototype cloud-based system has been created using a combination of C for the indexing and Java Server Pages (JSP) for presentation. Indexing runs as an off-line process, with file-based patterns constructed first and segments at the appropriate bit-length indexed across files subsequently. Initial cloud-based tests were conducted on an Amazon Small Instance (m1.small) with 1.7 GB memory and using a 100 GB chunk of elastic block store (EBS) for data and result storage. However, scaling up to the Uncovering Plagiarism, Authorship, and Social Software Misuse (PAN) Workshop 2009 dataset pushed us over the memory limits of such an instance. Rather than attempting to estimate the memory requirement, we detached the EBS, started an Amazon Large Instance (m1.large) with 7.5 GB memory, and tried again. Once more we hit a memory peak, so migrated similarly to a High-Memory Extra Large Instance (m2.xlarge) with 17.1 GB memory. The ability to transition between server sizes at such a rate, and not having to invent new data handling approaches to fit within system limitations or to procure new systems, was highly beneficial to the time taken to conduct these experiments.

Indexing used 9 GB memory and processed the 2009 extrinsic plagiarism corpus in 630 s. We achieve comparatively high scores for recall and precision (0.38 and 0.70, respectively, for the 2009 extrinsic corpus) in comparison to the 10 other competitors [14], which should readily put us in the top 5. Additionally, the winning system in 2009 took 12 h [15], though their compute infrastructure is not discussed, and the runner up reported a total processing time of 1 h 14 min [27] using 64 GB RAM and 8×3 GHz cores server. In a second experiment against the 2010 corpus, we consumed 17.4 GB RAM, processing took 26 min 30 s and achieved 0.39 recall and 0.96 precision, also sufficient for a top 5 result in the 2010 competition against 18 competitors [28].

A third experiment was performed using the news texts from Reuters Corpus Volume 1 (RCV1 [29]) against itself. Due to degradation of the media on which the corpus was stored, we were only able to use around 750,000 of the 806,791 in the entire corpus, representing most of 1 year of Reuters originated news for 1996/1997. We pre-processed the files by removing XML, although in principal this step may not have been necessary. Comparing the 750,000×750,000 files reports all instances of cross-copying between news reports, of which there are a reasonable number of indications that content has been republished or repurposed across news reports. Using the m2.xlarge EC2 instance as above, this took approximately 36 min to index and report all duplication. While we have not investigated these results exhaustively, examples are provided in Figs. 16.2 and 16.3 below.

16.6   Conclusions and Future Work

We have proposed a novel application of crowd, and cloud, computing for an Internet-scale information leak detection system and informally demonstrated how the detection can operate based on bit-string fingerprints extracted from documents. We believe that the document fingerprints we are generating are both computationally efficient and effective and can scale gracefully. Furthermore, we also believe that it should be possible for enterprises to make use of such an approach collaboratively without ever revealing the content of their queries – the mere fact that there is a long-length match across two companies should be of potential interest to both, and it may

417467newsML.xml.txt.sum

Minimum visible run length: 39
Maximum sorted run length: 98
Total number of extracts: 1432
Longest run: 639

Length	Word ID	Reference Doc Path	Reference Word ID
639	638	417467newsML.xml.txt	638
141	495	417472newsML.xml.txt	366
110	344	417472newsML.xml.txt	215
72	436	420889newsML.xml.txt	558
55	346	417584newsML.xml.txt	193
52	494	417473newsML.xml.txt	241
50	343	420889newsML.xml.txt	335
44	232	417472newsML.xml.txt	107

Fig. 16.2 An example of results reported for the RCV1 corpus. Note that the first result is due to the entire collection being cross-checked

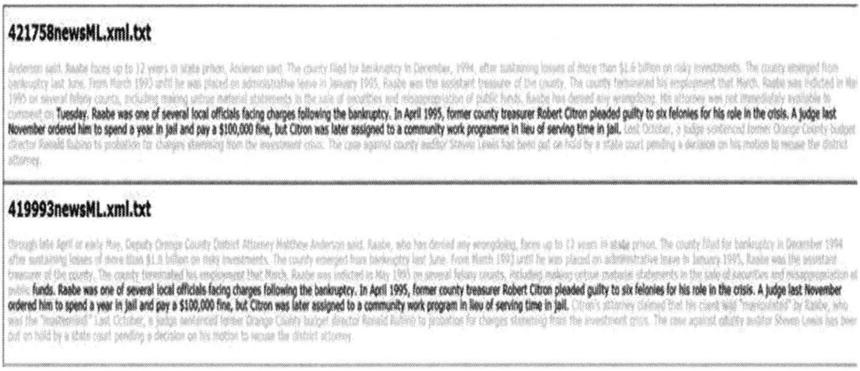

Fig. 16.3 An example of matching for two files from the RCV1 corpus

be possible to share yet further information about the contents of these repositories while still not revealing any private and/or confidential material. Such an approach can scale well in the cloud in two ways: first, scaling up as required to be able to trawl the entire Internet for specific sets of matches; second, scaling up per enterprise to allow for full crossmatching. The crowd is to be used when potential plagiarism is detected by the open Internet-facing detection service operating in the cloud. A cloud service can scale in order to meet demand, and the method used is relatively computationally efficient, but undertaking the entire task using a crowd would not prove satisfactory for a variety of reasons. We might also be able to identify wording variations which lead to detectable pattern variations; both the hits discovered and any derivative techniques used will be best assessed using human intelligence.

To detect duplication, our approach uses lossy compression and a pairwise matching technique. Through this, we showed that sub-paragraph length patterns can accurately identify near duplicates. This suggests that at Internet scale, a 64-bit system could be used with pairwise matching to identify near duplicates. Pairwise matching was chosen principally for ease of explanation and demonstration. Results also indicate that there is sufficient structure for fingerprint heuristic approaches to perform well. Other matching approaches should be evaluated, and further work is necessary to quantify the relationship between pattern length and false return rates. Furthermore, by varying the window size and step size, we will be able to evaluate the computational efficiency and detection effectiveness in relation to fingerprints and shingles. Use of shingles will avoid the impact of word insertions, deletions, or replacement with synonyms with minor grammatical modifications. Both approaches would be readily supported by reducing the length of the bit pattern and looking for a given N pointers to the same document or to the same, relatively contiguous, document segment. For multilingual use, the service would require only minor modifications for each language and to be able to treat Unicode. We believe our approach to be resilient to some degree against attempts to avoid detection through simple character translations – e.g., e → e (Unicode + 0435), h → h (Unicode + 04bb), v → v (Unicode + 03BD).

We are seeking to validate our work more fully by participating in subsequent SEPLN PAN Workshops.

Acknowledgments We gratefully acknowledge the support of Amazon in providing a grant to use Amazon Web Services (AWS), and in particular relating to use of EC2 and EBS for various experiments of ours. We are also grateful to Peter Wroble for the prototype indexing and detection system and near-duplicate viewer, and Henry Cooke, presently at the University of Plymouth, for conversion of prototype output to a format suitable for SEPLN 09 & CLEF 10 PAN workshops, and also for the post-indexing filter toolset.

References

1. Antonopoulos, N., Gillam, L. (eds.): Cloud Computing: Principles, Systems and Applications. Springer, London, UK (2010)
2. Harmer, T., Perrot, R., Lewis, R.: The PRISM on-demand digital media cloud. In: Antonopoulos, N., Gillam, L. (eds.) Cloud Computing: Principles, Systems and Applications. Springer, London, UK (2010)
3. Gentry, C.: A fully homomorphic encryption scheme. Unpublished PhD thesis, Stanford University (2009a)
4. Gentry, C.: Fully homomorphic encryption using ideal lattices. In: Proceedings 41st ACM Symposium on Theory of Computing (STOC), ACM, New York (2009b)
5. MessageLabs.: MessageLabs intelligence: 2010 annual security report. http://www.message-labs.co.uk/mlireport/MessageLabsIntelligence_2010_Annual_Report_FINAL-en.pdf (2010). Accessed 17 Dec 2010
6. Castillo, C., Donato, D., Becchetti, L., Boldi, P., Santini, M., Vigna, S.: A reference collection for Web Spam. SIGIR Forum **40**(2), 11–24 (2006), ACM Press
7. Gillam, L., Cooke, N.: Intellectual property escaped with the email? press F1 for help. J. Info. Assur. Secur. **3**(1), 16–26 (2008)

8. Wang, Z., Gemmell, J.: Clean living: eliminating near-duplicates in lifetime personal storage. MicrosoftResearchRedmond.http://research.microsoft.com/apps/pubs/default.aspx?id=70275 (2006)

9. Park, C.: In other (people's) words: plagiarism by university students–literature and lessons. Assess. Eval. High. Educ. **28**(5), 471–488 (2003)

10. Loutzenhiser, K., Pita, A., Reed, J.M.: Revisiting plagiarism in an internet era: how modern technology contributes to the problem and solutions. J. Coll. Teach. Learn. **3**, (2006). http://journals.cluteonline.com/index.php/TLC/article/download/1693/1673

11. Shulman, S.W.: Perverse incentives: the case against mass e-mail campaigns. Paper presented at the annual meeting of the american political science association, Hyatt Regency Chicago and the Sheraton Chicago Hotel and Towers, Chicago, IL. http://www.allacademic.com/meta/p209426_index.html (2007)

12. Teufel, S., Moens M.: What's yours and what's mine: determining intellectual attribution in scientific text. In: Proceedings of the 2000 Joint SIGDAT conference on Empirical methods in natural language processing and very large corpora: held in conjunction with the 38th Annual Meeting of the Association for Computational Linguistics - Volume 13. Association for Computational Linguistics, Stroudsburg, PA, USA (2000)

13. Dubin, D.: The most influential paper gerard salton never wrote. Libr. Trends **52**(4), 748–764 (2004)

14. Potthast, M., Stein, B., Eiselt, A., Barron-Cedeno, A., Rosso, P.: Overview of the 1st international competition on plagiarism detection. SEPLN'09 Workshop PAN. Uncovering Plagiarism, Authorship and Social Software Misuse. http://www.uni-weimar.de/medien/webis/research/workshopseries/pan-09/competition.html (2009)

15. Grozea, C., Gehl, C., Popescu, M.: ENCOPLOT: pairwise sequence matching in linear time applied to plagiarism detection. SEPLN'09 Workshop PAN. Uncovering Plagiarism, Authorship and Social Software Misuse. http://www.uni-weimar.de/medien/webis/research/workshopseries/pan-09/competition.html (2009)

16. Hoad, T.C., Zobel, J.: Methods for identifying versioned and plagiarised documents. J. Am. Soc. Inf. Sci. Technol. **54**(3), 203–215 (2003)

17. Rabin, M.O.: Finger printing by random polynomials. Center for Research in Computing Technology Report TR-15–81, Harvard University, Cambridge, MA, USA (1981)

18. Broder, A.Z.: On the resemblance and containment of documents. In: Proceedings of the Compression and Complexity of Sequences, IEEE Computer Society, Los Alamitos (1997)

19. Broder, A.Z.: Identifying and filtering near-duplicate documents, COM '00. In: Proceedings of the 11th Annual Symposium on Combinatorial Pattern Matching, pp. 1–10. Springer, Berlin/New York, CA, USA (2000)

20. Theobald, M., Siddharth, J., Paepche, A.: SpotSigs: robust and efficient near duplicate detection in large web collections. In: 31st annual international ACM SIGIR conference on Research and development in information retrieval (SIGIR 2008), SIGIR, Singapore (2008). ACM Press, New York, NY, USA

21. Wang, J.H., Chang, H.C.: Exploiting sentence-level features for near-duplicate document detection, proceedings AIRS '09. In: Proceedings of the 5th Asia Information Retrieval Symposium on Information Retrieval Technology, Springer, Berlin/Heidelberg, Germany ISBN: 978-3-642-04768-8 (2009)

22. Elhadi, M., Al-Tobi, A.: Use of text syntactical structures in detection of document duplicates. In: Digital Information Management. ICDIM 2008. Third International Conference on, University of East London, London, UK (2008)

23. Xiao, C., Wang, W., Lin, X., Xu Yu, J.: Efficient similarity joins for near duplicate detection, international world wide web conference. In: Proceeding of the 17th international conference on World Wide Web, Data mining: algorithms, pp. 131–140, Beijing, China. ACM Press, New York, NY, USA (2008)

24. Yang, H., Callan J.: Near-duplicate detection by instance-level constrained clustering. In: Proceedings of the 29th annual international ACM SIGIR conference on Research and Development in Information Retrieval, ACM Press, New York, NY, USA (2006)

25. Gillam, L., Marinuzzi, J., Ioannou, P.: TurnItOff – defeating plagiarism detection systems. In: 11th Higher Education Academy-ICS Annual Conference, University of Durham, 24–26 Aug 2010, UK
26. Damiani, E., di Vimercati, S.D.C., Paraboschi, S., Samarati, P.: An open digest-based technique for spam detection. In: Proceedings of ISCA PDCS 2004, pp. 559–564. ISCA (2004). San Francisco, CA, USA
27. Kasprzak, J., Brandejs, M., Kripac, M.: Finding plagiarism by evaluating document similarities. SEPLN'09 Workshop PAN. Uncovering Plagiarism, Authorship and Social Software Misuse. http://www.uni-weimar.de/medien/webis/research/workshopseries/pan-09/competition.html (2009)
28. Kasprzak, J., Brandejs, M.: Improving the reliability of the plagiarism detection system. Lab Report for PAN at CLEF. http://www.uni-weimar.de/medien/webis/research/workshopseries/pan-10/lab.html (2010)
29. Rose, T., Stevenson, M., Whitehead, M.: The reuters corpus volume 1 – from yesterday's news to tomorrow's language resources. In: Proceedings of the Third International Conference on Language Resources and Evaluation, LREC, Las Palmas (2002)

Index